WLD

HISTORY OF THE
NATIONAL ACADEMY
OF DESIGN
1825–1953

SAMUEL FINLEY BREESE MORSE

*From a miniature by Morse
in the permanent collection of the Academy.*

HISTORY OF THE

NATIONAL ACADEMY OF DESIGN

1825 - 1953

BY ELIOT CLARK, N.A.

NEW YORK 1954

COLUMBIA UNIVERSITY PRESS

TO
THE MEMBERS
OF THE
NATIONAL ACADEMY
OF DESIGN
PAST AND PRESENT

FOREWORD

LITTLE is generally known of the formative history of the National Academy of Design, and the significant part it has played in the development of American art. The only history of the Academy was published as long ago as 1865, and is now out of print. In the years that have passed since then, the Academy has continued to include in its membership the most eminent practitioners in the nation of the Arts of Painting, Sculpture, Architecture and the Graphic Arts. Important changes in the composition and in the Constitution of the Academy have taken place. In order to provide an accurate and up-to-date record, it is obvious that a new history should be written.

The publication of the present volume has been made possible by two men: Archer Milton Huntington and Eliot Clark. Over a long period of years Mr. Huntington has quietly fostered many institutions, including the Academy, in the fields of artistic and intellectual endeavor. It is due to his generous benefactions that the Academy is able to meet its increasing financial obligations, and is in a position to undertake the publication of this book.

But in order to write such a history, an author must be found who possesses not only an intimate knowledge of the history of American art, but also the patience for painstaking research in the voluminous Minutes of the Academy. These qualifications are happily combined in Eliot Clark; he is an authority upon the early history of American art, and has served for many years as the Academy's Corresponding Secretary.

On behalf of the Council and membership of the Academy, I take this opportunity to record our gratitude to these two men.

Lawrence Grant White
President

CONTENTS

LIST OF ILLUSTRATIONS

vel-

ARK

INTRODUCTION

ART, like other human activities and aspirations, is directly related to the economic, sociologic, and political conditions of a given time and environment. In consequence, the rise and early development of art in America arose from two distinct sources: the cultural and social aspirations of the opulent colonists, who continued the tradition of the mother country; and the more humble desires of the "lower class," who continued its folk-lore. From this social distinction came two disparate branches in the arts—one devoted to the agrandisement of the patron, and the other, less pretentious, fulfilling its own needs in "homemade" embellishments and the varied crafts of the artisan.

Socially, the craftsman had been regarded as a member of the working class, and the practicing of the arts, except as an occasional pastime, had been considered beneath the dignity and distinction of the elite. As there were no schools of instruction or native precedent in the arts, the craftsman emulated the works imported from England or copied his designs from engravings.

Portraiture, as the indication of family distinction, continued the tradition of the artisocracy in England. It was natural, therefore, that our early artists should seek instruction in the mother country and follow the style of its renowned practitioners, the artist being aided by his patron while studying abroad. Lacking such favorable opportunity, the uninstructed artisan developed his art by experimentation, and added to his livelihood as carpenter, blacksmith, or other occupation, the small reward of painting effigies, tavern signs, coaches, or over-mantel panels of local scenes.

The end of the Revolutionary War not only resulted in the independence of the former colonies and the formation of a new conception of government; it introduced a new era directly affecting the social and economic order of the republic.

the arts, the opening of the nineteenth century corresponds with ecline of the English masters in portraiture and, at the same time, the passing of their contemporaries in America. In France, the traditional continuity of the eighteenth century was abruptly severed by the French Revolution and the Napoleonic wars.

Thus in New York, at the beginning of the new century, the arts were given little consideration. Their practitioners were almost nonexistent. The aging John Trumbull, who followed the colonial tradition, was the sole important exception. The younger men, reared under the republic, reflected the equalitarian principles of its government. They matured at a time which brought the invention of the machine, the rise of new industries and means of transportation, and the forming of a new class of wealthy citizens who were to become the patrons of the new generation of American artists.

It was symptomatic of the time and the changes which occurred in social grouping that the new class of the wealthy aspired to cultural development, and thus became the friends and benefactors of the artists and members of the growing literary and professional circles of the city.

Although portraiture continued as the predominant art, the artist, joining in the romantic revival, was inspired by the "grand style" and the vision of a "nobler" form of art. The "primitive" stay-at-home, working in his own way, reflecting the local "mores" of his class, was entirely unaware of "academic" training or distinction, and had no relation to the "cultured" and opulent patron of the professional artist. The old masters were held in credulous veneration, leading the youthful artist to continue his study abroad. Lithography was to popularize the theme of "Americana" in the Currier and Ives prints, the name "chromo" being applied by the more sophisticated professional as the equivalent of "pot boiler." Thus the two sources of the art developed separately and represented two different aspects of American culture.

It is significant that the National Academy of Design, founded at the beginning of the second quarter of the nineteenth century, was concomitant with this social, economic, and political change, and grew up with the era of Jacksonian democracy that followed its birth. It thus provided an opportunity far the education of the American artist and the exhibition of his work at a time favorable for its reception and, by means of its organization, created a focus for the cultural interests of the city and the development of a national art.

ELIOT CL

New York City
September, 1954

HISTORY OF THE
NATIONAL ACADEMY
OF DESIGN
1825–1953

◆ ‖ ◆

ORIGINS: THE AMERICAN ACADEMY OF FINE ARTS FOUNDED IN NEW YORK, 1802 · THE NEW YORK DRAWING ASSOCIATION · CAUSES FOR THE FORMATION OF THE NATIONAL ACADEMY OF DESIGN · THE FOUNDERS

THE ISLAND of Manhattan, with its natural harbor at the confluence of the Hudson and East rivers, predestined New York City to become the paramount center of commerce and finance in America. At the beginning of the nineteenth century its growing population was to surpass that of Philadelphia; merchants prospered and wealth accumulated. But Philadelphia retained its cultural and artistic prestige. The spectacular career of Benjamin West was still remembered in the Quaker City, while Gilbert Stuart and Charles Willson Peale had added luster to the then seat of government.

The London studio of Benjamin West, court painter to George III and president of the Royal Academy, became the mecca of the young American painters as the eighteenth century came to an end. His fatherly hospitality and helpful guidance not only furthered their study but introduced them favorably to the art world of London and to possible patrons.

Gilbert Stuart arrived in London in 1775 and remained in England 17 years, where he attained marked success among the fashionables of the day. John Trumbull followed in 1780, Dunlap in 1784, Allston in 1801, Sully in 1809, and Morse in 1811.

This common artistic parenthood formed a bond in memory and fraternity which was to have fruitful results in the development of American painting and the founding of the National Academy of Design. In the practice of their craft the youthful artists brought back to America many of the formulas, methods, and techniques of the English painters which were to form the basis of their later practice and establish a sound foundation of instruction. The durability of their works testifies to the virtue of this tradition.

The war with England being over, the artistic brotherhood, remembering gratefully the hospitality of the mother country, stood apart from political controversy. William Dunlap related in his *History of the Rise and Progress of the Arts of Design in the United States* that once when King George was sitting for one of his many portraits by Benjamin West a

messenger brought him the declaration of American Independence. . . . "He was agitated at first," said West, "then sat silent and thoughtful, at length, he said, 'Well if they cannot be happy under my government, I hope they may not change it for a worse. I wish them no ill.' "

Washington Allston is quoted as saying: "England has never made any distinction between our artists and her own."

Returning to America as accomplished craftsmen, our artists missed the cultural environment of London, and lamented not only their lack of social status but also the absence of schools of instruction and public presentation of the artists' work.

In Philadelphia Charles Willson Peale was the first painter to organize the artists for their mutual benefit and to establish a school of instruction. Peale had studied in London under West from 1771–73, and was conversant with the methods of teaching at the school of the Royal Academy then but recently organized (1768). His first venture in 1791, the School for the Fine Arts, was short-lived and unsuccessful. In 1794 he started a second project, the Columbianum. "In this he was rather more successful. He collected a few plaster casts, and even opened a school for the study of the living figure, but could find no model for the students but himself. The first exhibition of paintings in Philadelphia was opened this year, in that celebrated hall where the Declaration of Independence was determined upon and proclaimed." The meetings of the Columbianum were held at the home of the founder, the sculptors William Rush and Giuseppe Ceracchi being among the members.

Some other artists, principally foreigners, joined in this plan; but the foreign artists, and Ceracchi at their head, separated from the Columbianum, and after the first exhibition it died. . . .

Ten years after Mr. Peale's first attempt, some of the most enlightened citizens of New-York, with a view to raising the character of their countrymen, by increasing their knowledge and taste, associated for the purpose of introducing casts from the antique into the country. These worthy citizens, though none of them artists, called themselves 'The New-York Academy of the Fine Arts.'

At the first meeting, held December 3, 1802, Edward Livingston was elected president of the Academy; Robert J. Livingston, treasurer; Dr. Peter Irving, secretary, together with six other directors.

The charter was not obtained until 1808. The words "New-York" were exchanged for "American," and the word "Fine" was omitted. We had then these gentlemen of every profession, but that of an artist, constituted by law an Academy of Arts.

Thus, Dunlap described the founding of the first Academy of Arts in America. Published in 1834, the book reviewed in retrospect the controversy between the layman and the professional artist, a controversy which eventually resulted in the founding of the National Academy of Design. But it should be borne in mind that in 1802, the date when the New-York Academy of the Fine Arts was organized, there were no artists of prominence residing in New York. Dunlap was engaged in other activities at this time; John Trumbull did not return to New York until 1804; Stuart was then in Philadelphia, Vanderlyn in Rome, Allston in England; the youthful Sully was starting his career in Virginia, Jarvis was unknown. The few craftsmen working in New York found their only means of livelihood in sign painting or attempts at profiles. Jarvis, coming to New York from Philadelphia, recalled that in 1805: "I was the best painter, because others were worse than bad—so *bad* was the best." (Dunlap)

In truth, the New York Academy had little concern with the practicing artist, but prompted by civic pride, it was an endeavor to bring together men of social distinction and affluence in cultivating an interest in the "Polite Arts." For the "Gentlemen" the study of art was a social accomplishment; there was little interest in its creation. The ancient world was held in credulous admiration. Associated with the fabulous past and the rise of Athenian democracy, Greek sculpture was regarded with veneration as the ultimate realization of "the sublime and the beautiful."

Prior to the founding of the New-York Academy of the Fine Arts, Robert R. Livingston, then chancellor of New York State, had been instrumental in organizing in 1791 the Society for the Promotion of the Useful Arts, over which he presided. Appointed Minister to France in 1801, he conceived the idea of enlarging this interest to include the "Polite Arts." (This indicates the prevalent distinction between the practical arts associated with the crafts of the working class, and the fine arts which were considered the special sphere of the social elite.) With this in view, while in Paris he formulated a definite program whereby casts from the antique were to be made from the originals in the "National Museum" (the Louvre) and sent to New York to inaugurate "the foundation of a school of the Fine Arts." A society was to be formed, the members of which were to defray the expenses involved by subscription, and the New-York Academy of the Fine Arts, which resulted from this preliminary program, came into being. Chancellor Livingston had solicited the interest of Napoleon Bonaparte, then First Consul of the French Republic, who, on being elected the first Honorary Member of the Academy, presented the society with twenty-four volumes of the prints of Giovanni Battista Piranesi as well as several volumes of drawings.

In 1803 the casts arrived from Paris, and, as we shall see, were to figure largely in the controversy which resulted in the founding of the National Academy, and were eventually to become the property of the younger institution. The casts included the *Apollo Belvedere*, the *Venus of the Capitol*, the *Laocoön*, the *Gladiator*, the *Silenus*, the *Grecian Cupid*, the *Castor and Pollux*, the *Germanicus*, the *Hermaphrodite*, the *Venus of the Bath*, the *Torso of Venus*, and busts of Homer, Demosthenes, Niobe, Euripides, Cleopatra, Brutus, and others.

The distinguished founders of the American Academy, echoing the classical revival and inculcating the prerequisites of the education of a gentleman, quite oblivious to the dynamic significance of their time, added to their civic and social prestige by their magnanimous effort to enlighten their countrymen. At first exhibited in the rotunda of the Pantheon in Greenwich Street, the casts were removed in 1805 to the upper floor of the Government House (later the Custom House), originally designed for the residence of the President of the United States; but not receiving public support after the first wave of curious interest, the exhibition was discontinued and the casts were placed in storage. In retrospect, it is interesting to observe that this quest of the ideal in the midst of commercial turmoil is a characteristic which is truly American.

In emulation of the New York Academy, a group of distinguished citizens in Philadelphia gathered together and likewise purchased casts in Paris, including several Roman examples then but recently installed in the Louvre, following Napoleon's Italian campaign. This resulted in the formation of the Pennsylvania Academy of the Fine Arts in 1805, a charter being granted in 1806. The first exhibition was held in 1807 in a building erected for that purpose. But in Philadelphia, as in New York, the artists, not being represented on the board of directors, had no control over the management of the Academy or its exhibitions. Thus there followed a similar controversy as in New York, between the professional artists and the directors.

Despite the worthy intention of the founders of the American Academy, their efforts met with little public response. Financed as a stock company, in shares of $25 each, and the stockholders being limited to 1,000, the Academy's membership included few artists. John Trumbull, as vice-president, was the only artist represented on the board of directors. The exhibition continued unchanged throughout the year. There was no opportunity for the practical study of art. After the first flurry of expectation, interest subsided and the institution was soon forgotten.

In 1816, under the presidency of De Witt Clinton, associated with Dr. David Hosack and several other influential citizens, an effort was made to revive the American Academy and further its original intention. A suitable building, formerly the Alms House (renamed the New York Institution), facing City Hall on Chambers Street being at this time vacant, the City Corporation placed several of the rooms on the second floor at the disposal of the American Academy. The rooms were redecorated, the casts from the antique were taken out of storage, a number of pictures were borrowed, and the galleries were opened to the public on October 25, 1816.

The pictures exhibited included Benjamin West's *Portrait of Robert Fulton*, his *Portrait of Benjamin West Painting a Picture of Mrs. West*, the *Lear* and *Ophelia*, all loaned by the widow of Robert Fulton; twenty examples by John Trumbull; eight portraits by Gilbert Stuart; a *Land-*

scape and Figures by Washington Allston; two pictures by Robert Leslie (one a copy after West) together with the engravings and drawings presented by Napoleon.

On the occasion of the opening, De Witt Clinton made an extended address, probably the first ever delivered before an art organization in America. It is a valuable commentary on the cultural trends of the time and the patronage of the "Polite Arts." Suffused with erudition, elegant quotations, and classical allusions, it was far removed from the life and welfare of the professional artist. Having reestablished the American Academy and delivered his oration, the former Mayor of New York City and future Governor of New York State thereupon retired from the presidency.

The exhibition attained considerable success, with attendance and receipts exceeding expectations. The by-laws were amended to include more artists on the board of directors in accordance with a legislative requirement insisting on eleven directors instead of five. In January, 1817, John Trumbull was elected president, the board including four artists and seven laymen. Professional artists, including painters, sculptors, architects, and engravers, were to be elected Academicians, limited in number to twenty, as were Associate members. Honorary Members were to be chosen both from distinguished professional artists and "amateurs." Encouraged by the favorable response, and envisioning a brilliant future, the directors entered into lavish expenditure to further the promotion of the Academy.

At this juncture, Colonel Trumbull offered to sell to the Academy several of his pictures for the sum of $10,000, the interest from which was to be paid as an annuity derived from the receipts of the exhibitions. However, the initial success of the exhibition was not sustained, attendance diminished, and in this embarrassing situation the institution was ultimately obliged to return the pictures to the president.

During the years 1817 to 1824, interest in the Academy steadily declined; the stockholders seldom attended meetings, and the burden of management fell upon the executive officers. The gallery was open throughout the year, with little change in the exhibition and no stimulating activity to engage public interest. There was likewise little opportunity for the display of current production. The growing number of young students were eager to study from the celebrated antiques, but the president was not sympathetic to the establishment of a school. However, permission was granted to draw from the casts between the hours of six to nine in the morning.

William Dunlap, the author of the *History*, was keeper of the Academy at the time, and was provided with a studio in the building, as was Trumbull. Arriving early one morning he found two young students, Cummings and Agate, waiting for the janitor to open the door. The janitor was an old Revolutionary soldier, "who had crossed on the ice from New-York to Staten Island, in the memorable winter." He would open the door when it pleased him. The occurrence which followed, and which had such unforeseen consequences, can best be told in Dunlap's words. The students

were turning away, when I advised them to speak of the exclusion to the directors. They replied, "that it would be useless," and at that moment one of the directors appeared, coming from Broadway towards them. I urged the young gentlemen to speak to him: but they declined; saying, they had so often been disappointed, that they "gave it up." The director came and sat down by the writer, who mentioned the subject of the recent disappointment, pointing to the young men, who were still in sight. The conduct of the person whose duty it was to open the doors at six o'clock A.M. was promptly condemned by this gentlemen, and while speaking, the president appeared coming to his painting-room which was one of the apartments of the Academy. It was unusually early for him, although now probably between seven and eight o'clock. Before he reached the door, the curator of the Academy opened it, and remained. On Mr. Trumbull's arrival, the director mentioned the disappointment of the students; the curator stoutly asserted that he would open the doors when it suited him. The president then observed, in reply to the director, "When I commenced my study of painting, there were no casts to be found in the country. I was obliged to do as well as I could. These young men should remember that *the gentlemen* have gone to a great expense in importing casts, and that they (the students), have no property in them"; concluding with these memorable words for the encouragement of the curator, "They must remember that beggars are not to be choosers."

We may consider this as the condemnatory sentence of the American Academy of the Fine Arts.

The youthful Thomas Cummings, later to become treasurer of the National Academy, has recorded in his *Historic Annals* the circumstances which led to the rupture with the American Academy resulting in the founding of the National Academy. Indignant at the indifference shown

the students, Cummings drafted a protest stating that the students should
be "sustained" in the privileges granted them by the directors. After he
had conferred with Henry Inman, with whom he was then studying, the
older man promised to use his influence in supporting the students. The
petition was submitted to Charles Cushing Wright, who in turn consulted
with Samuel Finley Breese Morse. The latter warmly sympathized with its
intentions.

The previous year (1824), Morse had been commissioned to paint the
full-length portrait of General Lafayette for the City of New York and
had gone to Washington, where Lafayette was the guest of the nation, to
make preliminary studies. While there he received the sad message of his
wife's death. It was thus at the time of his most sorrowful affliction and
solitary state that Morse received the petition on behalf of the students. He
at once invited several of his associates to join with him to consider a
means of improving the conditions for the mutual study of art, and suggested the possibility of forming an association "for the Promotion of the
Arts, and the Assistance of Students."

Acting upon this project, the artists of New York were invited to join
in a general meeting, to be held at the Historical Society on November 8,
1825, for the purpose of forming a Society for Improvement in Drawing.
This was indeed a historic occasion, it being the first general meeting of
artists ever held in the city for the advancement of their profession.
Asher B. Durand was appointed temporary chairman, with Samuel Morse
acting as secretary. The members then proceeded to ballot for officers, the
vote resulting in the election of Samuel Morse, president; Henry Inman,
vice-president; Asher B. Durand, secretary and treasurer. Following discussion, it was unanimously agreed that the artists present would unite in
forming an organization to be known as the New York Drawing Associa-
tion. The members present were: Samuel F. B. Morse, Henry Inman,
Asher B. Durand, Thomas S. Cummings, Ambrose Andrews, Frederick S.
Agate, William G. Wall, William Dunlap, James Coyle, Charles C.
Wright, Moseley I. Danforth, Robert Norris, Edward C. Potter, Albert
Durand, John W. Paradise, Gerlando Marsiglia, Ithiel Town, Thomas
Grinnell, George W. Hatch, John R. Murray, Jr., John Neilson, John L.
Morton, Henry J. Morton, C. C. Ingham, Thomas Cole, Hugh Reinagle,
Peter Maverick, D. W. Wilson, Alexander J. Davis, and John Frazee.

The rules adopted were simple: "That its members should meet in the evenings, three times a week, for drawing. That each member furnish his own drawing materials. That the expense of light, fuel, etc., be paid by equal contributions. That new members should be admitted on a majority vote—paying five dollars entrance fee. That the lamp should be lighted at 6, and extinguished at 9 o'clock P.M." Cummings relates:

The lamp was a can, containing about ½ a gallon of oil, into which was inserted a wick of some 4 inches in diameter—it was set upon an upright post, about 10 feet high. To give sufficient light, the wick was necessarily considerably out of the oil—and caused smoke. There was no chimney, and lampblack was abundant; added to that, some forty draftsmen had an oil-lamp each. The reader may easily imagine the condition of the room.

The room was generously loaned by the Historical and Philosophical Societies, also located in the old Alms House.

There was no thought at this time of holding exhibitions or in any way competing with the older institution. Without any conflicting ideas or proclamation, the artists were simply to meet in a practical way to further their study. Happy in working together in mutual helpfulness and criticism, they looked upon their association as a means of professional advancement. Secure in their self-supporting society, what was their astonishment when one evening John Trumbull, president, and Archibald Robertson, secretary of the American Academy, entered the drawing room unannounced. Trumbull with great dignity seated himself in the president's chair and summoning Cummings, who was in charge of the room, handed him the matriculation book of the American Academy, requesting that it should be signed by all of the members as students of the Academy. Cummings declined as did the others present. "The Colonel [Trumbull] waited some time, but receiving neither compliance nor attention, left in the same stately manner he had entered; remarking aloud, that he had left the book for our signatures, with the additional request that when signed, it should be left with the Secretary of the American Academy!"

On his departure, Cummings continues, the school was called to order and the question was proposed, "Have we any relation to the American Academy of Arts? . . . Are we their students?" The answer was unanimous: "None whatever." "We are not." Several of the smaller casts which had been loaned to the school by the American Academy were promptly returned and substitutes installed by Durand, Cummings, Frazee, and Ingham.

Not desiring to be alienated from the Academy or the members who supported it, the Association addressed a letter to the directors of the Academy stating that "it was their wish that there should be but one institution; and they held themselves ready to join, heart and hand, in building it up, so soon as it should be placed on such a footing, that they could unite in it with confidence and with well founded hopes of such a management, that the energies of all might be directed to the attainment of the noble ends of an Academy of Fine Arts." (Dunlap)

In response, the directors of the Academy appointed a committee of three to meet with a like number representing the Drawing Association. Morse, Durand, and Dunlap were appointed by the Association; Van Rensselaer, Coles, and Brevoort represented the Academy. The conference resulted in the directors agreeing to elect six artists as members of their board. Accordingly, six artists were unanimously chosen by the Association, but four of them not being stockholders in the Academy, $100 was paid to make them eligible. The nominations were sent to the Academy 17 days before the date of election. This being done, the artists rested, secure in their confirmation.

Some days before the election Dunlap and Cummings were walking together in the park. An old woman approached, seemingly a beggar, and asked if their names were Dunlap and Cummings. When they replied in the affirmative she placed a letter in Dunlap's hands and disappeared. The unsigned letter stated that only two of the artists nominated would be elected, and that the others, mentioned by name, would be defeated; it added that the information was reliable.

As prophesied, only two of the six candidates proposed by the Association were elected. They at once resigned; whereupon one of the directors, present at the meeting, declared that artists were unnecessary in the management of the Academy. The money appropriated by the Association was not returned. The associated artists thereupon resolved to found a new Academy to be governed by artists alone.

At a meeting of the New-York Drawing Association, held on the evening of the 14th of January, 1826, Mr. Morse the President, stated, That he had certain resolutions to offer the Association, which he would preface with the following remarks. . . . "Our negotiations with the Academy are at an end; our union with it has been frustrated, after every proper effort on our part to accomplish it. The two who were elected as Directors from our ticket have signified their non-acceptance of the office. We are, therefore, left to organize ourselves on a plan that shall meet the wishes of all. A plan of an *Institution which shall be truly liberal, which shall be mutually beneficial, which shall really encourage our respective Arts,* cannot be devised in a moment; it ought to be the work of great caution and deliberation, and as simple as possible in its machinery." (Cummings)

With this wise advice the president went on to say that the formation and history of other academies abroad should first be investigated; but that in the meantime an organization should be founded with its fundamental purpose defined. To effect this organization he divided the present members of the Association in three classes: professional artists, amateurs, and professional students. He then proposed, on the principle of "Universal Suffrage," that every member should nominate fifteen professional artists at the next meeting and that the fifteen receiving the highest vote should be declared elected members; that they in turn should at once elect from ten to fifteen more professional artists, either members of the Association or nonmembers; and that this body combined should have full power to govern the new organization, elect its members, and select its students.

In deciding upon the name of the new organization as the National Academy of the Arts of Design, the president included in the word "design" painting, sculpture, architecture, and engraving, as distinguished from the "Fine Arts" which added poetry, music, landscape gardening, and the histrionic arts. "Our name, therefore, expresses the entire character of our Institution, and that only."

On the fifteenth of January, 1826, in conformity with the resolution of the preceding meeting, the members of the Association assembled to elect the first 15 members of the governing body. On counting the ballot, the following members of the Association were declared the first 15 elected members of the National Academy of the Arts of Design: Samuel F. B. Morse, Henry Inman, Asher B. Durand, John Frazee, William G. Wall, Charles C. Ingham, William Dunlap, Peter Maverick, Ithiel Town, Thomas S. Cummings, Edward Potter, Charles C. Wright, Moseley I. Danforth, Hugh Reinagle, Gerlando Marsiglia. Those remaining in the Association after the election were given certificates of membership as students. The first 15 members met at once to consider the election of the second 15.

On January 18, Samuel Morse announced that, "the professional artists chosen at the last meeting of the Association had balloted for ten professional artists on one ticket, and five subsequently on separate tickets, and that the following gentlemen were those elected: Samuel Waldo, William Jewett, John W. Paradise, Frederick S. Agate, Rembrandt Peale, James Coyle, Nathaniel Rogers, J. Parisen, William Main, John Evers, Martin E. Thompson, Thomas Cole, John Vanderlyn, Alexander Anderson, D. W. Wilson."

Of the nonmembers elected, John Vanderlyn alone openly declined. Thus of the original founders sixteen represented painting; one, John Frazee, sculpture; two, Ithiel Town and Martin E. Thompson, architecture; six, Asher B. Durand, William Main, Moseley I. Danforth, Peter Maverick, Alexander Anderson, Charles C. Wright, engraving. Eleven students were admitted to the Antique School of the First Grade, three of whom were classified as amateurs.

The Committee on Publication presented its report, giving a particular account of the origin of the Association, of the conferences with the Academy of Fine Arts, and their result; and the new organization of the Association under the name of the National Academy of the Arts of Design, which report having been read was approved, and it was referred to the National Academy, as constituted by the previous Resolution of the Associated Artists, for publication. (Cummings)

The first meeting of the National Academy of the Arts of Design was held at the residence of Samuel Morse on January 19, 1826. Asher Durand was called to the chair, Charles Ingham acting as secretary. On motion of Samuel Finley Breese Morse the members proceeded to vote for officers. Samuel Morse was thus elected first president of the National Academy; Henry Inman, vice-president; Henry Morton, secretary; and Charles C. Wright, treasurer. Various committees were then formed to procure rooms for exhibitions, to devise ways and means of conducting the school, and to draft a code of regulations and by-laws. A Committee of Arrangement was to meet every Monday evening at the school for the study of the antique and for the transaction of business. The Academicians were to meet on the first Wednesday of every month at six o'clock.

At a subsequent meeting it was resolved "that any artist wishing to

become a member of this Academy before the adoption of the Constitution, may be so admitted by a *unanimous vote of the Academy* at a
monthly meeting." This was clarified by a further resolution to mean a
majority of those attending the meeting, stating, "that not less than 10
should form a quorum." (Cummings)

Thus was founded the first art organization in America whose membership was composed exclusively of professional artists.

· II ·

THE ACADEMY BEGINS: EARLY CONSTITUTIONS · THE SCHOOL ·
CHANGES OF LOCATION · CLINTON HALL

THE FIRST CONSTITUTION of the National Academy was read and approved
on December 16, 1826. Three hundred copies were printed, but no copy
of the original constitution is known to exist today. In 1828 a charter was
granted by the State of New York to continue until January 1, 1857, at
the expiration of which time the charter was extended for twenty years,
and in 1873 it was made perpetual. The initial charter states: "There shall
be established and located in the City of New York a Society by the name
of the 'National Academy of Design.' The object of the Society is the cultivation and extension of the Arts of Design, and its funds shall be employed in promoting that object."

The second constitution was printed in 1829. Membership was divided
into three classes: Academicians, Associates, and Honorary Members.
From the Associates alone, the vacancies in the body of Academicians
were to be filled. Active members were to be residents of New York City
and vicinity. Honorary Members were of two classes: nonresident professional artists, who on becoming resident were admitted as Academicians; and amateurs, patrons of the arts, and distinguished members of
other professions. (The last class of membership was eliminated in 1863.)
The various classes of membership were open to all without distinction of
sex. The annual exhibitions were to include the works of living artists not
previously exhibited in the Academy. Premiums were to be granted for
the encouragement of students, and rules were promulgated for regulating
the awards and the conduct of the students. The control and operation of

THE OLD ALMS HOUSE, BUILT 1795
LITHOGRAPH BY ALEXANDER J. DAVIS, A.N.A., 1825

*In 1816 the revived American Academy of Fine Arts was granted
permission by the City to occupy the second floor of the building,
without rent, for exhibiting pictures and the famous Antiques. The
American Museum occupied the first floor. It was here that the
New York Drawing Association was organized, 1825.*

THE ARCADE BATHS
LITHOGRAPH BY ALEXANDER J. DAVIS, A.N.A.

*Academy exhibitions were held in rooms
over the Arcade Baths, 1827 to 1830.*

the Academy was vested in the council, which was to be composed of Academicians only. With the exception of the clauses pertaining to Honorary Members, these basic conditions and classifications have remained unchanged. It will be noted that there was a definite distinction between active members, who were required to be residents of New York City, and nonresident artist members, who were called Honorary Professional Members. This accounts for the large number of Honorary Artists in the early membership. The administration of the Academy was vested in the active Academicians, but the Honorary Professional Members had equal privileges in exhibiting their works. Every encouragement was given to induce artists to exhibit their current work. If an Academician failed to exhibit in two successive years he was subject to demotion. Candidates for membership were chosen only from exhibitors in the Academy. Every Academician on being elected was required to present to the Academy within one year after his election an example of his work. In the constitution of 1839 every Associate-elect was required to present his portrait. This ruling has continued since its enactment, thus forming the invaluable permanent collection of the Academy. The restriction pertaining to nonresident Professional Members was rescinded in 1863.

The constitution mentions the duties of members; there seem to have been no special privileges. Officers, members of the council, and others serving the institution were given no remuneration. It was only thus that the Academy could hold its exhibitions and conduct its school without a deficit. There was no provision in the original constitution stating the *right* of a member to be represented in the annual exhibition. This privilege was not written into the constitution until half a century later. The many amendments and additions to the constitution that were to follow were concerned chiefly with the method of electing members, rules governing meetings and procedure, and methods of selecting pictures for exhibition and regulations pertaining to the election of members of the jury. The sole intention of the exhibitions of the Academy was to promote art by establishing a gallery wherein artists were given an opportunity to present their work to the public. Very few works submitted for exhibition were rejected. It was only when the production of works was greatly increased that a jury of selection became necessary. In consequence, the work presented was uneven in merit; but the artists of distinction were only too glad to welcome and encourage the efforts of other artists. This was the paramount significance of the Academy exhibitions. As the exhibition was enlarged and attained civic significance, criticism outside the profession developed. In 1847, Richard Grant White (father of Stanford White, and grandfather of Lawrence Grant White, a future president of the Academy), referring to adverse criticism, in an article entitled "The Arts," published in the *United States Magazine and Democratic Review*, stated in part:

But those who speak thus, forget that the Annual Exhibitions of the Academy of Design are not prize exhibitions of pictures which come up to a certain fixed standard, high or low, nor exhibitions of the works of members of the Academy, but of all pictures sent by living artists, and which have not before been exhibited in the Academy's rooms. These exacting critics reason without their host, seemingly ignorant that the object of this Annual display, is not merely to please the public and the successful artist of an exhibition of the best works, but to give the public some idea of the yearly progress of the Art, and both the artist and the public the opportunity of comparing the works of one painter with those of another.

The school was given the utmost consideration, with definite rules of regulation. Two members, or "visitors," attended the classes each week, one representing the council and one chosen from the membership in alphabetical succession. "Professors" were appointed by the council to deliver weekly lectures on painting, sculpture, architecture, anatomy, perspective, mythology, antiquities and ancient history. Any student of "good moral character" was eligible to study in the school, after examples of his work had been approved by the council or the "visitors." The students were classified in two grades: after preliminary probation the student was admitted to the second class and on further improvement he was advanced to the first class. The premiums were awarded for different degrees of attainment: for original designs in painting, sculpture, and architecture; drawings from the living model; and drawings from the antique and still life.

The formation of a library to bring to the members an opportunity of study was an initial project of the Academy. Books were costly and acquired only by the privileged few; there was no free public library; the history of art was not taught in college, and works on art were published abroad. A nucleus was formed by friendly donations, and many of the standard works were purchased. William Cullen Bryant added greatly to this interest through his lectures. In 1838, the council appropriated four hundred dollars to be used by the president during his sojourn in Europe for the purchase of books and engravings.

The library included works on the great masters, on the materials of the painters' craft, on drawing, anatomy, perspective, design, costume, architecture, antiquities, and engraving. Many works are now of historical and antiquarian value. At the annual meeting of 1844 it was resolved that $300 be appropriated annually for the acquisition of books; in 1848, a custodian was placed in charge of the library. The inventory of 1852 recorded some 300 volumes, and an extensive list of engravings, prints, drawings, costumes, medals, and paintings. The antique collection had grown considerably, numbering some 170 examples by the middle of the century.

The success of the Academy during the first decade of its existence fully justified the faith and promise of its founders. It was an "academy" in the true meaning of the word, stimulating learning and the advancement of the arts, as well as being of definite civic service. Without endowment or dues from its members, it had paid the expenses of the school and the annual exhibitions solely from the receipts of admission. The accounts of the treasurer are the best indication of attendance and the growing public response. The first exhibition did not meet expenses, and the receipts probably did not exceed $300. The receipts of the second exhibition held in 1827 were $532.46. In 1837 the total receipts were $4,198.66; but expenses increased likewise, amounting to $3,004.99. Some members thought that a surplus was quite unnecessary. The Academy, however, was fortunate in having a faithful watchdog in its treasurer, Thomas Cummings, who guarded and invested the savings with fruitful foresight. In his annual address of 1838 the president alluded to the flourishing condition of the Academy: "In the prospect of an increasing surplus in the Treasury, it is very desirable that the views of all Academicians should be concentrated upon one general plan. . . . We can never be truly an independent institution until we possess a building properly adapted to the purposes of an Academy, and wholly under our own control." The treasurer reported the Academy as *entirely out of debt;* a surplus in the Treasury, the greater part of which has been invested to form a fund for the future use of the Academy, in the promotion of its welfare."

In the autumn of 1829, President Morse sailed for Europe to be absent for several years. Under the circumstances, he felt he should resign his office, but the members unanimously prevailed upon him to retain the presidency, Vice-President Henry Inman assuming his duties until his return.

The former indebtedness mentioned by the treasurer was, strange to say, due to the receiving of gifts from abroad. "A singular matter to complain of; yet it was one which came near destroying the Institution. . . . The expensive transportation brought the Academy deeply, almost irrecoverably, in debt."

It was during Morse's residence in Rome that the gifts began to arrive; numerous crates of casts donated by friends of the Academy were shipped with transportation charges collect. The small amount of money in the treasury, which was to be used in paying the running expenses of the Academy, was not sufficient to meet the charges of delivery. In this dilemma

The Vice-President and the Secretary were authorized and directed to negotiate a loan on the plaster casts; but, unfortunately, *"imagery"* was a security unknown in the market. And it was an *"academic grief,"* that, long as they had been in the "school," they did not *"draw well"*—at least, not *"capitally".* . . . Money, it is true, could be had on *"plaster,"* if not "antique," not in the *"round,"* not "imagery," but modern, and well spread out on the "flat," on an indefinite number of bricks piled on a small portion of mother earth.

In this embarrassing situation, the treasurer proposed to the creditors that time payments be made with interest, assuring the gentlemen that as no funds were available, the only possible means of payment was from the receipts of the exhibitions, and if the Academy was not permitted first to pay the expenses of the exhibitions, no excess would be forthcoming. After much argument, the creditors reluctantly agreed and at the end of two years both principal and interest were paid in full, and the Academy was out of debt. (The debt had amounted to $2,140.) This resulted in a resolution that in the future no gifts would be received from abroad unless the transportation charges were prepaid; when two more packing cases arrived, the secretary was directed to refuse them.

The increasing number of exhibits and the growing attendance made it advisable to provide more gallery space. The Clinton Hall Association was at that time erecting a building on the corner of Beekman and Nassau streets opposite the Old Brick Church, and in 1829 the council offered

$500 for the annual rental of the second floor. This was accepted, but the first exhibition in the new building was not held until the spring of 1831. There was considerable discussion in regard to the color of the walls of the gallery. "The first choice was a '*negative* tea-green'—a light and admirable color. After some years, and many discussions, it was changed to a '*deep red.*' In 1859 it was ordered, and made of the deepest olive-green: little less than black. That, however, was quickly abandoned." (Cummings)

Henry Inman having changed his residence to Philadelphia, and Samuel Morse being still in Europe, William Dunlap was elected vice-president and chairman pro tem.

In October, 1830, the school was installed in Clinton Hall and arrangements were made to decorate the new quarters. The school was adapted both as a lecture hall and classroom, with a platform at one end and the seats arranged as an amphitheatre. The drawing boards were hinged to the back of the seats with a lamp affixed above each. The enrollment increased, and the attendance at classes and lectures was highly gratifying; "indeed, the little lecture room was often overcrowded." The lectures by William Cullen Bryant on ancient history elicited particular interest, being "filled with a fervid poetic fire"; Dr. Bush lectured on anatomy, with demonstrations; and a series of lectures by Charles Edwards on the most famous antique statues was later distributed in printed form.

The most favorable date for the opening of the exhibition was frequently discussed. "Circumstances determine it which cannot be foreseen—viz., the weather: if the Spring is a backward one, the later date is most acceptable; if warm and forward, the early one is preferable; though on no account so late as the 25th May." (Cummings) For the most part the exhibitions opened about the middle of April and closed the first week in July.

In the instructions to exhibitors for the exhibition of 1829 the catalogue announced that "works by living artists only, and such as have never before been exhibited by the Academy will be received. . . . No copies of Pictures, copies of Engravings, nor copies of Statues (except in enamel) will be received. . . . No picture or drawing will be admitted unless handsomely framed." No commission was charged on sales, and no picture was subject to sale if not owned by the artist. The expense for transportation of all works to and from the gallery was defrayed by the Academy.

The number of works which each artist was permitted to exhibit was unlimited. In the exhibition of 1830, Henry Inman was represented by 11 examples; William Dunlap by 10; Waldo and Jewett by 6, and so on. The Honorary Members and nonmembers represented included Washington Allston, John Trumbull, J. W. Jarvis, Rembrandt Peale, Thomas Doughty, Gilbert Stuart, Chester Harding, Charles Robert Leslie, and John Quidor. Thomas Sully appears for the first time in the exhibition of 1830.

In the annual report of 1846, the president advised: "the propriety of limiting the number of works presented by each contributor for exhibition —say to eight or thereabouts—not only that each may be more fairly exposed, but also with reference to a due regard to variety and interest in the aggregate."

An interesting test case occurred during the exhibition of 1835, which was settled by law. An exhibitor, being displeased with the disposition of his work, removed it from the walls. The Academy brought suit to determine the principle involved, stating to the court that it was not seeking damages. The judge upheld the Academy's contention, the picture was replaced, and the artist fined six cents.

President Morse being absent, the opponents of the Academy proclaimed that the Academy could not long endure without his vigorous leadership. The members lost some of their initial enthusiasm. The gallery space being now greatly increased, it was feared there would not be enough creditable work for an impressive showing. With this in mind it was agreed to break precedent and to have an exhibition limited to works exhibited in previous years. The result justified the resolution. Called the "Review Exhibition," it proved "highly successful"; it was at once a "Renovator," a "Reviver," and a "Restorer." Thus the new gallery was inaugurated with 201 representations. The experiment having accomplished its purpose, it was agreed that it would in the future be unnecessary to repeat it.

In the exhibition of the following year, 1832, a work in sculpture by Greenough created a heated ethical controversy of historic interest, revealing the attitude of "Public Opinion" relative to aesthetic morals. The subject, about three feet high and carved in marble, was entitled *The Chanting Cherubs*, and represented two children innocently nude. It was "fiercely assailed by 'Modistus,' who effervesced through the press for some time." But shortly after the closing of the exhibition, two life-size pictures by the French painter De Boeuf were displayed at the galleries of the American Academy, entitled the *Temptation* and the *Expulsion* in which Adam and Eve were pictured in the nude. "They were pronounced 'Great Moral Pictures,' and their exposition made a fortune for their exhibitor." (Cummings)

The moral controversy, however, had its reflection in the school. The antique statues had suffered conspicuous mutilation, and it was resolved by Ingham "that a plaster leaf be placed in lieu thereof." The motion occasioned considerable mirth, and although opposed by some, was adopted.

On December 5, 1835, the "Great Fire" devastated the area south of Wall Street and east of Broadway, leaving that part of the city in utter ruin. Water froze in the buckets and hose; the available supply was exhausted. Many of the old landmarks of the city were destroyed. The large exhibition room of the Academy, at Clinton Hall, was placed at the disposal of the civic body to care for the destitute sufferers. After the rebuilding of the lower section of the city, the residential section moved northward. Streets were laid out in the rural country surrounding Washington Square; streams were diverted underground. With the extension of the city limits, an era of building construction followed, the population increasing from 60,000 at the beginning of the century to over 200,000 at the time of the "Great Fire."

It was at this time that Dunlap proposed writing a *History of the Arts of Design in the United States*. Although the Academy was not able to subsidize the work, it was initiated and sponsored by the council and through the good offices of the treasurer, Thomas Cummings, subscriptions for the publication were solicited, resulting in doubling the amount named by Dunlap for the completion of the work, without which this basic source of information on the lives of the earliest American artists would have been lost.

· III ·

YEARS OF CONFLICT: THE FIRST EXHIBITION · CONTROVERSY BETWEEN
THE AMERICAN ACADEMY OF FINE ARTS AND THE NATIONAL ACADEMY
OF DESIGN · JOHN TRUMBULL AND SAMUEL F. B. MORSE · THE END
OF THE AMERICAN ACADEMY

IN 1826, the National Academy held its first exhibition. With no habitation or financial support, the first problem was to locate a suitable room.
This was found on the second floor of a dwelling on the southeast corner
of Broadway and Reade Street. The room was lighted by side windows
and measured 25 by 50 feet. Being open from 9 A.M. to 10 P.M., it was
lighted after dark by three gas burners, each with two lights only.

In this improvised gallery the first exhibition of the National Academy
was formally opened with conscious dignity and ceremony with guests by
invitation only. The members of the Academy received "*with a white
rosette in their button-holes.*" Those attending included "his Excellency,
Governor Clinton and suite, his Honor the Mayor, the Common Council
of the City, the Judges of the Courts, the Faculty of Columbia College, the
members of the American Academy of Fine Arts, and *persons of distinction* at '*present residing* in the city.'" (Cummings) The following day,
May 14, 1826, the exhibition was opened to the public.

The catalogue was prefaced with a brief introduction by William
Dunlap and Samuel Morse. "The Artists of the City of New-York have
associated . . . for the purpose of mutual improvement and the instruction of their pupils. They have no object in view but the advancement of
the Arts and the benefit of the Artists. . . ." Signed "Their good wisher,
W. D." Morse concluded his brief remarks by adding, "The only encour-

agement asked from the public at present is their attendance on the Exhibitions and Lectures." The 182 works displayed included paintings in oil and water color, drawings of machinery, architectural drawings, and engravings.

The exhibition continued until the first of July, and although well attended, did not meet expenses. The accounts being audited, the deficit was found to be $163, to pay which each member was assessed $7. The new venture was frowned upon by the supporters of the American Academy, and great effort was made by its members to improve its own advantages. Its library was increased, copies of Hogarth and Reynolds were added to the gallery, students were invited to study under instruction, and the rooms were to be "*warmed*, a thing never before attempted." The press also joined the American Academy in assailing the newly formed institution under the repeated signature of "Neutral Tints."

The first session of the school under the direction of the National Academy opened on November 15, 1826, in the rooms of the Philosophical Society, with an enrollment of 20 students. Classes were held every Monday, Wednesday, and Friday evening. To defray the expenses of the school for the ensuing year, a voluntary subscription was made by the members of the Academy. Dr. F. G. King was appointed professor of anatomy; Charles B. Shaw, professor of perspective. Two Academicians in rotation instructed the antique class. At the close of the season, two large silver palettes and two small ones were awarded as "premiums." "Every student on admission to the Academy will pay the Treasurer $5, being the proportion of expenses for fuel and light for the season. . . . Each student is requested to furnish himself with sperm or wax candles to draw by." It was at this time that Morse painted his "excellent likeness" of Dr. King, now in the permanent collection of the Academy.

The school reopened in the gallery where the exhibition was held, being now favored with gaslight. The lectures on anatomy and perspective were continued, and William Cullen Bryant was added to the faculty, giving lectures on mythology. Morse, Dunlap, Cummings, and others served alternately as instructors in drawing. Later James J. Mapes was appointed Professor of Chemistry and Natural Philosophy of Colors. His lectures were eagerly attended both by the students and by members of the profession. Several colors were tested for permanency and new ones added to the palette. The premiums offered incited keen competition. The decision of awards was made by a balloting of the students, followed by a balloting of the council; this was later changed to the decision of the students alone. As this created unfavorable rivalry, the council finally awarded the prizes. The premiums pertained to the artists' profession: a handsomely bound copy of Reynolds's *Discourses;* Cunningham's *Lives of the Most Eminent British Painters;* a gold and silver palette, and so on. The principle of instruction inculcated both mental and visual knowledge as well as technical facility. The school was considered of paramount importance to the significance of an academy, the deficit accruing from its operation being gladly paid from the scant funds of the treasury.

At the conclusion of the first season, President Morse delivered an address, and presented the premiums to the students in the chapel of Columbia College, then located at Church Street opposite Park Place. Beginning his address, Mr. Morse said: "The occasion of our first anniversary furnishes me with an opportunity, which I gladly improve, of explaining to you more at large the nature of those institutions among which we have lately ranked ourselves."

In an extended discourse, he then went on to present a historical survey of the formation and principles of academies of art.

Although [he said], it has been a disputed point whether, on the whole, Academies of Arts have a favorable effect . . . it does not therefore follow that we should teach nothing, nor that no system should be observed. . . . It has been urged against academies that, while they may encourage genius, they for the most part foster pretension and mediocrity. What should we think of the florist who should keep his flowers in total darkness, lest the same sun which invigorates the flower, should also warm into life the weeds which will spring up around it? (Cummings)

Continuing, he elaborated on the origin of academies for the improvement of art, under the protection of St. Luke in Venice, 1345; in Florence, 1350; in France, 1648; Vienna, 1704; Spain, 1752; Russia, 1758; Milan, 1800. Then followed a survey of the arts in England and the eventual establishment in 1768 of the Royal Academy of Arts under its first President, Sir Joshua Reynolds. The plan of the Royal Academy, as outlined by the artists in their petition to the King, was very simple: "1st. The establishment of a well-regulated *School,* or Academy of Design for the use of students in the arts; and, 2d. An *Annual Exhibition,* open to all artists of distinguished merit, where they may offer their performances to public inspection. . . . The whole government of the [Royal] Academy is vested in a President, a Council, and General Assembly, all the individuals of whom are professional artists." In concluding his remarks on academies in general, Morse summarized the origin and principles which they all held in common. First: artists were the first to organize European academies of arts; "In *all cases their entire government is entrusted to Artists*"; second: "the establishment of schools for students of art"; third: "*Premiums to incite the students to industry and emulation*"; fourth: "*an Exhibition of the works of living artists.*" (Cummings)

Specifically alluding to the newly formed Academy, he said: "*individual prosperity depends on the prosperity of the whole body*" and quoted D'Israeli: " 'an Academy . . . can only succeed by the same means in which originated all such Academies—among *individuals* themselves; it will not be by the favor of the *many*, but by the wisdom of the *few*. It is not even in the power of Royalty to create at a word, what can only be formed by the *co-operation of the workmen themselves*, and of the great task-master, Time.' " Before ending, the president emphasized the moral responsibility of an Academy in relation to the civic community.

On the publication of the president's address there followed an oratorical battle for the survival of the new Academy. The first broadside appeared in the *North American Review*. The extent of the article and the high level of its consideration was, in fact, a tribute to the new organization, as well as a revealing commentary on the "cultured" mind of the time. The unnamed author challenged the assumption and pretension of the Associated Artists and derided the name "National Academy." Ignoring the primal contention in the president's address as to what constitutes an academy and wherein the National Academy differs in its fundamental principals from the American Academy, the writer proceeded in a long abstract dissertation on the significance of the arts as an "ornament of society." Commenting on the rise of science and industry and the flourishing activity of New York as its center, he continued: "We are not prepared to see the American system, as it is called, extended to literature or the arts. It would be the worst possible policy for the artists. Painting and sculpture are not among the necessaries of life. Much as they improve and adorn society, a taste for them is not even the necessary accompaniment of a high degree of civilization."

Morse had alluded to the spurious "old masters" which were being introduced in New York and to their ready purchase by unsuspecting patrons, contending that it would be more worthy and helpful to encourage contemporary talent. To which the reviewer answered: "We would not have the arts degraded even in favor of the artists. . . . We can hardly hope that the masterpieces of ancient art are ever to be surpassed here or in Europe. The forms and occupations of society are growing every day less favorable to the highest efforts of the imagination. We live in an age of utility. . . . In this cultivation of the reason, the imagination loses its power. Eloquence, poetry, painting and sculpture, do not belong to such an age; they are already declining, and they must give way before the progress of popular education, science and the useful arts. . . . Argument is almost all the oratory of our time."

The authority of the *North American Review* made it incumbent upon Morse to reply. Despite the intellectual erudition of the author, Morse, point by point, illustrated the fallacy of his pretensions. With more faith and vision than the reviewer, the president, in a lengthy article, demonstrated not alone his intimate understanding of the arts and its practitioners but his ability to defend them. "In the last number of the *North American Review*, the article No. X. purports to be a critique on my discourse delivered before the National Academy of Design. In that article, written with much ability, and for the most part with courtesy, there are some strictures on the Institution with which I am connected, and on subjects relating to the Fine Arts generally, that I have thought it my duty to notice." He then reiterated the principles fundamental to all academies, adding that "individuals of a particular profession should best know how to manage what relates to that profession." In regard to the disparaging inference in the use of the name "National Academy," Mr. Morse countered by asking: " 'by what right' does the *Review* to which he has contributed, bear the name of *North American?* . . . yet who objects to its name, or thinks it worth while to write a page to prove that, because it is published in Boston, it should have a more limited title?" He then informed the reviewer that: "The catalogue of the sixty-four members of the Academy will show nearly all the most eminent names of the artists in the United States, not from New York alone, but from Philadelphia, Boston, Washington and Charleston." In the heated controversy which followed, the new Academy was greatly blessed in having an able spokesman as well as a distinguished artist.

Meanwhile the artists, undismayed by opposition, and firm in their solidarity, were engaged in arranging for their second exhibition. A more suitable location was found in the upper story of the Arcade Baths on Chambers Street. The room, about 25 by 50 feet, fortunately "sky-lighted," was leased to the Academy by a generous landlord for $300 a year. The exhibition opened May 17, 1827, and closed on July 5. "An entertainment was spread during the day, and a Committee of Academicians detailed to receive invited guests." There were shown 117 examples of "Original Works by Living Artists, never before exhibited by the Academy." (This rule has ever since been adhered to.) The gallery was lighted at night by 100 concealed gas burners, an innovation which proved decidedly successful, and the evening attendance exceeded that of the daytime. Receipts more than balanced expenses, but despite the favorable reception, hostility continued unabated. "Middle-Tint" again appeared in print, distributing handbills both of personal and general abuse. In defense of the Academy seven successive letters were published in the *Morning Courier* under the pseudonym of "Boydell." The letters impartially set forth in detail the formation, purpose and reasons for founding the new Academy, and probably constitute the most concise and authentic history of the confused controversy. They were said to have been written by Morse, but at a later time "Boydell" disproved this allegation.

The members of the American Academy had presumed that the National Academy could not survive merely from the receipts of its exhibitions and without capital funds. Dismayed by the opening of the third exhibition, the older institution and its supporters renewed their vindictive criticism. "Middle-Tint the Second" could find no good in the works displayed. "We wonder at the infatuation which has pervaded this community, in relation to this young illiterate aspirant! According to the plan laid down to, and pursued by the learned critics of our day, every artist of merit to be kept in the background, like stool pigeons in a field to gull the public, and thereby fill the pockets of Messrs. Morse, Ingham, Inman, Cole, and Cummings," and so on and on.

A new contributor to the controversy appeared in three successive letters published in the *Evening Post*. Signed "Denon" the articles were again attributed to Samuel Morse and excited bitter animosity on the part of John Trumbull. Morse, however, was temporarily away from the city, and did not learn of their publication until his return. "Denon" like "Boydell" gave a factual report of the principles of the National Academy, and wherein it differed from the American Academy.

The conflict of opinions between Mr. Morse, the President of the Academy, and the *North American Review,* has placed the whole subject very clearly before the public. . . . The American Academy of Fine Arts consists of nearly 300 stockholders of various professions, Lawyers, Physicians, Merchants, etc., etc., who have each paid $25 and who have each a vote in the choice of officers for directing the Institution. Merged in this body of the stockholders, were some of the few artists who belonged to the Academy before the formation of the National Academy, a meagre minority, and who must from the principles of the Institution always have remained a minority.

After citing the progress of the National Academy, the awakened interest in the arts, and the combined activity of the artists concerned, the writer concluded the first letter:

And now let us glance a moment at the difference in the natural advantages of the two Institutions. The American Academy of Fine Arts, with 264 patrons giving the sum of $6,600, to which add the receipts of at least 12 years of exhibitions, . . . rooms for *officers,* all rent free; and why is it in debt? What has become of all these funds? Where are its schools? Where its lectures? Where indeed is there any evidence of prosperity and of energetic and discreet government, at all answerable to the means given by its patrons, or to the reasonable expectations of the public who have been so bountiful to it?

In closing the writer stated that the National Academy maintains a school of 30 selected pupils, pays rent for its accommodations, has no city support, and yet is free from debt and rapidly rising in reputation. "The wish has been expressed in the public journals, and very often in common conversation, that there should be a *union of the two Academies.*"

The second letter considers the desirability of this union. Reviewing again the causes of dissatisfaction and the independence of the artists by forming their own association, the writer asks what would they gain by union? For the privilege of using the casts and the association with the patrons, the artists would lose their control under the government of the American Academy; furthermore the older institution was now burdened with debts, while the Associated Artists were self-supporting. Finally, what would the public gain?

Just so far as the arts are of public importance—just so far as it is proper that their direction should be under the control of those who best understand them.

Courts of justice are not placed under the control of physicians; medical degrees are not conferred by lawyers, nor the Chamber of Commerce composed of Artists. Why, then, should the concerns of the Artists be thought in better hands than in their own?

A third letter was drafted but withheld. By now many other anonymous writers had contributed to the controversy. A satirical "letter from Joe Strickland" to Samuel Morse introduced personalities. A final notice from "Denon" in the *Evening Post* warns against personal animosities.

Who cares a fig whether Mr. Morse is ambitious, or Mr. Trumbull unpopular among his brother artists? . . . . A truce, then, with personalities! The present aspect of the Academic controversy is particularly interesting. Philadelphia is an interested spectator; the controversy on both sides I find in the journals of our sister city. The contest has happily got into the hands of the two Presidents, and has assumed an official shape.

The argument had gained wide public attention and venomous articles continued to appear in the daily press. "Denon," who was erroneously thought to be Morse, was promptly answered by "A Patron," who asserted that the

communication had not the merit of a criticism, but was the mere putrid effusion of the most deadly feelings of an individual against the *very Institution in which he was hatched.* . . . Were I myself an artist, jealous of my fame, and wishing for some new machine other than my brush to raise me to the astonished admiration of the world, I might likewise endeavor to create some new three-legged animal to stride upon, and goad it on with a goose's quill, before the admiring multitude, to be gazed at. I might, perhaps, become the champion of one Institution, and, like a snake that is hidden, or a disease, spread my poison over the other.

Remarking that he is a friend of both Institutions, "Patron" continues:

I step forth to arrest the hand of an assassin, *knowing*, as I *do*, the cloak from under which the dagger sprung. I should deem myself accessary to the deed, were I to suppress from the public eye the source from which it came, and the malicious motive which put it into action. . . . I appeal to every fair and honest man, who has read the eulogy on the works in the New Academy which appeared in the *Morning Courier*, immediately after the opening of the Exhibition, and before the world was able to estimate, or critic to decide; and answer me whether such unbounded, fulsome praise, sounds like the language of the critic, or like the sounds of a man speaking his own fame to the world. . . . I would not endeavor to turn the public ear from the dulcet sounds of his smooth-tongued eloquence; but I would remind them, while they look in his smiling face, and listen to his plausible sounds, that the charm comes from a thing that creeps in the grass.

The final battle of the two academies was now culminating, and the leading protagonists were to face each other in print. An article in the New York *American* made this inevitable. Signed "A Lay Member" the writer began:

> During the course of last winter there appeared in the *Journal of Commerce* "A Reply to Art. 10, No. 58, in the *North American Review*, entitled 'Academies of Arts, and so forth,' by Samuel F. B. Morse, President of the National Academy of Design." And subsequently appeared seven letters signed "Boydell." These have since been published in pamphlet form and circulated, and are understood to be the acknowledged productions of Mr. Morse.
>
> Recently, since the opening of the spring Exhibition, several pieces have also appeared in the *Evening Post*, written in the same spirit and *style, possibly by the same hand*—particularly one of Friday, the 23rd inst., signed "Denon," on the union of the two Academies. . . . I am one of the early members of the original Academy—*lay-members*, I understand we who are not artists by profession are facetiously called.

In defense of the American Academy, the author presented in sequence the conditions leading to the impasse, with extended quotations from Colonel Trumbull's address before the Academy and an exposition of its government. Alluding to the artists as " *'seceders'*—men who had not the spirit to qualify themselves generally as electors," he asks, "It may well be doubted whether, in the present days of Christianity, there can be found an example so pure, of the exalted influence of the divine principles on any established society of Christians, as to have induced the majority to yield their opinions, and the elections of their officers, to the dictation of a small minority of dissenters; and could it have been expected here?"

Returning to New York, Morse was astonished at the tone of the letters, which he had not heretofore read. He at once published a letter in the *Evening Post*. With even tenor and self-command he repudiated the authorship of the letters mentioned and deplored the

indecency of publicly charging upon any individual what has been published anonymously, especially where principles, and not private character seem to have been the object of discussion. . . . I have not now time, nor is my mind in a state, to expose the *falsely colored* account of the origin of the National

CLINTON HALL
LITHOGRAPH BY ALEXANDER J. DAVIS, A.N.A., 1830

In its time, Clinton Hall was the cultural center of
New York. The Academy held its exhibitions here,
1831 to 1840.

Funeral Honours to Gen. Lafayette.

At a Meeting of the **NATIONAL ACADEMY OF DESIGN**, held on Tuesday Evening, the 24th inst., the following preamble and Resolutions were adopted.

Whereas, the President having communicated the invitation of the Common Council of this City to the National Academy of Design, to participate in the funeral solemnities in honour of Gen. Lafayette, to take place on Thursday, the 26th inst.—Therefore, Resolved, That we will attend in a body on the said day, in the place appointed by the City Authorities, wearing the usual badge of mourning, and taking such place in the procession as shall be assigned us by the Committee of the Hon. the Common Council.—Resolved, That the Secretary report these resolutions to the Hon. the Common Council.—In compliance with the above Resolutions you are requested to meet at the Council Room, Clinton Hall, on Thursday, June 26th, at 1 o'clock, P. M.

By order of the Academy,

A. B. DURAND, Secretary.

June 23d, 1834.

Academy of Design by the *Lay-Member*. This I propose hereafter to do, especially as it appears in at least a *semi-official* shape. . . .

One word, however, on the term *"Lay-members"*. . . . I resign all my claims to the *authorship*, and consequently to the *facetiousness* of this term: I not only never used it, but I do not recollect ever to have seen or heard the name before this morning applied to those who are not of the profession.

A Patron singles me out for a pretty full measure of delicate abuse. I have not known whether most to pity the passion into which the gentleman has wrought himself, or to be surprised at finding such an array of *"daggers"* and *"deadly shafts,"* and *"snakes,"* *"reptiles,"* and *"poison,"* and *"venom,"* . . . not a single point of public interest touched upon. . . . The thing may safely be left to itself.

The letter, which followed in reply to "A Layman," appeared in the *Post* under the title "Exposé of the Transactions between the Drawing Association and the American Academy of Fine Arts, previous to the formation of the National Academy of Design." Having been present at the conferences, Morse presented a factual account of the proceedings, and related just why and how the Drawing Association came to be formed.

In the autumn of 1825, there were found to be a considerable number of Artists in the city. They had but little social intercourse. There was no common place of meeting. The Artists, therefore, were for the most part unknown to each other. In October of that year, a few of them assembled at the house of one of their numbers in Broadway, for conversation on the state of the Arts. Their low condition was lamented, and the plan suggested, that if a few of us would associate for drawing, in the evenings of the approaching winter, it would be a pleasant mode of passing the time, combining improvement with pleasure. The plan suggested for a Drawing Association was at once acceded to, and the number consisting of but seven, at first determined to meet in a private room in Canal Street, and use the models belonging to the individuals of the Association. . . . The Association increased rapidly until most of the principal artists of the city were of our number, amounting in all to thirty-one, and we successively, as our numbers increased, occupied the rooms of the Agricultural, Historical and Philosophical Societies, through the generous indulgence of the gentlemen of these several Associations.

Then follow the events previously outlined, the point at issue being that the Associated Artists were not "seceders, mutineers, deserters, etc.," as they had formed an independent organization; and that the American Academy had acted in bad faith by not electing the six candidates nominated. Preceding the election a notice had been published, "to the stock-holders of the American Academy of the Fine Arts," informing its members of

the more than ordinary importance of the present election; involving no less than the union of the body of Artists with the Academy, or their separation from it. . . . At a meeting of the Committee of Conference, it was agreed that the next Board of Directors should comprise at least six Artists. The Artists accordingly balloted for six of their members to be submitted to the electors, who being the chosen representatives of Artists, it is to be understood that all or none will serve.

It had been claimed that the anonymous writer of this notice was an artist using it as a threat to the directors. "And now," wrote Morse, "what will be thought of these charges of arrogance, etc., when the public are informed that the dreadful notice was composed and sent to the papers by three stockholders of the American Academy of Fine Arts!"

Morse, it must be remembered, was the only writer involved in the controversy who wrote over his own name. John Trumbull now answered him as president of the American Academy. To best understand his reply, we must first consider the personalities and attitudes of these two artists.

John Trumbull was at this time seventy-two years of age. Born in 1756, he was the son of the noted patriot, Jonathan Trumbull, first Governor of Connecticut. Associated with a French family, the youthful son was attracted to the fine arts. He was much impressed by a visit to Copley. Dunlap tells us, "Copley was dressed in a suit of crimson velvet and gold buttons; and the elegance of his style and his high repute, impressed the future artist with grand ideas of the life of a painter." This notation summarizes Trumbull's aspiration. A brilliant scholar at Harvard, where he graduated at seventeen, his manner was courtly, his presence imposing, and his associates men of learning. But he was proud and oversensitive. Made deputy adjutant general under Gates at the outbreak of the war, he saw active service but resigned shortly thereafter, on a trifling matter involving a confusion in the dates on which he was commissioned. He sailed for England during the Revolution, was arrested in London as a spy, but was released after seven months confinement through the importunities of Benjamin West, under whom he was studying. Later he served as secretary to John Jay, then Ambassador to England, and was on the Commission of Claims at the conclusion of the war. Trumbull was thus thoroughly a man of the world. His portraits of Revolutionary heroes and his historical pictures brought him international fame. At the time of the Academical controversy he had but recently completed the four panels for the rotunda of the Capital at Washington. The work did not receive the applause anticipated, and Trumbull was in a somewhat bitter mood of disappointment.

Morse represented a younger generation of artists. Born in 1791, he was but thirty-five years of age when he assumed the presidency of the National Academy. His father, the Rev. Jedediah Morse, was the first American geographer; his maternal great-grandfather was the Rev. Dr. Samuel Finley, President of Princeton College. His mother's maiden name was Elizabeth Breese. Educated at Yale, he formed an early friendship with Washington Allston, which was to confirm him in his desire to become a painter. Allston had studied under West in London, and when he returned there in 1811, young Morse was placed under his guidance. Morse studied in the Royal Academy from 1811 to 1815, his progress being supervised by its venerable president, Benjamin West. He thus became thoroughly acquainted with the mode of teaching and the government of the Academy, a knowledge which was to prove invaluable in the formation of the National Academy. Attaining considerable success and honors in England, Morse returned to America with high aspirations as a historical painter, but finding no response to the "grand style," he turned to portrait painting, in which he attained distinction.

It will be seen that the two adversaries represented disparate ages and temperaments; Trumbull exemplified the traditional type of the colonial "gentleman," utterly divorced from the obscure position of the youthful artists then striving for livelihood and recognition; while Morse, equally cultured, championed the younger generation by furthering their opportunities for study and advancement.

Thus the culminating letters pertaining to the heated controversy were as uncompromisingly opposed as were the personalities involved. After quoting the salient points of Morse's letter, Trumbull inserted his own report as president of the American Academy in which he had proposed to the directors of the Academy "that, hereafter, of the eleven Directors authorized to be annually elected, six, at least, shall always be taken from among the Academicians, artists by profession," asserting that Mr. Morse knew "the election was conducted in conformity to that law, and that six artists, of whom he was one, were elected." Granting that the honor of organizing the Drawing Association belonged entirely to Morse, he conjectured that its ultimate aim was to revoke the charter of the American Academy, "to strip the obnoxious stockholders of their property, and to vest it in the President and Council of the Artists." The "Lay Member" had accused the artists of "mutiny and desertion." "He had some reason derived from analogy," said Trumbull, "for, in military and naval service, such is the language, and the penalty is death."

Alluding to the Gallery of the Fine Arts, of the splendid works displayed, and the benefits derived therefrom, he concluded "If artists choose to withdraw and hold themselves separate from such an Institution, from such gratuitous offers of the means of improvement, let them not ascribe blame to the Board of Directors." But heated words had been used in reference to Morse's "Exposé," "as being little better than the quibbling defense of a bad cause by a wretched pettifogger, who keeps out of sight the main questions, and buries truth and sense in a mass of sounding words."

Morse replied with dignity and moderation. After a brief introduction of vindication, in rebuttal he declared that Colonel Trumbull ought to know that the president and vice-president were members of the board of directors and that it therefore is composed not of 11 but of 13 members. This, however, was not the crux of the matter. "The American Academy is *not* an Academy. It is only (as its President has termed it), 'a sort of Benefit Club.'" In contrast "The National Academy is a real Academy for the promotion of the Arts of Design. Its plan was formed by Artists on sound and proper principles; the only principles on which Academies have been successfully established in other countries. . . . The Institution has prospered beyond the most sanguine expectations." Its members "have the satisfaction to believe that the great body of the stockholders of the old Institution are pleased with the success which has attended the new Academy, and they know that many of them have taken the pains to express their gratification."

Other reverberations followed. Trumbull and Morse were reviewed by Dunlap under the title of "Doctors Differ"; but the united support of the artists and the growing popularity of the exhibitions confirmed the validity of their purpose.

Overtures were made by the American Academy to unite with the new organization. Several conferences were held by their respective committees at which the members representing the council of the Academy were favorably disposed. However, when the project was proposed to the stockholders of the American Academy in 1833, Colonel Trumbull made an elaborate address urgently advising against the union. His opinion prevailed. In his report to the council, Morse read his reply to Colonel Trumbull's protest, whereupon it was ordered to be printed and distributed, with Colonel Trumbull's address as an appendix.

In 1836, conferences were reopened at the request of the American Academy. In his annual address of that year President Morse declared: "It is daily and hourly becoming of less importance to us whether the terms of union, as it is called, be settled; the difference of circumstances in which both now are, has made it a matter of comparative indifference to us." The members of the Academy, firmly convinced that artists should govern an academy of arts, had no wish to relinquish their successful independence.

The old Academy continued its lethargic existence for several years longer. Its stockholders and directors lost interest; the meetings were poorly attended and eventually the institution, lacking support, became financially insolvent. In 1832 the American Academy was ordered by the Corporation of the City to vacate its galleries in the old Alms House which it had occupied rent free for 16 years. This was a heavy blow. The president had urged the City Fathers not to "withdraw the particular protection from a Society which is yet too feeble to subsist alone and must sink without protection," but without avail.

At this critical moment the faithful David Hosack offered the Academy a lot in the rear of his residence on which a gallery was erected after designs by Trumbull, who incorporated in the building a studio for his own use. The venerable Dr. Hosack, who had leased the building and grounds to the Academy, and who was its main pillar of support, died in 1835. Colonel Trumbull resigned as president in 1836; his successors were Rembrandt Peale in 1837, and Dr. Alexander E. Hosack in 1839. As if to further the pathetic decline of the older institution and to deprive its former president of his spacious studio, a fire partly destroyed the upper story of the building in 1837, and a second more serious fire in 1839, starting in the library, injured many of the paintings and destroyed

the collection of books and prints, including the rare volumes of Piranesi.
(Cowdrey)

This proved to be the end. In 1841 the remaining works of art and
various properties were sold at auction, the National Academy lending its
galleries in which to conduct the sale. The pictures brought low prices
and were scattered among anonymous buyers. The casts from the antique were acquired by the National Academy, the only bidder, for $400
and became the "ornament" of the school for many generations, until
largely destroyed by fire in 1905.

In retrospect it will be seen that the two academies were founded on
basically different principles. It should be remembered, as Trumbull
pointed out, that at the time of the inception of the American Academy
(1802), there were few artists in New York, and there was no gallery in
which works of art could be exhibited. The importation of the casts
from the Louvre and the introduction of works by the old masters,
though many were no doubt spurious, stimulated an interest in art, and
brought about the establishment of the first museum in New York, an
example which was later followed in Philadelphia and Boston.

But times changed following the War of 1812. Industry flourished;
new enterprises were engendered; nationalism had a recrudescence; the
younger generation moved to the financial front. With the decline of
the colonial tradition, the student of art entered his profession under the
changed conditions of the growing republic.

It was at this stage that Samuel Morse came upon the scene. The
American Academy was composed almost entirely of well-to-do laymen. The aspiring student could not afford to join; there was little advantage in doing so. The younger artists, or "junior artists," as Trumbull
called them, were unknown to each other. It was, as we have seen, due
to the vision of Morse, as well as his unbounded faith and benevolence,
that the artists were united in a common need for the furtherance of their
art and livelihood. The National Academy was, therefore, founded upon
an entirely different principle than the older institution, and succeeded
because it responded to the conditions of the rising generation.

John Trumbull died in November, 1843.

Departed this life, the venerable Colonel Trumbull, aged eighty-seven years,
an artist and a gentleman. Whatever differences of opinion may have existed
as to his policy as President of the old American Academy, however he may

have proved deficient in his estimate of the rising generation of artists in his day, there is no doubt he acted in the full belief in the wisdom of his views. If fault there were, the fault was doubtless in his education. He was of the old school; his courtesy and urbanity of manner were worthy of imitation; his want of heartfeltness for the professional was severely felt by the younger artists.

So writes Thomas Cummings, who as a young student was present on the memorable morning when Trumbull appeared before the closed doors of the school, and whose protest eventuated in the Drawing Association and the National Academy of Design.

·IV·

AMERICAN PAINTING, 1825–1865: PORTRAITURE · LANDSCAPE ·
GENRE

EIGHTEENTH CENTURY commentators neatly classified the relative importance of painting into three categories: history, portrait and landscape.
The historical—including Biblical and other subjects—was associated
with the "heroic" and was considered the highest form of expression. In
this sphere the "old masters" were held to be supreme. Contemporary
portraiture, immortalizing the aristocracy and glamorizing the fashionables of the period, although bringing renown to the painters, was rela-
tively less esteemed. Landscape painting was considered a minor art.

Although "the portrait manufacturers"—to use Hogarth's phrase—
were fully employed and highly remunerated, the few artists who aspired
to the "grand style" of historical painting met with little reward. Benjamin West was enabled to carry out his large historical works only by
the favor and patronage of the king. Otherwise, profit from historical
painting came mostly from the sale of engraved reproductions or in the
proceeds from special exhibitions. John Trumbull, following the example of West, executed a number of historical works, the engravings from
which were widely distributed, but the original paintings remained un-
sold and were ultimately bequeathed to Yale University, the artist receiving an annuity which sustained him in his closing years. Morse, on
returning from England, endeavored to follow the same course, but met
with little success. Many of Washington Allston's important works remained in his studio until his death. Dunlap made a meager living from
the exhibition of his large religious pictures, which were shown in various cities by a traveling agent. Later this sort of exhibition was replaced
by the popular panorama.

The principal livelihood of the artist at the beginning of the nineteenth century was, as in England, derived from portrait commissions. It is not surprising, in consequence, that portraiture was predominant in the early exhibitions of the Academy.

In style and method our artists followed the English tradition. The painter inherited definite formulas. A young artist visiting Gilbert Stuart in Boston was honored by the master setting his palette: that is mixing the various hues of flesh color. The background was invariably painted a dark uniform hue to reveal the flesh coloring. There were few full-length or elaborated compositions. Before the advent of photography, these early American portraits remain the only visual records of our ancestors, treasured as family memorials or permanently enshrined in national museums or historical societies.

Thomas Sully forms the bridge between the colonial painters and the portraitists of the middle of the nineteenth century. On first going to London in 1809, he worked under the guidance of Benjamin West, but his fluent technique and coloring reflect the style of Sir Thomas Lawrence, who was to replace the elder artist as president of the Royal Academy. Sully made copious notes for the preparation of canvas, studied the pigments, mediums, and methods of the English painters, and followed their formulas in his practice. This accounts for the free, direct brushwork of the underpainting, and the fluid and colorful refinement of his final painting. During his long and successful career, Sully is said to have painted over 2,000 portraits. Residing in Philadelphia, he was elected an Honorary Member of the Academy in 1827, and exhibited there regularly until 1852. Of a most generous and friendly nature, he was a constant guide to younger artists, and published an informative technical treatise for the benefit of his students.

When John Wesley Jarvis came to New York in 1800 as a youth of twenty, there were no competent artists resident in the city. The time, however, was propitious. The rising generation of civic administrators and financiers were ready prospects for the painter. Apprenticed to an engraver, Jarvis said to Dunlap, who knew him intimately, "I made all my master's pictures, engraved them, printed them, and delivered them to customers." This was indeed a practical training. Shortly thereafter he "invented a machine for drawing profiles on glass." This proved a lucrative business, and with it as an introduction to the "fine arts" the artist began his career as a portrait painter. By 1808 he had raised his former price of $5 for small profiles to $100 for a head, and $150 for head and hands.

Jarvis passed most of the winter season in New Orleans and the South, where he was constantly employed. A bon viveur, extravagant and careless, he was, nevertheless, a prolific painter. His work was uneven, but at his best Jarvis was one of the most convincing realistic portrait painters in an age preeminent in portraiture. His rapidity of execution did not permit underpainting or the refinements of glazing. Dunlap writes that he "could not or would not see the merit of Stuart," asserting that Stuart did not "give the colour of nature." This statement is significant, for it marks a departure from the technical methods of the English tradition. When interested in a sitter, and in the proper mood, Jarvis attained a living characterization. He executed several official portraits for the City of New York and portrayed many of the notables of his time, but his wayward life ended in decline and impoverishment. He was represented in the Academy exhibitions from 1826 to 1834.

Cummings records in his Annals, January 14, 1839: "Died, John Wesley Jarvis. Mr. Jarvis was not a member of the Academy—he was however, one of the best portrait painters of his day—eccentric, witty, convivial—and his society much sought by the social. He died in extreme poverty, under the roof of his sister, Mrs. Childs." The council appropriated $35 for the "purchase of a drawing or other work as the family may be willing to part with."

Following the colonial tradition of his father, Charles Willson Peale, Rembrandt Peale was associated with Baltimore and Philadelphia. Elected in 1826 as one of the second 15 founders of the Academy, he exhibited there from the first exhibition until his death in 1860. His first studies abroad were in London during the last days of Benjamin West. Later, while he was resident in Paris, his portraits were highly praised by the celebrated David, who is quoted as saying that the best English painters in France were Americans, and Peale was offered an official position as portrait painter to the French government.

John Vanderlyn had worked in Paris before Rembrandt Peale's arrival. He was awarded the Napoleonic Gold Medal for his picture *Marius* in the Salon of 1808, the suggestion being made by Napoleon himself, who accompanied the jurors in making their selections. Vanderlyn was a companion of Washington Allston in Rome, where the *Marius* was painted, they being at that time the only two American painters residing in the Eternal City. Returning to America in 1815 after his prolonged residence and recognition abroad, the painter was bitterly disappointed at the mild reception given his work and also at not receiving a commission from the government to decorate the panels in the Capitol, which by preference were given to Trumbull. His famous idealized nude, entitled *Ariadne*, was thought by many to be immoral. Following the popular interest in panoramas, he conceived the idea of portraying the great cities of Europe, having made studies with that in view while abroad. In conjunction with the City Corporation, he constructed the rotunda in the City Hall Park in which to display his work. The reward of the project did not meet its promise, and after several attempts elsewhere, being financially embarrassed, he discontinued the undertaking. He executed a number of portraits of distinguished personalities, but, being very slow in procedure and exacting in the completion of his work, Vanderlyn was not in demand as a portrait painter. It is said that in several portraits he required 60 sittings.

He was sponsored by Aaron Burr, who had enabled him to go abroad in 1803, and it is a tragic but gratifying commentary that the protégé at the height of his fame provided for the needs of his former patron, then an impoverished exile in Paris. In the autumn of 1852, on returning to his birthplace at Kingston, ill in health, he asked a stranger for the means of a night's lodging. He was found next morning, in a miserable room overlooking a stable, dead in bed. Vanderlyn had declined membership in the Academy when elected with the second 15, but exhibited there on several occasions from 1830 to 1851, including his portraits of James Monroe and Zachary Taylor.

Washington Allston was esteemed with veneration as the living spirit of the great masters of the past. He epitomized the aspiration for the ideal. Both as a poet and a painter he was accorded universal esteem. Receiving high honors in England, made an associate member of the Royal Academy, and recognized as one of the most promising of the younger artists, on returning to America in 1818, ill in health, he lived in a dream world of nostalgic memory. Unlike his American predecessors in England, who had specialized in portraiture, Allston's vision was formulated by the Italian masters, imbued with the fervor of imaginative contemplation. Reticent by nature, he did not compete for popularity. His work was intimately known to but few of his contemporaries until his first collective exhibition in Chester Harding's studio in 1839. Absorbed in poetic and philosophical reverie, he passed his working days in the studio adjacent to his house at Cambridgeport. His pictures were the inner vision of his aesthetic contemplation, and much of his lifework remained secluded in his studio. His *Belshazzar's Feast*, the first full-sized study of which was made in London in 1817, remained unfinished at his death in 1843.

Nevertheless, Washington Allston was the one artist whom all agreed in venerating as a genius. This was true not only in America. Coleridge, with whom Allston was closely associated in Rome and later in England, said that "he was gifted with an artistic and poetic genius unsurpassed by any man of his age," while Wordsworth declared that Allston's portrait of Coleridge "is the only likeness that ever gave me pleasure." Washington Irving writes in reminiscence of Allston as "a man whose memory I hold in reverence and affection, as one of the purest, noblest, and most intellectual beings that ever honored me with his friendship." Griswold, in *Poets and Poetry of America* published in 1842, a year before Allston's death, summarized his eulogy: "Although Allston owed his chief celebrity to his paintings, which will preserve for his name a place in the list of the greatest artists of all nations and ages, his literary works alone would have given him a high rank among men of genius." This high praise was not sustained, but is a symptom of the cultural aspiration of the age.

Samuel Waldo was born in Windham, Connecticut in 1783. Like that of many other American artists, his early life was associated with the country. After many vicissitudes, he was able to go to London, where he studied for three years, being given helpful advice by Robert Fulton and the ever-faithful Benjamin West. His progress was slow but enduring. Made a director of the American Academy, he was instrumental in commissioning Sir Thomas Lawrence to paint a full length portrait of Benjamin West, which was displayed in the galleries of the Academy. In 1812 he was joined by William Jewett, whom he had met while executing some portraits in New London. Jewett had been employed as a coach painter, but was eager to improve his opportunity. Waldo received him in his family, and after several years of assistance and study, he entered into partnership with his master. Thereafter their pictures appeared under the double name. Jewett was particularly proficient in costume and lace work, but both were able portraitists. Their work appeared in the initial exhibition of the Academy, and they were jointly represented by innumerable examples in the years following. Waldo contributed five portraits, signed with his single name, to the exhibition of 1844.

The portraits of Chester Harding illustrate the severance of the colonial tradition, founded upon the English school, and derived from the technical formulas of the Flemish and Italian painters. They also show a change in the taste of the new patrons, for his fabulous career culminated in an unprecedented success in Boston, which prompted the remark of the aging Stuart: "How goes the Harding fever?" His success was due to obvious factual likeness, frankly stated, without the overtones of glazing or the enhancement of color and pigment quality. It also illustrates the rise of many young painters who attained temporary favor without proper preliminary training or a knowledge of aesthetic creation. Harding was elected an honorary member in 1828 and exhibited at the Academy from 1827 to 1859, his contributions including portraits of Daniel Webster and John Quincy Adams. He died in Boston in 1866.

Henry Inman entered the studio of John Wesley Jarvis in 1814 at the early age of fourteen. As an apprentice he assisted his master in painting backgrounds and accessories. Jarvis was then at the height of his production, and Inman accompanied him to New Orleans and other cities of the South. Before the introduction of drawing from the antique, the relation of master and assistant proved the most practical training in the painter's craft. On concluding his apprenticeship of seven years, Inman established a studio in New York, executing portraits in oil and miniatures. Thomas Cummings became his pupil at this time, and entered into partnership with his teacher in miniature painting. Thus the tradition continued.

Although Inman is known primarily as a portrait painter, his literary inclinations and poetical temperament drew him to the more romantic themes of anecdotal association. He was thus one of the precursors of genre and landscape painting. As one of the principal officers and founders of the Academy, as well as one of its most beloved members, he became a constructive influence in its growth. From the year of the first exhibition in 1826 until 1845, the year before his death, he exhibited at the Academy 150 pictures, mostly in portraiture. Suffering continuously from asthma, and in ill health in his later years, he was commissioned by several friends to paint the portraits of Wordsworth, Macaulay, and Chalmers. This proved a happy interlude in the tragedy of his closing career; it was a new beginning and a final farewell. He was honored by his fellow artists in London and had further prospects of distinguished sitters, but his declining health and the needs of his family necessitated his return. "It is hard to part with you, fellows," he said to a brother Academician when he realized the end was near.

An amendment to the constitution was proposed, "authorizing the payment of annuities to widows and children of deceased Academicians." A meeting was called to implement this decision but a quorum not being present, Miss Anne Hall, the only woman Academician, was persuaded to attend. One member being still needed, the Academicians adjourned in a body to the sick man's residence and in his presence the amendment was passed. "Sitting up in bed, supported by Mrs. Inman and the writer, poor Inman surrounded by his brother Academicians, and within a few days of his death, listened to a hasty reading, by his old friend Ingham, of the amendments, that were to give his wife and family the prospect of something, after his decease." (Cummings)

Inman died on January 17, 1846, and the funeral that followed was an impressive ceremony. "Never, never has been witnessed a more striking scene than that of the long and compact procession, comprising some of the most prominent persons both from this and other cities, following the bier of the artist on foot, for two long miles, on a cold winter evening." A public meeting was held at the Globe Hotel, as a result of which it was decided to hold a memorial exhibition of the late artist's work for the benefit of his family. The Art Union generously loaned its gallery, and the receipts from admissions after deducting the expenses ($1,913.32) were presented to the widow.

One of the most constructive personalities among the original founders, Charles Cromwell Ingham was a member of the council, and for many years vice-president of the Academy. He was born in Dublin in 1796 and was, on his arrival in New York at the age of twenty-one, already an accomplished painter. He achieved immediate attention on exhibiting his *Death of Cleopatra* in the old Academy of Fine Arts. Thereafter he found constant employment as a portrait painter and continued an active career until his death in 1863. His meticulous technique was suited to his gentle nature. His painting achieved a luminous and colorful transparency by means of repeated glazes. A prominent figure in the social life of the period, he became the most fashionable portraitist of feminine grace and beauty, his pictures having a miniaturelike perfection and finish which was much favored by the society of his time.

The most representative American portrait painter in the middle of the nineteenth century was Charles Loring Elliott. Born in the little town of Scipio, near Syracuse, in 1812, he seems to have had no regular schooling, but on going to New York worked for a short time under Trumbull. He later assisted John Quidor, whom Tuckerman refers to as a "fancy painter," in allusion to his imaginative interpretation of Washington Irving's tales. Following his instructor's example, Elliott likewise illustrated Irving, attaining some local recognition. But Elliott was a confirmed realist and he soon found his natural metier in portraiture. He was an excellent draftsman, with a fluid and decisive brush; his vision objective, without compositional accessories. Elected an Academician in 1846, he contributed annually to the exhibitions, being represented from 1836 to 1860 by 127 examples. A prodigious worker, he painted pictures uneven in aesthetic significance, but at his best Elliott ranks as one of our most distinguished portrait painters. Thoroughly American, his work represents the sturdy solidity and materialistic character of the personages of his time. His portrait of Mrs. Mary Ann Goulding, among several examples in the permanent collection of the Academy, is one of his finest achievements. He was highly honored by his fellow Academicians, and at his obsequies the casket was laid in state in the gallery of the Academy.

Benjamin West died in London in 1820, in the eighty-second year of his age. He was buried beside Sir Joshua Reynolds in St. Paul's Cathedral, the ceremony being attended by state dignitaries, noblemen and Academicians. After the turbulent era of continental war he had lived to see the restoration of peace, but with the abdication of George III he had lost the prestige and commissions of the court and also witnessed the passing of the great masters of English portraiture. In 1802, after the temporary reopening of the continent by the Peace of Amiens, West had journeyed to Paris to be present at the inauguration of the exhibition in the Louvre by Napoleon Bonaparte, then First Counsel of France. Attending the exhibition where his own *Death on the Pale Horse* was displayed, he had been received with high honors and found himself the center of unprecedented attention by the famous painters of France and the officials of state. The renown of his historical works had preceded him, the style of which found more favor in France than in England.

The passing of Benjamin West coincided in time with the dawn of a new era in art. After the Napoleonic upheaval and the romantic movement in literature, the quiet of peace and solitude gave a new meaning to nature. In England Turner revealed new visions of immensity in which the heavens were resplendent with ethereal transcendence, while Constable, more enamored of earth, discovered in his immediate environment the subjects of his pictorial realization. In France the classic revival of statuesque form was challenged by the more colorful themes of romantic association. Henceforth the artist was to find his subjects in his own visual experience. With the growing ascendency of the merchant class, landscape and genre painting were to prove a welcome diversion from the predominance of portraiture.

Landscape painting in America had heretofore been held in little esteem or was used only for backgrounds. It is true that many landscapes had been painted before the opening of the new century, mostly houses in a landscape setting, or pictures of estates, done by local journeymen who sought a living in various kinds of handiwork—sign painting, overmantel panels, coach painting, and the like, sometimes naïve and untutored, more often adapted from engravings. But landscape painting as a visual experience and contemplative interpretation of nature did not find expression in America until a later period and was concomitant with the attainment of independence and the romantic movement of the "return to nature." Thereafter, landscape painting enlarged the field of the painters' interest and was a welcome addition to the overburdened exhibitions of portraiture. The writers had preceded the painters in their poetic love of nature, which reflected the pantheistic and romantic philosophy then flowering in Europe. James Fenimore Cooper's novels were widely read; William Cullen Bryant's *Thanatopsis* was the poem of the day; Washington Irving's *Travel Sketches* and other works stimulated pictorial imagination; the romantic novels of Walter Scott were increasingly popular. Love of country and "freedom" became associated with "uncorrupted" nature.

The birth of American landscape painting corresponds, in point of time, with the founding of the National Academy. The rising generation of painters were also influenced by the patronage of a new generation, imbued not so much by the veneration of the old masters as by the more intimate environment and patriotic pride in local achievement. Under

VANDERLYN ROTUNDA, N. YORK PARK.
1823.

THE NEW YORK ROTUNDA
LITHOGRAPH BY ALEXANDER J. DAVIS, A.N.A., 1828

*Designed and erected by John Vanderlyn for the exhibition of his "panoramas."
On January 13, 1847, the first organization meeting of the Century Club was
held here, the members of the committee of management being composed of
Honorary Members, amateur and professional, of the National Academy.*

New-York, March 1st, 1836.

SIR.

The ELEVENTH ANNUAL EXHIBITION of the NATIONAL ACADEMY OF DESIGN, will open about the middle of April next. The object of the Exhibition is to give every Artist who wishes, whether belonging to the Academy or not, the opportunity of honourable competition with his brethren, by displaying his works, and leaving the public to form their own judgment, and make their own selections. The opportunity of sale for their productions is another inducement held out to the artists. The funds raised from the Exhibitions will be strictly applied, and with the greatest economy, to furnishing every facility for instruction in the Arts of Design, and to give greater effect to every succeeding Exhibition. By persevering in this system, it is believed that a taste for the Arts will be in the most direct manner promoted, and the character of the profession raised to its proper and natural dignity.

The Academy will be happy to receive the loan of any Work of Art in your possession, of the character hereafter to be mentioned. Should you favour them with any such works, they beg your attention to the following particulars:

1. All works to be exhibited, must necessarily be in New-York between the first and tenth day of April, directed to **J. L. MORTON, Secretary of the National Academy of Design, Clinton Hall.**

2. Such a description must be sent of each piece, as shall be suitable for the Catalogue, with the artist's name and address written, when practicable, on some part of the work: whether for sale; and if so, the price. Where to be returned after the Exhibition.

3. Works exhibited by the Academy, consist of Paintings, Sculptures, including Models in plaster or other composition, Architectural Models or Designs, and Engravings. All must be the works of living artists only.

4. No works which have once been exhibited by this Academy; no copies of any kind, (except paintings in enamel,) can be received.

5. The expenses of transportation and re-transportation, will be borne by the Academy.

6. The Exhibition will continue open from eight to nine weeks, during which time no work loaned for Exhibition can be allowed to be taken from the room.

Your obedient servant,

J. L. Morton
Secty N A

NATIONAL ACADEMY OF DESIGN,
    March 1, 1836.

Jacksonian democracy, the social caste and distinctions of English tradition were disappearing. The mercantile class supplanted the gentry of colonial inheritance as friends and patrons of the artist. The illustrious Honorary Members—Cooper, Bryant, and Irving—were all staunch Jacksonians.

The early landscape painters of America are alluded to as the "Hudson River school." This is a convenient designation, but it has little significance, for actually the titles of their pictures indicate that our painters traveled extensively. The method of their work gives a fuller meaning to the relation of the artist to his time. A careful adherence to nature was held to be an inviolable doctrine. This concept was associated with the current thought of the "uncontaminated" state of primeval nature. Every object should be represented accurately. In this sense our painters were naturalists, and to this end the artist made detailed drawings and studies directly from nature. But added to this was the assumption that the objects represented should be arranged in a correlated composition in accordance with the thematic invention of the painter. The composition was in consequence colored by the romantic imagery of current fiction and poetry. Scenes from Cooper and Irving were frequently used as illustrations, particularly those passages alluding to the grandeur and primitive wildness of nature, or the imaginative association of solitary horsemen or legends. A finished picture was not supposed to be a direct representation, and truth to nature did not imply the optical appearance of a particular place. As few original landscapes by European masters were known in America at this period, the composition was influenced by engravings after their work, particularly examples after Claude and Salvator Rosa. In a letter to Robert Gilmore dated December 25, 1825, Thomas Cole clearly states his intention: "The most lovely and perfect parts of nature may be brought together, and combined in a whole, that shall surpass in beauty and effect any picture painted from a single view. . . . He who would paint compositions, and not be false, must sit down amidst his sketches, make selections, and combine them, and so have nature for object he paints."

Thomas Doughty was probably the first native-born American artist to adopt landscape painting as a profession. Having served an apprenticeship as a leathermaker, in which trade he was discontented, he did not until his twenty-seventh year determine to try his luck at making pictures.

Without preliminary training other than occasional attempts, and a few lessons in drawing, he attained, by persistent practice, a sound knowledge of his craft and was rewarded with considerable success. Since in the meantime he had moved to Boston, he was made an Honorary Member of the Academy in 1827.

It was not, however, until the advent of Thomas Cole that landscape painting assumed major significance, bringing with it an appreciation and reward which opened a new field of artistic endeavor. Born in Lancashire, England, in 1801, Cole came to America with his parents in 1819. After various vicissitudes in assisting his father in the textile trade in Ohio and furthering, when opportunity offered, his natural love of drawing and painting, he arrived in New York in 1825. He worked in a garret of his father's house in Greenwich Street, and the first four pictures he produced there were placed in the shop of an acquaintance and sold for $10 each. This gained him the friendship of a Mr. Bruen, through whose generosity he was enabled to follow his desire to study from nature and to indulge his love of wandering in the wilds along the Hudson. On his return he painted from his studies three pictures which were placed in the window of Paff's art store. John Trumbull, in passing by, was at once arrested by their merit, and, purchasing one, *The Falls of the Caterskill*, hung it in his studio and invited the young painter to call on him. On his arrival, the elder artist was impressed by Cole's youthful modesty. "You surprise me," he said, "at your age to paint like this. You have already done what I, with all my years and experience, am yet unable to do." At the same time, Dunlap and Durand purchased the other two pictures. "His fame spread like fire," said Durand, and Bryant later added, "From that time he had a fixed reputation."

Cole's vital contribution was the interest which he stimulated in the direct study of nature, and his pictures and practice form the keynote and mood which was to be followed for a generation later. His pictorial theme responded to the romantic appeal of uncultivated nature, of scenic grandeur of "our aerial mountain-tops with their mighty growth of forest never touched by the axe, along the banks of streams never deformed by culture, and into the depth of skies bright with the hues of our own climate." (Bryant)

Conscious of the need of continuing his study in Europe, being lured by the praise of the old masters and the "higher style in art," Cole traveled extensively abroad. Writing from London in 1829 he comments in his notes on Art: "I have just returned from visiting Turner and his pictures. I had expected to see an older looking man, with a countenance pale with thought; but I was entirely mistaken." Although Cole admired his pictures, "they appear to me, however, to have an artificial look . . . chiaroscuro, colour, form, should always be subservient to the subject, and never be raised to the dignity of an end." Fresh from his naturalistic studies, our painter thought that Turner's pictures lacked "solidity" and were too sketchy. In stressing the effect of detail in relation to the whole, he added: "In confirmation of this doctrine I have only to appeal to Claude, Gaspard Poussin and Salvator Rosa." (Noble) Cole also visited Constable's studio, but the art of the latter seemed to have left no enduring impression.

In Paris, on visiting the Louvre, Cole was deeply disappointed in seeing the old masters replaced by an exhibition of contemporary work. "In landscape they are poor, in portrait much inferior to the English, and in history cold and affected. In design they are much superior to the English, but in expression false." The nostalgic lure of Italy, and the haunting aspiration of a "noble art," responded more to his romantic nature.

It was this transcendent conception of elevating the imagination in pictorial expression at the expense of his innate response to nature that led Cole on his return to America to compose his grandiose allegories, the *Course of Empire* and the *Voyage of Life*, which gained him popular renown. In high praise James Fenimore Cooper commented: "The series is a great epic poem, in which the idea far surpasses the execution, though the last is generally fine. . . . It is quite a new thing to see landscape painting raised to a level with the heroic in historical composition." But it was not this "new thing" that impressed the painters who found in Cole's earlier naturalistic work the guide to their continued study of "nature." This search for truth was not merely a fleeting visual appearance but a state of conscious realization which was clearly expressed by Durand when he wrote: "Every experienced artist knows that it is difficult to see nature truly; that for this end long practice is necessary. We see yet perceive not, and it becomes necessary to cultivate our perceptions so as to comprehend the essence of the object seen. . . . I maintain that all art is unworthy and vicious which is at variance with truth, and that only is worthy and elevated which impresses us with the same feelings and emotions that we experience in the presence of reality."

Asher B. Durand was born in Springfield, New Jersey, in 1796. His early association with country life formed the dominant mood of his nature, to which he gave his ultimate expression in later life. His father owned a small farm on Orange Mountain, but by trade was a watchmaker and silver smith, and also made or mended all sorts of contrivances. This mechanical facility was absorbed by the son, who at an early age was apprenticed to the engraver Peter Maverick in near-by Newark. Young Durand worked in that capacity for five years, at the termination of which he entered into partnership with his employer. It was not long thereafter that he surpassed his master in technical accomplishment, executing many plates after portraits of famous Americans, together with various commercial orders which formed the basis of his livelihood.

Engraving had been the only means of reproducing the works of the old masters and important contemporary works. It was by this means that American artists who had not had the opportunity to study abroad became familiar with these works. As large historical and religious pictures did not find ready purchase, the artist received his profit from the sale of reproductions. Engraving had become a major art, most of the work being executed in England and on the continent. On the completion of his picture *The Declaration of Independence*, Trumbull was in search of a worthy engraver. European masters of the art being excessive in price, he decided to entrust the commission to the youthful Durand. His judgment proved justified. Its publication established the reputation of Durand and provided an enduring historical document for the nation. It also stimulated the art of engraving in America, many reproductions comparing favorably with European masters.

Durand's last important engraving was after Vanderlyn's celebrated *Ariadne*, which he had purchased from the painter. The craft being very exacting and laborious, Durand turned to painting, and was rewarded for his "likeness" in portraiture by being commissioned to paint the portraits of all the Presidents. Those living he painted from life, and the others he represented by copying the works of previous painters. It was not until his return from European travel in 1840 that Durand devoted himself entirely to landscape painting, retiring eventually to the parental farm, where, amid the surroundings of his youth and the tranquility of nature, he lived until his ninetieth year.

Durand did not attempt the "grand style," nor did he emulate the mythical visions of Cole's later manner. It is true that while abroad he made some copies from the masters (the Academy owns two of his largest canvases—*Morning of Life* and *Evening of Life*—in which the preconceived theme is deliberately formulated), but his most personal achievement is attained in the less pretentious works, painted directly from nature. His palette had no echo of conventionalized tonality. He was not given to flamboyant color or to the deep resonance of the old masters. He worked in full sunlight, without forced contrasts or pre-arranged chiaroscuro; his key is in the middle register of variations of gray-greens and browns, receding to the ephemeral blue of the horizon and the luminous sky above. His brush is unhesitating, his painting clear and untroubled; the durability of his work is the final tribute to his sound craftsmanship.

Before mid-century our artists had explored the varied aspects of the American wonderland: its primeval forests, streams and mountains; the indigenous animal life; and the surrounding sea. In subject matter this may justly be called truly American. The dominant characteristic is visual accuracy, delineated on canvas with technical precision, thinly painted, but without the power of pigmented suggestion. The picture was likewise viewed with careful inspection and delight in the perfection of each detail. "High finish" was considered the indication of technical perfecton.

In the meantime New York had attracted foreign dealers, and numerous exhibitions displayed the work of contemporary European painters as well as that of the old masters. The most prominent and successful was the Düsseldorf Gallery. The meticulous realism and finish of the German painters met with immediate approval and had an appreciable influence upon the younger painters both in subject matter and technique. The religious picture was being replaced by the anecdotal or story-telling theme. To the older school it was thought to be a "low" form of expression lacking in elevated moral significance. But its virtue caused the artist to increase his interest in the local environment.

William Sidney Mount at once attained success in the new genre. As a student in the Academy School, making his living by sign painting, he first exhibited works of portraiture and imaginative subjects. But Mount had been born and brought up on his father's farm at Stony Brook, Long

Island, and scenes of boyhood haunted his memory. In the Academy of 1830 he exhibited *The Rustic Dance after a Sleigh Ride*, and in 1831, among other works, *Boys Quarrelling after School*. Washington Allston, recognizing the talent of the young painter, advised him to study the works of Teniers and Ostade. This may give a clue to his conception, but Mount had a humanistic affinity with his subjects which imbued his work with direct personal reaction. It opened an entirely new field of subject matter which was motivated by visual experience. Elected an Academician in 1832, and being encouraged by the popular appreciation and sale of his works, in 1837 he retired to the parental farm and thereafter devoted his art to depicting scenes of rural life. He contrived a studio on wheels drawn by a pair of horses, so that he could make his studies directly from nature. On one side was inserted a large plate glass window, and, since the wagon was provided with a stove and proper ventilation, Mount could work comfortably in either summer or winter. This accounts for the artist's factual documentation. A current writer alludes to Mount as "the comic painter of American life." It is true he had a sense of humor, and although not sentimentally anecdotal, his pictures illustrate the pastimes and frolics of country life as well as the sly onlooker's interpretation. Mount is an important figure in American painting, not alone in the perfection of his own genre, but because he created an interest in, and an appreciation of, a unique aspect of American life. The titles alone suggest his preoccupation: *Scene in a Country Tavern; Boys Trapping; The Blackberry Girls; Husking Corn; Dance of the Haymakers; Bird-egging; Bargaining for a Horse*, and so on. This interest is far removed from the tradition of West and Allston, or the grandiose conceptions of the "heroic" and the "sublime"; it inaugurated a new vision in American art.

Richard Caton Woodville is more directly associated with the Düsseldorf School. Born in Baltimore in 1825, he as a boy had the opportunity to study the pictures in the collection of Robert Gilmore, among which were examples of the Flemish School. One of his first efforts in emulation of the style was a small interior of a barroom with figures, which won local favor and determined the youthful artist to continue his education abroad. He passed several years in Düsseldorf, and after a brief visit home, he returned to work in Paris, then in London, where he died in 1856 at the early age of thirty-one. Although he was cosmopolitan in training and residence, his themes were of American origin, and the pictures which he sent to New York were greatly admired for their meticulous detail and "high finish." In 1845 he was represented in the Academy exhibition by *Scene in a Bar-Room;* several of his pictures were engraved and published by the Art Union as well as Goupil and Co.; while the pictures exhibited in New York after his death, notably *The Sailor's Wedding* and *Waiting for the Stage* established his enduring reputation. The popular *War News from Mexico* is in the permanent collection of the Academy. It may be noted that Mount and Woodville were among the first American figure painters to achieve financial success in their profession, apart from portraiture, and with a knowledge and technique adequate to their endeavor. Mount developed from local influence and training, while Woodville engendered the precedent of foreign study which was to dominate the following generation.

As the Western frontiers of the continent were extended, interest in the aboriginal life of the Indians stimulated pictorial possibilities. George Catlin joined a Western expedition in 1832 and, visiting the tribes bordering the Yellowstone River, made numerous portraits and studies of Indian life, which he later exhibited both in America and England with considerable success. He was the first artist to be elected to membership in the Academy after its founding, but resigned after some personal displeasure. Charles Bird King and Seth Eastman, both Honorary Members of the Academy, were pioneers of the Western scene, and Charles Deas, an Associate, exhibited at the Academy 18 pictures between 1838 and 1849, mostly of frontier and Indian life. Alfred Miller contributed authentic pictorial records of the mountain men, the trappers, the Indian encampments before the advent of the camera. These artists followed the adventurous life of the frontiersmen, sharing their trials and hardships.

The fabulous stories of the pioneers, and the wonders of the new land, likewise attracted the Naturalists, the most famous of whom, John James Audubon, attained international renown. He exhibited two pictures at the Academy in 1833, and in the same year was made an Honorary Member—his residence was then in New Orleans. John W. Audubon followed his father's example and exhibited continuously at the Academy from 1840 to 1857. Other painters depicted animal and floral life with realistic precision, thus adding scientific knowledge as well as artistic interest in the discovery of new species.

Of more humanistic significance, George Caleb Bingham portrayed the life of the trapper and river man. Born in Pennsylvania in 1811, he passed the greater part of his life in St. Louis, then the point of departure for the far West. Unlike his subjects, his art is in no sense unsophisticated, but composed with conscious dramatization and calculated effect. He exhibited eight pictures at the Academy between the years 1840 and 1848, but was otherwise little known in the Eastern states. In later life he was an active personality in the development of the Midwestern metropolis.

Thomas Birch devoted his art rather exclusively to marine painting, including several views of Niagara Falls. A resident of Philadelphia, he was made an Honorary Member of the Academy in 1833, and was a frequent contributor to its exhibitions until his death in 1851. Arthur Fitz-William Tait specialized in hunting pictures, game birds, and country life. Born in Liverpool in 1819, he came to New York in 1850, where his early work was popularized by the Currier & Ives prints. *Camping in the Woods, Maple Sugaring, Flushed, Retrieving, Mink Trapping*, indicate the nature of his subjects. *The Life of a Hunter. A Tight Fix* is today one of the most treasured collector's items of the Currier & Ives series, a single print being sold in 1928 for $3,000. Tait was a discerning naturalist as well as an exacting and capable craftsman. An annual contributor to the Academy exhibitions, he was elected an Associate in 1855 and an Academician in 1858. Living until 1905, he witnessed the impressionistic movement, so far removed from his meticulous and naturalistic rendering.

The work of George Henry Durrie was also widely reproduced by Currier & Ives. Living in New Haven, Connecticut, where he was born in 1820, he had a deep love of nature and the homely activities and attributes of New England farm life. His pictures of winter, made before the theme became stereotyped, still appear on popular Christmas cards. A frequent contributor to the Academy exhibitions, he first showed his work there in 1843. In contrast to the romantic themes of uncultivated nature, Durrie's interest was in the human environment. *Cider Making, Getting*

Ice, Feeding the Chickens, Home to Thanksgiving, illustrate the peaceful life of the self-sufficient farmer and his family.

Currier & Ives, "Printmakers to the American People," introduced the newly discovered reproductive process of lithography, the prints being made in black and white and colored by hand. With the invention of photography and more expeditious modes of quantity reproductions, as well as changes in pictorial style, the once popular "chromos," became obsolete, and the prints forgotten. With the return to the "American scene" and regional art in the twentieth century, the homely style of the primitives was revived and their anonymous authors became the prototypes of many "modern" painters.

The catalogues of the Academy exhibitions contain innumerable names of artists now forgotten, their work indicative of the popular sentiment of the time. As with the obsolete literature of the period, their work has a flavor more local than the more cultivated expression of their celebrated contemporaries. From the first exhibition of the Academy in 1826 to 1860, the names of 1,375 different artists appear in the annual catalogues. Of these 68 were Academicians, 55 of whom were painters, 3 sculptors, 2 architects and 8 engravers; 53 were Associates, including 48 painters, 1 sculptor, 2 architects and 4 engravers. During the same period 18 Academicians died; 14 painters, 1 sculptor, 1 architect, and 2 engravers; among the Associate members 6 painters and 1 engraver died. As a tribute and memorial to membership, an obituary was always inscribed in the minutes, and the band of mourning was worn by the members.

In the first quarter century after its founding, the Academy had become not only the paramount art organization of America, but as a body it was recognized in civic affairs and collective demonstrations. The Academicians were included in the annual commencement procession of Columbia College; in 1834 they were assigned a place in the funeral ceremonies in honor of General Lafayette; and in 1841 they marched in the solemnities marking the death of President William Harrison.

· V ·

SOCIAL AFFILIATIONS: NOTABLE HONORARY MEMBERS · THE SKETCH
CLUB AND OTHER GROUPS SPONSORED BY THE NATIONAL ACADEMY ·
THE ART UNION

BY 1830, New York had more than trebled the population of 60,000
inhabitants that it had had at the beginning of the century, but it was still
a small city. The boundary of city life was not much beyond Canal
Street. City Hall Park was the center of the city, and promenaders
frequented the Battery. The residential section was fast moving uptown.
Some of the more opulent citizens were already building around
Washington Square. The nation was entering upon an era of continental
expansion. Transportation was greatly improved; the old stage coach
was being replaced by railroads; steamboats were in operation; the Erie
Canal united the Hudson River with the Great Lakes. Industrialization
was followed by accumulated wealth. New York City became not only
the commercial center of the continent but also attracted many of the
most prominent personalities of the various professions.

Apart from the gratifying results derived from the annual exhibitions
and the establishment of the school, the Academy formed a nucleus for
cultural enrichment. The artists brought a fresh and welcome spirit to
the more active and sordid affairs of the business world, while members
of other professions, particularly the writers, found in the artists' circle
a congenial and stimulating environment. Although financially the poorest
of the group, the artist seemed carefree and untroubled, engrossed in the
study of nature and the associations of the romantic themes of his art.
The credulous veneration of the old masters was passing, and the patron

found a more living interest in the art and friendship of his contemporaries. The Academy numbered among its Honorary Members many of the most distinguished personalities of the period: William Cullen Bryant, Washington Irving, James Fenimore Cooper, Fitz-Greene Halleck, Henry James, Sr., Philip Hone, David Hosack, Luman Reed, Jonathan Sturges, Charles Leupp, and other notables of the city.

Of these Luman Reed was a most liberal benefactor and friend of the artists. It was due to his sympathetic and understanding aid that many of the younger artists were enabled to continue their careers. He commissioned Thomas Cole to paint *The Course of Empire*, and was one of the welcome patrons of the youthful William Sidney Mount. Most of the prominent artists of the city were represented in his collection, which included examples by Cole, Durand, Inman, Ingham, Mount, and others. To ensure a good light for his pictures he constructed a gallery over the top floor of his home in Greenwich Street, thus initiating one of the first private collections of American painting. His pictures were kept together after his death to form the New York Gallery of Fine Arts, later to be transferred to the New-York Historical Society. Jonathan Sturges continued the example of his father-in-law, Luman Reed, and as a friend of the Academy was to become its most constructive and helpful supporter in time of need.

One of the most fruitful outgrowths of the Academy was the Sketch Club, the first meeting of which was held in 1827. With memories of the Drawing Association still alive, there was always the thought of "getting together" by combining study with congenial fraternity. Morse, Durand, Cummings, and Ingham were at that time the instructors of the school, and Ingham suggested that it would be a good idea to meet at each other's studios as a means of exchanging thoughts and practicing impromptu sketching. One hour was given to drawing, the subject being proposed by the host, whose property the sketches remained. The membership also included writers and "lovers of art" who, during the hour of sketching, also proposed a subject, each author adding four lines to the total composition; the result frequently provided much hilarity. To avoid any embarrassment to the host, the refreshment stipulated at the first meeting was "figs, milk, and honey." The effects of this frugal repast did not suggest its continuance, and the more affluent members enlarged upon the menu. Eventually, the sketching was omitted and the club came to be called the Twenty-One, which name defined the exclusive limit of its membership.

In 1844, the Artists Sketching Club was organized, much on the same lines as the old Sketch Club, but without the lay members and refreshments. Meetings were held once a week in the Council Room of the Academy. The subject of the evening was not announced until the appointed time. Some of the titles give a clue to the contemporary tendency: "Too Late," "Charity," "Too Soon," "Just in Time," "Surprise," "Hard Case," "Catastrophe," and "Trying Hour."

The idea and pattern of the original Sketch Club as an Association for cultural and social intercourse was repeated many times throughout the century. The most prominent and enduring is, of course, the Century Club. The Sketch Club being permanently restricted in numbers, it was proposed in 1847, by John Chapman, secretary of the Academy, to found a new and more liberal organization to include in its membership the eminent men of all professions. A house was rented and its success was immediate. "The gatherings were looked upon as the most desirable of all the New York winter entertainments."

In the same year a third Sketch Club known as the New York Sketch Club was founded by the younger artists of the city including, among the elders, Honorary Members. This provided an opportunity of supplementing studio work with improvised studies, and a convivial way of bringing together kindred spirits. At a later date the Salmagundi Club was started, on the same principle, the meetings being held in the studios of the members.

Thus it is seen that the original conception of the New York Drawing Association and the founding of the National Academy resulted in the flowering of many offshoots for the cultivation of the arts and the opportunity of study.

As the Academy exhibitions were held only once a year, and as all works previously exhibited in the city were excluded, there arose a renewed interest in establishing a permanent gallery, free from those restrictions. In answer to this need the Apollo Association was organized in 1839. The paintings exhibited included both originals and copies. All works were for sale. Its purpose as announced was "for the promotion of the Fine Arts of the United States." Each member of the association subscribed $5 annually, for which he received an illustrated monthly bulletin, an engraving from an American painting, and a chance in a lottery, the winners of which received an original painting, medal, or statuette of an American artist, purchased from the funds contributed by the subscribers. These works were placed on exhibition at the gallery of the Association and were distributed by lot at the annual meeting in December. Honorary secretaries were appointed in different sections of the country to receive subscriptions and to transmit the awards.

It was anticipated that the receipts of admission would, like the exhibitions of the Academy, defray expenses. As this did not materialize the Association was reorganized in 1842 and admission was made free to the public. With increased attendance, the subscription likewise increased, and in the years following the venture attained a popularity far exceeding the fondest hopes of its founders. In 1839, 36 pictures were distributed to the winners in the lottery; in 1840, 14, and in 1841, only 7. After reorganization and the granting of free admission to the gallery, the number of pictures purchased from the receipts of subscribers increased to 35. Thereafter the membership was enlarged yearly, particularly in cities outside of New York. In 1849 the membership reached the spectacular peak of 18,960, with receipts totaling over $100,000. In that year 460 paintings were distributed, 20 small bronzes, 36 sets of outline illustrations, 250 portrait medals of John Trumbull, 150 of Gilbert Stuart, and 100 of Washington Allston. Thus the painter, the sculptor, and the engraver were equally employed, and their works distributed not only locally but throughout a wide section of the country. (Cowdrey)

The idea of the purchase and distribution of pictures by lottery was not new. It is said to have been originated by a French art lover under the title of Société des Amis des Arts. Its initial success was followed by similar projects in Berlin, Prague, Vienna, Düsseldorf, and London. When this idea was introduced in New York, the Academy was asked to cooperate in its promotion. Conferences were held by committees representing both organizations. It was evident that free admission to the exhibitions of the Apollo Association would compete with the annual exhibition of the Academy, which depended upon an admission charge for its maintenance. However, the council of the Academy, desirous of

an opportunity of showing pictures which were not eligible for exhibition under its own rules, offered rent free the use of the galleries in
Clinton Hall until the expiration of the lease in 1841.

At a meeting with the committee representing the Apollo Association,
a verbal understanding was reached that in its exhibition the Association
would refrain from presenting pictures which had not been previously
exhibited in New York. This was not confirmed in practice, and it led to
controversy. In a letter addressed to the Association, Mr. Morse, speaking
for the council, explained that the receipts from the annual exhibitions
of the Academy were the sole means of revenue, the very "life blood" of
its existence; that much of its public success was due to the "novelty" of
seeing the pictures for the first time.

All our funds are expended for the general good of the Arts, the officers, with
the single necessary exception of the keeper, perform their duties without
receiving a salary, the schools of the Academy are free. Their cost to the
Academy has been upwards of $5,000. Each student of the Antique School
receives his instruction at an annual cost of $12.50, and each student of the
Life School at an annual expense of $40. . . . If the Apollo Association should
adopt the plan of the Academy and present works not previously exhibited it
would seriously affect the interests and revenue of the Academy.

The President went on to say that there were innumerable works which
were not permitted to be shown by the Academy: the works of deceased
artists, copies from great works of Art, and the increasing number of
works previously exhibited.

If it selected such works for exhibition as come not in our plan there is no
interference, even more, there would be a positive gain to the Arts by such a
system, for it would cultivate a field upon which we do not propose to enter.

The only circumstances which would justify competition would be if
the annual production of pictures exceeded the possibility of showing
them in one institution.

Have then the annual productions of our artists so multiplied that our annual
exhibitions will not contain them? Our experience on this point is conclusive
to us. From 250 to 300 new works are the natural production of the year, our
walls have been filled and we have not excluded more than two or three works
for many years. The accommodations now at our command, will we think,
contain all the new works that are produced for exhibition within the year.
Another exhibition that should take the same class of works from our annual

exhibition must diminish the interest of the exhibition and consequently injure the Academy in all its interests.

After reviewing the nature of the previous conferences and the inference that the Association would not interfere with the interests of the Academy, the president concluded by asking

Will they [the Apollo Association] confine their exhibitions to those works, vastly more numerous, excluded by our laws from our exhibitions and leave us the exclusive exhibition of the works of living artists never before exhibited in the City of New York?

In answer to this appeal the chairman of the Apollo Committee abruptly replied: "That it is inexpedient to continue further negotiations in regard to the arrangement between the two institutions on the basis submitted in the communication of the President of the Academy." Fortunately, the management of the Apollo Association was changed, so that the president of the Academy could report at the annual meeting of 1842: "the modification of the plans of the Apollo Association by the present Board of Directors of that Society so as not to interfere with our exhibition system." In appreciation of this concession, the council resolved, "That in consideration of the known benefits to the Arts of Design from the present course pursued by the Apollo Association, the National Academy present to it for distribution among its members three hundred season tickets for the exhibition of 1844."

In 1844, the Association's charter was amended to change its name to the American Art Union. Because of the lure of the lottery, the Art Union flourished beyond the most sanguine expectations. As subscriptions increased, more paintings and engravings could be bought and distributed. The chance of winning a valuable picture, in addition to an engraving, for the annual dues of $5, was a tempting inducement. In 1849, Cole's series, *The Voyage of Life*, was purchased by the Art Union from the estate of the original owner and was offered as a prize in the lottery. When placed on view, after being extensively advertised, it was estimated that something like half a million visitors attended the exhibition during that season.

The annual exhibitions of the Academy were held in the galleries of Clinton Hall from 1831 to 1840. The largest receipts during that period were in 1838, amounting to $4,699.23, indicating an approximate attendance of 18,000 paid admissions. In his address of that year, before his departure for Europe, President Morse alluded to the growing prosperity of the Academy:

When we look back, as most of us can, to the total receipts of our first Exhibition, and find that we now receive in two days, as much as we then received in three months, the contrast is striking, and the result in the highest degree gratifying. . . . Hitherto, adversity and necessity of common defense have united us. We have now prosperity to try us, which, all experience shows, requires more moral courage to bear than adversity. . . . The state of our funds is such as very rationally to make us fix our minds upon some plan of building, either permanently or temporarily, with others. The City Library is about to build, and, in conversation, we have been led to believe that such arrangements might be made with them.

A building committee was appointed by the council and arrangements were made to lease the upper floor of the Society Library on the corner of Broadway and Leonard Street. This decision caused much discussion—it was too far uptown, the rent was double that of Clinton Hall, the stairs were too steep, it was too risky. It was in fact venturesome, as the Academy, according to the contract, was obligated to decorate the gallery at a cost of $4,000 or $5,000, which exhausted the treasury. The gallery was twice as large as the previous one, the wall space covering over 400 feet, "far superior to anything ever before presented, [and] gave an effect that was truly gratifying to the artist and visitor."

On the completion of the galleries, the sixteenth annual exhibition was opened on May 3, 1841, and continued until July 5. At this exhibition, 366 works were displayed. At the annual meeting, the treasurer reported a balance of $14! Despite the improvement of the galleries, the receipts of the next few years did not increase correspondingly. The Art Union proved a serious competitor. It was more centrally located, and admission was free. However, in 1847, the receipt of admissions totaled $6,278.22, the largest amount received in the new building. It was at this time also that free admission to the exhibition was granted to school children, which during several years numbered over 6,000 annually, thus indicating a total attendance of over 30,000 visitors to the exhibition.

The phenomenal interest in the Art Union created much activity on the part of speculators, and as there had always been a minor protest against the dictatorial methods of the Union, it was considered to be a culminating factor in challenging the lottery as a violation of state law.

THE EAST ROOM AT 663 BROADWAY
FROM THE *Illustrated News*, APRIL, 1853

*"The beauty and fashion that throng the rooms make it a place of agreeable
resort, independently of the paintings."* (Reprinted from the NEW MIRROR,
May 27, 1843.)

THE ACADEMY BUILDING ON THE NORTHWEST CORNER
OF FOURTH AVENUE AND 23D STREET

*The style of architecture was referred to as "revived Gothic." The building's
resemblance to the Doge's Palace at Venice caused it to be familiarly alluded
to under that name.*

As a result of the lengthy suit which followed, the judgment went against the Union, and in 1852, after thirteen years of activity, it was forced by law to end its spectacular career.

During that time the Art Union had unquestionably stimulated popular interest in art, and had benefited the artists by the increased sale of their works. But it had also created an artificial inflation appreciably felt by the depression which followed its demise. Cummings writes in his *Annals:* "Its sudden stoppage was therefore highly disastrous, and seriously felt for several years—indeed until the purchasing current returned to its proper and natural bed, from which it had been diverted." During the time of its operation, the Academy exhibitions suffered by its competition. At one time there was a thought of either combining the two organizations or having the Academy adopt the same means of operation. Happily neither course was necessary.

In retrospect, however, the plan of the Art Union and its efficient management contributed greatly to further an interest in a national art. It not only provided a suitable gallery with free admission to a continuous exhibition, and purchased the works of innumerable artists, but by means of its illustrated monthly bulletins, 80,000 copies of which were circulated in 1848, it incited the interest of those who were unable to attend the exhibitions or participate in its awards. The example of the Art Union was followed in five other cities, the most successful of which were in Cincinnati, Philadelphia, and Boston. Its most enduring contribution was the sincere endeavor of its sponsors who, after the demise of the Art Union, continued their efforts in furthering a permanent exhibition gallery. The remaining works of art in its possession were transferred to the New York Gallery and were later incorporated into the New-York Historical Society. Several members of the board of directors were influential in the founding of the Metropolitan Museum of Art, and thus, however irregular in its proceedings the Art Union may have been, its original purpose and great popularity was a definite factor in establishing a permanent museum for the people of the City of New York.

·VI·

ON A SHIP returning to America in 1832, Samuel Morse conceived the possibility of the electric transmission of words, making a penciled sketch of his theory of telegraphy. He is quoted as saying to the captain of the *Sully* before reaching port, "Well, if you should hear of the telegraph one of these days, as the wonder of the world, remember the discovery was made on board the good ship *Sully*."

It was not, however, until three years later that Morse was enabled to carry out his actual experiments, and it was in 1835–36 that he made his first telegraphic demonstration, successfully sending a message from one room to another. Morse was joined by his friend, Alfred Vail, whose father, Judge Stephen Vail, advanced money and facilities to enable the inventor to continue experimentation. In 1843 President John Tyler signed a bill by which the government appropriated $30,000 to construct an experimental telegraph line from Washington to Baltimore. The project having been endorsed by the inventor's former classmate, H. L. Ellsworth, then United States Commissioner of Patents, Morse invited his friend's daughter, Annie Ellsworth, to have the honor of wording the first telegram. The words were chosen from the Bible: "What Hath God Wrought."

"Morse slowly tapped out the message. Vail received it in Washington, where it was received with great cheers. That was the beginning of the telegraph industry as a service to the public, and it was heralded as having great possibilities for binding the young American nation of 26 states together."

While in Paris, Morse had met a fellow artist, Louis J. M. Daguerre, who had been conducting his first experiments in photography. Greatly interested in the possibilities of this new medium, and learning something of its process, Morse, on his return to America, applied his knowledge to further experimentation. It was at this time that John Draper joined the faculty of New York University (where Morse was now lecturing) as professor of chemistry. The two men proceeded to work on the new device. Daguerre had been able to photograph only stationary objects in bright sunlight. The problem now was to make photographic portraits that would require less time exposure. The success of their combined efforts at once made photography practical, and the new accomplishment created a great stir, particularly among the portrait painters. Was their art to be superseded by a less costly mechanical reproduction? "Certain it is that history and historic portraiture, and indeed every branch of history, will receive an extraordinary and impartial, and never-before obtained recorder, by photography." (Cummings)

George Templeton Strong comments in his diary (1841):

February 10. . . . Spent the morning variously and, among other things, looked in at Colman's with Post. He has some of the most distinct and perfect Daguerreotype pictures I ever saw, portraits especially. I think that invention succeeds best in buildings and statuary. I wonder if it can be employed to take facsimiles of paintings. . . .

Writing to a friend in a letter dated 1840, Thomas Cole alludes to the artistic controversy arising from the new invention: "I suppose you have read a great deal about the Daguerreotype. If you believe everything the newspapers say (which, by-the-bye, would require an enormous bump of marvelousness) you would be led to suppose that the poor craft of painting was knocked in the head by this new machinery for making Nature take her own likeness, and we nothing to do but give up the ghost. . . . This is the conclusion: that the art of painting is creative, as well as an imitative art, and is in no danger of being superseded by any mechanical contrivance." (Noble)

The continued development of the telegraph and its successful operation now absorbed its inventor's time and interest. Much to the regret of his fellow Academicians, Morse felt it incumbent upon him to decline reelection to the presidency. In 1844, Henry Inman having resigned as vice-president, Asher B. Durand was chosen to fill the vacancy, and in 1845 he was elected president, Charles C. Ingham taking his place as vice-president.

At a special meeting of the Academicians following the annual election, a "service plate" was presented to the treasurer, Thomas Cummings, as a testimonial of esteem "for the faithful and correct manner in which he has executed the duties of Treasurer of this Institution for twenty years." A press comment added "the financial affairs of the Academy have been managed with a business ability that is not often exhibited by artists, who are generally more noted for disregard of pecuniary interests than for undue attention to the prosperity of their worldly affairs." The treasurer was to continue to guide the Academy over many unforeseen and trying financial difficulties. If Samuel Morse had been the inspired godfather in the founding of the Academy, surely the vigilant Thomas Cummings was the wise guardian of its material support and maintenance.

In 1849, when the lease of the galleries above the Society Library on Leonard Street expired, the council thought it advisable to purchase land and to make plans for a permanent building for the National Academy. After much discussion of what would be the most favorable site, and after repeated difficulties in negotiation, a contract was signed to purchase, for the sum of $50,000, the property at 663 Broadway, formerly known as Browers Stables (the uptown terminus of the old bus line). The property lay between Bleecker and Amity streets, and had a Broadway frontage of 50 feet, and spread out 200 feet in the rear, adjoining Mercer Street.

The completion of the entrance building exhausted all available funds, and the committee in charge resigned. At this critical stage of the proceedings, two faithful friends of the Academy, Jonathan Sturges and Charles Leupp, were appointed trustees, and with their financial support and business acumen bonds of the Academy were issued, and the building was completed. The combined wall space measured 600 feet on the line; the 6 galleries were well lighted by day and illuminated by 300 gas burners after dark, altogether presenting "the finest Art Galleries in the country."

The first exhibition held in the new galleries was opened by an imposing reception on April 13, 1850. The most attractive feature of the design was the low staircase leading to the galleries. This "had been Mr. Ingham's hobby, and was ever known as the 'Ingham Stairs.'" Notwithstanding the greatly improved conditions, the receipts of the first exhibition were disappointing, amounting only to $3,066.61. This was no doubt due to the free exhibitions of the Art Union which were still going on at this time. In the meantime, however, the rental of the gallery at such times when not in use by the Academy helped greatly to pay the interest on the bonds. To further augment the funds and to liquidate a floating debt, it was proposed that the members each contribute a picture to meet this immediate need. The suggestion was favorably received. The president of the Art Union, being present at the meeting, stated that if the Academicians would contribute the pictures, the Art Union would purchase them en masse. Thirty-four members responded; a committee was appointed to appraise the pictures, which were accordingly sold for $2,000.

At the annual meeting of 1851, an amendment to the constitution was adopted which provided that the number of Academicians be raised from 35 to 50 and that the affirmative vote of two thirds of the members present be required for the election of candidates. Twelve members were elected in that year, including Jasper F. Cropsey, John W. Casilear, T. Addison Richards, James Smillie, George A. Baker, and Regis Gignoux. In the same year James Fenimore Cooper died. "As a friend to artists, and one who furnished an abundant harvest for art illustration, he deserves, and will receive, the lasting remembrance of the American artists." (Cummings)

Owing to the increased expenses and reduction in receipts, the school was closed from 1849 to 1852. Some of the students, however, continued the classes at their own expense. When the school reopened in October, 1852, the students were charged $5 entrance fee, it being the opinion of the treasurer that a small charge favored the student as well as the Academy.

On the occasion of the reception prior to the public opening of the exhibition of 1852, an innovation was introduced which proved highly gratifying. Guests were requested to attend in evening dress, and an elaborate collation was prepared during the evening. Although several similar occasions had been introduced, the twenty-sixth annual exhibition became famous for the Academy Reception. This inaugurated a series of artists' receptions during the following decade, eagerly attended by the society of the period and greatly enlarging the interest in art.

Notwithstanding the fact that the attendance at the exhibition was about the same as in previous years, the treasurer's account was balanced and the trustees reported that the revenue from the real estate was sufficient to pay the interest, taxes, and other charges against it. There was, however, an added debt of $13,000, owed to the two trustees who had generously loaned that amount. "It may therefore be safely said, that at no period since the Academy purchased its property, has so favorable a state of things existed."

The business activity of the city was now each year moving further uptown. Realizing the steady increase of property values in consequence, the sagacious treasurer proposed to the trustees the purchase of the adjoining properties on Mercer Street which included five or six old houses and lots. This was fortunately agreed to, and although delay and litigation were involved in clearing some of the titles, the entire purchase was consummated two years after negotiations had been started.

Recognizing the anticipated increase in the value of the property, Cummings proposed that it should be sold to realize the profit. This was approved by the council, and Thomas Cummings was authorized to effect the sale. Then followed a series of complicated negotiations and abortive sales, which placed the trustees in a difficult and embarrassing situation. The property was considered sold in February, 1854, a payment of $10,000 having been made in advance, with the final payment of $70,000 due upon delivery of the property in May. This was postponed until the first of July. But in the meantime a financial panic ensued. "Mammon's idol, gold, scarcely held its own; it too, perhaps, had almost to be tested before it was touched, so far was confidence lost." The purchasers were unable to fulfill the contract, a foreclosure sale followed, and the property reverted to the Academy.

The would-be purchasers had intended to convert the premises into a large music hall. The project was revived, the property resold, building and alterations continued, but again the purchasers, being financially insolvent, were unable to meet their obligations and work was discontinued. A foreclosure suit became necessary, and for a second time the trustees bought in the property. In the meantime the tenants in the adjoining building had refused to pay rent, and litigations ensued until finally, under able management, order was restored. When ultimately the entire property was permanently sold (in 1860) the gross yearly income from rentals amounted to over $10,000.

During all this precarious negotiation, the members entered into much controversy to which Cummings alludes humorously. Differing factions contended "that the Academy wanted no real estate—no property—a building only in which to exhibit Art"; "that the real estate should be sold for anything that it would bring"; "get rid of it anyhow"; "that art needed not money wherewith to forward it"; "that the Institution should not possess it"; "that money stultified and debased Art"; "that it was a clog in progress, and for that alone, should be immediately sold"; and again, by others, "that it should be held and leased, and the revenue only taken for Art purpose"; "that it should not be sold at all"; "that it would ultimately form a permanent support to Art and Artists."

Fortunately, the trustees were not confused or deterred by these varying pronouncements, and it was due to their excellent judgment and management of real estate that the future foundation of the Academy was established.

The Academy was now without home or habitation. The statuary was stored in Cummings's studio building, and a committee was appointed to rent temporary rooms for a suitable gallery. This proved a difficult problem, for since the committee was endeavoring to locate a site for a permanent building, it was thought advisable not to consider extensive remodeling of a temporary gallery. After many proposals and disappointments, it was decided to hold the exhibition in rooms over Dr. Chapin's Church, 548 Broadway, at a rental of $200 a month. The thirtieth and thirty-first exhibitions were accordingly held there from March to May, an earlier date than heretofore. Although the works were unsatisfactorily displayed, and the number of pictures reduced, the proceeds from admissions approximated those received at 663 Broadway. The following year, 1857, the exhibition of 548 works was held in the old galleries for one month only, from May 18 to June 20. The total receipts were

$3,861.75, the highest income covering a similar period up to that date. The new owner of the property offered to return it to the Academy at the price paid, but this was declined.

In the same year a building was being completed on the corner of Fourth Avenue and Tenth Street, the upper floors of which could be suitably adapted to the temporary needs of the annual exhibitions. Part of this space was leased for three and a half years, and later an additional section was included, the rent being increased from $1,500 to $3,000. The galleries, lighted by skylights and suitably decorated, proved highly satisfactory. The largest revenue received was $5,888.92 in the year 1859. Although subletting the galleries reduced the indebtedness, the deficit during the four years of occupancy from 1858 through 1861 amounted to $6,000.

In the spring of 1857, the building known as the Artists' Studio was erected on West Tenth Street. This became a second home of the Academicians, a gallery being included for the public exhibition of their work. The artists' receptions held in the building, at which time all of the studios were thrown open, were one of the social artistic events of the year. These artists' receptions had been inaugurated at Dodsworth's Dancing Hall in 1858, proving highly successful and largely attended by the elite of the day. The walls were decorated with pictures, and Dodsworth's orchestra added to the occasion. This artistic festival was imitated in Brooklyn at the Academy of Music, and later in Boston with equal success.

An event occurred in November, 1857, which well demonstrated the fraternal interest and unity of the members of the Academy. On learning of the death of William T. Ranney, an Associate Member, his fellow artists joined in creating a fund for the benefit of his bereaved widow and children. The annuity fund which had previously been adopted in the constitution had been discontinued for lack of resources. Unable, therefore, to give aid from the treasury, the members voluntarily agreed to contribute pictures. These were added to the remaining works of the deceased artist, the pictures were framed, and at the conclusion of the memorial exhibition were offered at auction, the auctioneer not charging for his services. The pictures of the artist returned a sufficient amount to pay for the mortgage on his home, while the $5,000 received from the sale of the pictures contributed by the members was invested for the benefit of the artist's family. Today, nearly one hundred years later, William Ranney is recognized as one of the few authentic illustrators of the Old West.

This spontaneous and heartfelt response stimulated an endeavor to create a permanent organization to aid impoverished artists and the needs of their bereaved families. The treasurer was requested to draft a plan to effect this purpose, which eventuated in forming the Artists' Fund Society, a fraternal institution that continued its beneficent activity for over half a century and was thereafter united with the Artists' Aid Society, which still carries on its helpful and much needed work. During the early years of the Society the members contributed pictures which were sold at auction, thus creating an initial capital of $20,000. This was followed by the payment of annual dues.

The Academy loaned its newly appointed galleries on Tenth Street for an exhibition of pictures by English artists, while at the same time the Art Union showed an exhibition of French artists. This was evidently operated as a commercial enterprise, but it gave our local artists an opportunity to study and compare the work of contemporary foreign painters. The French exhibition seems to have been the more approved.

During this period many inferior examples of foreign art had been exploited in New York and elsewhere. To check this unwelcome importation, a petition was presented to Congress by the Academy stating "that the present unrestrained introduction of foreign works of art, particularly paintings, is a subject worthy of your consideration and legislation. As against the importation of works of art of excellence, your petitioners offer no objection, and wish no serious impediment imposed to their introduction; such are of benefit to the artist, to art, and its general diffusion." It was a protest against the "worthless trash, benefiting none but the importer" and a plea to protect the standards of taste. It was therefore suggested that a duty be imposed on this class of work to deter its increasing exploitation. Forwarded to the Art Commission in Washington, it received no response.

After vacating the premises at 663 Broadway, the school was housed in the storage room of Cummings's studio building. There was little instruction or supervision, the students being allowed to govern themselves; the enrollment was reduced to less than ten, the average attendance to not more than three. Disorder prevailed, visitors came to be amused, a cast of the venerated antique was smashed to pieces, the few serious students resigned, and the school was closed.

Aware of the imminent disintegration of the school and realizing that the fault was partly due to inefficient organization, Thomas Cummings, with the approval of the council, assumed sole responsibility for its management. In reopening the school in November, free of charge, the director made a list of exacting rules informing the students that they would be strictly enforced. No visitors were to be allowed except members of the Academy, every student was furnished with a pass, no noise or smoking was permitted during study, the roll was called each evening, absence from three successive evenings forfeited the student's seat, the penalty for being absent six successive evenings without proper excuse was immediate dismissal.

The favorable response was immediate, the class of 1856 enrolling 52 students in the antique and 23 in the life class. At the end of the term a testimonial was presented by the students to the director, and the council also expressed its gratitude. The records of 1857 comment upon a "most successful season" with the enrollment being 91 students; and in 1858 "the order of the school is perfect"; the pupils "a credit to themselves, the instructors and the institution."

In March, 1858, a convention was called in Washington to appoint a commission relative to the decoration of public buildings at the Capitol. By request of the Washington Art Association, the council nominated Morse, Bellows, and Brown as delegates from the Academy. As a result of the conference, J. R. Lambdin of Philadelphia, H. K. Brown, and J. F. Kensett of New York, all members of the Academy, were elected as Art Commissioners to superintend the decoration of the Capitol with "Works of Art by American Artists."

The thirty-third annual exhibition inaugurated the new Tenth Street galleries with a full-dress reception, and for the first time music was introduced at an Academy exhibition. Open for 68 days, the exhibition was well received, and despite 26 rainy days, the receipts were greater than at any time since 1848. Five hundred and sixty works were displayed, the running wall-space aggregating 800 feet. The following year the receipts increased with 815 pictures exhibited.

At the annual meeting of 1859 Charles Ingham was elected vice-president, as the previous occupant of the chair, Thomas Cummings, felt it incumbent upon him to devote his entire attention to finances as treasurer, to which office he was elected. The council was increased from two to six members, not including the officers.

The sale of the Academy property at 663 Broadway, which had been pending since 1854, was finally and permanently effected in 1860—fortunately before the decline in real estate values that followed the outbreak of the Civil War. At the annual meeting of that year, President Durand being absent on account of ill health, the treasurer, Thomas Cummings, made the report. "I have the pleasure, gentlemen, to report to you the sale of your property, 663 Broadway, Mercer St., etc., for the sum, leasehold and fee, of one hundred and ten thousand dollars, to responsible parties. The proceeds therefrom, after paying all indebtedness of every kind, cannot fall much, if any, short of sixty-four thousand dollars . . . Mr. Leupp and Mr. Sturges, advanced the means for the purchase, and for which they stood in paternity, and during the years it has been in litigation for the title, and had to be held. . . . True friends they have been to you—such, indeed, as are seldom found, and you owe to them all you possess pecuniarily." After an extended address the treasurer concluded: "Charles M. Leupp is no more; yet not a word, a remark, or resolution passed by our body. That is discreditable; and it reflects severely on us. I trust the evening will not pass without its being remedied."

Before the conclusion of the meeting, the treasurer was awarded $1,000 to be paid by the trust, in tribute to his faithful and untiring effort on behalf of the Academy. During the annual dinner which followed, Jonathan Sturges being present, a vote of thanks was extended to him "As the best friend of the Academy" and somewhat later, portraits were made as a memorial to the two benefactors and trustees.

The accounts being properly audited and the trustees released, a third trust deed was executed with Sturges, Cummings, Edmonds, and Durand as trustees authorized to "purchase a site, and erect a building thereon, for the National Academy of Design."

During this period, numerous building sites were proposed and considered by the council, ultimately resulting in the choice of lots on the corner of 23d Street and Fourth Avenue which were accordingly purchased from William Niblo in November, 1860, for the sum of $50,000.

The outbreak of the Civil War was followed by a financial depression which affected real estate. The new owners of the Broadway site wished to return the property. This was not admissible, nor was foreclosure deemed advisable. Because of this unforeseen event, plans for the Academy's new home were held in abeyance until conditions improved.

Plans for the building were, however, presented to the council as a result of an architectural competition arranged by the building committee, and after continued discussion and alterations, the contract was awarded to Peter B. Wright in 1863. With this decision, the trustees were honorably discharged and the president and secretary were duly authorized to execute and attach the corporate seal of the Academy, affirming their permanent release.

In 1861, Asher B. Durand submitted his resignation as president of the Academy and as trustee of the building committee. Mr. Durand had been in ill health, and his resignation was regretfully accepted. As acting-president, Charles C. Ingham delivered the annual report in May of that year.

The great Rebellion has startled society from its propriety, and war and politics now occupy every mind. No one thinks of the Arts. Even among the artists, patriotism has superseded painting, and many have laid by the palette and pencil, to shoulder the musket—"Union for the Country" is the word on every lip, and the feeling in every heart. Let us not, however, in our love of country, forget our love of art, nor forget that if union is good in the nation, it is also good among the artists; and as unity in a nation is absolutely necessary to command the respect of mankind, so a united body of artists is equally necessary to obtain the respect of Society.

Alluding to "the flourishing state of the essential part of our Institution, the Schools," Ingham continued,

In this ever-changing community, where ambition has unlimited scope, and Young America treads on the heels of Old America, and essays to push her from her stool, the Academy has maintained a calm position, and in thirty-six years has had but two Presidents.

Stating that he desired to forego the honor of standing for his own nomination he concluded,

To Mr. Morse is justly due the compliment that he should be the President that shall introduce the Academy into the building they are about to erect, and which it is expected our excellent Trustees will in a short time have completed. It is to be wished that in all things we could be as unanimous as I am sure we will be in our vote of thanks to our late President for his long and faithful services.

Mr. Morse in his reply stated his reluctance to resume the presidency, having been "so long out of the traces of Art"; but being persuaded by so many of the members, "that in view of the case, the feeling of paternity is strongly moved in my heart, and I cannot forget the early travail with my honored Associates, which brought into existence the National Academy of Design." In accepting, he concluded: "I make one condition, however, to wit: that one term only of the Presidency must be considered as the utmost limit of my acceptance." Morse no doubt recognized that, after the unexpected resignation of Durand, a year's interim would be needed to allow sufficient deliberation in regard to the election of his successor. Henry Peters Gray was elected vice-president. Twelve new Academicians and 16 Associates were chosen on the same occasion.

During the war period, an unprecedented number of exhibitions and sales were conducted in the city, with increasing prices received. Leeds' Annual Native and Foreign Production Sales were continued in the galleries of the Academy. The proprietor stated in response to a request from the author of the Annals: "Sixteen years ago we commenced the fancy auction business, and connected with it the sale of pictures. We have had regular sales every week since that period, with few exceptions." In the beginning purchasers were unwilling to pay more than $2.50 for a picture. As taste improved, so did the prices. It was then determined to have annual sales, which had amounted to from $20,000 to $30,000. "At the present time there appears to be hardly any limit to the price persons will pay, if the quality of the painting will warrant the price." The most prominent sale of the period was the collection known as the "Düsseldorf Gallery," which had been continuously exhibited over a number of years and included both old and new American and foreign pictures. The proceeds of the sale amounted to $45,000. This ended the existence of the only permanent gallery in the city, as the Art Union had been discontinued earlier. The Academy was free of contending rivals. The International Art Union and the Foreign Artists Experiment were likewise discontinued. The increase of prices received was attributed to the inflation caused by "Greenbacks." Yet in England, where the gold standard prevailed, pictures also sold for unprecedented prices, the celebrated

Bicknell Collection of 145 examples realizing at auction the enormous sum of nearly $300,000.

"In the time of war or rebellion, it could not be expected that the Fine Arts should receive much attention; and the knowledge of the many absent at the seat of war, either as soldier, or in the Art Corps illustrative, it was thought the Schools would not be well attended, or even, perhaps, called for. It was quite the reverse. The entries were about fifty in the Antique, and twenty-five in the Life." However, as the war continued and successive drafts followed, the enrollment declined.

As the lease of the Tenth Street galleries terminated May 1, 1861, the annual exhibition was opened at an earlier date, March 20, and was continued for one month only. The following two years, the thirty-seventh and thirty-eighth annual exhibitions were held in the Derby Gallery, and although the accommodation was unsatisfactory, the number of exhibits increased and the receipts likewise. The price of the catalogues was raised from 12 to 15 cents, due to the increased cost of paper!

At the annual meeting of 1862 Samuel Morse retired, much to the regret of the members, and Daniel Huntington was elected President. Huntington had been elected an Academician in 1840, and thereafter became an active member of the Academy, joining the council in 1842 and serving on various committees of arrangement. Born in New York in 1816, he received his academic education at Hamilton College. After graduating he studied under Morse and Inman, and was thus trained in the direct line of traditional portraiture. In 1839 he worked in Florence, and revisited Italy at several later periods. Renowned for "catching the likeness," he might be termed the official portrait painter of his generation, reflecting the style and taste of the period. His work in genre was equally well known and popularized by engravings.

During his long tenure of office as president of the Academy, from 1862 to 1870 and from 1877 to 1890, he proved an able administrator. His profound integrity and the esteem in which he was held, not only by his fellow Academicians, but by the distinguished citizens of the city, brought to his office a distinction and stability which added greatly to the prestige of the Academy. Living until 1906 he had witnessed the many currents of social and aesthetic change but his sound and liberal judgment remained ever a constructive force.

Active preparations were now made to start building on the property at 23d Street and Fourth Avenue. As the purchase price of the ground was $50,000 and the amount available in the treasury $60,000, the property was mortgaged for a ten-year period. The remaining amount not being sufficient to cover the cost of building, which was estimated at $80,000, it was proposed to create a fellowship fund. The constitution being amended to authorize the fellowship Vice-President Henry Peters Gray was appointed chairman of the committee (with J. F. Kensett and George Baker as the other members) to solicit contributions. This undertaking proved a brilliant success, far exceeding expectations. It had been proposed to endeavor to raise $100,000; but the members of the committee confessed that if they were successful in raising one-fifth of that amount they would be highly gratified. In a few weeks time the total amount proposed was subscribed. In his report to the Council the chairman of the committee exclaimed in elation, "Gentlemen, we confess ourselves the most astonished parties in the matter, when we announce to you *that we have done it!*" Among the donors of $1,000 was the Academy's first president, Samuel Morse.

In his annual report, President Huntington, in commending the committee, humorously alluded to "the zeal with which they have hunted the men of taste and fortune from their homes to Wall Street, and from Wall Street again to their homes, till they pinned them to a Fellowship."

A contract having been signed for the excavation of the new building, on April 18, 1863, at six A.M., Daniel Huntington lifted the first shovel full of earth. In October of the same year the council resolved to hold a formal ceremony in celebration of the laying of the cornerstone. The following announcement was accordingly issued by Corresponding Secretary T. Addison Richards:

The Academicians, Associates, Fellows, Honorary Members, and Students of the National Academy of Design, Members of the Press, and the Artists of the city generally, are hereby invited (without other notice) to assist in the Celebration of the Laying of the Corner Stone of the New Academy Edifice; and are requested to meet the Council at two o'clock, in the afternoon of Wednesday, the 21st Inst., at the Century Club, 45 East 15th Street, between Union Square and Irving Place—to proceed thence in a body to the Academy grounds, at the corner of Twenty-third Street and Fourth Avenue, where the exercises will commence at three o'clock P.M. Should the weather be stormy, the ceremony will take place at the same hour, on the first fair day thereafter.

The day chosen was auspicious. The sun shone brightly, and although the season was late October it was pleasantly warm. The janitor led the procession bearing a copper box in which had been placed, in the presence of the council, the various articles which were to be deposited in the cornerstone. The clergy, accompanied by the president of the Academy, followed; then the guest speakers with the council, the Academicians, Associates, the Fellows and Honorary Members, the students, artists, the literary representatives, the press, and ordinary citizens.

At Union Square the procession passed around the statue of Washington, and every head was uncovered in honor of the Father of his Country; the sculptor, H. K. Brown, was present among the Academicians. Greeted by the band as they approached the site of the building, the dignitaries and the Academicians took their allotted place on the platform which had been erected on the 23d Street front. It was indeed a memorable celebration.

Following the invocation, the president introduced the vice-president, Henry Peters Gray, chairman of the fellowship fund. After recounting briefly the origin and development of the Academy, Gray asserted that "this is the first Academy of the Fine Arts this side of the Atlantic, the first instance of the building of an Academy of Design, not only in the United States, but on the continent, governed and directed entirely by artists, carried on strictly under Academic regulations, and dependent heretofore wholly on our own resources. And now, strongly wedded to public sympathy by a new order of members, its Fellows." It was deeply regretted that Samuel Morse had to be absent from the city and was thus unable to be present as the youthful dream of the founders was about to be realized.

Parke Godwin, the distinguished orator and citizen, next addressed the assembly. He spoke of the horrors of war, and the frightful conflict then at its height, but reviewing the great periods of the past wherein art flourished after heroic struggles, he prophesied the efflorescence of the arts after the triumphant reunion of the states. "These ages were great, because the spirit of the people, raised by the mighty events in which they participated to celestial heights of enthusiasm, energy and

National Academy of Design.

MDCCCLXIII.

ORDER OF EXERCISES,

AT THE CEREMONY OF THE

Laying of the Corner-Stone

OF THE

NEW ACADEMY EDIFICE,

At the corner of Twenty-Third Street and Fourth Avenue

(*At 3 o'clock, P. M., Wednesday, October 21st.*)

INVOCATION, by the Rev. FRANCIS VINTON, D. D.

MUSIC.

INTRODUCTORY REMARKS, by the PRESIDENT of the Academy.

ADDRESS, by PARKE GODWIN, Esq.

MUSIC.

REMARKS, by Professor S. F. B. MORSE, Ex-President of the Academy.

MUSIC.

ADDRESS, by WILLIAM CULLEN BRYANT, Esq.

MUSIC.

ADDRESS, by Hon. GEORGE BANCROFT.

MUSIC.

ADDRESS, by the Rev. H. W. BELLOWS, D. D.

MUSIC.

The Laying of the Corner-Stone,

Preceded by the offering of a SILVER TROWEL to the President of the Academy, by the Builders, through the Architect,

P. B. WIGHT, Esq.

MUSIC.

ADDRESS, by Rev. E. H. CHAPIN, D. D.

MUSIC.

VOLUNTARY ADDRESSES.

Committee of Arrangements.

THOMAS S. CUMMINGS,   HENRY PETERS GRAY,

THOMAS HICKS,   GEORGE A. BAKER,

T. ADDISON RICHARDS.

unity could but overflow in all the appropriate intellectual manifestations."

The venerable poet William Cullen Bryant, Honorary Member and
Fellow of the Academy, expressed again the general regret that

Professor Morse, to whom the cause of Art in this country, and the cause of
Science throughout the world, owes so much, is not here to address you in a
more impressive manner than I have the ability to do. . . . For my own part,
as an early friend of the Academy, I, too, have some title to say a word or
two on an occasion like this. I was a witness of its birth, nearly forty years
since. I lent its Founders such an aid as a daily press could give, and its pupils
accepted from me a short course of lectures on the Mythology of the Ancients. . . . When this Institution came into existence I could count the
eminent artists of the country on my fingers. Now, what man among us is
able to enumerate all the clever men in the United States who have devoted
the efforts of their genius to the Fine Arts.

The eminent historian, George Bancroft, also a Fellow of the Academy,
delivered the next address. "The occasion on which we meet is full of
earnestness and promise. . . . I have a favorite belief that in this nation, beyond any other, art is destined to thrive and attain its highest
result." Commenting upon the basic freedom of the republic, and of the
universal sentiment and sympathy of its people, he responded to the
thought of the previous speaker, and concluded, "I have nothing to
add, except the hope that the gleam of light which shines on us today,
from the undoubting patriotism of our artists, may be like the wing of
the halcyon on the stormy wave, the harbinger of joy, and life, and
triumph and peace."

In an eloquent and spirited address, the Rev. Dr. Bellows, also Fellow
and Honorary Member of the Academy, spoke of the elevating significance of art and its benefit to the community.

Has anybody ever considered what the influence of the honor and dignity paid
to the Fine Arts repays a community, in the gradual effect it produces upon
the whole style of architecture, house building, furniture, costume patterns
and decorations of every kind, gradually creeping down to the humblest
ramifications of life? . . . We cannot, as sagacious and prudent citizens, as
tax-payers and lovers of peace and order, do too much to naturalize Art, in
all its forms, among us. I consider every print-shop window a public teacher,
and a guarantee of civic order. . . . Gentlemen, no city is great whose
wealth has not crystallized into beauty; no materialism supportable which
has not blossomed into the rich clusters of art.

Referring to a recent visit to Washington where he watched the dome of the Capitol being completed, the speaker concluded: "Art must finish what artisans began. The symbolic Statue of Liberty, cut by Crawford's dying fingers, must surmount the dome of the Capitol; and Art must occupy the last and highest place in the temple that enshrines the Constitution of our Nationality."

The architect of the building, Peter B. Wright, then presented the trowel to the president. "Fear not to injure it, as it is made for a practical purpose. When in after years it is preserved as a memento of this event, its stains and scratches will be of far greater value than the metal of which it is made."

On receiving the trowel the president responded:

In the name of the Artists, and more especially of the Members of the Academy whom I have the honor to represent, I thank you, Sir, and through you, those who have united with you, for this beautiful and appropriate present. I am glad that it is a trowel, and that it is of silver. I remember that distinguished American artist, the late Charles R. Leslie, once saying, "We hear a great deal about the 'golden glow,' but give me in preference the delicate lustre of silver, which, by its purity and refinement, far better suggests the subtle and modest tints which form the greatest beauty of coloring."

After the mortar had been spread, the box was buried in the corner-stone. It contained, among other mementos, letters of Abraham Lincoln, the *Historical Annals of the Academy* by Thomas Cummings, and medals of its previous presidents, Samuel Morse and Asher B. Durand.

The concluding address was given by the Rev. Dr. Chapin, Honorary Member of the Academy, and the benediction by the Rev. Dr. Vinton. Of the original founders of the Academy only five were then living: Morse, Cummings, Ingham, Durand, and Evers. Charles Ingham was to die in December of that same year, but happily was present at the dedication.

The building, when completed, was a fitting edifice for the new era inaugurated by the end of the Civil War, and was to become the focal center of the art activities of the nation. The building occupied a site about 80 feet wide facing 23d Street, and approximately 100 feet long on Fourth Avenue, on the northeast corner (a site now occupied by the Metropolitan Life Insurance Company). For the first time in its history the Academy had ample space for the installation of its properties, the proper equipment and lighting for its school, and appropriate galleries for the presentation of its annual exhibitions.

The façade was designed in the so-called Gothic style then being revived in England, and in general appearance resembled the Doge's Palace in Venice, in consequence of which it came to be known under that appellation. The decorative ornamentation was modeled after the forms of our native leaves and flowers, designed by the stone carvers under the supervision of the architect. The walls of the basement level were of gray marble, with bands of North River gray stone. The first story was of white marble with similar gray bands; the third story was of white and gray marble patterned in oblong blocks, while the whole was surmounted by an arcaded cornice of white marble. There were no windows in the upper story, but circular openings were inserted, designed with tracery, for ventilation. The entrance was supported by columns of red Vermont marble, and enriched with sculpture. The architect contrived to combine beauty and utility.

The basement was appointed with apartments for the janitor. Above it a hall 16 feet high was provided for the casts, and the school proper occupied three studios, the entrance to which was on Fourth Avenue. The formal entrance on 23d Street was approached by a double flight of stairs, from which one entered a spacious hall running the entire length of the building. The Fourth Avenue side was occupied by the reception rooms and the library, the council room and the lecture hall. The main interior stairway led to the galleries above, in the central hall of which were displayed the works composing the permanent collection of the Academy. Opening from this were four spacious galleries for painting and one for sculpture, all being lighted by skylights, the latter having also side lights.

The Academicians could well be proud of this handsome and imposing structure, the visible and material result of their early aspirations, and a symbol of the development of the fine arts in America.

·VII·

THE FIRST meeting of the council in the new building at 23d Street and
Fourth Avenue was held in March, 1865, and arrangements were made
for the inaugural reception and the opening of the annual exhibition.
But on hearing of the death of President Lincoln the council called a
special meeting on April 15 to draft fitting resolutions, as a result of
which the opening was postponed until April 29.

Daniel Huntington, then president, read a touching letter from Samuel
Morse, in which the former president wrote:

It is with pleasure that I now send you the accompanying portrait of Washington Allston by C. R. Leslie, which I purchased a short time ago for the
purpose of presenting it to the National Academy of Design. Please present
it to the Academy in my name as a slight testimonial of my continued interest
in an institution which, in its birth and infancy, I devoted the best days of my
artistic life, and which at this moment of its public success in a special manner
recalls to my memory the pleasures as well as the pains of its early history. In
the review of the past it is one of the most gratifying reflections that though
compelled to engage in controversy with friends, which for a time threatened
permanent alienation, time, with the ascendency, on both sides, of a mutual
disposition to unite in the furtherance of a common and public good, has
long since obliterated in a substantial conciliation, all the asperities incident
to a state of conflict.

After congratulating the Academy on the erection of its edifice, and
prophesying its future growth and enlargement he added:

I also take this opportunity to ask the acceptance of the Academy of a valued relic of my excellent master, which seems a fitting accompaniment to his portrait. It is a pencil which he last used upon his picture of Belshazzar's Feast and on the very day of his death. It was the gift of Mrs. Allston to me, and has an interest more than personal, the color was still fresh on it when I received it. I surrender it to the keeping of the Academy, the most appropriate depository for its preservation. (Cummings)

This thoughtful tribute was indeed a living torch handed from one master to another, the veritable symbol of tradition, the faithful bond of continuity, and truly a most auspicious gift for the inauguration of the new gallery and a legacy for the new generation, the past and the present united.

Previous to the inauguration, Thomas Cummings announced his retirement as treasurer of the Academy. This was a sudden and severe loss to the council. It was accepted with deep regret and heartfelt appreciation of his great service to the foundation and maintenance of the Academy. Thomas Cummings had been an officer of the Academy for forty years, and was in truth its principal executive and financial manager during that time, as well as the most influential and active director of the school.

In his appealing letter of resignation the treasurer expressed his reluctance to part with his active participation in the council, stating that the time chosen was the beginning of the fiscal year and therefore the most favorable for his successor. With rightful pride could he assert, "That during the many years I have held office—the many trials, commercial revolutions—and even the period of rebellion—every creditor has received his demand in full, and the Academy has never been the loser of a cent, a position I trust the Institution will long be permitted to enjoy to its benefit and credit." (Cummings) It was indeed an exceptional achievement, and one which was to benefit not only the Academy but the future artists of the country at large.

James A. Suydam was appointed by the council to fill the unexpired term as treasurer, and at the annual meeting he was duly elected to that office. Alas, he was not long to remain. The council received the sad news of his death on September 15 of that year. An artist of much promise, he had been elected an Academician in 1861, was treasurer of the fellowship fund, and had been of great service in promoting the interests of the Academy. In his will he bequeathed to the Academy the sum of $50,000 to establish a permanent fund, "the income of which shall be appropriated by the Council in such manner as they in their discretion shall deem most desirable to the purposes of instruction in the Arts of Design." In addition he left a valuable collection of contemporary pictures to the permanent collection of the Academy, which the committee appointed appraised at $12,821. Edward Greene was elected to fill the vacancy, and John Kensett succeeded as treasurer of the fellowship fund.

The council at this time was in correspondence with the government on several problems of national interest. The Director of the Mint consulted the Academy relative to designs for the national coinage. A committee of sculptor members was appointed to act in an advisory capacity. The council petitioned the government to enact a law providing copyright protection for works in the visual arts. Copies of the petition and a circular letter were sent to artists in Boston, Philadelphia, Cincinnati, and Chicago for signatures, and also to members of Congress representing those districts. The council also petitioned Congress to place a duty on the permanent importation of contemporary works of art. The auction rooms and dealers' galleries were being flooded by the commercial exploitation of foreign pictures.

On acquiring the property at 23d Street, the council had on repeated occasions appealed to the state legislature to exempt the Academy from taxation. Although it was favorably and worthily presented, the war years were not propitious for its enactment. In 1866, the counsel for the Academy, Charles Tracy, prepared a formal petition which was signed both by artists and by many influential citizens of the city. Acting for the Academy, Vincent Colyer presented the petition to the legislature at Albany. "After six weeks of persevering effort his labors were crowned with complete success and he returned with a copy of the law, delivering it to the officers of the Academy on the evening of the day it passed the Senate and was signed by Governor Fenton." (Minutes) The tax on the property at that time was about $3,000 a year. The exemption has continued until the present time.

In his annual report for the years 1865 and 1866, President Daniel Huntington summarized the events and progress of the Academy. The inaugural exhibition was highly gratifying, the receipts from admissions being $13,000, with some 40,000 persons attending the exhibition. "By agreement with the Council the Artists' Fund Society had its exhibition in our galleries, the net profit to each institution being $1,402.89." The construction of the building cost $172,000 and the site $50,000. There still remained additional carving and interior decoration to be done that would approximate from $10,000 to $15,000. In November, 1865, the architect, Peter B. Wright, reported the cost of the building, including the architect's commission of five percent, to be $176,621.54. A mortgage of $50,000 was placed on the building and held by the Seamen's Bank for Savings, at six percent, payable in two years, nine months from date. A balance remained in the fellowship fund of $41,000, the interest from which would pay the interest on the mortgage.

The fellowship fund had become, aside from the income from the exhibitions, the main support of the Academy. At this time there were over 800 members, with applications steadily increasing. Four thousand season tickets were issued to the Fellows, and a special diploma was awarded in recognition of membership. One principle, however, the president emphasized particularly, that the resolutions of the founders should be perpetuated, and that the professional members should have absolute control. "Better that the building should be levelled with the dust and we begin again without a dollar than to yield an iota of the right of artists to govern an Academy of Art." (Minutes) The expenses of the first year in the new building amounted to $16,000; this, however, included the continuing cost of completing the interior. The year's subscriptions to the fellowship fund aggregated $50,000.

The income from the winter exhibition of 1868 amounted to $9,889; the total profit of the year was $16,000.

At the suggestion of Emanuel Leutze, T. Addison Richards, then corresponding secretary, was appointed resident keeper of the Academy. His new duties were to act as general supervisor and to attend to needed supplies. Mr. Richards occupied this double office for many years. He was given an annual stipend of $1,000 which was later increased to $1,250 and eventually to $1,800. A salesman was added to the staff; his functions included increasing the fellowship fund. This did not prove entirely satisfactory. Later a salesman was paid on a weekly basis for the exhibition period only. This was again changed, the salesman being employed on a commission basis, receiving five percent of sales, the Academy retaining the same amount. This proved mutually beneficial.

The sales recorded in the president's report of 1871 amounted to $24,000.

In 1870 the receipts from admissions increased to over $11,000, as did the receipts from the sale of pictures, prompting the president to report that

New names, new ideas, and plenty of old ideas in new dress have appeared, the dry bones of the ancients are coming to life, brightened by the rich juices of *Copal en pâté*. . . . There is a reaction in favor of American art. . . . We are informed a number of gentlemen are forming collections exclusively of American Art. . . . While it is important we should maintain a united front, it is equally important we should possess a large and liberal spirit toward every class of honest workers. From the noblest efforts of creative and poetic art with its abstract treatment, through all the phrases of the historic and picturesque, the naturalistic and the realistic, even to the elaborate and minute reproduction of the facts and phenomena of nature which delight the eye of the scientist, all shapes and views of truth should be represented. An Academy of Art should take broad and liberal views, and never submit to the tyranny of a single and arbitrary theory. (Minutes)

The expense of maintaining the Academy, including the exhibitions and the school, presented perennial difficulty. Whereas the receipts from the exhibitions showed a surplus over cost of operation, the expenses of the school and the interest on the mortgage combined to cause a deficit averaging about $3,000 each year. It was realized by the finance committee that this could not continue indefinitely. Although the foundation was secured by the great increase of the Academy's property and the appraised value of the works of art and other possessions, there was an embarrassing absence of available cash. Subscribers to the fellowship fund had virtually ceased. The older generation of patrons had passed. To meet this deficiency, in 1870 the council determined to borrow an additional $15,000 to be drawn upon for the support of the school. It was further decided that a committee be appointed to interest new subscribers, and in addition, that the members should donate pictures to be sold for the benefit of the Academy. Both of these undertakings proved highly successful. Although several times postponed, the exhibition and sale of pictures resulted in a net return of $4,000, the auctioneer offering his services free of charge. Several of the Academicians also subscribed amounts varying from $50 to $500 aggregating $1,057.76. Fellowship subscriptions amounted to $2,500 and contributions for reducing the mortgage $1,565.52; the total amount received aggregated $9,030.38.

The year 1876 celebrating the National Centennial coincided with the fiftieth anniversary of the first exhibition held by the National Academy. To mark this double occasion and to further the interest in art, a group of distinguished citizens, cooperating with the Metropolitan Museum and the National Academy, organized a benefit exhibition known as the New York Centennial Loan Exhibition. This proved an event of unusual significance. The exhibition included many examples by popular French painters who continued to be "best sellers" during the last quarter of the century, among them Gérôme, Boldini, Zamacois, and Madrozo. Mrs. A. T. Stewart insured two works by Gérôme for $30,000 each. The gross receipts from the exhibition amounted to $51,250 and the net profits were $39,907. Of this amount 60 percent was donated to the Academy and 40 percent to the Metropolitan Museum. Mrs. Stewart made an additional donation to the Academy of $2,000. This enabled the treasurer to reduce the mortgage on the building to $5,000 and within a short time the Academy was free from debt and the burden of paying interest.

The Academy's income for 1877 came to $15,432, exclusive of donations, and the expenses were $11,895. The sum of $3,400 was received from rental of the galleries, the most prominent annual exhibitions being those of the American Water Color Society and of the Society of Decorative Art.

The Academy sustained a sorrowful loss in 1879 in the death of its faithful treasurer, E. D. E. Greene, who had served in that office since 1865. George H. Hall was appointed to fill the vacancy.

The amendment to the constitution of 1869, which ruled that "no Academician shall be eligible to the office of President or Vice-President for more than two consecutive years," was annulled by unanimous vote at a special meeting held in 1878, the clause being omitted. This accounts for the short terms of office of the succession of Academy presidents after Daniel Huntington: Henry Peters Gray, William Page, J. Q. A. Ward, and Worthington Whittredge. Daniel Huntington was reelected president in 1877 and continued in that office until 1890. William Page was elected vice-president, T. Addison Richards continued as corresponding secretary and keeper of the academy.

The reception at the opening of the annual exhibitions each year continued to be one of the important social events of the season. Many guests arrived early to have first choice of the pictures. Sales reached unprecedented heights. At the annual exhibition of 1882 the receipts from sales totaled $35,000, paid admissions $7,794.28, indicating an attendance of over 30,000 spectators. The following year, with the reopening of the autumn exhibition, the sale of pictures for both exhibitions amounted to $48,554.

The period from the inauguration of the new building to 1880 was one of continuous concern and activity in the conduct and development of the school. The income from the Suydam Fund provided a substantial foundation, but the yearly cost of operation averaged between $4,000 and $6,000. The deficit was a heavy burden, but it was willingly shouldered.

The goal of the school was to maintain a high standard of work, and to provide not only visual and technical training, but also a thorough analytical knowledge of anatomy and perspective. The student entered in the antique class and, after proper preparation and achievement, was advanced to the life class, and later was initiated in painting. The program was in accord with the training followed by the artists of that time who had studied abroad. The difficulty, as in the past, was to provide regular and systematic instruction by the Academicians, who formerly had given their services without remuneration. For the school term of 1867, the members who were appointed to instruct served for two weeks in rotation and were paid $10 for each session. The instructors at this time included Daniel Huntington, William Page, Eastman Johnson, Henry Peters Gray, and George Baker.

In 1869 the school committee recommended that it would be advisable to employ one member of the Academy to instruct the students regularly, supplementing which, lectures should be given periodically on anatomy and perspective. This suggestion was approved by the council, and Lemuel Wilmarth was appointed instructor to attend the school two sessions each week, being paid $10 for each criticism. This was further implemented in 1870 by specifying that the instructor attend the evening sessions, and three day sessions at a yearly salary of $1,500.

Classes for men and women were held separately (the male model in the women's life class was not permitted to pose entirely in the nude, and the members of the class were required to be over twenty-one years of age). The curriculum provided for an elementary class, the antique class, the life class, and a class in painting. Dr. William Rimmer was employed to deliver a course of lectures on anatomy, receiving an annual fee not to exceed $100.

Prior to 1870 the enrollment in the school did not exceed 100 students. The trustees of the Cooper Union proposed uniting their art school, composed of some 200 students, with the school of the Academy. Considerable negotiation ensued, the council reaching an agreement in principle. There were, however, certain conditions in the charter of the Cooper Union that could not be changed. Among these was a clause insisting that the name of the Union should be used jointly with that of the Academy. Ultimately the council withdrew its previous decision, and the amalgamation was not effected. In the meantime the number of students attending the Academy had steadily increased. In the annual report of 1875, 251 students were recorded, 131 being in the men's class, and 120 in the women's class. A second instructor was appointed to assist Professor Wilmarth.

The corresponding increase in the cost of running the school accounted for the annual deficit in the treasurer's report. It was suggested that the pupils be required to pay a nominal tuition. This was opposed, first, because of the apprehension that the exemption from taxes might be revoked, the charter stating that the Academy conducted free schools, and second, because of the enduring ideal of the founders.

The sum appropriated for the maintenance of the school was determined by the council. During the summer recess of 1875, many members were absent from the city, and there was no quorum at the council meetings until late November. There being no funds available for instructors, models, and other school expenses, the school was closed during that time. This led to dissatisfaction among the students. In this unhappy condition a group of students joined together and in conference with their teacher, Professor Wilmarth, formed a self-governing, cooperative class. The name given to the new venture was suggested by one of the Academy pupils, Theodore Robinson, as the Art Students League. Thus the new school grew from the Academy and followed its initial purpose—a school governed by artists for the study and promotion of art on a noncommercial basis. Professor Wilmarth remained their instructor.

Finding no means of continuing the school without the partial support of its students, the council appointed a committee composed of

J. G. Brown and E. Wood Perry to formulate plans for its reorganization. In the meantime Charles Tracy, counsel for the Academy, was requested to determine the question as to whether there would be a legal violation of the charter if the students of the school were required to pay a tuition fee. Mr. Tracy based his conclusion on the wording of the charter: "So long as the same shall be devoted exclusively to the advancement of the Fine Arts or be used as a free school of design and no longer." In defending the right of the Academy to charge tuition fees, he stated:

The exemption is upon conditions that the building be either devoted as specified *or* used as specified. If the building should be occupied otherwise than in one or both such ways the exemption would cease, but while it is occupied in either of these ways the exemption continues. . . . Instruction in the Arts is one of the most direct methods of effecting the advancement of the Fine Arts, and taking payment for such instruction is as legitimate as taking payment from visitors on entering the exhibitions. . . . Payment in both cases is incidental and is a considerable means of carrying out the general intention, namely to give advancement to the Fine Arts.

He pointed out that the word "Design" as used in the charter of the Academy referred to the fine arts, specifically, painting, sculpture, architecture, and the graphic arts rather than industrial or commercial design. "So long as the school is one of Design in the Fine Arts the first condition is complied with. The question above submitted is therefore answered in the affirmative." (Minutes)

Acting upon this advice, the school committee recommended that, "Whereas it is impossible in the present condition of the finances of the Academy to provide sufficient instruction in the Schools and to the end that such efficient instruction be provided, be it resolved that the following fees be charged to the students payable monthly in advance from and after the first day of January, 1877." A special meeting was called on December 18, 1876 to consider and act upon the report. The committee proposed, and the council approved, twelve resolutions pertaining to tuition, to the curriculum of the School, to examinations required, and to the regulations pertaining to attendance, conduct, and instruction. It was first agreed that Professor Wilmarth be reengaged as instructor with a salary equal to one half the receipts from the students' fees for the year, the compensation of any assistants to be paid for by the instructor. The fees to be charged were as follows: antique class: for students intending to become professional artists, $5 per month; for amateur students, $10; life class: for students intending to become professional artists, $6 per month; and for amateurs, $12.

In the meantime, during the absence of Professor Wilmarth, the Academicians, J. G. Brown, Thomas W. Wood, and Henry Peters Gray voluntarily conducted instruction without remuneration. In his presidential report, Worthington Whittredge, commenting on the school, stated that

All the students this year appear to be young men and women who have made up their minds to make Art their profession, [as compared] with many who crowded our Schools formerly, who to all appearances were chiefly anxious of the renown of passing through the Academy Schools in order to get places to teach in seminaries or elsewhere, studying art as an accomplishment. Some of the students were very talented and have made remarkable progress. (Minutes)

When tuition fees were required, considerable disagreement arose, and enrollment was reduced to about 40 students. The president made a formal protest to the council, being supported by many of the Academicians. At the annual meeting of 1877 the question was brought before the members attending and after much discussion it was resolved: "That the resolution of the Council in December last, establishing a charge to the students in the Schools for tuition, is deemed inadvisable and that said resolution be rescinded." The motion was carried by a vote of 24 to 16.

Under the new regulations and instruction, and as a result of free tuition, the enrollment increased to 200 pupils by 1879. The *esprit de corps* was excellent. In the meantime the interest from the Suydam Fund had decreased by nearly $1,000. To reduce the deficit an annual matriculation fee of $10 was required to be paid by each student. The amount received approximately covered the cost of models. This ordinance continued in operation for the next half century.

The casts from the antique had from time to time been restored and supplemented. In consultation with Sir Alfred Eastlake, president of the Royal Academy, several casts from the Elgin Marbles in the British Museum were added to the collection, and the sum of $1,000 was appropriated to purchase in Europe photographic reproductions of drawings by the Italian masters.

Medals were offered as prizes, competitive examinations being held at the end of each term. The first medal was awarded as a memorial to the late James Suydam, donor of the fund; the second medal in honor of Charles Loring Elliott, whose widow had bequeathed $1,000 for that purpose. These awards continued annually, the president presenting the medals after addressing the students at the close of the term. The medals were cast in silver and bronze, the Suydam medals being awarded in the life class, the Elliott medals in the antique.

The period under consideration witnessed many amendments and additions to the constitution. With the steadily increasing number of artists and the growing national significance of the Academy, new problems arose, the solution of which was not provided for in the former constitution. The most insistent cause of complaint was relative to the exhibition privileges of Academicians and the powers of the Hanging Committee.

The words "Hanging Committee" first occur in the minutes of 1865 as distinguished from the former Committee on Arrangements. There had previously been no special jury of selection, as no precedent had been formed. The evolution of the system as we know it today was a gradual development. Several amendments and additions to the constitution were necessary to effect this change. The first reference to this subject occurs in the president's report:

It has been proposed that hereafter all works received shall be deliberately reviewed and their merits decided before they are placed on the walls, and that a proper time shall be taken after the hanging for careful consideration to correct the mistakes, by these means more justice may be done and possibly the annual growl of varnishing day a little softened. . . . It is important that members should freely discuss all measures of reform or progress and urge them forward by resolutions and action. The old stereotyped ways will no longer serve. (Minutes)

It was proposed that a fall and winter exhibition be held. The opposition contended that this would lower the standard of the exhibitions as there were not a sufficient number of new pictures worthy of being exhibited. The motion was, however, passed in 1867, it being favored as a means of increasing receipts from admissions and furthering the sale of pictures. The result was definitely successful. Special Academy Receptions were held during the winter exhibitions with elaborate collations.

In 1867, 76 works were represented by members and 97 by nonmembers, this relative number varying considerably with each year. During the winter exhibitions the Suydam collection was displayed; the galleries were open free of charge on Saturdays and closed on Sundays.

The American Water Color Society, founded in 1866 with Samuel Colman as its first president, was granted permission to exhibit collectively in conjunction with the winter exhibition of the Academy. This marks the increasing interest in the water-color medium, and the separation in hanging of oil and of water-color pictures.

It is amusing to note in passing that when a portrait of Homer D. Martin was presented to the council (to qualify him for Associate membership), "The Secretary was instructed to return it to Mr. Martin with the request that it be better finished." Not being able to identify the artist, one of the members asked Winslow Homer if he knew who painted it, whereupon Homer responded: "Why I painted it. I tried to make it look as much like a landscape as possible." The portrait is now in the permanent collection of the Academy.

A special meeting of the Academicians was called in June, 1869. Particularly to be considered were amendments pertaining to the management and the direction of the exhibitions. The control of the affairs of the Academy had been previously vested in the council; this was modified to read: "During their term of office they shall have entire management of the affairs of the Academy, subject to the control of the body of Academicians, provided that the power to mortgage or otherwise dispose of the Real Estate belonging to the Academy rests solely in the Academicians." The previous method of selecting works and arranging the exhibitions had been vested in the council and two additional Associate Members. The amendment provided that this new jury should be elected by written ballot and be composed of "Three Academicians not members of the Council or officers of the Academy, who shall constitute the Committee for selecting the works of art and arranging the exhibitions of the Academy for the year, no member of the Committee to be eligible for two consecutive years." This is the first indication of the committees of selection and of hanging being elected by ballot rather than appointed by the council. The powers of the Academicians as a body were thus more fully represented in conducting the business and direction of the exhibitions of the Academy. The later ruling was, however, to cause much controversy, since it placed absolute authority in the hands of only three representatives.

The first challenge was made by John La Farge in a letter of protest written to the council. La Farge had been elected an Academician in 1869 and had served actively on several committees in cooperation with the council. Two pictures which he had sent to the annual exhibition of 1874 had not been placed by the Hanging Committee. There was at this time no mandatory provision in the constitution to ensure the representation of works by members of the Academy. As we have seen, the former amendment granted absolute authority to the Hanging Committee of "Selecting the works of Art and arranging the exhibitions of the Academy for the year." In his considered letter of justified protest the writer stated:

I cannot admit that having passed through the ordeals of election for Associate and Academician, I can be deprived of its advantages by the mere will of this Committee of three men. Such an action would be the reversal of the judgment of the entire Academy that I have deserved the right of expression in Art and that I hold an assured position in the profession. Such an action would be in discord with one great advantage that an Academy of Science or Art offers to the members of the profession, namely a place and means of recognition so well established as to secure for the artist and scientist a sure chance of being heard. The great danger, the great difficulty in the life of all men who live in the intellect, is to secure such a hearing for a permanence; for this, Academies are the one great resource.

Referring to changing conditions and personal dislikes he added:

To meet this great need in moments of danger by keeping a place and opportunity open is the great value of an Academy apart from educational tradition, to the Artist or man of Science. It would not be worth his while laboring to attain this position if it were revocable at will or subject to an annual struggle. . . . Expecting action in the direction I have indicated I shall beg of you to submit this to the Council. (Minutes)

The secretary, in response, expressed the regret of the council "that you or any member should find cause to complain of the arrangement of the exhibition and it fully agrees with the spirit of your general proposition that the status of an Academician should assure to him at all times the right to be fully represented by his works on the walls of the Academy." The secretary then stated that, inasmuch as the constitution by its recent amendment granted to the Hanging Committee the sole right and power of "selecting the works of Art and arranging the exhibitions of the Academy for the year," the council was thereby deprived of its authority in making any changes in the decision of the committee. "It, however, deems the question which you have raised, namely, the rights and privileges of Academicians in the exhibitions, to be of such grave import, it will request the President to bring the subject to the notice of the general body of the Society in order that such action may be taken as shall be thought needful." (Minutes)

Following a resolution proposed by Mr. La Farge, a proposal was made "That a committee of five be appointed by the Chair to consider the subject of a revision of the Constitution, and to report any changes it may deem necessary at the next Quarterly Meeting of the Academy."

Mr. La Farge asserted in his resolution "That the Academy of Design in its exhibitions does not propose to exercise judicial functions and to decide between different schools and methods in Art, but that it believes the interests of Art to be best aided by the exhibition of all that has obtained sanction in the artistic community." This passage is of significant historical interest, for it voices for the first time a division of opinion relative to the new movement then coming into being, and asserts that the Academy should not act as an arbiter of style but should recognize accredited achievement.

In the exhibition circular of 1875 contributors were advised "that those works that have been seen at any club or other exhibition will be considered to have been exhibited and are therefore ineligible." This caused considerable agitation, the council questioning the legality of this arbitrary interpretation of the constitution. Sanford R. Gifford sent in his resignation, which happily was not accepted. The original article in the constitution stated, "No work previously exhibited by the Academy should be re-eligible to an Annual Exhibition." This was implemented by a ruling enacted in 1847: "Whereas, it is important to preserve the novelty of each Annual Exhibition of the Academy, by a strict exclusion of all works of art that have been previously exhibited publicly in the City of New York, it is therefore Resolved, that in future, no work of art, that has been publicly exhibited in the City of New York, be admitted in the Annual Exhibitions of the Academy, and that due notice be given to exhibitors to that effect."

In his *Annals*, Thomas Cummings, who was present when this resolution was proposed, comments in part as follows: "It was not done at a meeting legally constituted to do it. No notice, as required, was given. There was not the requisite vote to constitute it a law. It has, therefore, no legal existence." The resolution fell in abeyance, as there was no agreement on the exact interpretation of the clause "publicly exhibited." In later editions of the constitution the ruling was omitted.

After obtaining legal advice, the council, in replying to Mr. Gifford's letter of resignation, stated that the authority rested entirely with the Hanging Committee. At a later meeting, however, it was resolved, "That the resolution of January fourth regarding pictures shown at clubs is in our judgment wise and calculated to enhance the interests of the exhibition [but] that finding it not to be within the jurisdiction of the Council it is hereby repealed."

It was an embarrassing situation. The council was without any power to determine the works eligible for exhibition or to select the works to be hung. President Huntington, in addressing the members at the annual meeting of 1875, declared:

This question should be determined by you at once. We did not believe that in giving the Hanging Committee the *selection*, so much stress was intended to be laid upon that word as to exclude all uses and powers of the Council in determining the character of the works to be exhibited, making the Council entirely subservient to the Hanging Committee on this important part of the Academy's business. . . . I recommend to you an immediate change in the Constitution, giving back the power to the Council, or if this cannot be done, to a chosen part of it, which, with the present Hanging Committee shall have this so-called selection. I further recommend to you to expunge from the Constitution forever, so far as you can do it, the words "Publicly Exhibited." (Minutes)

At a special meeting of Academicians in April, 1877, the following amendment was proposed and adopted: "After the election of the new Council, at the Annual Meeting shall also be elected by written ballot three Academicians who together with two Academicians to be appointed by the new Council shall constitute the Committee for selecting the works of art and arranging the exhibitions of the Academy for the year; no member of this Committee to be eligible for two consecutive years." Thus we witness the gradual development of the present jury of selection, which was ultimately to be entirely elected by the balloting of the full membership.

At the same meeting it was voted: "That in our Annual Exhibition hereafter each Academician shall be entitled to have two pictures hung on the line (excluding the corridor) provided the space occupied thereby shall not exceed eight feet." This ruling, by reserving the best places in the galleries for the Academicians, proved unjust to many of the gifted younger artists who were not members, and was one of the principal causes of opposition which led to the founding of the Society of American Artists in the same year.

In reporting for the council at the annual meeting of 1877, the president, in alluding to the recent amendments, asserted:

It is certainly desirable that the fairest opportunity should be afforded to every exhibitor, and at the same time the privileges of members should be respected. It is surely not too much to ask that every member should be entitled to at least one good place on the line, and ought we not to rule that no work of an Academician shall be excluded without the joint consent of the Committee and the Council. These discussions remind us of the importance of care in the election of new members. . . . If, however, after years of faithful and successful labor we receive an artist into our body we should stand by him. (Minutes)

In the presidential report of 1878, Daniel Huntington, in referring to the absence of works by many previous exhibitors, but not mentioning by name the newly formed Society of American Artists, commented upon its cause:

It may not be amiss to allude to some distrust of the perfect fairness of the Academy towards the rising and younger artists, partly by the passage of the so-called "eight-foot rule" so soon after tumbled into the lumber room of the past. The absence of the new and perhaps stormy element has undoubtedly caused some stagnation and weakened the exhibitions—we need all the vital forces—unity among ourselves is essential in maintaining our position as American Artists amidst the overflowing torrent of foreign competition. If we have been slow to acknowledge the merits of the younger men, if we have barred the door of entrance too obstinately let us correct the error in a magnanimous spirit. Among the younger men whose works for years have proved talents, there are several that we should welcome into our body. Let us in the elections today show a discriminating liberality, be generous as well as just and thus send some new and hot blood through our old veins.

A provision was made in 1880 "that all contributions to the Academy Exhibitions shall be sent and removed at the expense of the contributor" and that pictures sent from out-of-town be delivered to an agent for delivery.

In 1882 it was resolved that the Hanging Committee should be enlarged and that instead of three Academicians elected by ballot and two appointed by the council, five Academicians should be chosen in alphabetical rotation, the council appointing two Associate Members to add to their number. The names of all eligible Academicians were placed in a hat, and the first name drawn (which proved to be that of Samuel Colman) was to head the list forming the committee, the other members following alphabetically. Any member unable to serve was called upon the following year. At the same time, the autumn exhibition was resumed to provide greater opportunity for exhibitors. In 1885, William Hart, chairman of the Hanging Committee, stated in his report that 1,160 pictures had been received and that from this number, 665 were hung; he recommended reducing the Hanging Committee to three members, the entire body selecting the pictures to be hung. In the annual report of 1886 the alphabetical rotation of selecting the Hanging Committee was questioned:

There has been savage work this year—the grumbling has been fierce—and the rights and privileges of Academicians have not been fully considered, or even clearly understood. . . . I confess there is just cause for complaint. When an artist has been admitted to the Academy, his name and honor should be precious in the esteem of all of us—and at least one good place in the Exhibition assured. . . . It is suggested that a Jury of Reception, separate from the Hanging Committee, should decide before the arrangement begins, thus dividing the responsibility.

This is the first suggestion of the advisability of a separate jury of selection. After repeated discussion and several adjourned meetings, an amendment to the constitution was passed in December of 1886. This provided that six members of the council, not officers, be added to the previous seven members, to form a "Committee of Selection, the duty of which shall be to determine which works of art shall be accepted for exhibition." In alluding to the spring exhibition of 1887, President Huntington reported favorably upon the new ruling: "The Committee of Selection has proved a power which has freed the Exhibition from a load of uninteresting material. . . . This elevation of the standards will have an effect to stimulate the efforts of established artists, to rouse the ambition of rising ones, and to terrify only those who dread the danger of the fight for victory." (Minutes)

The question of the rights and privileges of members was frequently discussed, there being no definite ruling in the constitution in regard to the exemption of members from submitting their contributions to the committee of selection. In reference to this controversy, Daniel Huntington suggested: "Ought we not to have some definite and binding rule regarding contributions by members—both Academicians and Associates? For instance Academicians to have the right of two pictures, and Associates one, simply by virtue of their membership." This was similar to the thought as expressed by John La Farge thirteen years before; it was to remain unresolved until a decade later.

The gallery space was, in the meantime, proving too limited to hang all of the pictures accepted by the committee of selection. The Hanging Committee reported in 1889 that of the 1,352 works received, 547 were placed, including 21 pieces of sculpture; but that 174 pictures, which had passed the jury, could not be hung for lack of space. It was not until 1896 that a definite ruling was made stating that all works accepted by the jury of selection must be placed by the Hanging Committee, and that no work rejected by the jury would be permitted to be hung. It was also definitely ordered that each Academician should be entitled to be represented by three works at each regular exhibition, and each Associate by at least one work.

The jury of selection and the Hanging Committee were continually undergoing modification and change. The eventual result was the democratic system of selection by ballot. At a special meeting of Academicians in 1891, after several amendments and counteramendments, it was voted that "The Hanging Committee shall consist of two Academicians and one Associate, chosen by ballot at the Annual Meeting. This Committee with the addition of twelve Academicians and five Associates, chosen by ballot at the Annual Meeting, shall constitute a General Committee to select works of art for exhibition."

During these years, the Academy also experienced important changes in membership. The artists of the old school were gradually passing, while the newly elected members represented the younger generation that had recently returned from foreign study.

The active membership of the Academy as recorded in 1883 consisted of 92 Academicians and 83 Associates, the number in each class being limited to 100. The candidates nominated were chosen only from the current annual exhibition. The Associate-elect was required to present his portrait within one year after his election, failing which, unless a proper excuse was offered, his election was declared void. An Associate not exhibiting in two successive annual exhibitions was dropped from membership. There seems to have been no regulated mode of nomination. A two-thirds vote of the Academicians, providing a quorum was present, was required for election. If a candidate came within two votes of the required two thirds, he was entitled to reconsideration. It was not until 1896 that a definite ruling in regard to the mode of nomination was approved. Each Academician was entitled to nominate in writing five Associates as Academicians, and each Academician and Associate were equally entitled to nominate ten candidates for Associate members. The candidates receiving the largest number of votes at the Annual Meeting were declared elected, provided that the vote was not less than two thirds of the members present, and also that the candidates elected did not exceed the number of vacancies. A subsequent ruling permitted both Associates and Academicians to nominate candidates for Academicianship. This was again overruled, but ultimately it was sustained.

It will be seen that, in the period under consideration, the modern exhibition system was gradually evolving, as indicated by the corresponding changes in the constitution. With growing competition, the standard of the exhibitions was greatly improved, while the honor of being represented encouraged the younger artists to contribute, with the additional hope of becoming nominated for membership. In the 'eighties and 'nineties the candidates elected to membership included many of the most gifted artists of the period, artists who were later to be recognized as the leading masters of the American School. The list is a long one, the most prominent painters including John W. Alexander, Edwin A. Abbey, Cecilia Beaux, Robert Blum, Edwin Blashfield, Frank W. Benson, Kenyon Cox, William M. Chase, Thomas W. Dewing, Frederick Dielman, Thomas Eakins, Thomas Hovenden, H. Bolton Jones, Francis D.

Millet, Thomas Moran, J. Francis Murphy, John Sargent, Edmund Tarbell, Abbott Thayer, Dwight W. Tryon, Frederick P. Vinton, Douglas
Volk, Horatio Walker, J. Alden Weir, and Irving R. Wiles. Of the
sculptors, Augustus Saint-Gaudens and Olin Warner were elected in
1889, Herbert Adams in 1899, and Daniel Chester French in 1901. There
were no architects elected during this period.

The painters in water color, as we have noted, had organized the
American Water Color Society, most of the members of which worked
in both mediums and were members of both organizations, their annual
exhibitions being held in the galleries of the Academy. Other organizations exhibiting at the Academy from time to time included the New
York Etching Club, the Artists Fund Society, the Salmagundi Club, and
others.

The increase in attendance and sales during the 'eighties indicates not
alone the popularity of the Academy exhibitions but also the prosperity
of the purchasers. But sales varied with the general financial conditions
of the country, and during the next decade they gradually declined, although the receipts from admissions remained more or less constant. The
presidential report of 1895 alludes to the sales in the autumn exhibition
as being greater than the previous year while "We have reason to be
proud of the present Annual Exhibition, now drawing to a close, for
its superior excellence over those of previous years and it is gratifying to
learn that the public has shown due appreciation of this fact in purchases,
although there has been some falling off in attendance." (Minutes)

Conditions suddenly changed with the financial panic of the following year. President Thomas Wood, in his annual address, reported

The present business depression rather increasing than diminishing, which has
affected us for a year or more, has proved disastrous to our present Annual
Exhibition, both in attendance and sales. This collection, probably as representative as any in the country, although held in this time-honored building
devoted to art, near the centre of the city, with four different lines of street
railroad cars passing its doors, has met with such poor recognition from the
public, that the gate receipts and sale of catalogues will hardly pay the cost
of the Exhibitions. The sales of pictures have been very meagre also, giving
little or no encouragement to the artists of this country.

Since the advent of "Free Art" so called, many foreign dealers have opened
houses upon Fifth Avenue for free exhibitions. The West is flooded with
cheap foreign pictures, mostly forgeries, and Western Exhibitions go now

to Europe instead of New York for their collections. Altogether the prospect for American Art at this time, is anything but encouraging. (Minutes)

In fact this date may well mark the end of an era. Winslow Homer complained bitterly about low prices and lack of sales; most of the life-work of Thomas Eakins remained in his studio. Albert Ryder seems never to have thought of selling his pictures, content in the realm of reverie. The Paris trademark, as in fashion, was the sign of the *haute monde*. An American painter working in France had the edge over his confreres at home.

But there was to be a new awakening. The astute American collector began to think of financial returns. As a patron of the arts, Thomas B. Clarke had for many years promoted American painting and was inti-mately associated with the art movements and artists of his time. Over a period of years, seeking counsel from the artists themselves, he gradually formed the most representative collection of contemporary American painting of his generation. The sale of his pictures in 1899, which in-cluded 39 examples of Inness, and 31 by Homer, was the most en-couraging and hopeful event of the time in the furtherance of American art. The unprecedented increase of prices received at auction over that of the original price paid the artist at once stimulated the interest of other collectors and encouraged dealers to recognize the possibility of profit in sponsoring American painting. The prominent art dealers in New York represented international concerns and controlled the market. The old relationship between patron and artist had passed. The era of the dealer was at hand. It required great courage, however, to deal in American art in competition with European dealers. The name of William Macbeth should be honored for both his wisdom and his faith in being the first dealer to promote exclusively the work of American artists.

·VIII·

THE SOCIETY OF AMERICAN ARTISTS: STEPS LEADING TO THE FORMATION OF THE SOCIETY · THE SOCIETY MERGES WITH THE NATIONAL ACADEMY

THE SOCIETY of American Artists was organized in 1877. Of the twenty-two original members, twenty either were members or were to become members of the National Academy. The list included John La Farge, George Inness, R. Swain Gifford, Samuel Colman, Homer Martin, Thomas Moran, and Alexander Wyant. Walter Shirlaw was the first president. Previous to the building of the Fine Arts Galleries at 57th Street, the annual exhibitions were held in various galleries as opportunity and finances prompted: the Kurtz Gallery, the Yandell Gallery, the National Academy, the American Art Galleries, and one summer in the Metropolitan Museum. In 1885 no exhibition was held. From 1889 to 1892 the exhibitions were held at the Fifth Avenue Galleries. Within five years the membership doubled.

The inception of the idea of the Society took place in June, 1877, in the studio of Helena De Kay, when she with Saint-Gaudens, Wyatt Eaton, and Walter Shirlaw inaugurated definite plans for exhibitions. The Society cannot rightly be called a secession from the older institution as most of its members also exhibited at the Academy. The movement was a protest against the preference given the older Academicians and the enactment of the ill-advised "eight-foot-line." The previous year several of the pictures of the newcomers were given conspicuous positions in the favored south gallery, while some of the work of Academicians was "skied." This imposition could not be tolerated by the older artists of established reputation, hence the enactment of the ruling, which in the year following was fortunately annulled. The majority of the younger men in the Society were of the generation born in the 'fifties and early 'sixties, and had only recently returned from the art schools of Munich and Paris. Preoccupied with technique, direct painting, and optical reaction, they looked upon the meticulous finish of the older genre painters as sentimental story telling.

The Munich School was represented by William Chase, Charles Miller, Frank Duveneck, Otto Bacher, Frank Currier, Frederick Dielman, Henry Murhman, Frederick Freer, and Walter Shirlaw. Works by several of these painters had been favorably shown at the Academy both before and after their sojourn in Europe.

The artists trained in the French schools represented three general groups: students working under the supervision of Gérôme, Lefebvre, Boulanger, and other masters at the Beaux Arts and the Académie Julian; those working in the studio of Carolus Duran; and others influenced by Bastien-Lepage and Dagnan-Bouveret, great names in the French capital. Monet and the Impressionists also made many converts. Of the first group, Edwin Blashfield, Will Low, Kenyon Cox, and George de Forest Brush were the most prominent. The impressive compositions of Brush in which he depicted the nude form of the American Indian are the most accomplished conceptions in the Academic tradition. The early work of J. Alden Weir reflects the naturalism of his friend Bastien-Lepage. Theodore Robinson, an early member of the Society, was the pioneer of American impressionism, the influence of which grew with the work of Robert Vonnoh, Childe Hassam, John Twachtman, Willard Metcalf, and others. The Düsseldorf influence and the "Hudson River school" were conspicuously absent from the exhibitions.

The constitution of the Society of American Artists was sufficiently brief to be printed in the catalogue of 1883. The board of control was composed of four officers and three additional members elected at the annual meeting. The committee of selection consisted of nine members elected by ballot, three of whom formed the Hanging Committee. No contributions to the exhibition were exempt from being submitted to the jury. The point of departure was in the method of selecting the pictures. The signature of the artist was concealed before his work was presented to the jurors. During the first ballot no discussion was permitted. Pictures were rated by each juror with numerals, 90 being the highest, the verdict decreasing by tens. The total number received was then marked on the back of each picture. Those receiving no mark were rejected. All remaining pictures were then placed in a row, the highest numbers being first. On the second ballot, a two-thirds vote decided at which number further rejection should begin. In the exhibition of 1882 all pictures numbered below 30 were rejected. It was a complicated system requiring several days in judging. In the constitution of 1901, the method of selection was simplified, the jury being increased to 27 members. A special committee was appointed by the jury to invite a determined number of pictures exempt from the jury of selection. Works receiving the affirmative votes of two thirds of the jurors present were marked 1; those receiving a majority vote were marked 2; those receiving less than a majority but more than a third were marked 3; those receiving the negative votes of two thirds of the jurors were marked "R"—rejected. All works marked 1, 2, and 3 were then reexamined, and by a two-thirds vote of the jurors, their rating could be either raised or lowered. (This system was later adopted by the Academy.)

The Hanging Committee was obliged to hang all works marked 1; those marked 2 and 3 were hung at the discretion of the committee relative to space available, number 2 having the preference. After the completion of the hanging, the exhibition was reviewed by the jury. All works marked 2 and 3 remaining unplaced were again viewed. Any picture not hung could by a two-thirds vote be admitted, and by a two-thirds vote a picture placed could be removed, or its position changed.

This exacting procedure used by the Society was a reaction from the jury rules then prevalent in the Academy. The number of pictures and the amount of space permitted to any one exhibitor was determined by the jury; thus preferred pictures by a single artist were given more space than was permitted by the Academy. In the later years of the Society, younger artists representing new trends were given much the same treatment as that received by the elder artists of the Society, when as youths they first submitted their work to the Academy jury.

In the twenty-eighth and final exhibition of the Society held in 1906, 1,500 works were submitted, of which 448 were hung. The attendance, including the reception and school children admitted free, totaled 12,909. The price of admission was 50 cents. The final enrollment of the Society included 134 members, each member being required to pay $10 in annual dues, in default of which he was dropped from membership.

In the meantime the original protest against the Academy was subsiding. The iconoclastic young men of the 'seventies and 'eighties were now the conservatives of the Society. From the time the first exhibition of the Academy was held in the Fine Arts Building in 1900 to the exhibition of 1905, the Society of American Artists also held its annual exhibitions in the same building, in which it was a founding stockholder. It was becoming obvious that the character of the work exhibited by the two institutions were each year more similar, and that the majority of the members of one organization were also members of the other. Recognizing these facts, the council of the Academy proposed that the board of control of the Society be approached with the view of uniting the two organizations. At a special meeting of the council held at the Century Association on March 22, 1905, it was resolved "That a committee of three be appointed by the President, and that the Society of American Artists be asked to appoint a similar Committee, these two Committees to confer together with a view to ascertaining on what conditions and in what manner, if at all, a consolidation or union of the Academy and the Society of American Artists may be effected, and to report to the Council and the Board of Control of the Society of American Artists respectively." (Minutes) President Dielman, Harry Watrous, and C. Y. Turner were appointed to represent the Academy; Kenyon Cox, Samuel Isham, and Robert Henri were appointed by the Society.

A series of conferences followed, resulting in a printed report unanimously approved by the council of the Academy and the board of control and advisory committee of the Society, which was to be sent to the membership of both organizations preparatory to calling meetings for its consideration. In the preface to the report the committee of conference presented a general summation of its reasons favoring the union.

In considering the question of a possible union between our two greatest Art Societies it may be well to note the extent to which the two bodies are already identical in membership. Fifty-one of the present Academicians, or a clear majority not only of the ninety-eight actual but of the possible one hundred Academicians, are members of the Society, as are forty-four out of ninety-five Associates; while out of a total membership of one hundred and thirty-four there are only thirty-nine members of the Society who are in no way connected with the Academy. The Academicians have a Council of eleven members, of whom all but two are members of the Society. The Society has a Board of Control of five members, of whom three are Academicians and one is an Associate, and an Advisory Board of four, of whom two are Academicians and one an Associate. More remarkable still, four members of the Council of the Academy are also members of the Board of Control or the Advisory Board of the Society. . . . If the Society has become more conservative, the Academy has become more liberal, and today, the two exhibitions, held in the same building and managed, largely by the same men, are so nearly alike that it would sometimes be difficult to know, if one were set down suddenly in one of them without a catalogue, which of the two it was. . . . It is evident that such duplication of function causes great waste of effort and labor, and that the two bodies are doing work which might be better and more economically performed by one.

The committee pointed out the need for a great exhibition building, in which something like an American Salon may be held. . . . The greatest obstacle to the attainment of such a building is the indifference or distrust of the public, who believe the artists of the country to be split up into bickering sects and warring parties. Let the pacification which actually exists be made apparent, let the artists of America form a dignified, united, and powerful body, and they have but to ask for what they want.

For such a body there could be no better name than the "National Academy of Design" but it would, obviously, need to be a more flexible organization than that of the Academy as now constituted. If the Academy shall be willing to so amend its constitution as to secure this flexibility, the Society can afford to sink its identity, feeling that its work has been done.

The report then outlined the essential changes mutually agreed upon by the representatives of both organizations. The principle of these were the extension of the privileges of the Associates and the reconstitution of the jury system. It was recommended that the number of Associates be unlimited and that "all members of the Society not already Academicians or Associates should become Associates," and also that "the Associates should have voting power in the election of new Associates and in the nomination of Academicians, and an equal voice with the Academicians in the choice of juries, and an equal chance to serve upon juries." After consultation with the legal advisors of both the Academy and the Society a *Memorandum of Agreement* was formulated, including the amendments to the constitution and by-laws of the two organizations which would be necessary to carry the agreement into effect. In addition to the above proposals it was agreed that the number of Academicians be limited to 125 painters, 25 sculptors, 25 architects, and 25 engravers.

In the first election held by the Academy after the execution of this Agreement, the 25 painters and 5 sculptors receiving the highest vote in nomination shall be declared Academicians, and thereafter not more than ten Associates altogether may be annually elected Academicians. . . . Each Academician and Associate shall be entitled to exhibit one work exempt from the Jury of Selection. . . . All the property now owned by the Society of American Artists, consisting of 62 shares of the American Fine Arts Society, 5 Second Mortgage Bonds of the United States Steel Company, and all the funds on hand in cash and deposit in the Greenwich Savings Bank, ($7,416.52), shall be transferred to the National Academy of Design. . . . That such prizes as shall have been given to the Society of American Artists for distribution at their exhibitions, shall, if possible, be transferred to the National Academy of Design, to be awarded in accordance with existing terms or upon conditions to be agreed upon with the donors.

Minor rules and regulations pertaining to meetings, methods of selecting pictures, and other details agreed upon, were added to the by-laws. The new constitution proposed for the Society was presented in four brief articles so stated as to confirm the amended constitution of the Academy, the fourth article stating "All provisions of the Constitution except the above, and all by-laws and rules heretofore adopted are hereby repealed."

A special meeting of Academicians was held on February 21, 1906, to act upon the report of the committee on conference; 36 members were present. Each article was voted upon separately and approved, as was the new constitution of the Society. The vote was then taken on the report as a whole; it carried with only one dissenting vote. At the following meeting on March 14, a letter received from the secretary of the Society confirmed the agreement. "The Society of American Artists has the honor to inform the National Academy of Design that the report of the Committee of Conference on the union of the two Societies after the unanimous approval of the Board of Control, was unanimously approved by the Society-at-large at a Special Meeting of the Society of American Artists held this evening." (Minutes) It remained only to transfer the lease of the Society and the prizes, to properly legalize the proceedings. The union of the two organizations was accomplished and completed on April 7, 1906.

·IX·

CHANGES IN PICTORIAL CONCEPTION: THE DÜSSELDORF SCHOOL · THE
TONALISTS · MUNICH · PARIS · THE SALONIERS · IMPRESSIONISM

THE PERIOD from 1850 to 1875 is often referred to as the Golden Age
of American painting. Certainly this is true if the affluence and acclaim
of the artist are indications of his significance. The era of Reconstruction
after the Civil War resulted in an unprecedented prosperity for the
victors. The material progress and development of the West did not
engender cultural or artistic activity. The fine arts were centered in the
East. Apart from New York, Philadelphia, and Boston, there seemed little
need or evidence of the manifestations of the "over soul." In Boston the
"transcendentalists" colored the cultural and philosophical aspirations
of the time, while in New York the financially successful merchants
beautified their luxurious homes with the painter's art. The lyrical mood
of the earlier poets permeated the romantic sentiment of the generation
that followed with a love of nature combined with introspective musing;
Walt Whitman was a "still small voice"; Thoreau was known to but a
limited circle. The wilderness was giving way to cultivated fields, and
"God's first Temple" was replaced by man's.

In a general way one may for comparison classify the artists of this
period into two groups, one representing artists who, after receiving local
training, continued their studies abroad, and the other representing artists
who were educated in and worked in America.

In the first and more numerous group may be included the Academicians who worked abroad in their early careers and received European
recognition before returning to America. It was this body of artists that
received greatest applause and reward. Excellent artists and consummate

craftsmen, they matured in their work at an early age; but thereafter, satisfied chiefly with remuneration, their work became repetitious and static.

In the latter group we find several of our most eminent artists, to be considered later, who, evincing talent, developed and progressed slowly, reaching their full maturity in later life at the end of the century.

The meticulous detail and finish of the contemporary Düsseldorf painters, both in genre and landscape, made a great appeal to the American patron, while the success of the Düsseldorf schools drew many artists to Germany. In its own provenance, it was an excellent school, many of its students attaining the desired goal. It inculcated fixed methods and principles, instead of engendering personal expression. This was particularly apparent in technique and draftsmanship. The picture was a means of telling a story, generally of a sentimental nature, and, in landscape, naturalistic and descriptive detail was emphasized more than creative expression. Naturalism was further stimulated by the Pre-Raphaelites in England and the persuasive writings of John Ruskin. In fact Ruskin, as an artist, was represented in the Academy exhibitions of 1855 and 1856.

Eastman Johnson was one of our first painters to reflect the new style. After studying two years in Düsseldorf he visited Holland with the intention of going on to Paris and Italy, but captivated by the "little Dutchmen," he remained in The Hague four years, successfully competing with the local painters in portraiture and genre. By the time he returned to America, his technical proficiency eminently qualified him to depict the characteristic life of his time. *The Old Kentucky Home* popularized his art, and when it was shown at the Paris Exposition of 1867 it was highly praised. The nostalgia for the Old South engendered a sentimental interest in Negroes, depicted not in toil and slavery, but in carefree indolence and reverie. The songs of Stephen Foster accompanied the melancholy longing for days that were no more. But Johnson did not continue the commercialization of this theme.

Remembering his youth in his native state of Maine, the painter depicted the life of the woods and the farm: *Boiling Day* in the sugar camp, corn husking, and the study of local character. Free from the meticulous finish of the German school, this aspect of Johnson's work forms the transition to the painters of the American scene that followed, and marks Eastman Johnson as one of the key figures in the American tradition. In later life he devoted himself entirely to portraiture, the field in which, as a youth, he had first won recognition.

In contrast to the intimate life depicted by Johnson, Emanuel Leutze, born in southern Germany in 1816, devoted his art to historical compositions and patriotic conceptions. His father, a political dissident, came to America and settled with his family in Philadelphia. Of a romantic and adventurous nature, the son showed a youthful proclivity for painting. He had little formal education, but having attained recognition and commissions in portraiture he was in 1841 enabled to go to Germany, where he studied in Düsseldorf under Karl Friedrich Lessing and became one of the noted masters of the German school. He returned in 1859 to America, where his work was highly acclaimed, and he received important government as well as private commissions.

Leutze conformed to the aesthetic philosophy of Lessing, best expressed in Leutze's words:

For a beginner in the Arts, Düsseldorf is probably one of the very best schools now in existence, and has educated an uncommon number of distinguished men—the consistency and severity of the mechanical portion of the art taught at this school, are carried into the theory, and have led, by order and arrangement, to a classification of the subjects, which is of essential service; and soon confirmed me in the conviction that a thorough poetical treatment of a picture required that the anecdote should not be so much the subject, as the means of conveying some one clear idea, which is to be the inspiration of the picture.

Briefly, the general idea should come first, and the anecdote taken from history or life should illustrate the theme.

This theory was thoroughly exemplified in his *Western Emigration* which decorated the staircase of the new wing of the Capitol. Leutze was, however, more American in his subject matter than in his treatment of it. His series devoted to the discovery of America—*The Landing of the Northmen,* episodes from the life of Columbus,—and his *Washington Crossing the Delaware,* were popularized in reproductions. Although Leutze had little influence in the tradition of American painting, his fame and mastery of his medium were symptomatic of the culture of his time. Leutze was elected an Academician in 1860, and was represented at its exhibitions by many of his major works from 1844 until his death. He was an intimate and helpful friend of many of the Academicians both in America and Europe. Leutze was appointed to succeed Lessing as president of the Düsseldorf Academy, but the honor came too late for his knowing. He died in 1868 in Washington.

It was in landscape painting, however, that the artist received the highest reward and acclaim, with the well-established Hudson River school holding a strong place in popular favor. The public participated in the painters' discoveries. Nature was viewed on vacation, not as the scene of the farmers' toil, but in the spirit of holiday. The mountain was ascended for the view; the woods were invaded for the cascade; sites were selected for the panorama of winding river and distant mountains; the colors of sunset were proclaimed in ecstasy. The naturalist had an eye for nature's wonderland, of plants and flowers and season's change. The glamor of autumn was a pageant of delight, the brilliant colors beyond compare. In city parlors the memory was evoked by the painter's art.

The most renowned and successful painter of the period was John Frederick Kensett. Born in Connecticut in 1818, he, like many of our early artists, began his practice and maintained his livelihood as an engraver, in the meantime painting as a recreation. In 1840 he joined Durand, Casilear, and Rossiter on a painters' holiday in Europe, tramping along the Rhine, through Switzerland and around the Italian lakes, passing several winters in Rome and the vicinity of Naples, combining the study of nature and art, thus inaugurating a classical tour which many others were to follow. His picture of Windsor Castle, exhibited at the Royal Academy, was purchased by the Art Union in London, where his work was particularly favored. Kensett first exhibited at the Academy in 1838, but it was not until his adventure abroad that his name again appears; he was represented in 1845 and thereafter by numerous examples of English and Italian landscapes through which he was first known. After he had returned to America, he was elected an Academician in 1849, and for many years served on the committee of arrangements and on the council.

The mature period of Kensett's work belongs entirely to America. Versatile in subject matter, he worked in the White Mountains, the Adirondacks, the Housatonic Valley, and along the coast of New England. His work shows penetrating vision, and his brush is facile and decisive. A superior draftsman, he renders nature's intricate forms with accuracy and precision. The word "naturalistic" would best describe his style. His discriminating selection brings clarity to nature's confusion. Not given to tonal envelopment, the glamor of color, or dramatization, his pictures when seen today show a well-conceived unity and distinguished reserve. His studio was one of the centers of attraction during the New York season and the Artists' Receptions. The sale of his remaining pictures, following his death in 1872, realized at auction more than $150,000.

It has been remarked that several of our painters received distinction and honors in England and the continent before settling permanently in their native country. Jasper Francis Cropsey is a notable example. Born on Staten Island in 1823, he was a precocious child, frail in physique. At the age of twelve, he received a diploma from the Mechanics Institute for a detailed model of a country house and, thus encouraged, became an architect's assistant. A few years later he designed several buildings, including a Gothic church at Rossville.

Cropsey's first pictorial work, entitled *Italian Composition*, combining architecture and landscape, was favorably received at the Academy exhibition of 1843, and the following year he was represented by five examples, as a result of which he was made an Associate member in 1844 and an Academician in 1851. Following the precedent of Kensett and others, Cropsey visited England in 1847 and made a scenic tour of the continent by way of Switzerland and the Italian lakes, passing the winter in Rome, where he occupied Cole's former studio. The pictures of this period, painted in the country surrounding Rome and Naples, are a tribute to his achievement, as clear and brilliant today as when first executed. His *Lake Nemi* in the permanent collection of the Academy is a representative example.

Returning to America in 1849, Cropsey found his subjects in the White Mountains; Greenwood Lake, his former home; Lake George; and Newport. Several of his pictures were purchased and engraved by the Art Union. In 1856, preparatory to going abroad again, he conducted a sale of his pictures and sketches, realizing over $8,000. This favorable result was later imitated by several of his contemporaries.

Cropsey remained in England seven years and established a distinguished reputation, several of his pictures receiving conspicuous praise, notably a large canvas, *Autumn on the Hudson River*, shown at the London International Exposition in 1862 and *Richmond Hill* exhibited at the

Royal Academy. A contemporary critic wrote an elaborate description of the former picture,

American artists are making the untravelled portion of the English public familiar with the scenery of the great Western Continent. . . . The singularly vivid colors of an American Autumnal scene, the endless contrast of purples and yellow, scarlets and browns, running into every conceivable shade between the extremes, might easily tempt a painter to exaggerate, or revel in variety of hue and effect, like a Turner of the forest. . . . The result is a fine picture, full of points that are new, without being wholly foreign and strange to the European eye. It will take the ordinary observer into another sphere and region, while its execution will bear any technical criticism.

A second commentator, in a laudatory description of the *Richmond Hill*, concludes:

A student of nature so faithful to his task as Cropsey, and with a pencil so fearless, may rest easy about the reputation of his works, which, like those of Turner, may stir up the critics of the present, yet be worshipped by the Ruskins of the future. (Tuckerman)

Although often in feeble health, Cropsey lived until 1900, and was annually represented in the Academy exhibitions. His later work, however, did not augment his earlier achievement. It is interesting to note, in passing, that Cropsey designed the stations of the elevated railroad in New York, some of which are still in use on Third Avenue.

It will be seen that our painters abroad, in England, Germany, France, Belgium, and Italy, were not only highly praised in exhibitions of international significance, but were considered as having made a distinctly American contribution. Commenting upon the American section at the Paris Exposition of 1867, a local critic wrote: "Every nation thinks that it can paint landscape better than its neighbors; but it is not every nation that goes about the task in a way peculiar to itself. No one is likely to mistake an American landscape for the landscape of any other country." (Tuckerman) The particular emphasis was upon clarity and directness of execution, with fidelity to local characteristics. Every detail near and far is rendered with precision; there is no textured suggestion of form—the sky is luminous and expansive, the horizon gives a sense of space and endless distance.

Other eminent Academicians associated with the so-called Hudson River school were Worthington Whittredge, Sanford Gifford, John

Casilear, and a host of other painters who popularized the current vogue.

Born in Ohio in 1820, Worthington Whittredge was at an early age practicing his art in Cincinnati, drawn thither by the patronage of a group of leading citizens, who, following the precedent of the East, had formed collections of both European and American artists, and also encouraged local talent. Sully, Jarvis, Harding, and others had found remunerative employment there. Nicholas Longworth, in particular, sponsored many young painters, helping to give Cincinnati the distinction of becoming the nursery of several of our most distinguished artists. Without previous instruction, Whittredge began painting landscapes in the environs of Cincinnati. Achieving local recognition and commissions, he was enabled to further his technical study in Düsseldorf. Andreas Achenbach, who with Lessing was the leading master of the Düsseldorf school, had been represented in the private collections of Cincinnati, and the young painter was fortunate in being under his instruction for three years. A close friend of Leutze, during the summers he was also joined by the American painter, William S. Haseltine, in sketching tours on the Rhine and in Switzerland. After extensive continental travel, he established a studio in Rome, where he remained four years, returning to America in 1859. His foreign pictures were sent directly to his patrons in Cincinnati.

Whittredge was first represented in the Academy in 1846, but it was not until 1860, when he settled permanently in New York, that he became an annual contributor, being made a member in 1860, and serving as president from 1874 to 1877. His portrait by Leutze in the permanent collection portrays a striking personality, indicating penetrating understanding and dignified reserve. Although his work is associated with the intimate landscape of New England, he was also one of the early painters to explore the pictorial possibilities of the Far West by joining a government expedition under General Pope in 1866.

William Stanley Haseltine was elected an Academician in 1861 at the early age of twenty-six. Born in Philadelphia, he attended the University of Pennsylvania for two years and at the same time studied painting under Paul Weber. Continuing his schooling at Harvard University, he graduated there in 1854. Shortly thereafter he went to Düsseldorf to become a pupil of Andreas Achenbach, and while there formed a lasting friendship with Leutze, Whittredge, and Bierstadt. Returning to the States, he painted along the New England coast and at once attained wide recognition. The pictures of this period are rendered with naturalistic knowledge and technical precision. In 1869 Haseltine established his residence in Rome, and with the exception of several visits to the States, remained there until his death in 1900. His home and spacious studios in the Palazzo Altieri were a favored rendezvous of the art circles of the city. The pictures of southern Italy and Sicily reflect the enchantment of nature's colorful moods imbued with romantic reverie. With the revived interest in nineteenth century painting, exhibitions of Haseltine's work have been held at the Fogg Art Museum, the Addison Gallery of American Art in Andover, Massachusetts, and other centers from coast to coast. His son, Herbert Haseltine, the noted animal sculptor, is a present member of the Academy.

The pictures of Sanford Gifford reflect his visual adventures in rural America, the joy of picturesque discovery. His parental home at Hudson, New York, looked across the river to the Catskills, and his youthful admiration of Thomas Cole determined the style of his future study, the revelation of scenic beauty. Versatile in his choice of subjects, he painted the mountains, lakes, and rivers on his varied excursions, sketching directly from nature, and composing his larger pictures in the studio. Elected an Academician in 1854, he was represented in its annual exhibitions until his death in 1880. His studio in the Tenth Street building actively united him with his fellow Academicians. Several of his later pictures introduced a new theme of misty silhouette and graduated forms, eliminating the detailed rendering of his predecessors.

John Casilear, born in 1811, continued the tradition of Cole and Durand, and like the latter began his livelihood as an engraver, at which he attained distinction. He accompanied Durand on his European travels, and, on returning to America, devoted his art to landscape painting.

The discipline of engraving furthered his technical proficiency in the precise rendering of form. His work illustrates the ingratiating aspect of nature, of lakes and mountains and secluded pastures amidst peaceful tranquility. His first contributions to the Academy exhibitions of 1833–34 were engravings, but in 1836 and thereafter he was represented by landscapes, several of which, we note in the catalogue, were loaned by Durand, Kensett, Knoedler, and others. Elected an Associate as an engraver in 1833, he became an Academician in 1851, serving thereafter several terms as a member of the Council and participating in the receptions on Tenth Street, where he had his studio.

The scenic appeal of landscape inaugurated by Thomas Cole was followed by his pupil, Frederic Edwin Church. But Church had a more scientific mind and was not given to the lure of romantic association or allegorical allusions. He was essentially a naturalist. As a topographical draftsman, he is unexcelled. Born of wealthy parents at Hartford, Connecticut, in 1826, he was able to indulge his yearning for pictorial exploration which led him to the *Heart of the Andes;* to Mexico; to the tropical islands of the West Indies; to the icebergs of the North; and, later in life, to the classic lands of Greece and the Near East. As a youth he had lived for a time with Cole at Catskill and was inspired by the devout sincerity and accomplishment of his master. His own style and individuality is, however, apparent in his earliest efforts—methodical and technically precise. The form is developed from the details of which it is composed. For Church, truth to nature is not simply a temperamental optical impression, but a rendering of naturalistic fact and phenomena. In this aspect of his art he is the pictorial successor of Alexander von Humboldt, with whose work he was conversant, having occupied the very house in which the scientist lived in Quito, Ecuador. When exhibited in London, Church's landscapes were greatly admired, exciting the interest and praise of Ruskin, particularly the illusionistic effect of the painter's *Niagara.* Likewise in Paris, at the Exposition of 1867, his work was highly praised. "The originality of this artist, more than his technical skill with the brush, entitles him to the leading position." (Tuckerman)

From boyhood, Church recorded natural phenomena in innumerable studies in paint and pencil. The collection bequeathed by his son to the Cooper Union museum forms a veritable naturalist's paradise of pristine expanse. As he worked on prepared nonabsorbent paper panels, his fluent direct painting is as fresh and enduring as when first executed. Several splendid examples are in the permanent collection of the National Academy. Church first exhibited at the Academy in 1845, was elected an Associate in 1848 and an Academician in 1849. The most successful practitioner of his period, he retired after his foreign travels to his country place near Hudson, overlooking the Catskills, and, being crippled by arthritis, devoted much of his time to erecting a mansion which is a veritable symbol of his life, combining details reminiscent of his exotic adventures with the prevailing style of the Victorian era.

The picturesque discovery of unknown lands created a sense of curious wonderment, of the grandeur of primitive nature, the immensity of mountains, of tropical verdure. As Church's fancy had turned to the tropics, so at the same time Albert Bierstadt was discovering the scenic glory of the Golden West. In 1858 he accompanied General Lander on a government exploration over the Oregon Trail and made numerous studies of the mountains, of the buffalo hunt, and of life in camp. From this local material he composed his famous picture, *The Rocky Mountains*, which was to establish his reputation. The highest peak depicted was named after the commander of the expedition.

Albert Bierstadt was born in Düsseldorf, his father having been a soldier in the German army. At an early age he came to America where his parents settled at New Bedford, Massachusetts. The pictures of his cousin, Hasenclever, had been exhibited in America, and this probably inspired the youthful aspirant to follow the profession of an artist. It was natural, therefore, that he should study in the Düsseldorf Academy, where he was enrolled in 1853. While there, he formed intimate friendships with Leutze, Gifford, Whittredge, and Haseltine, who together sketched along the Rhine, in Switzerland, and later in Rome and southern Italy. Returning to America in 1857, he exhibited his pictures at the Academy the following year. He was elected an Honorary Member in 1858 and an active Academician in 1860. His Alpine studies had prepared him for his western adventure. In a letter written from camp in the Rocky Mountains the painter comments: "The mountains are very fine; as seen from the plains, they resemble very much the Bernese Alps. . . . The Indians are as they were hundreds of years ago, and now is the time to paint them. . . . The color of the mountains is like those of Italy." (Tuckerman) Thus his European training and experience haunted his imagination in the West.

At a time when little was known pictorially of the fabulous West, the novelty of Bierstadt's grandiose conception greatly impressed the eastern spectator. He had discovered a pictorial mine as rich in return as the gold in California. His success was immediate, his pictures being eagerly bought or commissioned. His *Storm in the Rocky Mountains* sold for $35,000; *Landers Peak* for $25,000. The former picture when exhibited in London caused extended praise and commentary. In a lengthy article published in the *London Saturday Review*, the critic writes: "In an age when some hold the theory that art may be dispensed with, and that mere copyism is enough, we welcome a man like Bierstadt, who, though as devoted a lover of the grandest scenes in nature as any painter who ever lived, is, at the same time, given to plotting and planning for purely artistic ends." (Tuckerman)

Bierstadt continued his Western exploration in pictures of the recently discovered grandeur of the Yosemite Valley. Others followed in his way, but the old master lived to see his work overshadowed as its novelty waned. He died in 1902 at his home on the scenic heights of the Hudson, overlooking the Palisades.

Of quite different temperament and training, Thomas Moran envisioned the Southwest as the miraculous materialization of an enchanted dream. The Painted Desert, the pinnacled glory of the Grand Canyon, the turbulent rivers, the scintillating horizon, the cloud drama—all combined to create a rainbow land of romantic, miragelike glamor. Moran accompanied Major Powell in his exploration of the Colorado River. The diminutive water colors and drawings of his visual experience are unsurpassed in their revelation of transcendent expanse and sensitive suggestion. Captivated by the ethereal color of Turner, he reveled in its natural realization, and brought to his art a personal technique and craftsmanship worthy of his vision. Moran was elected an Academician in 1884. His diploma picture, *Three Mile Harbor*, was painted at East Hampton, Long Island, after he had discovered its old-world charm; there he continued to have his summer residence and studio. Moran lived until 1926, deploring modern improvisation. In one of his last reviews of the Academy Exhibition, he said to the writer, "A picture can never lie. If a painter is not sincere it will reveal itself on its surface."

Although William T. Richards did not attempt the panoramic vista or the grandeur of scenic landscape, his naturalistic preoccupation and dexterous technique follow the example of Frederic Edwin Church. He was known in his later years particularly as a marine painter, but all his direct studies of near-by landscape display his knowledge and meticulous observation of nature's intricate detail combined with the mastery of his artistic intention.

The painters of this period are known in our museums of today by their large exhibition pictures. It is regrettable that their sketches and more intimate studies are not more generally known, for therein one realizes the initial vitality of their work. Before the advent of the modern tendency in the 'eighties and 'nineties, the painted form was represented with naturalistic accuracy, the picture to be viewed at close range. There was no thought of pigmented suggestion, volume, or carrying power. The delight of the spectator was largely in verisimilitude rather than in purely aesthetic appreciation. Optical shock was not premeditated. Pictures, heavily framed in gold and hung one above the other, were related to the parlor of the period: elaborate mantelpieces, stuffed furniture, heavy curtains, dimly lighted both by day and by night. The interior reflected the opulence of the owner. He counted his treasures by number and evaluated them accordingly.

In the 'seventies and 'eighties the Düsseldorf influence began to wane. Paris and Munich became the centers of principal attraction. Most of the students underwent the preliminary requirements and discipline of the current academic curriculum but later followed their several ways. In Paris the most eminent teachers were Gérôme, Laurens, Boulanger, and Lefebvre. The accredited schools, and also the most popular, were the Beaux Arts and the Académie Julian. The Beaux Arts, under government control, required strict entrance examinations, not only in drawing but in the allied arts. Julian's was less discriminating. Then was the culminating period of Meissonier, Gérôme, Bouguereau, Bonnat, and a host of celebrities who controlled the salon. One had to follow the official line or be excluded. The same period in Europe witnessed the turbulence of a new generation of creative artists who were to have a decisive influence in American painting.

Before 1870 there was little conflicting opposition or technical controversy in the Academy. With the return of our artists from the continent, divergent views and aspirations reinvigorated and stimulated the contending styles.

The younger men thought the Academicians old-fashioned; later they were themselves to be distinguished by that designation. The word "Academic," formerly a tribute of distinction, came to be used in a negative sense. Retrospectively, one may trace four general tendencies resulting from the new movements in Europe. The "Barbizon" influence predominated, leading to definite specialities of landscape, figure, marine, or animal painting; in portraiture and genre the salon style was the most evident and salable, competing with the dealers in French art; the most vigorous and controversial group reflected the Munich training; while in the 'nineties the impressionists created a veritable furor of opposition and aesthetic regeneration.

William Morris Hunt, associated with Boston and Newport, studied in Düsseldorf in 1846, but not content with its teaching, worked in Paris for several years in the atelier of Couture. It was not until his friendship with Millet at Barbizon that he developed his ultimate style. With profound vision and prophecy, he acquired a group of Millet's pictures, a purchase made possible by a Boston patron; thus he recognized the genius of his master, before he was rightly appreciated in the French capital. Through his work and teaching, Hunt had an enduring influence on his contemporaries which was to mature in the 'seventies. As early as 1856 he was represented in the Academy, and he continued to be for several years thereafter.

William Page was one of the last echoes of a vanishing age in which the artist was imbued with the nostalgic veneration of the masters of the past combined with the realization of tonal unity, the fusion of romance and reality. Of an introspective nature, deeply relegious, he was never satisfied with his achievement. This led him to continuous experimentation in technical methods and the elusive overtones of pigmentation and glazes. In consequence much of his work deteriorated with time. Nevertheless several of Page's pictures have a unique significance, quite unusual at the time, notably the *Young Merchants* and the *Portrait of Mrs. Page* executed while he was in Rome. In middle life he was enabled to carry out his cherished wish to study in Italy, where he remained eleven years. As a personality Page was highly esteemed by his intimates and in later years formed an enduring friendship with George Inness, the two artists having a common interest in the doctrines of Swedenborg. Elected an Academician in 1836, three years before his sojourn in Italy, on his return to America he became active in the affairs of the Academy, and was elected president in 1871.

Henry Peters Gray was more popular, his pictures combining classical allusions with the sensuous idealization of Venetian prototypes. This appealed particularly to the knowing amateur who could parade his knowledge of classical lore and enjoy at the same time the ingratiating charm of youthful beauty. Gray was an accomplished technician, having made a particular study of Titian during his residence in Italy. Although he did not respond to the direct vision of the contemporary scene, his pictures reflected the cultural taste of his time and were much admired at the Academy exhibitions. Both as vice-president and president of the Academy he did much to promote the liaison between patron and painter.

The famous triumvirate, George Inness, Alexander Wyant, and Homer Martin, began their careers in landscape painting under the prevailing style and methods of the Hudson River school. In maturing, Inness made several sojourns in Europe and was familiar with the work of Corot and Rousseau, as well as with that of Turner and Constable; Wyant had studied in Düsseldorf; while it was not until later life that Martin went to France, not to study in the galleries, but to find a sympathetic retreat in which to paint. In the meantime the foreign dealers in New York were introducing the work of the Barbizon painters, the firm of Cottier and Co. being the most prominent. To the connoisseur accustomed to the meticulous finish of the older school, the new style seemed by contrast to be merely a "daub" demonstrating technical incompetence and uncontrolled manipulation of paint.

It is evident that the painters of the new movement were not following a popular or lucrative style, but each was seeking freedom of expression, the outcome of an individual urge. The dominant trend was opposed to meticulous finish and the elaboration of detail; the creative endeavor was to achieve the relation of the part to the whole by means of coordinated tonal values. Whereas their predecessors delineated each component part of the composition with naturalistic accuracy, the painters of the tonal movement emphasized the unity of visual impression.

George Inness was the foremost master of American landscape painting during the years of his activity. His portrait by Daniel Huntington in the permanent collection of the Academy indicates the intensity of his temperament. Elected an Associate in 1853 and an Academician in 1868, he made his first contribution to its exhibitions in 1844, followed by innumerable examples until the close of his career in 1894. It is altogether too simple to classify Inness as a follower of the Barbizon school. His life-work covers a vast evolution from the scenic beauty of pastoral landscape to the ultimate synthesis of tonal form. Continually experimenting in

method, his dramatic and impetuous temperament and his decided individuality transcend the clichés of contemporary fashion.

Inness was born in the year when the National Academy was founded,
just at the dawn of American landscape painting. His early work is
based upon the direct observation of nature, and the knowledge derived
from this study brought to his later painting that freedom of expression
and creative improvisation which is obtained only from direct experience.
Maturing at a time when the Düsseldorf school was in the ascendant, he
was not, however, lured by the imitative appeal of superficial detail.
"Knowledge must bow to spirit." His versatility and his dramatic use of
color have no counterpart in European painting. "Fullness of tone" is
attained only by "fullness of color." Interpreting the "moods" of nature,
his art is a synthesis of the sensation of reality and the vision of a mystic.
A follower of the doctrines of Swedenborg, Inness transformed his belief
into the principles governing his art, emphasizing always the relation
of the part to the whole as a means of suggesting the inexpressible. His
daring innovations were at first misunderstood and heatedly criticized,
but his later acclaim caused unprecedented prices to be paid for his pictures, which in his lifetime he did not realize. His first European recognition came from Benjamin-Constant, who on a visit to New York, was
greatly impressed by his pictures. But Inness is unfortunately little known
in the Europe of today, and scarcely represented in its galleries. He remains, nevertheless, one of the significant masters of his generation.

Alexander Wyant is much more limited in expression. Never an
opulent colorist, he was a master of tonality, rendered in variations of
neutral hues, subtly enveloped in ambient atmosphere. His early work,
as in the well-known *Mohawk Valley*, is representative of the culmination of the Düsseldorf teaching. In 1871 he joined a government party in
western exploration, but being of delicate physique and unable to endure
the hardship, he was stricken with paralysis of the right side, and thereafter was obliged to paint with his left hand. He was elected an Academician in 1869; his admirable *Self-Portrait* in the permanent collection of
the Academy is a unique example by one who devoted his art otherwise
exclusively to landscape. Wyant's mood is pensive and serene, imbued
with introspective brooding. He was one of our first painters to use
textures suggestive of nature's intricate pattern. Not overinventive in

design, his composition is formally arranged, its significance dependent on muted tonality and the carrying power of vibrant chiaroscuro.

Like Inness and Wyant, Homer Martin evolved his art from the early naturalistic studies of local subjects, to the deliberately designed composition evocative of his subjective intention. Unlike Inness, he was not given to impetuous emotion or improvisation. His mature work is the result of prolonged contemplation. Lackadaisical by nature, he was forever postponing execution. As he worked over long periods before completing his conception, his major works are limited in number. His finest achievements have a solemn solidity and an elemental design significant of his poetical intention. Martin had a sharp wit and ironical humor as well as a comprehensive understanding. He was one of the elite in literary and artistic circles. Whistler facetiously introduced him to a gathering at a London club: "Gentlemen, this is Homer Martin. He doesn't look it," the allusion was to his rather bulbous nose and unkempt habit. Martin was elected an Academician in 1874 before his style had ultimately matured.

George Fuller is an anomaly in American painting. After venturing in portraiture, on the death of his father he returned to work the parental farm at Deerfield. There his introspective nature indulged in reverie, entirely unconscious of the outer world and public display. It was not until the last decade of his life that his work, on being exhibited in Boston, received universal acclaim. Elected an Associate in 1853, his *Self-Portrait* suggests the melancholy remoteness of his later style.

It is sad to reflect that Ralph Blakelock was an inmate of a public institution, his mind deranged, at the time eight of his pictures, privately owned, were being sold at public auction for over $40,000. The famous *Moonlight*, now in the Toledo Museum, alone sold for $20,000. Lyrical by temperament, a lover of music, he could not bend his artistic integrity to commercial competition. His visual experience was transformed in the alchemy of the imagination. He reveled in the lacquerlike quality of paint, the subdued resonance of deep texture-toned pigment, and the dark lace-like tracery of foliage silhouetted against the evening sky. A poet in paint, his work has a universal significance, the emanation of his creative vision. His belated election as an Academician in 1916 came when his active career had ended. He had many imitators, some of whose work passed under his name, but his style was too limited to produce a creative progeny.

Albert P. Ryder was nurtured in the romantic milieu of his youth. Although a student in the Academy school, he was not responsive to formal education or the dictates of a teacher. A recluse by nature, he had no desire to compete with his contemporaries. He was conversant with the tonal unity of the Barbizon painters shown at Cottier's, who later sponsored his own work, and particularly by the open sea- and landscapes of Dupré, with their heavy, unctuous pigmentation; but his creative imagination was his own child, naïve in its significant simplicity, its well-resolved form being the visual manifestation of his poetical conception. Ryder was reluctant to part with his dream children and kept them with him until they were fully matured. This overpainting and the heavy use of varnish was, in many examples, not conducive to durability, although it produced the illumined tonal quality which is inseparable from its mystical allure. The art of Ryder attained creative fulfillment in the untranslatable significance of correlated color-form as expressive of an indwelling and transcendent idea, the pictorial sublimation of his imagination. He was not interested in abstract design as such; the form grew from the theme.

One windy day in March, an artist friend entering Central Park saw a diminutive figure running to catch some fleeting sheets of paper. Ryder had been writing poetry. He was elated when one praised his poetry. His pictures he reserved for the few. Although deeply devoted to his intimates, he shunned art circles and social gatherings.

The tonal school continued well into the twentieth century. Dealers reaped the harvest with soaring prices. The minor artists of the style are today comparatively little known. The achievement of Samuel Colman is worthy of perpetuation. His smaller canvases, often related to travel in the Near East, have distinguished quality, somewhat reminiscent of Alexandre Decampes. Horatio Walker echoed the manner of Millet in his dramatization of the Canadian peasantry; D. W. Tryon followed the bucolic mood in highly sensitized tonal arrangements of evanescent evening; Henry W. Ranger portrayed woodlands in autumn with vibrant variations in gold, an artist of comsummate mastery within a limited theme; J. Francis Murphy won general esteem in the tonal simplicity of upland pastures in which surface color-quality attained its final expression.

Meantime the "saloniers" returning from Paris were preoccupied with technique and draftsmanship. This found expression in figure painting, interiors, illustration, and mural decoration. It was essentially a studio art. The early work of Thomas Dewing, Harry Watrous, George de Forest Brush, Francis Millet, H. Siddons Mowbray, Hamilton Hamilton, Kenyon Cox, Edwin Blashfield, and others reflects the teaching of their respective French masters. Thomas Dewing sublimated his aesthetic conception in the detached distinction of fastidious ladies in ethereal drawing rooms, a world apart from reality, yet temperamentally real. George de Forest Brush found his subjects in his own children and in motherhood. His work is imbued with the spirit of the Florentines. Not swayed by passing fashions, he saw the universal in the particular, and achieved monumental distinction. His method was a return to the old masters. Hamilton Hamilton perfected his craftsmanship, and attained the fulfillment of his artistic premises. Kenyon Cox and Edwin Blashfield remained strictly within the confines of their academic training. Both men were also members of the Society of American Artists, as were Millet and Mowbray. John La Farge stood apart from the realistic trend of his time. Of French parentage and ancestry, he spent his youth in the literary and artistic salons of Paris. Profoundly intellectual, he was enamored with the color tonalities of Delacroix and the structural significance of the old masters. His traditional background covered a vast area, uniting the mysticism of the Far East with the sensuous reaction of visual experience.

Robert Blum, a member of both the Academy, to which he was elected an Academician in 1893, and the Society of American Artists, was one of the most brilliant technicians of the period. His initial style was greatly influenced by Mariano Fortuny; his later work shows his reaction to the aesthetic significance of the Japanese. Versatile in many mediums, he excelled in etching, illustration, easel painting, and mural decoration. His murals in Mendelssohn Hall, when seen in place, corresponded to musical moods and rhythms. The color scheme reflects the pastel studies which he made for the murals.

The Munich tradition springs from quite other sources. In his later years Leutze referred to Munich as having the best school of painters on the continent. As an art center it was drawing students away from Düsseldorf, and was to become the rival of Paris. Its growing fame attracted particularly the American students of German ancestry. Frank Duveneck was to herald its significance in America. In alluding to his youthful days and his departure for Europe, the reminiscent master said: "When I stood on board the ship, Rubens wasn't in it." Thus the keynote of the style. Hals and Rubens were the gods of Munich. The old Pinacotheca became the veritable studio of the students. Their studies were placed in comparison beside the Dutch and Flemish masters. The brush takes precedence over the pencil, color-form over line. Paint quality was emphasized rather than finish, direct visualization rather than anecdotal fancy. Wilhelm Leibl was the foremost master of the realistic revival in Germany.

While still working at the school, the youthful Duveneck was an acknowledged leader; indeed, he conducted a class on a painting tour of Italy. He returned to America where his work, on being exhibited in New York and Boston, created a furor of heated controversy. The direct brushwork and powerful impasto were daring innovations in contrast to the reticent technique and meticulous method of the French tradition. Sargent proclaimed Duveneck "the greatest brush of his generation." His etchings of Venice, when shown in London, inspired Whistler to visit the city of the lagoons. Masterly in conception and execution, they remain among the finest achievements of the modern needle, unhappily a medium in which the master was not to continue. He was a member of both the Society of American Artists and the Academy; his fame belongs to his early period. Retiring to his birthplace in Cincinnati, he devoted his later life to teaching. His experience and wisdom flowered in his pupils; his own work remained neglected.

The "Duveneck Boys" added technical vitality to American painting. William Chase, working with Duveneck at Munich, became in his early work the most proficient practitioner of the movement. The addition of bitumen to the palette, to simulate the resonant depth of the masters, proved an unfortunate innovation, causing cracking and pigment deterioration, and also tending to give a sameness in tonality. The work of Frank Currier was much admired in his time, while the youthful John Twachtman, who worked with Duveneck in Munich and Italy, produced some striking improvisations. Alluding to the bituminous style, Twachtman in later life referred to his early work as "black as your hat." But the pictures painted in Venice and of the New York harbor have decided distinction and vitality. Walter Shirlaw also began his career in Munich. His large canvases of Bavarian farm life, reflecting the influence of his environment, show an intimate knowledge of his subject and mastery of his medium. He was elected an Academician in 1888, and was also a member of the Society.

The Munich manner did not long survive its inception. Criticism followed fashion. The period following the Franco-Prussian War released the creative energy of French aspiration, and produced a galaxy of painters, united under the popular appellation of "the impressionists." The twilight mood waned in the presence of the sun, and Paris became the dominant art center of the western world.

The first collective exhibition of the impressionists was held in 1874. Degas had said that his great desire was to "surprise a living moment." It was this immediate visual experience, transmuted by the temperamental reaction of the beholder, that transformed the former studio conception into a living realization. Its aesthetic sources are manifold.

In the background of Manet's portrait of Zola one notices the Japanese prints on the studio wall. This symbolizes, as it were, the keynote of the movement; realism expressed in the terms of design rather than naturalistic representation, the contemporary world revivified by space-form arrangement. The angle supersedes the classical curve; the simplification of planes challenges the illusionistic modulation of the round. When Courbet derided Manet's *Olympia* as resembling the Queen of Spades, the latter responded that Courbet's ideal was a billiard ball. The eye level is raised, the horizon placed high on the canvas, the angle of vision reduced. Monet and Pissaro had their eyes opened in the museums of London; Turner was a revelation. Black is eliminated from the impressionistic palette. The painter works directly in the open light. The sun is in the ascendant. The analytical research of the chemist, Chevreul, decomposes the prism; light is made vibrant by the juxtaposition of broken color. The recluse returns from the heights. The human habitat becomes alive, the city and its environs a playground of delight. The immediacy of the moment is paramount.

Whistler innovated the new aesthetics in the decorative arrangement of tonal form. The voice of the aesthete was heard in sophisticated circles.

Ruskin was dethroned. In America a fresh breeze wafted from across the Atlantic. The studios hummed with heated debate.

In the 'sixties and 'seventies journalistic commentary had been largely adulatory, with elaborate descriptions and interpretations of individual pictures. The approach was literary rather than aesthetic. Even in Paris, innovations were strenuously opposed. A critic of the Paris Exposition of 1867, alluding to Whistler's contributions, writes, "Three of the oil paintings are blurred, foggy, and imperfect marine pieces. The fourth is called the 'White Girl' and represents a powerful female with red hair, and a vacant stare in her soulless eyes. She is standing on a wolfskin hearth rug—for what reason is unrecorded. . . . There is some boldness in the handling and a singularity in the glare of the colors which cannot fail to divert the eye, and to weary it." (Tuckerman) At the same exposition, American progress was heralded by the panoramic pictures of Church, the American themes of Eastman Johnson, and the landscapes of Kensett. When Theodore Robinson won the Shaw Prize at the Society exhibition of 1892, one knowing critic advised that in order to view the picture effectively and bring it into focus, the spectator would have to be at the end of a tunnel. One was accustomed to examine a picture at reading distance. A decade later Winslow Homer was to place a small placard on the frame of his picture reading, "Please stand away ten feet." The point of view was changing. The artist had a horror of being "skied." In the galleries of Europe and America pictures had been hung three deep. Greater care was now taken in the arrangement of pictures. Totality of effect, rather than the examination of a part, began to impress the critics, catching up with the artist's intention. The Ruskin-Whistler legal controversy had proved an international cathartic. The *avant garde* of the 'nineties led the way. On the other hand, it was pitiful to witness the disregard of the veterans, who after being relegated to the attic, are now revived as modern discoveries. E. L. Henry, William T. Richards, J. G. Brown, Jasper Cropsey, Albert Bierstadt, Worthington Whittredge, and others preeminent in their time, lived to see their work critically abused and neglected. A host of forgotten artists of the mid-century, whose work once adorned the Academy walls, are now being restored to honor and perpetuity in the much applauded Karolik Collection permanently installed in the Boston Museum.

Manet had wittily remarked, "One year one paints purple, next year one paints more purple." Purple and blue now predominated over the traditional "brown sauce"; everything was enveloped in refracted light. Absorbent canvas permitted opaque pigmentation; varnish was discarded. Luminosity was associated with a high key rather than transparency—complementary color contrast rather than light and dark modulation. "Values" was the key word of the period. The model left the studio to bask in sunshine. Literary allusions declined as the painter saw his subject in visual awareness and decorative arrangement. Impressionism had triumphed by repetition.

The American artists associated with the impressionists had all passed through the rigorous discipline of the Paris ateliers. The initial members of the impressionists' group formed a close circle, each distinctive in personality, but interchanging aesthetic ideas. The Players Club was a favorite rendezvous. Somewhat disdainful of the Academy, they nevertheless respected its tradition and prestige. By the close of the century the impressionists' formula had become accepted. Durand-Ruel had initiated the movement in New York in 1886 with alluring financial returns. In fact, the New York branch was largely instrumental in sustaining the Paris house, enabling Durand-Ruel to continue the purchase of works by the French masters, many of which eventually came to America. The walls of the Academy brightened. The initial shock of optical innovation had passed. The pioneers became the elders of the style and gracefully merged with the Academy; but their followers had not their aesthetic sensibility or the vital spark of discovery. Commercialism destroyed artistic integrity. The fabulous increase in prices created false values.

Theodore Robinson was a pioneer of the new aesthetic. His conception responded to the immediacy of visual impression and spontaneous improvisation. A student at the Academy school, he was also one of the founders of the Art Students League. Later he assisted John La Farge in mural decoration. In France he joined the group at Grez, enjoying the companionship of Robert Louis Stevenson and Will Low. With several young Americans, including Willard Metcalf, he explored the countryside about Rouen. Stopping at Giverny, he was unaware that Monet had established his studio there the year previous. This proved a happy retreat and greatly influenced his artistic destiny. It is difficult to appreciate the antagonism which his work engendered when exhibited in New York.

The high key, the brilliant color, the divided brush stroke, proved a daring innovation. Today his sensitive technique seems almost effete, his discriminating vision and direct painting frankly recording the optical impression. Suffering continuously from asthma, he did not live to consummate his distinctive talent, but he had an invigorating influence upon his American contemporaries. Most of his major works are associated with the French countryside both in figures and landscape, but his picture, the *Canal*, in the Pennsylvania Academy, with its blue sky and radiant sunshine, is a revelation of the local scene and an indication of the way which others were to follow. His portrait of his friend Will Low, in the permanent collection of the Academy, is one of the first examples in American portraiture demonstrating the broken stroke as a means of color modulation. A wreath was placed over his last picture shown at the Academy, though he did not live to become a member.

As we have seen, John Twachtman's early work reflects the Munich influence. In France his palette changed to variations of gray. The unctuous bituminous impasto is abruptly displaced by the fluent flow of untextured surface. The pictures of this period, many of which were painted in Holland, reveal a highly sensitive personality and are among his finest achievements. In the 'nineties his style is again transformed to the higher key of the impressionists. The accent is on the constructive division of color-space, the simplification of form and luminous tonality. He characterized the local scene with discriminating observation. Although quite remote from Whistler in effect, the older master stimulated his aesthetic awareness. This is noticed particularly in his etchings, and the fastidious delicacy of the pastel studies.

In reviewing the evolution of the art of J. Alden Weir, one is impressed by his indwelling integrity, the search for the right form and manner to express his intention. He combined a masterly control with ever-seeking innovation. His art responds to the continuous deepening of contemplative impression. Reticent by nature, he was nevertheless a leader, his judgment being greatly respected. Commissioned while still a young man in Paris to select works for an American patron, he enriched our museums by several masterpieces, notably Manet's *Woman with a Parrot* and *Boy with a Sword*, both in the New York Metropolitan Museum of Art. As a student at the Beaux Arts, he was beloved by his companions and became a devoted friend of the noted Bastien-Lepage.

The still lifes with flowers, and the early portraits, low in key, brilliant and decisive in execution, are among the finest examples of the period. His final style is emphasized by opaque pigmentation, designed to enforce the interrelation and totality of form content. The landscapes painted at his summer home in Connecticut have an individual flavor and local characterization which transcends their inclusion within the confines of any verbal classification. Elected an Academician in 1886, he served as president during the years 1915–17. He was always a champion of youthful aspiration, rather than a moderator, his encouragement based always on integrity of purpose.

Childe Hassam's work is as distinctive as his name. His personality is reflected in his manner. A member of the Society of American Artists, he joined the Academy when the two organizations were united in 1906, and became an active contributor after that date. Hassam made the short brush stroke and the division of color an integral element of style. His conception is deliberately decorative. He eschewed the typical appeal of the picturesque and the dramatization of subjective mood. His pictures have the allure of a holiday—of joy in painting and delight in living. His art reflects the unperturbed spirit of youth; the flags of the nation are never at half-mast.

Robert William Vonnoh was distinguished equally as a portraitist and as a landscape painter. A precocious talent, at the age of fourteen he entered a lithographic house in Boston, supplementing his work by study in the Massachusetts Normal Art School, where in 1879 he became an instructor. This enabled him to go to Paris in 1881 where he continued his study at the Académie Julian under Boulanger and Lefebvre. Returning to the States in 1883 he was awarded a gold medal in Boston for his portrait of John S. Converse, which had previously attracted attention at the Salon. This was followed by numerous commissions, one of the most impressive of which is the portrait of Dr. S. Weir Mitchell in the Pennsylvania Academy, a lasting tribute to his distinction. But it is in landscape painting that his art is associated with the American pioneers of impressionism and the vital rejuvenation of color. Alluding to a picture by Vonnoh in the Munich exhibition of 1892, Richard Muther, in his *History of Modern Painting,* writes: "Never yet was war so boldly declared against all conventional usages of the studio; never yet were such barbaric means employed to attain an astounding effect of light." This transformation to the prismatic palette was due to Vonnoh's second sojourn in France from 1887 to 1891, when he devoted much study to the figure out-of-doors and the scintillating vibration of light. Attaining unusual success on his return to America, he in later life divided his interests, while his youthful vitality was lost during the turmoil of war and the controversial trends in style which followed.

Abbott Thayer cannot be conveniently classified. His self-portrait in the permanent collection of the Academy reveals the true signature of the man, reticent and frank but also uncompromising and courageous. A retrospective review of his work demonstrates his continuous development. A master of his craft, he illustrates in his early work his technical foundation combined with intense visual concentration, low in key but emphatic in characterization. A naturalist by instinct, he had an innate affinity with nature's hidden secrets. It was this psychic approach, united with keen visualization, that ultimately universalized his theme—realism and idealism united in the terms of his medium. His embodiment of American womanhood is a classic tribute, the ideal clothed in living realization. Always appreciated and highly respected both as a man and artist, Thayer refrained from controversial issues, traveling much of his way alone. Honored by many awards, he never competed in the market and remained aloof from commercial temptation and notoriety. His style grows from mature contemplation rather than improvisation; but when the theme was determined the execution has an immediate finality. Associated with the younger group of the Society he was, however, elected an Academician before the merger of the two institutions, his diploma picture, a landscape, being presented in 1901.

· X ·

PROGRESS AND PROBLEMS: INAUGURATION OF PRIZES · CONTROVERSY
RESULTING FROM THE USE OF GLASS OVER PICTURES · SALE OF 23D
STREET PROPERTY · PURCHASE OF PROPERTY AT 109TH STREET AND
AMSTERDAM AVENUE · THE NEW SCHOOL BUILDING

WHEN Samuel Morse, in his speech given at the end of the Academy's
first season, outlined the basic conditions inherent in the development of
academies abroad, he stressed the need for a system of prizes to encourage
students in fruitful competition, but nobody thought of awarding prizes
to the artists represented in the annual exhibitions of the Academy. In
1883 Thomas B. Clarke, long a patron and friend of American artists,
offered the first annual prize to stimulate exhibitors. To this proposal the
secretary, T. Addison Richards, replied: "The Council have received
your proposal to endow a yearly prize of three hundred dollars for the
best American Figure Composition shown at the Annual exhibition of
the Academy. They accept your most liberal offer with great pleasure
and will endeavor to administer the trust in the best interests of art." As
the exhibitions were dominated by landscapes, the prize may also have
been an effort to promote figure painting. The conditions governing
the award required that the recipient be chosen by balloting of the exhibitors, including members of the Academy and nonmembers, provided
that 50 or more exhibitors voted and that the winning picture received
at least one third of the votes cast. The council ruled that no Academicians
would compete for the prize.

In the same year Julius Hallgarten endowed a trust of $12,000, the
interest of which was to be used for awarding three prizes for the best

paintings exhibited at the Academy by artists under thirty-five years of age. The bequest also included an endowment of $5,000 to be used for the most deserving students of the school as the council might decide. The year following this bequest, the council was grieved to learn of the sudden death of Mr. Hallgarten in Davos, Switzerland. "Being at the time still in the very prime of his life, it was hoped that he would live many years to witness the fruits of his liberality. Happily his good deeds survive and his name will live in the memories and hearts of the many who will enjoy his generous bounty in the years to come." (Minutes) To honor his memory a group of distinguished citizens commissioned Daniel Huntington to paint a portrait of him, which was presented to the permanent collection of the Academy.

In 1886 Norman L. Dodge offered an annual prize of $300 to be awarded for the best painting exhibited by a woman. This was the first prize to be restricted to a particular sex.

The Hallgarten and Dodge prizes were to be governed by the same rules as pertained to the Clarke prize. This method of award operated satisfactorily for the first few years after it was instituted. In 1884, 106 votes were cast for the Clarke prize, and the award was given to C. F. Ulrich, who received 49 votes. But in the following years it became increasingly difficult to obtain the necessary quorum. It was accordingly proposed that the method be modified. The jury of award was thereafter to be composed of five members—three Academicians and two Associates—elected by a balloting of the exhibitors at the annual exhibition. This change was approved both by Mr. Clarke and Mr. Dodge, but owing to the death of Mr. Hallgarten, the previous method of awarding the prizes given in his name had to be continued. This, however, proved impracticable. In three successive years no award could be made as the required 50 exhibitors were not present at the meeting called for that purpose. To eliminate this difficulty it was ruled in 1894 that the Hallgarten prizes be awarded by the jury of selection. Permission to make this change had already been granted by Albert Hallgarten, legatee of the estate.

A question which had prompted much discussion and was to continue to be debated for several years concerned the use of glass over pictures. The exact date that glass was first introduced is not stated, but in 1884 it was "resolved that no oil painting covered with glass will be admitted to the Academy Exhibitions." Pictures had become a necessary ornament in the luxurious homes of the 'seventies and 'eighties, and the use of elaborate frames and protecting shadow-boxes covered with glass corresponded to the dark walls, velour hangings, and plush coverings of the interior in vogue at that time. In May, 1886, the rule prohibiting the use of glass over oil paintings in the exhibitions of the Academy was rescinded; but in November of the same year the resolution permitting its use was in turn repealed. Winslow Homer complained that in looking at a glass-covered picture he could see only the reflection of his bald head. The question was again considered at a meeting of the council in January, 1888, and the previous prohibition was again overruled. As the members were divided in accepting the authority of this decision, a special meeting was called in February by requisition of six Academicians to determine the issue. A motion was made by E. W. Perry and seconded by Homer Martin to sustain the original prohibition. A lengthy and heated debate followed. When the vote was finally taken, 17 members voted in favor of the motion and 19 in opposition, and the resolution was lost. This however did not pacify the opponents. At the regular business meeting of December in the same year Mr. Perry returned to the attack and repeated his previous motion. On this occasion 27 Academicians were present and the resolution was carried. This prompted President Huntington to remark in his annual address: "The plate glass barriers were carried by storm. The glass was shattered to fragments at the first blow. Reactionary measures, may at some future day, restore the flattering delusion." (Minutes) His prophecy proved justified when, by a subsequent ruling, the use of glass became optional with the exhibitor. In the days of open fires and gas burners, glass over pictures no doubt served as a protective covering, but its fashionable use in the decade following was more concerned with flattering embellishment and purchasing appeal.

When the plans for the building on 23d Street had been approved, the members of the Academy thought that ample provision had been made both for its exhibitions and its school. The building was, in fact, the finest serving the purpose of art in America. But contemporary vision can seldom see future trends and developments. In the 'eighties and 'nineties the increase of pictures and students overcrowded the galleries and classrooms. In the school this was partly due to the increased enrollment of women. Although numbers varied from year to year, the average was well over 200. The number of students registered in 1891 was 294, of whom 121 were women. A women's life class had been added which caused an English visitor to remark that "The Royal Academy had not dared to establish such a class." (Minutes) In the school, visual training and exactitude of rendering were encouraged rather than individuality. On reviewing the work of the school in 1886, President Huntington commented: "The drawings exhibited prove that accuracy and completeness can be united with breadth and simplicity of style without loss of force or delicacy." This discipline was supplemented by work in the composition and sketch class. The class in painting was reserved for advanced students, a charge of $10 monthly being considered necessary to meet the additional cost of instruction and models. In 1883 there were only ten students in this class—a number which, however, was doubled in the next decade. Lectures on anatomy and perspective were continued, the former under the enlightened instruction of Thomas Eakins, the latter under Frederick Dielman. A class in modeling was introduced in 1889, directed by Olin Warner, but was discontinued owing to lack of pupils. Etching having become an adjunct both of the artist's livelihood and craft and a complete etcher's equipment having been bequeathed to the school, the council appointed the veteran James D. Smillie to conduct a class in that medium. In 1889 Professor Wilmarth, who had introduced so many aspirants into the profession, retired as instructor of drawing, having served the school faithfully for twenty years. Edgar M. Ward, who had assisted Wilmarth, was appointed in his place, and the teaching staff was further enlarged to include Will H. Low, Charles Noel Flagg, C. Y. Turner, and Francis C. Jones, who instructed a painting class in still life. The growing need for enlarged accommodations, and the fact that the studio of the life class had been deprived of daylight when an adjoining building was erected on Fourth Avenue, caused the Academy to rent the building recently vacated by the Art Students League at 143 East 23d Street to serve this purpose.

In 1893, for the first time in its history, the chairman of the school committee could report that the school was conducted without financial loss. This was partly due to the Elizabeth Fogg Bequest in 1892 creating a fund of $30,000, the interest to be used for the furtherance of the school. The Harper Lecture Fund of $250 annually supplemented lectures pertaining to the curriculum. This included lectures on costume, illustra-

tion, and "the locomotion of animals." William F. Havemeyer, who, at
the time, requested that his name should not be publicly announced,
donated $1,500 for two European scholarships to be awarded to the most
deserving students. The interest of the students was further stimulated
by the formation of the Society of National Academy Art Students,
which held monthly meetings at the school, with exhibitions of their
work, lectures, and entertainment.

To advance the interests of the school, and to gather further information in regard to future plans of building, the council commissioned S. R.
Koehler, who was to visit the leading art centers in Europe, to report
on the mode of instruction, the equipment of buildings, the size of
galleries, and the distinctive differences characterizing the various institutions abroad.

With the approach of the much-heralded Columbian Exposition—the
famous Chicago World's Fair of 1893—it was proposed that it would be
appropriate to hold a loan exhibition in the galleries of the Academy,
not alone to celebrate the occasion, but (with the financial success of the
centennial loan exhibition in mind) to gain funds to reduce the mortgage
on the Academy building. With this in view, a joint committee was
appointed, consisting of three members of the Academy and Thomas
B. Clarke, Samuel P. Avery, and James A. Garland, Fellows. After a conference held at the Century Association, the latter three members were
invited to outline a plan covering the nature of the exhibition and its
operation. Henry Marquand, Cornelius Vanderbilt, Herbert A. Bishop,
H. O. Havemeyer, and the president of the Academy were added to the
committee. As many of the most important works by American artists
were to be shown at the Exposition in Chicago, it was decided that the
Academy exhibition should be composed only of foreign masterpieces of
painting and *objets d'art*. The Academy was to insure all pictures loaned
to it and to employ guards day and night to assure their protection. The
exhibition was held from June to November, 1893. Although an unquestioned artistic success, the "disastrous silver panic made it a financial
failure." There were few visitors to the city during the summer. "The
hotels were nearly empty." With further promotion and advertising in
October, the attendance increased; but the final balance sheet was fatal,
showing expenses totaling over $16,000 and a deficit of $6,726. Instead of
decreasing the loan as anticipated, the council felt obliged to increase

the mortgage on the Academy building from $60,000 to $68,000 to meet necessary expenses.

In his presidential address at the annual meeting of 1895, Thomas Wood announced the passing of the last surviving founder of the Academy, Thomas Seir Cummings, in his ninety-first year. He had lived in retirement for many years at his country home in New Jersey and was personally known to but few of the members present. In paying tribute to his memory and his faithful and untiring service, the president said, "It was to his sound financial management that much of the success of the Academy is due." In the same year George Inness had passed from the living. "The sudden death of George Inness in the zenith of his fame, must be felt as a great and severe loss to us all, and especially this Institution which has been honored by his great accomplishments. Most of you who are present today were never acquainted with the intense individuality manifested in his positive utterances, his enthusiasm and devotion to his work." (Minutes) George Inness died at Bridge of Allon, Scotland, August 3, 1894. The funeral services were held in the rooms of the Academy.

A very touching tribute to membership in the Academy was disclosed by the will of Jules Emile Saintin in which he bequeathed to the Academy all his pictures and all the studio effects of which he died possessed. Born in France in 1829, the youthful Saintin established his studio in New York in the middle 'fifties and was made an Associate of the Academy in 1861. First represented in 1857, he exhibited 52 pictures between that date and 1861. Returning to France, he was awarded medals in 1866 and 1870, and was decorated with the Legion of Honor in 1877. In 1883 he was similarly honored in Munich. Accepting the entire bequest would have involved tremendous inheritance taxes and transportation costs, so the council requested permission to make selections from the bequest and appointed Frederic Bridgman, then living in Paris, to make the selections. The examples in the permanent collection of the Academy attest the distinction of Saintin's work and provide a testimony of his membership.

The general superintendence of the Academy building had for many years been under the care of the "keeper," T. Addison Richards, who also acted as corresponding secretary. To relieve Mr. Richards of this double burden, it was thought advisable to employ a nonmember to devote his full time to this service and increase his duties. In 1890 Mr. C.

S. Farrington was appointed to this position and the title of "keeper" was discontinued. Mr. Richards retired as secretary in 1892, after forty years of faithful service. "During the many years he has held office, he has conscientiously studied the highest interests of the Institution, aided it by his judgment, adorned it by his taste, scholarship and refinement, and endeared himself to our members by his kindly, genial and affectionate intercourse." (Minutes) Other changes had taken place in the official administration. "Reminded by advancing years, that it is wise to lay down responsibility in good time," Daniel Huntington expressed his wish to retire. T. W. Wood as vice-president presided at the annual meeting of 1891 on which occasion he was elected president, F. D. Millet was elected vice-president. The following year J. C. Nicoll was elected corresponding secretary.

The need for more space for the school and the extension of the galleries resolved itself into two propositions: the first was to remodel the existing building and add a top floor gallery; the second was to sell the property and build anew further uptown. Architectural plans were made for enlarging the building, but this idea roused objection because of the great expense entailed and the undesirability of an additional flight of stairs. Meantime the business section of the city was steadily moving uptown. Twenty-third Street had become a main cross-thoroughfare, and property values had risen correspondingly. With wise thought, the council purchased two adjoining houses on 23d Street, to protect the lighting of the galleries from the west, and with the prospect of enlarging the Academy building. Number 51 was purchased in 1888 for the sum of $40,000, half of which was paid in cash and $20,000 borrowed on mortgage from the Artists Fund Society. The second house, Number 49, was purchased in 1890 for $46,750. Each house was rented by the Academy for $2,000 annually. To make the second purchase possible, a mortgage of $60,000 was negotiated on the main building. This enabled the Academy to terminate the remaining balance of $10,000 owed to the Artists Fund Society.

During the summer of 1894, the treasurer, James D. Smillie, conferred with representatives of the Metropolitan Life Insurance Company concerning an offer to purchase the entire property of the Academy. A special meeting of the Academicians was called in November to receive the report of the treasurer and to act upon his findings. After the reading of the report and the conditions of sale, a formal resolution was offered authorizing the president and treasurer to execute a contract of sale incorporating the terms set forth and, with the combined approval of the Metropolitan Life Insurance Company and the council of the Academy, to consummate the sale. When the resolution was voted upon, of the 41 members that were present, 40 voted affirmatively, one member did not vote. The provisions of the sale are transcribed in detail in the minutes of the Academy. In accepting the offered sum of $610,000, the Academy included a provision by which it would be permitted to lease the main building, with the right of subletting, for a period of two years. This extension of time was to continue until the historic structure was demolished in 1899. In the meantime, a modification of the contract was confirmed whereby the Metropolitan Life Insurance Company agreed to pay the Academy $340,000 on delivery of the deeds for the two houses on 23d Street, the remainder of the purchase money to be paid on the delivery of the deed of the Academy building.

A committee to explore the possibilities of a new site had first been appointed in 1885, and during the following decade many other committees were to continue this search. In 1892 the Fine Arts Building at 57th Street, financed jointly by the Society of American Artists, the Art Students League, and the Architectural League, was formally opened. It was in these galleries that the annual exhibitions of the Society were being held. In January of 1895 the Architectural League proposed to the council of the Academy a plan for the affiliation of the various art societies of New York. At the business meeting of Academicians in December of the same year it was resolved that the Academy should maintain its absolute independence of all other Societies, and "that it is the expressed wish of this body that no funds of the Academy shall be used for acquiring an interest in any property unless the sole, separate, entire and absolute ownership of said property shall stand in the name of the Academy." (Minutes) It was imperative, therefore, that a building site should be definitely determined. With this in view three special meetings of Academicians were held in March, 1896, without, however, reaching a decision. It was not until the following November that the discussion was resumed. Various locations were presented by their respective sponsors. In brief, the contention was between sites south of Central Park and north of Central Park. To come to a decision it was therefore "Resolved that the officers and members of the Council, together with Messrs. J. C. Nicoll, Harry W. Watrous and E. Wood Perry, are hereby appointed a committee on site and plan, with power to select and purchase such site as, in their judgment, is the best one obtainable for carrying out the object of the Academy, and that upon the purchase of a site, the committee is requested to prepare and submit to the Academicians some plan for the further action of the Academy." (Minutes)

Thomas Moran proposed an amendment that the council and three additional Academicians should be elected by ballot to serve as a committee on site and plan. This was accepted and other names were placed in nomination. Fifty ballots were cast, 26 being necessary for a choice. The council received 38 votes, E. Wood Perry 33, J. C. Nicoll 29, Harry Watrous 32. Other votes were scattering. It was moved that the vote on the council be made unanimous and it was so done. Mr. Perry then called for a poll on the resolution as amended; this resulted in 47 votes in the affirmative, one negative, two not voting. Notwithstanding this resolution, a meeting of Academicians was called February 3, 1897, to hear the final reports of the committee on site and plan and to vote thereon. Mr. Beckwith presented his views favoring the site at 109th Street; Mr. Perry set forth the advantages of the 57th Street site. The chair ruled that no other locations could be proposed or voted upon. After prolonged discussion the ballot was then taken. Fifty-seven members being present, the roll was called and each member deposited his ballot in a sealed box to be counted by the committee at its next meeting. The council met with the committee on the following day. The result of the ballot was as follows: in favor of the 109th Street site, 40; in favor of the 57th Street site, 16; one vote was opposed to both. Thus after twelve years of exploration, consideration and discussion, the final decision was made.

The choice of this seemingly unpromising site was motivated by the vast project of the building of the Cathedral of St. John the Divine and plans for the development of that section of the city centering around Columbia University. The bridge across the Hudson was at this time expected to be erected at 110th Street. All this resulted in the immediate enhancement of surrounding real estate. In two years time the appraised evaluation of the Academy property increased from $60,000 to $112,000. In 1905 the Academy was offered $260,000 and in 1911 $375,000.

Plans for the proposed building and means of raising funds were at once formulated. Six prominent architectural firms of New York were invited to compete in the presentation of designs, the rules governing the competition to be made by the competitors in consultation with the committee on site and plan. The award was given to Carrère and Hastings, the committee "finding their plan more nearly the fulfillment of all the needs and requirements of the Academy."

Because of the outbreak of the Spanish-American War and the resultant unsettled state of finances, the council postponed signing contracts for construction. At the general business meeting held in December, 1898, it was proposed to begin immediately the erection of a temporary building at 109th Street to provide rooms for administration and meetings on the first floor and studios for the school on the upper floor. At the close of the school season, the Academy properties were to be moved to this temporary building, which was to be completed before that time. The building at 23d Street was to be surrendered to the Metropolitan Life Insurance Company on June 1, after the Academy had received the balance of the purchase money of $235,000. Of this sum, $175,000 was to be invested as a building fund.

To raise the necessary funds for the construction of the permanent building, a committee of ways and means was appointed by the council to act in conjunction with an advisory committee. The first meeting of this committee was held at the residence of Henry Marquand. The members attending included Bishop Potter, who presided; Thomas W. Wood, president of the Academy; James M. Hart, vice-president; J. C. Nicoll, secretary; Frederick Dielman, chairman of the building committee; and Henry Marquand, Jacob Schiff, William Dodge, Seth Low, Levi P. Morton, Perry Belmont, and Charles Barney. John Carrère represented Carrère and Hastings.

Mr. Nicoll presented the plan and reasons favoring the erection of a temporary building at an approximate cost of $17,000. This was freely discussed. Mr. Carrère proposed an alternate plan of erecting a foundation and the first and second floor of that portion of the permanent building to be devoted to the school, the same to be covered by a temporary roof at a cost estimated at $100,000. It was however concluded that it would be more expeditious to erect the temporary building at once, so that the school could be opened in the autumn, after which, with enlarged resources, the building of the main edifice facing Cathedral Parkway could be started. The chair then appointed a subcommittee of three members to represent the advisory committee in consultation with the ways and means committee, expressing the belief that the project would meet with immediate success in raising the necessary funds. This plan was accordingly approved by the council and ratified at the general meeting of Academicians.

The brilliant hopes of the committee were, however, not to be realized. In his report at the annual meeting of May, 1899, the president conceded "that the conviction is forced upon us, that the large sum needed to build the new Academy must come by slower degrees and will take a longer time to secure than we had hoped for." He reminded the members that the Metropolitan Museum of Art and the American Museum of Natural History, although supported by the city, had been in process of construction for many years. At the same meeting Mr. Beckwith, chairman of the ways and means committee, announced that the committee "regrets to state that it has encountered considerable apathy and ignorance in the public mind regarding the institution; subscriptions amounted to only $64,450." It was then suggested that temporary galleries should be erected to be used until such time as a suitable endowment fund could be raised. At a subsequent meeting of Academicians this proposal was put to a vote; eight were in favor of the motion and seventeen opposed.

It therefore became imperative that suitable galleries be engaged for the annual exhibition the following year. This had in fact been under consideration for some time, the first meeting being held at the Century Association in June, 1899. The following October, at a special meeting of Academicians, several prospective galleries were considered, but were not approved as they lacked proper space. It was then proposed that the galleries of the American Fine Arts Society be rented for the annual exhibition of 1900. This was carried unanimously, and the chairman was authorized to sign a lease engaging the galleries from December 17, 1899, to January 27, 1900, at a rental of $1,720.43. Thus, at the opening of the new century the Academy was to begin a new career, little realizing at the time that its annual exhibitions were to be held in this same gallery for the following forty years.

Meantime the school building had been satisfactorily completed, the library and art properties installed, and a jubilant "house warming" of the members was given on November 20, 1899. This happy reunion was, however, far removed from the former haunts and memories of the members. Although intended only as a temporary necessity, it was not to prove in the many years that followed a sympathetic environment, owing to unfavorable changes in the vicinity.

At the annual meeting of 1901, the ways and means committee made its final report, requesting that the committee be discharged and its duties be taken over by the officers and members of the council. In reviewing the work of the committee, Mr. Beckwith stated that in many ways the temporary building had been an "obstacle" in gaining subscriptions, as many prospective subscribers, when interviewed, replied that when the Academy was ready to start the permanent building "they would consider the matter." In this uncertain stage of the proceedings it was suggested that the committee investigate the possibilities of a municipal site nearer the center of the city. With the assistance of John Cadwallader, who had drawn the charter for the Public Library, and several other influential citizens, the Academy petitioned the municipal authorities for permission to build on the site of the old Arsenal facing Fifth Avenue, as that building was to be demolished. This created a heated controversy in which the press of the city engaged, public opinion being agitated against it.

A NEW CENTURY: PRIZES AND BEQUESTS · THE SCHOOL · FIRE · THE SCHOOL THROUGH THE FIRST WORLD WAR AND UNTIL 1925

SEVERAL BEQUESTS and prizes were presented to the Academy during the opening decade of the twentieth century: the Maynard Prize of $100 and the Proctor Prize of $200 for portraiture; the Barnett Prize of $200 for sculpture; the Isidor Medal for figure painting; and the Saltus Medal for Merit. The Inness Gold Medal for landscape painting, first presented in 1901, was discontinued in 1918, and unhappily the Dodge Prize for women could no longer be offered. Mr. Woodbury Langdon of the Archaeological Institute offered an annual prize of $100. To encourage students in etching, Mr. E. Hackley Barheydt endowed a fund of $6,000, the interest from which was to be used to further this art and to be known as the Albert H. Baldwin Fund.

Also for the students was a "traveling scholarship" for study abroad, generously donated by Miss Ella Mooney in memory of her father, which provided $700 each year. The first such scholarship was awarded to Maurice Sterne; the second to Leon Kroll. The president reported in 1905 that Mr. Sterne "informs us that he has two paintings hung in the Champ de Mars Salon, as well as two etchings. Moreover that one of his etchings appears in the Gazette des Beaux Arts." In alluding to Leon Kroll, Will H. Low, chairman of the School Committee, reported in 1909: "As his predecessor was able to win five out of six possible prizes at the Julian School in Paris, so in his turn, Mr. Kroll has won the most important prize of the year in the same school, a prize for which all the various ateliers which compose it competed. So it will be seen that by its more advanced pupils and in individual cases the School of the Academy is not without merit." (Minutes)

The most important contribution, as far as the Academy exhibitions were concerned, was the Altman Bequest established by the will of the late Benjamin Altman in 1913.

I give and bequeath to the National Academy of Design, in the City of New York, the sum of one hundred thousand dollars for the benefit, encouragement and advancement of Art in the United States, the same to be kept as a separate fund the income thereof to be used as follows: For the best figure or "genre" painting by an American born artist, a First annual prize of $1,000.00, and a Second prize of $500.00; for the best landscape painting by an American born artist, a First annual prize of $1,000.00, and a Second prize of $500.00; the awards to be made from time to time, by the members of the Academy, or constituted in such a manner as shall be in accordance with the custom of the Academy.

The Altman award is a title of distinction, and has added greatly to the contributions to the annual exhibitions.

The most significant and far-reaching bequest was to come from a fellow member of the National Academy. Henry W. Ranger, one of the most distinguished American landscape painters of his generation, after acquiring a considerable fortune, had in his later years contemplated making a bequest that would provide for acquiring representative works by American painters to add to the collection of paintings in the National Gallery at Washington. To this end he consulted the attorney for the Academy in order to carry out his intention the best way possible. Mr. Ranger's thought was not merely philanthropic. His purpose, fundamentally, was to further the development of American painting by placing chosen examples in public institutions, and after a designated time, permitting selections from these examples to be made by the National Gallery to form a permanent collection.

Mr. Ranger bequeathed to the Academy his entire estate, including all of his remaining pictures. The will specifies concisely the nature of the bequest.

I direct that my entire residuary estate be paid over to the National Academy of Design, the principal to be kept invested and the income thereof to be spent by the Council of said Academy in purchasing paintings produced by American artists, at least two thirds of such income to be spent in the purchase of works by artists who are forty-five years of age and over, it remaining optional with the Council to spend the remaining one third, or any part thereof, in the purchase of works by younger artists. All pictures so purchased are to be given by the Council to art institutions in America, or to any library or other institutions in America maintaining a gallery open to the public, all such gifts to be upon the express condition that the National Gallery at Washington, administered by the Smithsonian Institution, shall have the option and the right, without cost, to take, reclaim and own any picture for their collection, provided they exercise such option and right at any time during the five year period beginning ten years after the artist's death, and ending fifteen years after his death, and, if such option and right is not exercised during such period, the picture shall remain and be the property of the institution to which it was first given. The words "America" and "American" as used above shall be construed as equivalent to "North America" and "North American" respectively. (Minutes)

In providing that two thirds of the income be used in the purchase of paintings by artists over forty-five years of age, Mr. Ranger's expressed belief was that an artist's most representative work was created in mature age, after the cumulative training and experience of his earlier years. In delaying the selection for the permanent collection in the National Gallery, the interim of time elapsed would permit a fully considered judgment.

The will of Henry Ranger was probated in 1916. Unhappily, another will of a later date than the first was also presented. The second will proved to be false but involved the Academy in costly litigation over a period of two years. The total estate aggregated approximately $416,000. The sale of pictures realized $76,811. Debts and expenses of administration reduced the total to $315,283.86.

From the date of the will's enactment until 1952, 142 paintings were purchased by the council, costing a total of $321,300. Of these, 21 paintings have been permanently assigned to the National Gallery, 27 paintings have been permanently assigned to public institutions, and 94 paintings have been temporarily assigned. Ranger Fund purchases are represented in 39 states. This wide distribution includes most of the museums in small cities, as well as the museums of the principal cities of the nation.

Joseph Pulitzer established by his will a bequest, the interest from which was to provide for an annual traveling scholarship of $1,500 to be awarded to a student of art in a national competition, the fund to be administered by Columbia University, and the award to be made by the Society of American Artists. As the Society had merged with the Academy before the time of his death, the awards were made by a committee appointed by the council of the Academy. Works submitted in competition include the graphic arts, sculpture, painting in oil and water color, with the jury of selection representing artists specializing in each of these mediums. The annual response demonstrates keen national interest in the competition. Announcement of the award is made at the same time as the awards in literature and drama. The will, probated in 1914, stipulated that the Pulitzer awards would not be operative until or after Columbia had established a school of journalism for three years. The first traveling scholarship was, therefore, not awarded until 1917, from which date it has continued annually with one exception (in 1944).

In the closing decade of the nineteenth century the Academy classes had been overcrowded, the number of enrolled students approaching 300. Moreover, in the old school, surrounded by encroaching buildings, the lighting of the studios was unsatisfactory. There was no proper room for a class in sculpture. In the new school at 109th Street there were ample accommodations; the studios facing north on Cathedral Parkway provided unobstructed lighting. But, like the members of the Academy, the students missed the sympathetic associations of the old building, and they were far removed from the artistic activities of the city, as well as from Academy exhibitions.

As a bill was pending in Albany to obtain tax exemption on the newly acquired property, the council thought it advisable to follow the original policy of free tuition. Accordingly the classes in the antique, the composition classes, and the lectures on anatomy and perspective were made free to all students who could pass the required examinations. In the life class as well as painting and still life, a charge was made to cover such expenses as models. It was the intention of the new school committee to concentrate on quality rather than quantity, so that "When a student leaves the School of the Academy he may be more fully equipped to strive for success in his art career than would be the case could he only make a good Academy drawing." In consequence, of the 285 applicants who sought admission during the term of 1899–1900, only 111 were admitted; the following year, 142 of the 280 applicants were enrolled.

A new class was inaugurated in cooperation with the Numismatic

Society and the Archaeological Institute, the special object of which was the training of students in the art of designing and modeling of coins and medals, and ultimately of the cutting of dies for their production. It was also hoped that this class would promote an interest in establishing a larger school for sculpture. Summer classes were inaugurated in 1900 with an enrollment of 78 students. The etching class continued under the faithful guidance of James D. Smillie, who "gave his services freely."

FIRE. Saturday morning, March 18th, (1905) at about 7 A.M., Mr. Davis, the janitor, notified me by telephone that the building was burning. About 8:30 I arrived on the scene and found the fire practically extinguished. The firemen were removing the last portions of the roof preparatory to flushing it so that all chance of fire should be removed. The President, Mr. Dielman, was assisting removing the pictures from the etching classroom, the roof of that portion of the building still occupying the attention of the firemen. Upon examination I found a hole in the Antique classroom floor about ten feet wide and sixteen feet long, with some of the charred joists quite gone—all of the roof destroyed. (Minutes)

So wrote C. Y. Turner, chairman of the house committee. The cause of the fire was not known; electrical experts said it was not caused by faulty wiring; the fire marshal asserted that it had started between the floors. There was no fire on the first floor, but the falling debris and timbers and the flooding of water and smoke had ruined much of the interior and many of the pictures and objects of art. The collection of casts which had been purchased from the old American Academy, and many others which had been added, were almost totally destroyed. Many of the paintings and prize drawings by former students were ruined, as well as many historical records, including those of the school. The most valued paintings, which hung in the general meeting room, were happily removed. Those that remained were badly damaged by water and smoke. A copy of a Rubens painting by Morse was completely destroyed. The heroic and hazardous efforts of the firemen alone saved the building from total destruction. After the arrival of agents from the insurance company, all undamaged property could be removed to the Liberty Warehouse. "Janitor Davis and helper, Charley, with the assistance of four or five students, removed 257 pictures uninjured." All others were removed from the walls and placed under tarpaulins within the building, to await the adjustment of the insurance company. "A lamentable result of the fire was the death of fireman William Brown, of Engine 76, caused by injuries received when the ceiling and roof of the Antique room caught him in its fall. He had been in the service only a few weeks. Every Academician will heartily approve the action of the Council in appropriating the sum of $100 for the relief of the widow and children of the unfortunate victim." (Minutes)

The loss caused by the fire in material value was fully covered by insurance. The loss on furniture and fixtures was adjusted at $2,683.72, on pictures at $6,815.00, and on the building at $8,730.00, a total of $18,228.72.

The Art Students League and the Metropolitan Museum of Art generously offered their services and placed all available accommodations at the disposal of the Academy. Columbia University at once proffered assistance and acted immediately. "Without a roof tree on Saturday morning, on Monday morning at the regular hours, the classes were being reorganized in the Building of Columbia University." The Academy office was also transferred to Columbia. "It is probably an unprecedented event that a whole institution should be transplanted over night and in active running order at a day's notice." (Minutes)

A special meeting of the council was held on May 3 to consider a proposal that had been made by Columbia to unite the Academy School with the university in a combined School of Fine Arts. The proposal, which had been previously drafted by President Butler, was discussed in detail, section by section. After several amendments were made, the council approved the agreement and voted that it be submitted to the general meeting of Academicians with a recommendation for its adoption.

The agreement was accordingly placed before the Academicians at the annual meeting of 1905; 25 consecutive pages pertaining to the discussion are recorded in the minutes of the Academy. President Dielman prefaced his remarks by saying that there were three cardinal points involved; first, "the integrity of the Academy as an institution; secondly, the integrity of its property; and thirdly, the best interests of art education in this city or country." The president made it clear that the council did not contemplate the disposal of any of the present funds or property of the Academy. He told how Columbia offered the site; the funds required, estimated at $500,000, were to be raised by public subscription. The faculty of the Academy school was to be independent of control by the university. "The Dean—that is, the Managing Officer of the Faculty of the School of Fine Arts—cannot be appointed by Columbia unless we consent to such appointment by nomination."

John F. Weir was the principal spokesman for the opposition. Mr. Weir began by saying that he believed the Academy, through its friends and supporters, could raise the necessary funds to erect a proper building on its own premises, and thus be entirely free from any dependence upon the university. Although Columbia's chief contribution to the Academy faculty would be mostly concerned with its school of architecture, still the professors of this school would outnumber the representatives from the Academy. Mr. Weir feared that the institution would probably become known as the "Columbia School of Fine Arts," though it had not been so named in the agreement. The pupils could not be matriculated as students of the National Academy.

As director of the School of Art at Yale University, Mr. Weir could speak with the authority of experience. "Art under the University scheme seems to be very loose and indefinite. The only idea is that a University has only to do with the theoretical, historical or technical past, and therefore a School of Art in connection with a University is not a professional school." He then went on to say that Yale University had initiated the plan of employing only professional instructors in their respective schools. This he highly approved.

The distinction I would make is this: Here is a body, a professional body, National Academy of Design, the members of which are a professional body of artists. The question is whether that body can maintain its position in the future as in the past, as it is maintained in France or England or elsewhere, by passing it under the University Scheme. Could it go up to Yale and fall under our department there, which has a $400,000.00 foundation and buildings and collections, and not lose its identity as a professional body with its own professional school?

In favor of the agreement, a second speaker, after an extended exposition, affirmed:

The final question is, is it more important today that the Academy should keep entirely and absolutely its control of its schools, without any connection with them, or that one great Art School in the Arts of Architecture, Painting, Sculpture and Music, should be combined, and the only chance that we have to get such a school is by combining with Columbia, and it is for us to decide what to do.

In summation, the fear expressed by the opposition was that if the Academy school were conducted under the general jurisdiction of the university, eventually the professional artists, as instructors, would be dominated by the Academic education required by the university. It was the renewal of the old, old question: should the artist have control in the training of artists and be the judge of his own craft?

After much rugged opposition, a compromise was finally reached, it being resolved that a committee of five members be added to the council, with power to act. Of the 47 members who were present, 29 voted in favor of the resolution. At a special meeting of the council held on January 22, 1906, the agreement with Columbia University, having been revised and perfected, was voted upon for final acceptance. It was resolved "that the President be authorized to execute this Agreement and that the Corresponding Secretary be instructed to affix the Seal of the National Academy of Design." Thus the formal conferences ended; but the agreement was more readily drawn up than it was fulfilled. The necessary building funds were not forthcoming, and while plans for the school were held up, the council was concentrating its efforts on increasing subscriptions to make possible the construction of a permanent building to enlarge its annual exhibitions. It was not until 1914 that the agreement with Columbia signed in 1906 was formally dissolved by mutual consent.

The school term for 1905–6 opened in the restored building in October. "It is believed that the building and its contents are in much better condition than before the fire and at least $1,500 has been added in the way of betterment, yet leaving a net balance unexpended of nearly $4,000." The enrollment of students had by now increased to such an extent that the classrooms were again overcrowded. A class in sculpture was established in 1907 under the direction of Hermon MacNeil, but the only available space was the cellar, where the students worked under artificial light. As the proposed fine arts school to be erected in cooperation with Columbia was not foreseeable in the near future, the council authorized an addition to the present building at a cost not to exceed $15,000. This was completed in 1908.

Under the chairmanship of Will Low, the school committee gave great thought to the conduct of the school and methods of betterment. A series of lectures were delivered by Kenyon Cox, Samuel Isham, John F. Weir, Edwin Blashfield, Howard Pyle, and Frederick Crowninshield. The class in sculpture was favorably installed. This marks

a distinct advance toward an Art School of a higher grade than the country yet knows; a school having the character, and hoping to attain with time the authority of the great art schools of the Old World. But to make a beginning of such a school is no easy task and, as every school attains its position as much from the character of the students as from its instructors, a determined effort must be made to elevate the class of pupils applying for admission to the School. For some reason, whether through our change of location and establishment in this remote quarter of the city, or from the abolishment of our fees for instruction, a class of pupils now frequent our classrooms that is totally different from the average student of ten years ago.

In complaining of the lack of discipline and frequent disorder in the classes, the chairman advised that a professional artist be added to the faculty to be in permanent charge of the school. "By 'proper conduct,' the present School Committee desires to define a decent maintenance of order sufficient to enable a student to work without distraction, but it nowise seeks to limit the traditional liberty of the art student, in so far as it does not interfere with the liberty of his neighbor." (Minutes)

The atelier system, common to European schools, was then suggested as a method more favorable to the consistent development of the student. "This would abolish all the special classes by progression through which a student's art education has been entrusted to different special instructors, and would enable the student, on his entrance and progress through the school, to become and remain the pupil of the same master from the Antique to the Life and painting classes." This, the chairman continued, would also obviate the danger of teaching becoming perfunctory through too much repetition of a restricted phase of study.

In the report of the school committee for 1907–8, the chairman could say

The new system was accepted with great enthusiasm by the students and if any doubt as to its desirability as a system existed in the minds of any of the instructors, these were quickly restored by the new interest which they have one and all found manifested by their classes. . . . But the work of an art school, in its highest sense, does not stop with the study of the model and the lessons imparted by the instructors, however efficient they may be.

He went on to say that it would be very helpful and greatly appreciated by the students if some of the members of the Academy would visit the school from time to time and review their work; thus the students could form personal contact with the artists whose work was known to them in the exhibitions, and the members would be reminded that the Academy included "virtually every artist of rank in the Eastern section of the States and each and every one of these has, beyond doubt, some message to impart." In this respect no other school would have such great advantages.

In 1909 over 300 applicants registered, of which 280 were accepted for instruction. Although the exhibition of their work compared favorably with other art schools, "the majority of our pupils are very young, mentally" and "the advanced students are comparatively few." It was a disputed question as to whether only the more gifted be received as students, or the school should be allowed to increase in numbers. It was pointed out that the first course of action, by reducing the number of students, would allow more time for individual instruction. The school committee solved this problem by dividing the school in two sections, the preparatory and the advanced. The first section would not only provide an opportunity to judge the student's progress, but would also fulfill the obligations of a tax-exempt institution. The second section would raise the standard and conform to the aesthetic requirements of the Academy as an art institution.

Before America's entrance into the First World War, the school's activities were not affected by the conflict raging in Europe. They were, in fact, extended. In 1914, a course of lectures on architecture was established in conjunction with the sculpture class, under Adolph Weinman. In 1915 the Academy appropriated a room for instruction in mural painting in collaboration with the Society of Mural Painters and the Beaux Arts Architects. Fourteen day classes and four evening classes were conducted under eight instructors, the enrollment numbering 425 students. Lectures were given in composition, perspective, anatomy, history of painting, and architecture. Prizes and medals aggregating $800 were awarded annually. The Mooney Traveling Scholarship of $700 was postponed during the war. The running expenses of the school in 1915 totaled $14,000; the receipts $4,000.

President Weir, in his annual report, stressed the significance of etching, an art in which he was an accomplished master: "I must refer to the class in etching, which is an admirable means of interesting students in searching for line and looking for things in light and dark." At a special meeting to consider the aesthetic direction of the school, Kenyon Cox recommended that "the insistence on Composition is a matter of vital importance"; he suggested "plans for the next season along such lines as will give this work a much larger and more important part in the School work." Herbert Adams, in his annual report for 1918, reiterated the statement of this need: "The intelligent, faithful student learns to draw well, and this can be said of but few other schools at the present time. Many learn to paint well, but I am of the opinion that the system we have inherited fails to stimulate and cultivate the all essential thing for an artist, his imagination, his love of composition."

The school was to play an active part in America's war effort. It established an Art War Relief. Funds were contributed by the Academy to purchase materials for making garments and hospital dressings. Three war orphans were adopted by the students with funds received from a benefit concert. The council posted a bulletin at the school:

The National Academy of Design has gone on record as upholding the Government of the United States in the present war, and it is requested that all students not in sympathy with this action will resign their membership in our Schools before further action is necessary, as we have no desire to have among our loyal students those who are opposed to our boys represented on our service flag, now in preparation, who are risking their lives in upholding the cause of liberty, and civilization. The National Academy of Design has no room for students who are disloyal either in act or talk. (Minutes)

During the war years the enrollment dropped to as few as 219 students. Many had been called into service, and others were to follow. Because of the prevalent social unrest and subversive activities, it was thought advisable to make a statistical classification of native and foreign-born students. Of the 367 students enrolled in 1918, 156 were foreign-born, including 84 of Russian birth, 30 of Italian birth, and 26 of German birth. This check was continued.

In 1921, many students whose applications met Academy requirements had to be refused admission because of lack of room. At that time, 506 students were enrolled. Of this number, 181 were foreign born, including

95 of Russian birth, 51 of Italian birth, and 33 of German birth. The school committee reported "that numbers are not always the highest recommendation for a scholastic institution," advising that examinations be more exacting and "the weeding out of such students as had not evinced sufficient ability or shown enough progress to warrent their return next term." Notwithstanding, "much excellent work was accomplished, some of specially high quality, and much earnestness and generally regular attendance prevailed, especially in the Life classes." A new course of lectures on the graphic arts was introduced by Joseph Pennell. It was well attended and created much interest. During these years, the school deficit ran from $4,000 to over $6,000.

·XII·

THE OPENING of the first exhibition of the Academy in the Galleries of the American Fine Arts Society marks not only a change of scene but, coinciding with the opening of the new century, it marks the beginning of a new era and the passing of the "Old Guard." The administration was taken over by younger men. In the elections of officers at the annual meeting of 1899, President Thomas Wood withdrew his name, and on the third ballot Frederick Dielman was elected president. Harry W. Watrous was elected corresponding secretary. At the annual meeting of 1900 Mr. Watrous offered the following resolution:

Resolved that the National Academy of Design express its profound sense of loss in the death of our esteemed fellow members, Jared B. Flagg, William L. Sonntag, William S. Haseltine, William H. Beard, Frederic E. Church, Charles F. Blauvelt, and Alfred Jones whom all wise Providence has taken since our last Annual Meeting. These men belonged to the rugged "Old Guard" of the Academy and were leaders in the fight for Truth as they saw it. They had convictions and lived true to them. They were American artists and were proud of it as we of them. And while many of us now carrying on the work they have relinquished never came within their orbit, their names are familiar to us through the loving voices of their contemporaries and are echoes of a time when America had a distinctive School, and the Academy under their guidance represented it in the highest sense. Their work is finished, they have signed it, and we can say of each "well done, thou good and faithful servant." (Minutes)

This sentiment could rightly be applied to the roll call of the departed in the closing years of the century.

One of the first constitutional amendments indicative of new trends was enacted at a special meeting in May, 1900. A rule which had been in force since the inception of the Academy was eliminated by striking out the words: "The election of Academicians and Associates shall be made only from exhibitors at the regular exhibitions of the year of their proposal for membership." The ending of this restriction was to have favorable results. The number of candidates eligible for election was enlarged, and the membership was further nationalized. A second ruling, that of opening the galleries on Sunday and charging no admission, was indicative of sociological changes of deep significance in the mores of the time. The closing of the galleries on Sunday was taken for granted in the early days as a customary recognition of the Sabbath. After mid-century it had annually been disputed, but the "Old Guard" had always stood adamant.

Concomitant with this latter change was the passing of the friends and patrons of the elder members, who had been stalwart supporters of the Academy.

The admission fees of the annual exhibitions had in the past, with few exceptions, measurably exceeded the cost involved, and the profits were used to support the school. In fact this was the initial premise in the founding of the Academy, its very "life blood." But, in 1898 the expenses of the exhibition exceeded the income, and after that date a favorable balance was not always assured. Added to this problem was the growing influence of dealers in foreign art who were cultivating a new patronage. Lamenting this change, Thomas Wood, in closing his last presidential address, remarked: "The large sums paid in this country to foreign painters, especially for portraits, and the meagre support given to our own artists by Americans, is rather discouraging to American art; but let us still hope and pray that the patriotism of this country may in time extend even to the Art of our own land."

President Dielman complained on several occasions of the lack of cooperation of many members in not sending work to the annual exhibition. In the exhibition of 1901, only 45 out of the 92 living Academicians were represented; only 34 of 62 Associates contributed. "Of the 271 names of exhibitors in the Seventy-Seventh Annual Exhibition only 40 were those of Academicians or Associates. . . . While the facts show conclusively that our exhibitions are not held in the interests of our members to the detriment of the claims of outsiders, this large non-participation of members is to be deeply regretted."

During the first five years of occupancy of the American Fine Arts Gallery, receipts from the sale of pictures fluctuated from $8,640 in 1900, to $13,720 in 1903, to $13,265 in 1905, to $11,740 in 1906. The attendance varied likewise; the receipts from admissions in 1900 totaling $1,268.95, while the deficit of the exhibition ran between $1,000 and $1,500. It was fortunate, however, that the total income of the Academy during these years exceeded the annual expenditure. Altogether, as the president reported, the financial accounting was in excellent state.

At the autumn meeting held in November, 1906, "The President called attention to the fact that this was the first time in the history of the Academy when Academicians and Associates were present with equal powers for the business of the meeting, and he further extended on the part of the older members a hearty welcome to the newer element, congratulating them as well on the infusion of new blood." (Minutes)

The annual exhibitions became truly national. This was apparent also in the great increase in the number of artists resident in New York who had originally come from distant states, as well as in the nation-wide representation in the art schools and among students returning from abroad.

The eighty-second exhibition of the Academy, held in 1907, was the first annual exhibition to be given after the union with the Society of American Artists. The sale of pictures brought $12,050. The entire receipts, including admissions, sale of catalogues, and advertising and commissions on the sale of pictures, came to $4,319.20; the expenses were $5,218.70. Although not differing greatly in this respect from previous exhibitions, the result was encouraging. The affiliation and cooperation of the new members demonstrated the wisdom of consolidation.

A total of 1,434 works, of which 1,364 were pictures and 70 were sculpture, were submitted to the jury. Of these only 429 were placed on exhibition, including the 78 examples which were exempt and the 2 which were invited. The protest of those rejected followed. This caused unprecedented commentary from the press and might be considered historically as the beginning of "modern" prejudice against what was erroneously termed "the policy" of the Academy. In reference to this negative attitude, President Dielman, in reviewing the exhibition in his annual address, affirmed: "Legitimate and intelligent criticism of our policy and methods, publicly expressed, we must be prepared to hear and regard, particularly when they reflect sentiments current among the body of our fellow artists. But it may be questioned whether ignorant abuse and willful misrepresentation should be suffered without protest; and latterly the privileges which part of our Press seems to enjoy of being irresponsible and unjust has certainly been abused." After mentioning the large number of rejections the President continued: "In the expression of disappointment and discontent that reached them, certain laborers on the press saw grist for their own mill. . . . Is it anything less than unblushing impudence that emboldens any newspaper writer on art and miscellaneous topics to set his individual judgment against that of thirty professional painters and sculptors and to represent that body as incompetent, ignorant, or jealous and afraid to encourage new genius?" One critic "informed its readers, on editorial authority, that the policy and methods of the Academy are precisely those of a labor union, and its attitude toward the outsider that of the latter toward the 'Scab.' " This was, however, far from being the prevailing reaction of the visitors to the exhibition, which was conceded to be of "exceptionally high quality." (Minutes)

The controversy that continued was to have much the same relation to the Academy as that which transpired in its inception, as to whether artists are competent to organize and control their institutions and to judge the works to be exhibited, or whether the "layman" and critic should be the arbiters of art and its presentation.

The period from 1906 to the beginning of the First World War marks a notable increase in the production and representation of sculpture. There was not, however, nor had there ever been a suitable gallery for the presentation of sculpture. In 1905 only 13 examples of sculpture were represented; in the winter exhibition of 1911, 167 pieces of sculpture were received by the jury and of this number 67 were placed. In the same year it was resolved that "So long as the Academy is forced to exhibit in the present restricted galleries, one gallery shall be set aside for sculpture at each Winter exhibition of the academy, and that no sculpture shall be accepted at the annual Exhibition of the Academy. . . . all sculptors elected as members of the Jury shall serve on the Jury of the Winter Exhibition." From this date also the sculptors were more fully represented in the membership of the Academy. Frederick W. MacMonnies, Hermon MacNeil, C. H. Niehaus, Edward C. Potter, and Frederick Roth were elected in 1906; Isidore Konti in 1909; Lorado Taft and Adolph Weinman in 1911; A. Stirling Calder in 1913; Robert Aitken in 1914. It was not, however, until a decade later, with the growing opportunity for sculptors, that this class was considerably augmented. In 1908, through the generosity of Frank Jay Gould, the riding stable which adjoined the Fine Arts Building and which belonged to him was placed at the disposal of the Academy, and a comprehensive display to sculpture was held in conjunction with the winter exhibition. Unhappily this favorable opportunity was not extended.

The building at 23d Street and Fourth Avenue had become a part of the past.

Our dear Old Building as you know has vanished from the site on which it stood for nearly forty years. It has reappeared in many of its features and much of the old body, in a structure connected with the Church of Our Lady of Lourdes, at Amsterdam Avenue and 142d Street, and if it is true as has been stated, that a saving was effected to that church of some $129,000, by making use of our cast off building, then the Academy may congratulate itself that through it, Art has once again in these later years come effectively to the service of the Church. (Minutes)

Subscriptions to the new building fund had slowly increased to $78,500. At this juncture, J. Pierpont Morgan volunteered to donate $100,000 if another would add the same amount, but this challenge met with no response.

The organization of the Fine Arts Federation of New York in 1897 had successfully united all the art societies in New York to cooperate in furthering the artistic interests of the city as well as to guide and promote civic improvement. The certificate of incorporation stated: "That the particular objects for which the Corporation is formed are, to ensure united action by the Art Societies of New York in all matters affecting their common interests, and to foster and protect the artistic interests of the community." The first five directors signing the certificate were J. Q. A. Ward, George W. Maynard, John M. Carrère, George B. Post, representing sculpture, painting, and architecture; and the distinguished layman, Edward Hamilton Bell. Recognizing the limited space provided by the American Fine Arts Building on 57th Street and realizing the need for a larger center in which all of the art organizations would have an equal opportunity to exhibit, the members of the Federation gradually endeavored to materialize such a project.

The council of the Academy, unable to obtain sufficient funds to erect its own building, now concentrated its effort on furthering this project through its appointed delegates in the Federation and its members on the board of directors. In conformity with this plan a letter was drafted by Kenyon Cox to be sent to the presidents of the different art societies forming the Federation.

On behalf of the National Academy of Design I beg to entrust to your Society, for such action as it may see fit to take, the following proposition regarding the needs of the Art Societies of New York. First: There is urgent need for more adequate facilities for the exhibition of works of art in the city. The galleries now available are far too small and are no longer properly lighted and there is no possibility that New York can take its proper place as an art center until a commodious exhibition building is erected. Second: Among the Art Societies in this city the National Academy of Design is best fitted by its position, its endowment, and the representative nature of its membership including, as it does, workers in all the plastic and graphic arts, to assume the initiative in securing such a building as is necessary. Third: Such a building should be large enough to contain permanent quarters for the various art societies centered in New York, together with galleries large enough to permit of simultaneous exhibitions by all the exhibiting Societies, on a larger scale than the present exhibitions, so that the output of the year in American Art may be seen at one time and place. These exhibitions would be held by various Societies under their own rules as to juries and admissions but, under an amicable arrangement, for one admission fee. Fourth: Such a building should be centrally situated, easy of access, with permanent and unobstructed light, and should have sufficient architectural beauty and monumental character to be an ornament to the city, and a fitting house of Art. Fifth: In view of the importance of Art education and culture to the community it seems fit that the city should be asked to supply the site for such a building and that private liberality be applied to for contributions toward the necessary funds for erection and maintenance. These propositions embody the intentions of the National Academy of Design. If they can be accepted by the other Art Societies of New York, the artists of the city will be in a position to make such a united demand upon the city authorities as can hardly be neglected. (Minutes)

While these proceedings were going on, a definite plan of agreement was formulated under the direction of Howard Russell Butler.

In 1906 the National Academy of Design united with the Society of American Artists, thereby enlarging its membership and at the same time liberalizing its Constitution. Its present desire is to carry still further the work then begun by bringing all the artists of New York into a form of union for a practical purpose. It abandons the intention it long held of securing a building for its own exclusive use and now proposes to devote its means and its prestige to the joint benefit of the art Societies of New York. It is fortunately able to contribute to this plan not only its proper share of the rental of the proposed building and a substantial amount toward a maintenance fund for running expenses thereof, but it recognizes the fact that none of the other societies is in so fortunate a position. (Minutes)

The Societies who were to sponsor the plan included: the National Academy of Design, founded in 1826; the American Water Color Society, founded in 1866; the American Institute of Architects, New York Chapter, founded in 1867; the Architectural League of New York, founded in 1881; the New York Water Color Club, founded in 1890; the National Sculpture Society, founded in 1893; the Municipal Art Society, founded in 1893; the Society of Beaux Arts Architects, founded in 1894; the Society of Mural Painters, founded in 1895; and the Society of Illustrators, founded in 1902.

The plan and agreement set forth in legal form the various terms and conditions pertaining to the project. The title was to be the National Academy Association. "All exhibition space shall be free of rent to the parties hereto, but in lieu thereof, all admission receipts shall belong to the said Association. . . . The expenses of hanging and arranging exhibits shall be borne by the parties making such exhibits." The Academy agreed to set apart on its books $200,000, to be designated as a maintenance endowment fund, the title thereof remaining in the National Academy of Design, but the interest thereon to be paid annually to the Association to be used for running expenses. Other sources of revenue would include the rental of the galleries when not in use for the combined annual exhibitions, the rental of permanent quarters to the cooperating Societies, the rental of rooms for lectures, and so on.

By the spring of 1912, "Howard Russell Butler reported that all the constituent Societies had signed and executed proper papers of agreement of the National Academy Association, and that the act of creating the

Charter had passed the Senate on the Eleventh of March and was to pass the assembly before the adjournment of the legislature." Although it had become evident that the municipal authorities would not grant city property, President John Alexander "stated that he was much encouraged by a prospect of obtaining a most desirable site." Meantime the constitution and by-laws of the National Academy Association were being prepared for presentation.

Harrison Morris, formerly director of the Pennsylvania Academy of Fine Arts, was engaged to promote the project; Howard Russell Butler was the leading spokesman for the Academy. A site adjacent to the Grand Central Terminal seemed assured but the plan was not consummated. George A. Hearn advocated the extension of the 57th Street property, offering $10,000, and a loan of $80,000. Unhappily, this generous benefactor passed away the year following his proposal.

John W. Alexander worked valiantly for the Association. He retired from the presidency in 1915, because of failing health. The Academy regretted the loss of his administrative guidance and was later saddened by the news of his death. He was succeeded by J. Alden Weir.

With the outbreak of the First World War in Europe, financial advisors warned that the time was not propitious for building. With the entrance of the United States into the war, all efforts were then devoted to furthering the national cause and the project was held in abeyance. In his address at the annual meeting of 1918, after stressing the effect of the war on the fine arts, President Weir stated for the council: "It was felt that any attempt at this time to push the project of the new building would be not only futile but unwise, and no effort has been put forth in this direction." The plan never fully revived. The realization of a noble aspiration to unite the arts in a common cause, for a common need, was still to be but a vision for the future.

Throughout its history the Academy had been invited to cooperate in the formation of international exhibitions. This was continued in 1908 when the Academy accepted the request "to take, decorate and hang a gallery with fifty paintings, water colors, black and white and sculpture, of representative works by American artists, to be selected under the supervision of the Academy" for the biennial exhibition at Venice. This complimentary solicitation, however, entailed considerable responsibility and expense.

With the beginning of the conflict in Europe there was no appreciable change in the Academy exhibitions, as indicated by the attendance and sales. To mark the ninetieth exhibition in 1915, the galleries were opened free to the public. The attendance rose to 38,618 as against 16,280 for the previous year. In the winter exhibition of the same year, 1,752 pictures were submitted to the jury; 158 works by members and 211 by non-members were placed; 14 works by Academicians and 16 by Associates were rejected. Again, this created much dissension. Commenting upon the subject at the meeting of academicians, President Weir stated:

In reference to the hanging of the Winter Academy of which I stand sponsor, I wish to say that the experiment, which, although I advocated it, was done at too great a sacrifice to those who had rights which were not considered. . . . Now, Gentlemen, many of us here today were revolutionists when we were outside this institution, who are reckoned now among the most conservative. . . . We want to be liberal, but not at the expense of the Academy. . . . Yet do not think that the Institution was inaugurated for any other reason than to uphold as high a standard in the Art as possible, and this first of all, and for that object this Institution must stand. (Minutes)

In the winter exhibition of 1917, 194 works in sculpture were received, of which 57 were placed. Of 309 pictures hung, 86 were exempt.

After America's entry into the war, the number of works received was considerably reduced. Attendance and sales dropped sharply. Every facility was bent to the needs of the war effort. In cooperation with the Liberty Loan Drive, stocks were transferred into war bonds aggregating $20,000. The annual dinner was canceled, and the sum of $1,000 appropriated for that purpose was donated to the Artists War Emergency Fund. The service flag showed 54 stars; later these increased to 78. The sons of many members were also "at the Front." The unique work of Abbott Thayer on *Protective Coloration in Animals* formed the basis of American camouflage techniques. Everett Warner, Charles Bittinger, and Frederick Waugh headed the War Camouflage Department in Washington. "War Targets," used as range finders, were voluntarily painted by many of the members. This system, adapted to indoor training for artillerymen, was not at the time officially recognized by the War Department. In England and Europe lithographic copies had provided means of large distribution. In America the training corps were obliged to use originals, some 130 or more being executed. The artists were instructed by army officers in regard to function and requirements. War posters were designed under the able direction of Charles Dana Gibson, without expense to the government. Weekly meetings were held at the Academy and Salmagundi Club for stimulating effort and to receive instruction.

On the conclusion of the war, the council could give its undivided consideration to the more immediate concerns of the Academy. The artists of the city marched as a unit in the victory parade. But this patriotic unity did not extend into the aesthetic differences that had been suspended during hostilities, augmented by the Russian revolution, and the social, as well as the political unrest that followed. The Armory Show preceding the war had let loose a bombshell, as if to foreshadow the actual combat. In Europe the art schools had been closed. Academic discipline and regulated instruction ceased. The American students in Paris had temporarily returned, but not without the brush being charged with a new kind of explosive. The Academy school and exhibitions continued as if nothing had happened to disturb their serenity. The aggressive dissidents of the 'eighties, now in control, were placed on the defensive.

Herbert Adams succeeded J. Alden Weir as president of the Academy in 1917. The ever-youthful spirit of the latter could not stay the hand of destiny. Failing health caused him to decline reelection. His great integrity and liberal understanding had transcended aesthetic differences. His death in 1919 was greatly lamented within and outside the Academy.

The most pressing problem was still lack of adequate exhibition space. But no progress had been made either in enlarging the American Fine Arts Society building or in raising funds to create a new center. The Academy Association, once so bright a prospect, had faded away as an unfulfilled dream. The unity of the artists made possible by the merger of the Academy with the Society of American Artists, was now made apparently impossible by the increasing opposition of new cults and tendencies. Artists had increased in unprecedented numbers, not alone in New York, but throughout the country. Works submitted to the Jury of the winter exhibition of 1922 totaled 1,827. These included painting, sculpture, and the graphic arts. Of these, only 553 could be placed. Nearly 1,000 paintings were rejected. Exhibition costs had likewise increased. In order to maintain the American Fine Arts Society, rental of the galleries had to be doubled. Printing costs of catalogues and other services rose accordingly. Other exhibitions held in the galleries did not have to carry the heavy burden of the Academy. Attendance diminished, as did sales. The annual deficit of the Academy exhibitions approached $10,000. This could not continue indefinitely, but there seemed no immediate remedy. A special committee was appointed to contrive means both of reducing expenses and changing the exhibition program. The report was brought before a special meeting of the members and freely discussed. The predominant thought was to endeavor to create a greater diversity between the winter exhibition and the annual exhibition. The constitution and the tradition of the Academy made it imperative to make the annual exhibition open to all contributors. The winter exhibition was not so conditioned. It was suggested that the winter exhibition should be limited to members only, but this was not sustained. The idea of group exhibitions was proposed, but possible favoritism caused its rejection. The special committee was dissolved, and the responsibility was assumed by the council. All suggested changes were blocked by the lack of space and funds. During this extended period, Francis C. Jones acted as treasurer. The Academy was fortunate in having such a competent administrator and guardian of its finances.

The maintenance of the school imposed an additional financial burden. After the war, the enrollment steadily increased without added matriculation fees. The care of the permanent collection of the Academy, including the works by members, as well as a vast collection of engravings, etchings, and numerous donations, was a department in itself, ably supervised by George W. Maynard. A regular librarian was employed to take charge of the library, the books being available for study by the students. The upward cost of models and studio properties augmented the annual deficit which increased to $6,000, a sum that would have maintained the school for many years at the time of its inception.

In the past, the substantial funds of the Academy were accumulated by the sale of its real estate and subscriptions to the fellowship fund. Now the latter was not augmented, while the major property held by the Academy at 109th Street had, owing to changed conditions in the neighborhood, greatly declined in value.

Herbert Adams presided over the Academy during the trials of the war period, and retired from office in 1920. His energy and executive ability, as well as his wide field of experience and knowledge, made him a worthy administrator. He was succeeded by Edwin Blashfield, who continued in office until 1926.

·XIII·

ART IN TURMOIL: "THE OLD GUARD" · THE AMERICAN TRADITION ·
WINSLOW HOMER · THOMAS EAKINS · "THE YOUNG RADICALS" ·
REALISM · END OF AN ERA

BY THE END of the nineteenth century, the invigorating influence of those artists who had matured in the 'eighties had been widely assimilated. The shock of innovation had passed. Although distinctive styles arose, the predominant trend was one of eclecticism. It represented a sophisticated aestheticism, with decorative rather than naturalistic significance. The predominant influence was a blending of the Whistlerian-Japanese linear-space conception with the *plein air* color of the French impressionists. From the extended panoramic vision in depth, which characterized the classical composition of the older painters, the angle of vision was reduced, the skyline raised. Scenic grandeur was no longer in fashion. The continent had been explored and depicted. The romanticism of uncultivated nature gave way to the near-by environment of intimate surroundings. The arrangement of subject matter and the immediacy of optical reaction became the theme of the painter.

Estranged from the new aesthetic conception, the remaining members of the old school lost the youthful inspiration of their early work, and repeated the traditional in uninspired but competent uniformity. Although Frederic E. Church lived until the end of the century, he had been crippled with arthritis, and produced little work after 1880. Albert Bierstadt lived until 1902, but his name had passed into history; Jasper Cropsey, who achieved fulfillment early in his work, was no longer exhilarated by fresh discovery; he continued to paint what the new generation dubbed "chromos." John Bristol passed away in 1909. J. G.

Brown worked through the first decade of the new century. On returning from the Pan-American Exposition at Buffalo in 1902, a fellow Academician boasted "that there were more people standing before my picture
than any other artist except one. The only trouble was, they all had
their backs to my picture and were looking at J. G. Brown's." Samuel Colman lived until 1920, but devoted much of his thought to his masterful
work entitled, *Nature's Law of Harmonic Unity*. He was thus, unsuspecting, a pioneer of the analytical movement that was to follow. Gilbert Gaul
was a forgotten name, though he lived until 1919. An old acquaintance,
meeting him without recognition, was startled to hear him say, "You
don't remember me. I *was* Gilbert Gaul." E. L. Henry continued to
paint until 1919, his early work unremembered, himself classified as one
of the "old fogies." His *Waiting for the Train* now hangs in the Metropolitan Museum, a historical documentation of great veracity. William
Magrath, whose early work showed great integrity and competence,
died in London in 1918. *On the Old Sod,* also in the Metropolitan,
attests his distinction. Charles Miller continued to exhibit. One of the
first Americans to study in Munich, he was looked upon as a remnant
of a past age. Thomas Moran, one of the stalwarts, prospered in old age
as the classic painter of the romantic West. James C. Nicoll, so popular
in the 'seventies and 'eighties, lived until 1918. E. Wood Perry, elected
an Academician in 1869, one of the active and constructive figures in the
institution, a close friend of Winslow Homer, died in 1915. His pictures
were favorites in many homes. Walter Shirlaw, elected an Academician
in 1888, the first president of the Society of American Artists, so brilliant
in the Munich period, lost the virility of his early promise; his was a name
highly respected at his passing in 1909, but with no further projection.
James Smillie and his brother George, both prominent in water color
and etching as well as painting, lived to see the new century, but the
heyday of their popularity had passed. Worthington Whittredge, one
of the masters of American landscape, found his work neglected. Of
utmost integrity and technical ability, he was saddened in his later life
when his work was labeled "Hudson River school," an appellation which
he declared in his autobiography to have been given in derision by an
art critic of the New York *Tribune*. T. W. Wood, former president of
both the Academy and the American Water Color Society, also passed
the turn of the century. In his early work he explored the homely

domestic scene with telling characterization and discovered the pictorial possibilities of negro life in the South. Daniel Huntington, the dean of portrait painters, a personality of sound and liberal judgment, was ignored by the younger generation. Huntington and Eastman Johnson died in the same year, the year of the union of the Society of American Artists with the Academy. Johnson had been active in both organizations, and was highly respected as one of the pioneers of American genre, as well as a distinguished portraitist.

In his annual address, President Dielman paid tribute to these eminent masters of American painting by saying,

No events that we might be called upon to chronicle could signalize more clearly the fact that we are standing on the border of a new era in our National Art, none could symbolize more forcibly the passing of the old, the advent of a new order, than did the departure from our midst of our veterans and leaders—Eastman Johnson and Daniel Huntington. . . . It is all the more significant falling in the year that has brought with it striking features in the development—adapting it to new conditions—of that institution with the growth of which both men were so long and intimately associated. . . . Reaching the age of eighty-two Eastman Johnson never did grow old; he retained ever his interest in younger men and their work, and gave them generous recognition. . . . [Daniel Huntington, in his ninetieth year] "treasured the memory of a day in his childhood on which he visited the studio of an artist who had moved among and painted the men and events of the Revolution, retaining a vivid impression of the dignified appearance, the courteous, old-time manner of its occupant—John Trumbull. (Minutes)

Although in their old age the work of these artists who had attained distinction in early life was by-passed with changes of aesthetic fashions, the deep undercurrent of the American tradition persisted. It was not until the first decade of the new century that the work of two of the most representative American painters became universally proclaimed, although both artists were then in declining years, their lifework accomplished.

Winslow Homer and Thomas Eakins were contemporaries, but their ways did not cross. Born in 1836, Homer was eight years the senior of Eakins. The work of the two men was utterly dissimilar in style and intention. Decided individualists, they had one fundamental trait in common; both lived and experienced the life they depicted. Uninfluenced by the eclectic movement springing from France, Homer and Eakins represent the basic integrity of the American tradition, derived from the environment in which they lived. Not given to self-promotion or social popularity, each artist realized the deep significance of visual reality. Both were decided realists, in the deeper significance of that word, which implies a conscious affinity with the subject pictured. Homer projected his invigorating leaven into the future. Eakins was the culmination of a long tradition. Conceiving his theme in three dimensional form, he depicted the envelopment of light as the revelation of structural embodiment. It was this realization that attuned his art to the younger men of the new century and to their reaction against the atmospheric vagueness and optical illusion of the *plein air* school. Both Homer and Eakins were essentially masculine in their materialistic conception, making no compromise with the more ingratiating appeal of feminine allure. The light and dark extension of the palette was incompatible with the high key of the impressionists. Values were registered in the terms of black and white rather than coloristic modulation and complementary vibration. Homer used contrast dramatically, light against dark; Eakins used contrast structurally

Homer was made an Associate of the Academy in 1864 and an Academician the following year, at the age of twenty-nine. His early work as an illustrator left a lasting influence on his pictorial conception. He first worked as a wood engraver in Boston. On his arrival in New York in 1859, he occupied a studio in the New York University building in Washington Square. Eastman Johnson had then but recently established his studio in the same building and, as a mature artist, was the most highly recognized genre painter of the period. His pictures of life in the South had popularized his fame. Homer was a familiar figure in the artistic fraternity centering around the Square. John La Farge was an intimate friend, as was Homer Martin; but the three men, though sympathetically related, were too individualistic to have a common aesthetic goal.

With the outbreak of the Civil War, Homer was commissioned by *Harper's Weekly* to make illustrations of events at the front. The pictures resulting from this experience established his distinction as a painter as well as illustrator. Homer had the satisfaction of seeing his *Prisoners from the Front* included in the Paris Exposition of 1867. It seems strange to envision Homer in a studio in Montmartre, and there is little influence in his work of the French sojourn.

It is characteristic of Homer's individuality and art that he made no repeat performances. He might well have augmented his success in continuing to paint his memories of the war or his very accomplished compositions of negro life in the South. But Homer was a visualist and worked from direct impression. His pictures follow the changes of scene—Gloucester, the Adirondacks, Houghten Farm—all intimate impressions of personal experience imbued with individual identification with his subject and formulated in the terms of his art. His portrayals of the coast of England and fisher life at Tynemouth in the early 'eighties, formed a transitional period, with a deliberate attempt at picture making in water color. Although winning recognition and sales, it was not the manner which Homer was to follow.

The practice of working in water color as a means of direct expression was, however, to create Homer's style. It was this abbreviated dramatization, combined with lifelong introspection, that resulted in the masterpieces of his final period.

The familiar portrait of the recluse was but a mask for his personal protection and uncompromising independence. To the fisher folk at Prout's Neck, where he retired in the early 'eighties, he was familiarly know as "Win." He was always a friend to those in need. His father and brothers had large holdings in the growing summer resort, in which Homer shared. When the summer colony departed at the end of the season, Homer was in his real element.

Homer exhibited annually at the Academy until his retirement from the city. When *Gulf Stream* was exhibited at the Academy in 1906, Homer already had been acclaimed as the foremost realist of American painting. When the picture was presented to the jury, the chairman was so impressed that he wrote enthusiastically to the director of the Metropolitan Museum, and in response, the picture was at once purchased for that institution.

Homer was not a member of the Society of American Artists, but he exhibited there in 1896 at the invitation of his old friend, John La Farge, then president of the Society. In the exhibition of 1903, his striking picture, *Early Morning after a Storm at Sea,* was poorly hung in the small gallery and drew unfavorable criticism. Homer was deeply offended and did not exhibit at the Society of American Artists again.

Thomas Eakins devoted much of his mature life to teaching. His early training under Gérôme suited his nature completely. The exacting discipline and insistence on the fundamental laws of construction conformed to his methodical and scientific predilection, an interest which endured throughout his career. Never an ingratiating or popular painter, his art portrayed his intimate associations—portraits of friends or admired personalities, youthful scenes of outdoor activity, hunting, sailing, rowing, and sports that revealed masculine virility. He was more concerned with material facts than with passing effects. His special interest in anatomy drew him to the dissecting rooms and the hospitals of Philadelphia, resulting in the much discussed masterpieces, the *Gross Clinic* and the *Agnew Clinic*.

Eakins's uneventful life was passed in the surroundings of his father's home in Philadelphia, in which he was reared and died. He was not a familiar figure in New York, although he instructed the class in anatomy at the Academy school for many years. He had already exhibited at the Academy from time to time when his impressive self-portrait qualified him as an Associate member. The large picture, the *Wrestlers*, was presented when he was made an Academician in 1902. Elected a member of the Society of American Artists, where his *Gross Clinic* had won him honored acclaim, he later resigned after his work had been refused by the jury on three successive occasions.

Eakins's teaching and art stood like an enduring rock against the ever-changing waves of impressionism. In Philadelphia a small group of students, then venturing in illustration, gathered together for sketching and an exchanging of ideas. Robert Henri, somewhat older and more experienced, was the painter of the group. All were interested in the city scene rather than the fleeting effects of landscape. Henri, Glackens, Everett Shinn, and John Sloan moved to New York. Gradually their work appeared in exhibitions. Everett Shinn held a one-man show of pastels, street scenes in winter, impulsive, impressive, immersed in city mood, spontaneous in execution. Henri went to Paris. More sophisticated, his technical talent responded to the flat brushwork of Manet and Hals; the insistence was on planes, rather than the atmospheric envelopment of broken color. Sloan and Glackens followed the call of illustration, giving humanistic interpretations of city life, the passing crowd, the café and music hall, all expressed in vitalized line, reminiscent of Cruikshank, Rowlandson, and the racy English illustrators who worked before the advent of the camera and the halftone. Realism was revitalized. Painting was an exciting recreation, with no eye on the picture mart. Others of like persuasion joined the group which was to become known as the "Eight." They adhered to no aesthetic program or "ism," but were held together by the cementing bond of sincerity: there was Ernest Lawson, with his opulent, unctuous brush, an intuitive colorist and vital impressionist; George Luks, selecting his models to echo his mood, a painter of impetuous virility and penetrating characterization. The "Eight" gave but one united show at Macbeth's; the youthful exuberance departing, each was to follow his own way. Henri became a dominant influence as a teacher, inspiring many of the new generation with the significance of vitalized living and daring. Black was restored to the palette; atmospheric harmonies were renounced; contrast of light and dark was dramatized; and the picture plane was moved forward. Before the advent of "abstraction," the American scene had become the vogue.

John Sloan was a consistent individualist. Deeply immersed in the problem of social welfare, he was a profound humanitarian, and his awareness was illumined by both the pathos and the humor of the unsuspected moment. Sloan exhibited at the Academy between 1906 and 1909; but after 1909 he ceased to submit his work and later declined nomination. Believing in equality of opportunity, he organized the Society of Independent Artists in 1917, with the slogan of, "No Jury, No Prizes." Where anyone could exhibit on payment of a fee, without consideration of merit, the exhibitions were naturally miscellaneous. This experiment in the freedom of artistic expression was justifiable, but it gradually faded away. Glackens became absorbed in coloristic experimentation, flavored by Renoir, and the exhilaration of spirited visual impression. Everett Shinn continued his initial urge, in sketches of the fantasy of city life, the ever-moving crowd, and the haunting nostalgia of an unknown rendezvous. Robert Henri, an active force in the Society of American Artists, was voted an Academician in 1906. Ernest Lawson was elected in 1917, William Glackens in 1933, Everett Shinn in 1943.

The work of the youthful George Bellows made an immediate im-

pression; he was the right man at the right moment. His frank, unin-
hibited nature brought to his painting a natural vitality. His impressionable sensibility and intuitive power of absorption were augmented by
intense concentration and the faculty of visual dramatization. Jay
Hambidge, the analytical theorist, entered the artistic arena at this time,
and Henri and Bellows became eagerly absorbed in the architectonic and
geometric structure underlying composition. This had a decisive influence on Bellows's picture planning, far removed from theoretical
"abstraction," but forming the structure of realistic dramatization and
compositional integration. Bellows was honored by the highest awards
in the profession and was elected an Academician in 1913. His early death
was a greatly lamented loss.

Realism and impressionism reinvigorated painting and extended the
artist's field of observation. Method and technique had been transformed.
The artist stood before his easel, viewing his work at long range; the
mechanism of the brush was from the arm, not from the wrist. The
artist worked directly before the subject, the brush obeyed the eye with
spontaneous precision. The preliminary lay-in was in mass, not in line.
Pigment quality was valued more than "finish," carrying power more
than naturalistic detail.

The opening years of the new century witnessed great changes in
city life. In the age of steel the "skyscraper" was to accent perpendicular
contours. Apartments were taking the place of private houses. The
moneyed barons from the West, building on upper Fifth Avenue, broke
the deadline of 59th Street. At night the city was resplendent with light.
In the galleries electric lighting outmoded the ingratiating effects of
chiaroscuro. The honk of the motor horn drowned the more familiar
hoofbeat. Speed transformed the time sense. The mechanization of the
robot age was dawning.

The foreign population in New York had increased immeasurably,
each nationality congregating in a separate quarter of the lower city.
With little or no understanding of the American tradition but discontented with their homeland, the new immigrants arrived with visions of a
land of plenty. Living in the slums, their dream unrealized, many gave
eager ear to the promises of socialism. Greenwich Village had become
a center of young intellectuals. Writers, artists, adventurers, strays from
all parts of the country championed the cause of the underprivileged,

of whom indeed they were a part. In the day of the "muckrakers," the common foe was the captain of industry and the capitalist. The novelists found new themes in the tragedy of the impoverished and exploited; the artists discovered their subjects in the underworld and on the streets of the foreign settlements. The old New Yorker was passing. Traditional culture was taboo. Reality was equated with the masses. Squalor was thought more realistic than luxury.

This new milieu directly affected the artists' ideology and temperament. The "pretty" picture had become effete and effeminate. The palette changed from light prismatic scintillation to the opaque tones of the lower register. Direct impasto was considered more masculine and forthright than broken color and illusionistic vibration. Solidity, volume, carrying power became the new clichés. Manet replaced Monet. Thus the opening years of the new social revolution had its response in the arts, starting the trend which was to promote the differentiation between the so-called "progressives" and "conservatives," a division which was to be accentuated in the years that followed. Unsympathetic toward the Academy, the radicals nevertheless largely made their early reputations on the walls of its exhibitions. It is ironic to observe that, with repeated innovations, the "progressives" of the period are now overshadowed by the "moderns" who followed.

Less influenced by the radicals of city germination, the landscape painters retreated to the country. Many of the resorts now renowned for their art colonies found their inception in this formative period. Birge Harrison discovered Woodstock and established a growing class of talented pupils. His work in teaching was to be continued by John Carlson, followed by the "modernists" of a later generation. Eugene Speicher was an early summer resident and remains the dean of the colony. Edward Redfield, Daniel Garber, William Lathrop, Robert Spencer settled at New Hope, Pennsylvania, later to be joined by John Folinsbee and Harry Leith-Ross, who had migrated from Woodstock.

Gloucester had for many years attracted artists. Before the coming of motor power, the harbor was peaked with sails. John Twachtman was to paint his last pictures there at the beginning of the century. But it was not until the summer classes started that easels were seen everywhere. Provincetown was but a scattered village with a single boardwalk in the early days of Charles W. Hawthorne. His large class brought it growing popularity, while the Provincetown Players introduced the Greenwich Village element. Winslow Homer created interest in the Maine coast. George Bellows and Rockwell Kent were flavored by his austere realism. A group of young Academicians and members of the Society visiting friends at Prout's Neck on their way to Ogunquit wished to pay their respects to the old master. On being informed of this, Homer replied that he did not care to meet any enthusiastic young students. The party included Bruce Crane, Edward Potthast, Walter Clark, Will H. Drake, and the author, then but a boy.

Connecticut had always been a near-by haunt for New York painters. Outcropping rocks and stone fences accentuated the contours of friendly hills. Weir painted at Branchville, where he had his summer studio. Twachtman remodeled an old house outside Greenwich. His winter landscapes were painted there, and the familiar waterfall was in his back yard. As New York extended its boundaries and suburban life encroached, the artists likewise moved onward. Before the coming of the motor, the painter's range was limited to his immediate vicinity. The Griswold House at Old Lyme proved a hospitable rendezvous. Henry Ranger, William Howe, Carleton Wiggins, Willard Metcalf, Childe Hassam, and Frank Vincent DuMond worked there in the early days of the century. With the growing art colony and summer classes, the senior artists sought more secluded pastures. Henry Ranger established his studio at Noank, Connecticut, where across the inlet on Mason's Island he found his subjects in the golden glow of autumn oaks or springtime trees in early leaf. Charles H. Davis had long been resident at near-by Mystic, now the center of a summer colony and an art gallery. The Housatonic Valley is a natural painters' habitat. Willard Metcalf worked near Danbury, Ben Foster at Cornwall Bridge, Luis Mora at Gaylordsville, while Robert Nisbet remains the dean of the group at Kent. Frederick Waugh lived at Kent in the 'twenties. He had remodeled an old farm house in a sequestered valley and at the time had decided to renounce the sea. A master craftsman with tools, he transformed the large barn into a studio and became absorbed in painting spirit pictures which he envisioned in dreams. He also collected gnarled roots of ancient cedars and wrote and illustrated a book entitled *Gnomes*, which foreshadowed the cult of modernistic sculptured form. A voyage to the West Indies revived his interest in the sea and tropical waves drowned the evanescent spirits of dream. He was renowned for his masterful marines, and dealers would have no other subjects from his brush. Nearer the sea, at Province-town, where he passed his later days, his pictures with their vivid visualization and brilliant manipulation of paint never lost their vigorous improvisation. The Kent Art Association was organized during this period with Robert Nisbet as president and Spencer Nichols, George Laurence Nelson, and Eliot Clark among the founding members.

At Dover Plains, across the hills from Kent, William Howe found models in his cattle, which likewise attracted Glenn Newell, while the winter landscape appealed to Harry Waltman and Arthur Powell.

Walter Clark was first to paint at the little village of Chadds Ford, Pennsylvania, the headquarters of Washington and Lafayette during the battle of the Brandywine. For several seasons during the spring and autumn he was joined by Bolton Jones, Edward Potthast, Will H. Drake, and Eliot Clark. Howard Pyle later conducted his class in illustration there, the old military headquarters being converted into studios. Among his pupils was N. C. Wyeth, who was to make his home there, and it is there also that his son, Andrew Wyeth, continues his brilliant career.

After the adventurous days of the "Wild West" and its scenic dis-covery, painters returned to the secluded habitations of the Indian villages. Ernest Blumenschein was lured to Taos, to be followed by E. I. Couse, Walter Ufer, Victor Higgins, and others who have given celebrity to the colony. Santa Fe, one of the oldest settlements on the continent, was to become more modern. John Sloan was a summer resident for many years, and other easterners, both writers and painters, found in its old-world charm a captivating and enlarging experience. Albert Groll revealed the fleeting effects of cloud formation and evanescent color of desert expanse, while William R. Leigh recorded the life and country of the Navajos.

Edward Redfield was the "strong arm" in landscape painting. His large canvases, made at one standing, have a singleness of impression, enforced by the immediacy of visual reaction, and technical intensity of improvised brushwork. Unlike many of his contemporaries, he did not make small sketches. His robust nature demanded a large surface. Redfield introduced a new vision in the painting of winter landscape, entirely free from subjective association, truly American in its forthright presentation of the local scene. His initiative started a vogue which many were to follow. The brilliancy of sunlight on snow made a telling note on the Academy walls. Gardner Symons popularized the motive with masterly command of the medium, an authentic interpretation of the scintillating glamor of snow magic. Elmer Schofield, more reserved, was essentially a painter's painter. His brush stroke has a controlled significance, the composition its just relation, the flat surface its intentioned effect. The general trend of the era was away from introspection, imagination, or the overtones of sentimental association. The keynote was visual realism and technical virtuosity.

In portraiture John Singer Sargent was the dominant international personality of his generation. Born in Florence, of American parents, he as a youth of seventeen entered the studio of Carolus Duran, and at once demonstrated his precocious talent. The facile technique, the fluid paint, and seeming ease of execution marked his own signature from the start; but behind this instinctive awareness, the vision and aesthetic understanding were united. Before the Sargent manner became commonplace through imitation, his work was a revelation in the possibilities of fresh paint. His subjects are never arrested in static pose, or calculated prearrangements. The composition is born from the impact of the personality, the naturalness of pose and surrounding milieu.

In the age of Boldini, Ziem, Madrozo, and Rico, Sargent was never seduced by the bait of best sellers. His pictures of the streets of Venice, or courtyard with figures, are unforgettable memories of place and character, interpreted with aesthetic as well as visual sensitiveness— the magic of the painter's temperament. Sargent had a remarkable sense of objectivity; he stood apart from his subject, quite above flattery, and yet with a penetrating understanding of character. He cannot rightly be superficially labeled as being superficial. If his influence was unhappy in his innumerable followers, he remains the master of his metier and of his time. Water color added to his recreation in travel. A consummate master of the medium, he by selection and elimination illumines his chosen subject, unobserved by others. In the era of analytical dissection which followed, his work remains unclouded in spirit, with the rare fragrance of an enlightened vision. Sargent presented his self-portrait when made an Associate of the Academy, and a portrait of his friend, Monet, when he qualified as an Academician in 1897.

William Merritt Chase was likewise symptomatic of his time. His pictures reflect his personality. Enthusiastic and receptive, he encouraged and furthered talent wherever he encountered it. As a teacher, his radiation was contagious, starting many of our gifted painters on a brilliant career. Somewhat fastidious, but discerning, his judgment was discriminating and sound. A master of still life, in which he could display the bravura of brushwork, his style was, nevertheless, flexible. In his studio interiors he combined creative arrangement with the intimate charm of family life. The many portraits by Chase in the permanent collection of the Academy, as contrasted to his official portraits, are among his happiest achievements. Chase, as we have seen, was one of the leaders of the Society of American Artists, but he had been prominently represented in the Academy before the birth of the younger institution, and remained one of its most brilliant contributors. He was elected an Academician in 1890.

Several of the distinguished Academicians had established their permanent residence abroad, and were placed on the absent list, thus allowing, at the time, an extension of the number of resident Academicians. Among the most prominent were Elihu Vedder, Edwin Abbey, Frederic Bridgman, Alexander Harrison, and Gari Melchers.

Elihu Vedder was as unique in personality as in his art. Entirely uninfluenced by contemporary trends, as an individual his vision was contemplative and profound. Retiring to Rome in 1866, on his occasional visits to New York he regaled his intimates at the Century Club, and enlarged his garrulous dissertations in his *Digressions of V.* In an era when realism was in vogue, Vedder found his natural expression in subjects of symbolical allusion. Born in 1836 and living until 1923, he produced comparatively little during his long life. His illustrations for the *Rubáiyát,* so sympathetic to his nature, enlarged his recognition, although the *Lair of the Sea Serpent* and the *Lost Mind* had previously indicated his imaginative trend. His understanding of significant form made his style particularly adapted to mural decoration, and he was happy in receiving several commissions, among them his work in the Congressional Library. Vedder was made an Academician in 1865 at the early age of twenty-nine.

The art of Edwin Austin Abbey may properly be divided in two major periods, both in regard to style and medium. Before his departure for England, he was known for his illustrations and etching. In this genre his work is highly sensitive and utterly charming, imbued with aesthetic imagination and wrought with consummate craftsmanship.

In the later period, when he worked in London, his art in painting is associated with the murals commissioned in America, his historical episodes, and his portrayal of the Coronation of King Edward VII. Working in color on a large scale involved problems, the solution of which was not inherent in his early training. His painting is entirely consistent within its premise, and, being definitely illustrative, achieves its intended purpose, but may lack that monumental and significant simplification which relates the mural to its architectural setting and the distance from which it is to be seen. In his American period Abbey was closely associated with his fellow craftsmen, and was one of the members of the Tile Club, the records and illustrations of which appeared in *Harper's Weekly* and later in book form. The club was one of the last offshoots of that fraternal conviviality and cooperation reminiscent of the Old Sketch Club, and the original New York Drawing Association. Abbey is represented in the permanent collection of the Academy by his portrait, painted by John Alexander, and by a study for a mural presented when he was made an Academician in 1902. He was greatly honored in London, where his sepulchre in St. Paul's Church is beside that of his renowned contemporary, John Singer Sargent.

Frederic Bridgman and Alexander Harrison both studied under Gérôme, and were thus accomplished draftsmen, but in their work they followed quite separate ways. The former found his subjects, as his master had done, in Algeria and the Near East; the latter responded to the visual discoveries of Bastien-Lepage and naturalistic impression. Both artists were honored in the salons of Paris, as well as in the Academy, becoming noted exponents of the art of their time. Harrison was an innovator in the revelation of light, and its naturalistic effects, as well as a sensitive craftsman. His later work, in twilight mood, of waves in elongated rhythm, breaking on the beach, have never been surpassed. A subject new at the time of its inception, it has since become banal by endless repetition.

American painters working in Paris and London established a decided prestige, not merely as followers of a current trend, but as rightful leaders in their profession.

Gari Melchers found his subjects in Holland, painted not in the popular mode of Israels, and others of the Dutch school, but seen in the light of his own personality, without sentimental association. Decidedly masculine, his brush is authoritative, his creative conception related definitely to his medium, without the overtones of ingratiating allure. Returning in later life to live in Virginia, he served occasionally on the juries of the Academy, where his sound judgment was always respected. He was elected an Academician in 1906.

At the beginning of the century, new names appear in the catalogues of the Academy, many of which were to add renown to American painting. Artists were still specialists in their chosen field. Landscape dominated the exhibitions, reaching the culmination of realistic illusion with a truly local American significance. The old religious reverence of nature had passed. Thomas Cole would have considered the blatant effect and improvised brushwork a desecration of nature's shrine. Our painters responded to optical impression rather than contemplative reverie. There was, nevertheless, great diversity of expression and individuality in the work of Edward Redfield, Robert Spencer, Daniel Garber, Hobart Nichols, Albert Groll, Gardner Symons, Charles Davis, Elmer Schofield, Chauncey Ryder and others too numerous to enumerate. Portraiture attained freedom and freshness of expression in the work of Wayman Adams, John Johansen, Sidney Dickinson, Leopold Seyffert, and Louis Betts. Figure painting witnessed a revival with new significance and individuality. Charles W. Hawthorne, Eugene Higgins, George Bellows, Robert Henri, Eugene Speicher, Leon Kroll, Maurice Sterne, made their debut in the Academy in the first quarter of the century, and were to become Academicians. Gifford Beal vitalized landscape with figures. A strong group of visualists depicted the sea with realistic vigor and dramatic effect: Frederick Waugh, Howard Russell Butler, Paul Dougherty, William Ritschel, occupied places of honor on the Academy walls. The list of artists first appearing at the Academy dominated the exhibitions from the Atlantic to the Pacific.

The large galleries of the American Fine Arts Society prompted artists to execute large canvases for striking effect, with a view to prize awards. The small anecdotal picture of an earlier generation had become old-fashioned. But in the meantime the private house was disappearing, apartments had little wall space, museums were becoming overcrowded, gifts were more carefully considered. The broad technique of the exhibition picture was not suitable to small dimensions.

·XIV·

THE SISTER ARTS: ARCHITECTURE · SCULPTURE · ENGRAVING · ETCHING

At the time of the founding of the Academy, the "arts of design," other than painting, were little developed or practiced. Architecture, sculpture, and the graphic arts had in consequence comparatively few representatives in the early membership of the Academy. The exhibitions were devoted almost entirely to painting as the preceding chapters indicate.

At the opening of the nineteenth century there were few professionally trained architects in America and little public demand for their service. In domestic architecture the owner collaborated with the builder who followed the traditions of his craft.

Jefferson, after his return from France, considered American architecture uncultured. Imbued with the spirit of the classical revival, he conceived architecture in the grand style, founded upon the Romans and the plans of Palladio. Governor Clinton, in his presidential address before the American Academy, alluded to Jefferson, saying, "Although I am not prepared to go the whole length with a distinguished countryman, and to say that the genius of architecture seems to have shed his maledictions over our land, yet it must be admitted that too little attention and encouragement have been given this important art." (Cummings)

Although the Academy was conceived of as a school of instruction and a means of exhibiting contemporary works of art, the architect, although an integral practitioner of the arts of design, had little opportunity of exhibiting his works, his creation being the building itself! No school of architecture had been inaugurated. The helpful and needful function of the architect as a member of the Academy was to be in extending the conception of the visual arts, particularly in their relation to sculpture and mural painting, as well as in constructively participating in the wider field of administration and the fraternity of artists.

Of the founding members of the Academy, only two were architects—Ithiel Town and Martin Thompson. With the exception of several Honorary Members, including Charles Bulfinch, architect of the national Capitol, and Alexander Jackson Davis, elected an Associate in 1828, this number was not to be extended until the beginning of the twentieth century.

The firm of Town and Davis, possibly the first to organize in the profession, were of conspicuous service in promoting a knowledge of architecture, not only by the important buildings that they planned, but by means of their comprehensive collection of drawings and lithographs of the architecture in New York City. The immense library which Mr. Town assembled, including most of the major works on architecture, painting, and sculpture published in Europe, formed the first comprehensive source of reference established in America. The firm designed many of the important public buildings and churches of the period, including the state capitols of Connecticut, Indiana, North Carolina; the city hall at Hartford, Connecticut; the customs house, New York; the patent office, Washington; the Merchants' Exchange, Clinton Hall, and the Astor Hotel in New York, as well as many prominent residences and churches in the city.

The architects to be elected at the opening of the new century dominated the architecture of the period. The first was Charles F. McKim in 1907, followed by Cass Gilbert, W. R. Mead, John Carrère, Thomas Hastings, Henry Bacon, George Post, John R. Pope, Bertram Goodhue, and Walter Cook. Charles A. Platt, elected in 1911, might equally have been represented in other arts which he practiced with distinction, notably etching. The architects have, therefore, added greatly to the honor roll of Academicians.

Since the first two decades of the century, the membership representing architecture has increased considerably, now numbering 23 Academicians and 16 Associates. Two architects have been elected presidents of the Academy: Cass Gilbert and Lawrence Grant White.

Sculpture, as a profession, was practically nonexistent in America prior to the founding of the National Academy. The few commemorative commissions were given to the celebrated Houdon: the imposing Washington at the state capitol in Richmond, and the busts of John Paul Jones and Robert Fulton, the first casts from which are in the permanent collection of the Academy.

The fanatical Giuseppe Ceracchi, renowned as a sculptor in Europe, fired by the French Revolution and the turbulent spirit of "freedom," arrived in America in 1791 with the express purpose of executing a monument to Liberty. In view of gaining favor with the government, the sculptor executed marble busts of Washington and other statesmen, including Hamilton, Jefferson, John Paul Jones, and John Jay. His model for a statue of Liberty, receiving the praise of Washington, was presented to Congress for consideration, but the magnitude of its design and the estimated cost of its execution caused Congress to decline the project. Failing in his endeavor, the unhappy Ceracchi returned to Paris where, becoming implicated in a plot to assassinate Napoleon, he was condemned to the guillotine in 1801. It was this Ceracchi who had joined with Peale in organizing the exhibition and school of art known as the Columbianum. (Dunlap)

Although antique sculpture was held in veneration, there was no opportunity for an American sculptor to obtain commissions or any means of learning the craft. Its native birth grew from the instinct to carve in wood, making toys, emblems, and figureheads for ships, as well as mortuary designs in stone. William Rush thus developed as one of our first American sculptors. His professional occupation was in ship carving, which was then much in demand. "When in a hurry he used to hire a wood chopper, and stand by and give directions where to cut; by this means he facilitated work with little labor to himself." (Dunlap) Perhaps his friend Ceracchi inspired him to attempt other subjects, when time would permit. His symbolic *Water Nymph* excited much attention, in particular when it became known that the sculptor had used as his living model one of the lovely young ladies of the community, the story of which suggested Thomas Eakins' several pictures of *Rush Carving His Allegorical Figure of the Schuylkill River*. Rush also executed busts of several venerated personalities, including Linnaeus and Washington, and thus initiated portraiture in American sculpture. As all of his work was executed in wood, the originals have perished. Fortunately the *Water Nymph* was later cast in bronze.

The importation of casts from the Louvre and their relation to the classical revival was of paramount significance. This ideal was, in a nebulous way, associated with Independence. Its immediate result was, however, in introducing the method of instruction in drawing from the cast, rather than the living model.

The only sculptor included among the founders of the Academy was John Frazee. Evidently no others in New York were known. The life story of Frazee is a typical example of the trials and vicissitudes facing one who aspired to be a sculptor in early America. Dunlap records that when a boy "his [Frazee's] principal amusement, when not at work, was to cut the forms of familiar objects out of boards and shingles, and to chalk figures on the doors. His reward for these efforts was to have his ears boxed, and the prediction that he would be a limner." Being apprenticed to a bricklayer, he was obliged, in addition, to wait at the bar of the tavern, of which his employer was the proprietor. His technical skill was first exhibited when he inscribed on the foundation stone of a bridge, the name of its builder and the date—1808. This was the first work in stone of the eighteen-year-old future sculptor. The success of this effort encouraged him to become a stonecutter. Entering into partnership with his brother in New York, he established a firm of marble works, executing mortuary memorials and mantelpieces. His first attempt in the round was a copy of a bust of Franklin, followed by a portrait of his mother, which was shown in the first exhibition of the Academy.

The history of sculpture in America, as in the other arts, begins with the demand for the product, and the opportunity of livelihood. With America's winning independence, came the desire to see the heroes of the Revolution and the eminent statesmen of the time immortalized in marble. John Frazee was one of the first American sculptors to work in this exacting material. His important works included portrait busts of Chief Justice John Marshall, John Jay, and Daniel Webster. Seven portraits were commissioned for the Boston Athenaeum. Frazee lived until 1852 and thus witnessed the growth of an art of which, in America, he was one of the founders.

Like their predecessors in painting, the sculptors who were to follow sought the most favorable environment and sources of instruction. The excavations in Pompeii and the scholarly work of Winckelmann and others of the classical revival stimulated world interest in "the glory that was Greece and the grandeur that was Rome." Italy, particularly Rome, became the mecca of American sculptors.

Horatio Greenough occupies much the same place in Early American sculpture that Washington Allston does in painting, both being venerated in their respective arts. In fact, the elder artist was to form the mind of the youthful sculptor and guide him on his way. This led to Rome where, at twenty years of age, Greenough arrived in 1825. In a letter to Dunlap, the sculptor writes: "Allston . . . was to me a father in what concerned my progress of every kind. . . . So adapted did he seem to kindle me, making me no longer myself but, as it were, an emanation of his own soul." If Allston was his spiritual guide, James Fenimore Cooper was his practical one. Recognizing his talent and realizing his need, the writer commissioned Greenough to execute a group in the round suggested by a detail of angelic children in Raphael's *Madonna del Trono*. Apart from his own fancy, Cooper thought that the subject would have greater appeal than the more austere work of Michelangelo, in which the sculptor was then absorbed. It was this work, *Chanting Cherubs*, said to be the first group executed in marble by an American sculptor, that was exhibited at the Academy in 1832, and that drew the much discussed criticism from "Modestus" about the nudity of the children. In gaining recognition for his friend, Cooper had in mind proposing to the federal government that a statue of Washington by an American artist be placed in the Capitol. Upon the recommendation of influential friends in the government, the commission was given to Greenough. Double life-size, Washington is portrayed seated, the torso nude, the limbs draped in formal folds. For those who had conceived of the hero being on horseback or in military accoutrement, the statue, although praised by the sophisticated, was a shocking surprise, and was the object of much ridicule from the general public.

Cooper persuaded Lafayette to sit for Greenough, the General requesting that the novelist be present. Samuel Morse, being in Paris at the time, also attended several sittings, the triumvirate of Americans thus paying homage to the great French patriot and the memory of Washington. The portrait was considered a more living likeness than the formal bust executed by David d'Angers. "As Lafayette himself expressed it,

THE JURY OF SELECTION FOR THE ANNUAL EXHIBITION, 1907

FRONT: *Samuel Isham; Robert Henri; Francis Luis Mora; Kenyon Cox; Frederick Dielman; Irving Ramsay Wiles; Hugh Bolton Jones; Charles Yardley Turner.* BACK: *Edward Henry Potthast; William Henry Howe; Henry Bayley Snell; Carlton Theodore Chapman; Elliott Daingerfield; Frederick George Richard Roth; Louis Loeb; Edwin Howland Blashfield (behind Mr. Loeb); Ben Foster (seated); William Thomas Smedley; John White Alexander (seated); Frederick Weller Kost; Henry Willson Watrous; Francis Coates Jones; John Francis Murphy; George Willoughby Maynard; Emil Carlsen; William Sergeant Kendall (seated); Herbert Adams; Leonard Ochtman.*

THE ACADEMY BUILDING BETWEEN
CATHEDRAL PARKWAY AND 109TH STREET
CHARCOAL DRAWING BY CHARLES CHAPMAN, N.A.

*Erected in 1899 as a temporary structure to house the
school, which was there from 1899 to 1948. In the background is the unfinished Cathedral of St. John the Divine.*

one is a French bust, the other an American." Greenough was represented in the Academy by numerous works from 1832 to 1848, having been elected an Honorary Member in 1828. He died shortly after his return to America in 1852.

Of the comparatively few sculptors elected Academicians during the first fifty years after the founding of the Academy, the greater number studied or worked in Italy. The environment was congenial, living was less expensive, models and competent assistants were obtainable. Of the Honorary Members in sculpture, Hiram Powers was the most celebrated. Born in the same year as Greenough (1805), his early aptitude in making effigies in wax and various mechanical devices created an interest in his talent. Sponsored by several gentlemen in Cincinnati in 1837, he was enabled to go to Italy, and established his studio in Florence. Receiving numerous commissions in portraiture from both America and England, his work won great favor, his studio being frequented by distinguished personalities from many countries. His famous *Greek Slave* won him international acclaim and established his permanent reputation, and was followed by other idealistic figures of allusive connotation. In portraiture, his work was praised by contemporaries for realistic fidelity and likeness. Powers lived in Florence until his death in 1873. He was elected to the Academy as an Honorary Member in 1837.

As Powers reigned in Florence, so Thomas Crawford was the dominant American sculptor in Rome. He was born in New York in 1813, and considering his comparatively short life of forty-four years, his production was prodigious. It consisted not only of many minor works, but also of the monumental commission for the decoration of the pediment of the senate wing of the Capitol, and the bronze doors, as well as the heroic figure which surmounts the dome. His equestrian statue of Washington was first unveiled in Munich, where it had been cast in bronze. It received great applause from his fellow craftsmen, and its unveiling in Richmond was a national event. At his death in 1857, Crawford was the most renowned sculptor of American birth.

In the age of Thorwaldsen and Canova, American sculptors working in Italy shared their prestige in international renown. Henry Kirke Brown received his early training in Europe, worked in Italy for four years, but returned to his native country to practice his profession. His work first appeared in the Academy exhibition of 1847, the year after his return from Italy. Elected an Academician in 1851, he exhibited continuously thereafter, being represented in the exhibition of 1850 by 13 examples, including busts of Thomas Cole and William Cullen Bryant. He was the first sculptor in America to master the art of casting in bronze. His most important work is the equestrian statue of Washington in Union Square, commissioned by the citizens of New York. Brown was also the first sculptor to use the native Indian as a model, in such notable works as *Indian and Panther* and *Aboriginal Hunter*.

There being no school in which to study the mechanics of the craft, Brown's studio might be considered as the first practical training school in which younger men could learn the craft while assisting the master, a practice which was happily to continue in the evolution of the American school of sculpture. It was a blessing to break the prestige of Rome.

The first to avail himself of this opportunity was the youthful J. Q. A. Ward, a name to become notable in the annals of American sculpture. The cooperation of master and assistant enabled the student to earn an honorable living while practicing his craft, truly the most vital mode of instruction. Ward was active throughout his career in the councils of the Academy and the direction of the school, and furthered the integration of the sculptor members in the constructive administration of its purpose. He represents the middle period of the art in America, the bridge, so to speak, that made it possible to study and to execute commissions in America. As with the painter, the livelihood of the sculptor was in portraiture. In his many notable representations of contemporary personalities, Ward was the outstanding master of his time. He also found interest in sculpturing Indian subjects, making his models in wax from life in the far West, the most notable result of which was the popular *Indian Hunter*. Likewise, he was among the first American sculptors to portray the Negro, as in his celebrated *Freedman*, where a seated semi-nude Negro with broken shackles symbolizes liberty. Ward was elected an Academician during the Civil War. In later life the sculptor regretted that his many commissions in portraiture did not allow him to develop further his more imaginative conceptions.

From the founding of the Academy until 1889 only 16 sculptors were elected as Academicians, seven of whom, being nonresident, were made Honorary Members. Two Associates were elected during the same period.

The Centennial Exposition held in Philadelphia in 1876 awakened in-

terest in contemporary European art. The repetition of the antique motif
had lost its original appeal. The new generation was more interested in the
living present. The school of Rome declined. As in painting, Paris became
the center of creative production and instruction. The new era in
American sculpture was founded not upon the interpretation of the
antique, but was gained from the knowledge derived from the study of
the living model.

Augustus Saint-Gaudens, who was to give new meaning to sculpture,
was born in Dublin in 1848. His father, a shoemaker by trade, was from
the town of Saint-Gaudens in southern France; his mother was from
Dublin. The family migrated to America when Augustus was an infant,
and the child matured in the light of a new world, with no natal memory
of the old. Apprenticed to a cameo cutter, he was forced by this exacting
art to develop intense concentration and corresponding discipline of
hand and eye. During this time, the youth attended the drawing class at
Cooper Union and likewise studied at night, for two years, in the life
class of the Academy.

At twenty years of age, enrolled as a student of the Ecole des Beaux
Arts under Jouffroy, working in the class with Mercié, Bastien-Lepage
and other brilliant students, Saint-Gaudens was already well prepared as
a draftsman and technician. Then followed three years in Italy, where
the realistic appeal of the early Italian sculptors made a more lasting
impression than the idealizations of pseudo Greek replicas.

Returning to New York after six years of study, he established his
enduring reputation with his first important commission, the *Farragut*,
and proclaimed the advent of a new era in American sculpture. Thereafter, each successive achievement added to his fame.

Saint-Gaudens brought to his creations a living realization. Without
stylized preconception, each theme passed through the alchemy of the
mind, and was executed with the consummate mastery of his craft—
body and spirit united in the embodiment of his vision.

Saint-Gaudens served on the council of the Academy and was elected
an Academician in 1889. He was also one of the founding members of
the Society of American Artists. A committee of Academicians, in
cooperation with others, was instrumental in having a replica of his
Lincoln placed in London, instead of the previously chosen one by
George Gray Barnard.

If the creative genius is not transferable, the example of the master and the training of his assistants were of immeasurable value. One of the most gifted and brilliant of these was Frederick MacMonnies. Susceptible, in addition, to the virtuosity of his French contemporaries, MacMonnies brought a renewed awareness and exciting stimulation to the art, which was to give it new vitality.

Daniel Chester French developed in the cultural society of a distinguished New England family. Of a sensitive nature but favored by environment, he was not to know the early trials of others who had to fight for survival. It is impressive indeed that with little technical training, other than a short stay under Ward and his own youthful experimentation, he could at the age of twenty-three execute the *Minute Man* and receive the acclaim of the elite of Boston at its unveiling in 1875. The many monumental works which followed added greatly to the distinction of American sculpture, and incited others to follow in the path of glory. Elected an Academician in 1901, he was always a pillar of reliance, with a serene nature and thorough balance.

After the merger of the Society of American Artists with the Academy, followed by the holding of two annual exhibitions, the sculptors were given more ample opportunity to display their work. The sculptor membership and cooperation in the administration of the Academy increased greatly after that date. Many of the then youthful sculptors, later to attain renown, were first made known in its galleries.

In the first three decades of the new century, the list of sculptors elected as Academicians, represents the honor roll of their profession. Daniel Chester French, elected in 1901, was followed, in the order of their election, by Karl Bitter, Phimister Proctor, Charles Grafly, Frederick MacMonnies, Hermon MacNeil, Charles Niehaus, Edward Potter, Frederick Roth, Isidore Konti, Lorado Taft, Adolph Weinman, Robert Aitken, Stirling Calder, Paul Manship, Paul Bartlett, James Earle Fraser, Evelyn Longman, Bessie Potter Vonnoh Keyes, Anna Hyatt Huntington, Mahonri Young, Chester Beach, Edward McCartan, John Flanagan, Charles Keck, Rudulph Evans, Harriet Frishmuth, Cyrus Dallin, and Malvina Hoffman.

Continuing the tradition of their eminent predecessors, the present membership includes 48 Academicians and 35 Associates in the sculptor class. It is unfortunate that the limitations of gallery space do not permit the proper presentation of work in sculpture, and that, being above the ground floor, it does not allow the exhibition of works on a large scale. In the absence of this, however, the work of the sculptors may be publicly viewed in the many examples in their permanent locations in New York and other centers throughout the country.

Engraving has a double significance in the early development of art in America: the technical accomplishment of the craft itself, and the fact that it was a means of reproducing works of art executed in other mediums. It was in the latter aspect that our artists became familiar with the masterpieces of the past, as well as with contemporary production, and this was to have an important relation to their aesthetic conception. More humbly, our first native engravers found employment in embellishing silverware and ornaments, as well as designing documents, bank notes, and federal currency.

In a review of nineteenth-century painting, engraving has an added significance, as many of our artists were first trained in this craft, the exacting discipline of which, with its insistence on line, brought to their painting a high degree of technical control and organization. Thus, many Academicians honored as painters were first proficient as engravers. Of the founding members, five were classified as engravers. During the nineteenth century this number was not greatly augmented; three were elected as Honorary Members, five as Academicians, and five as Associates.

Early American engravers were virtually obliged to invent the technical methods of their craft by improvised experimentation. There were no schools of instruction or competent masters from whom to learn the craft. Three generations of Mavericks, each son named Peter, practiced engraving, the grandfather beginning as a silversmith. Peter the Second was employed as a bank note engraver, but also essayed portraiture after paintings. He has, however, a special distinction in the development of engraving as the master to whom Asher B. Durand was apprenticed, and also as one of the original members of the Academy.

The career of William Main, also a founding member, is an unhappy illustration of the lack of recognition of a competent craftsman. He accompanied the Italian engraver Gondolfi to Florence but, being deserted by his master, gained admission to the studio of the celebrated Morghen. Returning to New York, he could find employment only in engraving visiting cards and door plates. Seeking other opportunity, he copied a portrait of Bishop Hobart by Waldo and Jewett, but its publication brought no reward. After several other competent efforts, being in delicate health, he retired to the country and became a farmer.

Moseley I. Danforth was one of the most accomplished of our early engravers, but his later work was executed in London. Learning the rudiments of the craft as an apprentice in the Hartford Engraving Company, he continued self-study by copying Morghen prints. On arriving in New York he supplemented his technical work by drawing in the Academy school, at the same time being elected one of the first fifteen members of the Academy. Danforth was highly recognized in London where, as a close friend of his fellow Academician, Charles Leslie, he reproduced many of the latter's pictures as well as others by contemporary English artists.

The art of Charles Cushing Wright is a tribute to his indomitable will and versatility. Born in 1796, orphaned at an early age with little schooling, he ran away to enlist in the War of 1812. He was wounded and, after many trying vicissitudes, was apprenticed to a jeweler and watchmaker under whom he worked as a silversmith. There he learned to smelt and plate metals and to temper and sharpen steel tools. This practice led him to experiment in copper engraving, while gaining some knowledge of the craft from *Kendall's Pocket Encyclopedia*. By experiment and application Wright attained proficiency in the art, and in 1818 worked with Peter Maverick and Asher B. Durand in the engraving business in New York. The following year he journeyed to Savannah and Charleston. It was in the latter city that he was given the opportunity of executing his first commission as a medalist—an intaglio portrait of General Charles Cotesworth Pinckney.

Returning to New York, Wright joined Asher B. Durand in the bank note business. It was at this time that he became one of the first fifteen founders of the National Academy, being then classified as an engraver. His mature accomplishment and his historical distinction is, however, as the first medalist of America. Before the mechanical means of reproduction was invented, the sculptor was obliged to work directly on the steel. Making his own tools and inventing the process without instruction required the most exacting craftsmanship as well as the creative interpretation of an artist. Wright's first portraits were intaglios, his later work was carved in bas-relief, from which the dies (or matrices) were sunk in steel by a screwpress, as were the editions of medals into gold, silver, and bronze. His masterpiece is the *Independence* portrait of Washington, followed by medallions honoring his contemporaries— Henry Clay, Daniel Webster, Andrew Jackson, De Witt Clinton, the actor Edwin Forest, and others. He also designed the original seal of the Academy. The check list of his engravings, excluding purely commercial work, numbers 15 plates; that of his medals, which he considered his real life work, more than 77 examples.

In the middle period of the art of engraving countless examples were made after American paintings. In this the Art Union was an important contributor, commissioning American engravers each year to make reproductions from American paintings to be distributed annually to their subscribers. In this way the work in both arts became widely circulated in the states, and greatly stimulated the growth of native production.

In the middle of the century, several graphic artists were honored as Academicians—F. O. C. Darley, Alfred Jones, J. F. E. Prud'homme, and James Smillie. John Casilear, a pupil of Durand and originally elected as an engraver, became more noted as a painter. James Smillie was in constant employment and greatly enlarged the field of the art. He was the father of two future Academicians, James D. Smillie and George Smillie, both of whom were to continue the American tradition.

With the introduction of mechanical methods of reproduction, the function of engraving on metal, in its commercialized aspect, became obsolete. Two masters of the art of wood engraving, Timothy Cole and Henry Wolf, in their reproduction of world masterpieces, were the last distinguished practitioners of their particular craft.

As recorded by Dunlap, the first historical information on the art of wood engraving in America was given in lectures by Abraham Mason at the National Academy, repeating his lectures given in London in 1829. The art itself was first practiced in America by Alexander Anderson. Although educated as a doctor, he began his professional career as a wood engraver in 1794, being engaged to make illustrations for the publisher, William Durell. Copying prints by Bewick, the English engraver, entirely without other technical guidance, Anderson made his own tools, and by continuous experimentation perfected his craft, the example of which was to be successfully followed in the further development of wood engraving as a means of reproduction during the middle of the century.

The rise and development of etching as a creative art in America follows quite different origins from the evolution of engraving. The word "painter-etcher" indicates only the double craft of the artist, as the technical methods used in each process are utterly opposed; it does, however, imply that the etcher is an original creator, and is not using the art as a means of reproducing the work of others executed in a different medium. This at once has primal significance in the technique adopted by the etcher and his treatment of the selected subject. Toward the end of the century, the renown of the French etchers and, more directly, the art of Whistler, was to have a decisive influence on the style of American etching. The art had its native precursors in the very able work of Thomas Moran and James D. Smillie and, as we have seen, the latter initiated the class in etching at the Academy, which was continued by Mielatz and others with much success.

As as artist, Whistler emphasized the particular nature and limitations of each medium in which he worked. In etching, its significance was in design, as expressed in the creative characterization of line. It was this distinction that governed the etchings of J. Alden Weir and John Twachtman. There was no attempt at purely naturalistic illusion. The etching of Frank Duveneck is more amplified. A veritable genius of the art, his etchings of Venice, executed before Whistler popularized the subject, seem to have been full-blown without preliminary evolution— a consummation and an end, for Duveneck did not continue the art. Otto Bacher was in Venice at the same time and continued his work with enduring results. The invigoration of the youthful group, and the psychic stimulation of Munich, created a freshness and vitality which were to wane in America. Robert Blum and William Chase executed a few notable plates, but their major art of painting diverted its continuance.

The revival in etching, as exemplified in the exhibitions of the Academy, does not begin until the first decade of the twentieth century, with the election of Joseph Pennell as Academician in 1909. Pennell's association with Whistler, his virile and temperamental personality, as well as his distinction in the art, made him the champion of the younger generation. His lectures at the Academy school were enthusiastically attended, while as a distinguished writer on the technique of the craft, as well as a master publicist, the promotion of the art was greatly enhanced.

After the consolidation of the Society of American Artists with the

Academy, when two exhibitions were held during the season, the graphic artists were given the small, middle gallery for the display of their work. Here many of the younger etchers, later to become masters of the profession, made their initial public appearance.

Of the 25 living Academicians in this class, John Taylor Arms was the first to be elected in 1933, Allen Lewis in 1935, Louis C. Rosenberg in 1936, and Arthur Heintzelman in 1937, the remaining members all being elected after 1940. Ernest Roth, elected in 1928, known both as etcher and painter, chose to be represented as an Academician in the painter class, as the separation of the membership in classes was not in force at that time. All of the 32 living Associate members in the graphic arts were elected after 1937.

It will be seen, therefore, that the practice and interest in the art has been greatly furthered in the present century, resulting in one of the most accomplished groups of craftsmen in the world today. The section of the graphic arts in the present Academy exhibitions is, owing to lack of space, represented only by the members of the Academy.

·XV·

THE ACADEMY CONTINUES TO FLOURISH: THE CENTENARY · EXHIBI-
TIONS IN WASHINGTON AND NEW YORK · CULTURAL AFFILIATION
WITH NEW YORK UNIVERSITY · PRESIDENT BLASHFIELD DEFINES THE
ROLE OF THE ACADEMY · SEARCH FOR A NEW HOME CONTINUED · THE
MEMBERSHIP COMMITTEE

THE ART CENTER of New York City had gradually been moving uptown.
Although the old Tenth Street building would always have distinguished
occupants, and several artists continued to linger around Washington
Square, the establishment of the Holbein Studios on either side of West
55th Street between Sixth and Seventh Avenues drew a large contingent
of the profession to that locality. Next were erected the Sherwood
Studios on West 57th Street, their famous neighbor, Carnegie Hall, and
a row of studios on West 67th Street. The Holbein Studios were built
as taxpayers; the lower section served as stables; the upper floor, with
unobstructed skylight, made perfect studios. The aroma of paint and
turpentine mingled with the air of the stable. The studio was a workshop
only, without separate apartments for living. The occupant supplied his
own coal and heat; as the studio was without modern conveniences, the
rent was cheap. The fashionable receptions of Tenth Street days had
passed. Without the distraction of the telephone, the brotherhood of
painters and sculptors were in their rightful realm of work. When the
Society of American Artists and the National Academy moved to West
57th Street, the area was consolidated.

Business also moved uptown, and conditions changed. Rents increased;
an artist could no longer afford a private studio. Living *en famille*,

the painter saw his picture in its more intimate surroundings; the studio was consciously decorated. As we have seen, many painters moved to the country. The familiar relations of painter and patron, so helpful in earlier days, declined, as did also the wider cultural relations with members of other professions. The art dealer became a necessity. Reputations were made on exhibition walls. Coincident with this was the more decoratively considered arrangement of hanging; fewer pictures were displayed; frames were narrowed, glass was eliminated. This promoted more intense competition. A greater number of works were submitted and, consequently, a greater number were rejected. As in the theater, the critic pronounced the current judgment.

After the move from the old building at 23d Street, and with the school located in a separate building, the genial old-time camaraderie and social reunions became but memories of the past. For the new generation, the Academy was centered in the annual exhibitions. The American Fine Arts Gallery never was the heart or the home of the founders' dream.

The one hundredth anniversary of the founding of the Academy was now approaching, and great plans were made for its celebration. It was proposed to give a retrospective exhibition in addition to displaying the work of present members. The prime difficulty was the lack of proper space and of necessary funds to make the exhibition possible. The Academy being a national institution, Douglas Volk suggested the happy idea of opening the exhibition in Washington. This was greeted unanimously. Conferences were opened with the director and president of the Corcoran Gallery of Art. Favorable response was immediate, and a provisional agreement was reached pending its ratification by the trustees. In a letter dated December 31, 1924, and addressed to President Blashfield, Mr. C. Powell Minnigerode, director of the Corcoran Gallery, wrote:

It is a source of great personal satisfaction to me, as the Director of this Gallery, to know that the Centennial Exhibition of the National Academy of Design is to be held in this building. The National Academy of Design is the oldest and largest organization of artists in the country. The record of its accomplishments, the many noted painters and sculptors who have been honored members of the Academy during the one hundred years of its existence, its tradition, its history, and the priceless service which it has rendered to the cause of art in America are all important factors which were recognized by this Gallery in the action of the Trustees as conveyed to you by Mr. Glover's letter of the 29th instant.

Confirming the agreement, Mr. Glover wrote, in part:

As you know, this Gallery was established for the purpose of "encouraging American genius," and the suggestion contained in your letter is, therefore, one which comes distinctly within our scope. . . . It is a pleasure to give you the assurance that the National Academy of Design will find our doors open wide to receive them, and that a most cordial welcome will be awaiting you and your colleagues. I am glad, too, to say to you that when the time comes, you may confidently count upon the fullest cooperation on the part of Mr. Minnegerode, the Director of the Gallery.

The limited amount of available space in the American Fine Arts Gallery made the problem in New York more difficult to solve. Mr. Edward Robinson, director of the Metropolitan Museum of Art, expressed his regrets that the museum did not have available galleries for such a large showing, explaining that

The amount of wall space, which I understand the exhibition would call for, would make it necessary to strip a very considerable number of our galleries, and the situation this year is doubly complicated by the fact that we are just starting with the installation of our new wing. . . . In view of the exceptional importance of this exhibition and the close relations which have always existed between the Academy and this Museum, I wish it might have been possible.

Fortunately the Grand Central Galleries had been recently completed, and the directors generously offered them for the Centennial Exhibition, rent free, to follow the exhibition in Washington. This was unanimously accepted by the Academy, and the detailed conditions mutually agreed upon. The dates being decided upon and arrangements concluded, the council devoted its attention to the promotion of the exhibition. John Ward Dunsmore was appointed director, and Charles T. Heaslip was employed to manage the publicity and to raise funds through donations. Members contributed individually, and also helped to add considerably to the list of fellowships. Two booklets were published, one outlining the history of the Academy entitled *The First Hundred Years*, the second telling of *The School of a Thousand Stories*. Mr. H. Harrison Morris, a devoted friend of the Academy, donated $1,500 for the publication of the first; Mr. John Fry contributed $1,300 to defray the cost of the second. Both booklets were printed in editions of 10,000, and were distributed through the country.

In conjunction with the celebration of the Centennial, the council organized an expansive plan to explore and promote the possibilities of creating an endowment fund that would enable the Academy to consummate its ideal of erecting a permanent building that would have suitable accommodations for exhibitions, and would allow the enlargement of the functions of the school. The program was not to be in the nature of a drive, but was rather to seek the cooperation of several prominent citizens who had expressed a deep interest in furthering art in America. The plan contemplated a total fund of $6,000,000. "The income from one million dollars of this fund will be devoted to the presentation of semi-annual, free, public exhibitions in cities throughout the United States. The remaining $5,000,000 will be devoted to the development of a new art school." The idea of the school was in the nature of a college of Art "to give students an opportunity to acquire a classical and academic education at the same time as they are mastering the fundamentals of their art."

President Edwin Blashfield desired to extend the cultural and theoretical education of the art student as well as his visual and technical training. Recognizing that in the formative period of youth it was essential to train the hand and eye, he felt that at the same impressionable and receptive age it was equally essential to develop the mind and the imagination. To this end conferences were held with the chancellor of New York University with a view of coordinating certain educational courses in the university with the practice of the arts in the Academy school. In this exchange, an approved student working in the Academy school, by taking certain courses at the university and passing the required examinations, would be eligible for a B.A. degree; while a student at the university, specializing in the arts, would be permitted to attend the Academy school, thus gaining credits for the same degree. The conferences were held in February, 1922, and a formal affiliation of the Academy with New York University was approved on April 3 of the same year.

Although few students actually took advantage of this opportunity, the arrangement is as valid today as it was at the time of the inception. Many institutions of higher learning do not employ art teachers who have not received an approved degree; this restriction prevents the great majority of artists most highly recognized in their profession from teaching in such institutions should they desire to do so. George Moore relates in his memoirs of the same conditions existing in England, citing the particular example of a painter of national distinction who, being in need of livelihood after the war, was not permitted to teach painting without taking a prescribed course in order to qualify for the particular institution. As recently as 1952, the councils of the National Academy and of the National Sculpture Society united in sending a letter to the American Federation of Arts calling attention to this unfortunate condition.

In a formal addess to the Academicians at the business meeting of March 11, 1925, President Blashfield commented on the present and future prospects of the Academy.

Between our hope of building a home and the wish to prove that our Centennial Birthday finds us vigorous and progressing, we of the Academy should realize that we have reached a highly critical moment of its life.

Recognizing that there existed an aesthetic division in the arts as well as differences in regard to the purpose and prospects of the Academy, he stressed the need for the unity and cooperation of all the members.

Fortunately, human nature provides us with just the two groups we require; the so-called practical and the so-called idealists. These two groups are, in a way, like the Right and Left in a Parliament. We *must* have them because we are human. There are advantages and disadvantages in such an equation, but, in order to succeed—and success at this time is vitally necessary—we must reconcile Right and Left, at least enough to persuade all to pull together, neutralize the disadvantages and push the advantage.

Contrasting the idealist who is apt to isolate himself, and the practical man, who keeps the wheels going around he continued,

right down the middle of the Academy runs a dividing line of sentiment which tries hard to keep the practical and the ideal in view at once.

For some years past, many severe statements have been made regarding "the Arts of the Academy of Design." But the rolls of the Academy include such a majority of the most eminent painters, sculptors, engravers and architects, that condemnation of the art of the National Academy of Design, is just simply condemnation of American Art. Every now and then a group of men holding some view, which for the moment is an advanced one, falls away temporarily from the Academy and exhibits elsewhere. But it is not fatal, indeed it is in part a healthy reaction. It is only what happens surely to the Wheel of Fortune and of Fashion, which turns incessantly and returns with certainty, to the point from which it starts. Mr. X.Y.Z., who is famous now at the top of the wheel, is bye and bye nowhere, or at the bottom of the wheel. Soon, as the wheel turns, he, or at any rate his kind of art, is in the sunshine again. The younger men who, on their way home from an exhibition, damn us older men as devitalized conservatives, will very soon be damned themselves and placarded with the same epithet, by a newer group of younger men who have attached themselves to a spoke of the wheel that is one ahead, and on the upward curve. . . . Some members who rarely attend meetings criticise freely. Have we any of us a *right* to blame exhibitions which we did did not help either to frame or to combat? (Minutes)

In his address Mr. Blashfield had touched upon two conditions which are ever recurring: the practical and material operation of the Academy which is carried on by the council; and the critical opposition pertaining to differing aesthetic opinions within and without the Academy, which is not within the province of the council to judge or control.

The Centennial Exhibition in Washington was officially opened on October 17, 1925.

The ceremonies were impressive. After releasing the cord across the entrance, the President and Mrs. Coolidge, escorted by the Officers and Council of the National Academy of Design, and of the Corcoran Galleries, mounted the Grand Staircase and traversed the various galleries, while the great throng of guests came on behind and lined the balconies and sides of the stairway. Among the distinguished guests were the Secretary of State, several Ambassadors, Officers of the Army and Navy, and the cream of Washington official society.

This indeed was an unprecedented honor in the art world and added greatly to the national significance of the Academy, which gained in consequence much favorable publicity, both critics and artists being loud in their praise.

Representing the "Arts of Design," the exhibition included 364 paintings, 52 works in sculpture, 72 examples of the graphic arts, 24 architectural drawings, and 24 miniatures. The attendance during the four weeks of the exhibition approximated 50,000 spectators, with added social functions of delegations representing various clubs and art organizations throughout the country.

In his illuminating preface to the comprehensive and profusely illustrated catalogue, Mr. Blashfield stated, "Let us say that conservative, like other Academies, ours has been, but we hope, conservative of the best. The champion of continued rather than sporadic progress, it has nevertheless upon its rolls the names of nearly all of the most original and individual thinkers among American artists."

Following the exhibition in Washington, the Centennial opened in New York at the Grand Central Galleries on Tuesday evening, December 1. The galleries proved inadequate to accommodate the vast throng of over 6,000 guests who attended the reception, and many departed without entering, owing to the congestion. Footmen in old-time livery attended the entrance and landing, while beautiful models in colonial costume sold catalogues in the gallery. The total attendance of over 30,000 was not as large as in Washington, owing possibly to the Christmas season and the admission charge of one dollar. The exhibition continued until January 3. The wall space being more limited than in the Corcoran Gallery, the committee of arrangement was obliged to hang a double line, which was unfavorable to proper presentation. "In nearly all instances the critics were not only sympathetic but enthusiastic in praise— even those who seemed to favor the more radical movements in art."

Taking advantage of the wide national publicity attending the Centennial celebration, the council now revived the plans for the National Academy Association. It was apparent that with a suitable building and endowment, public interest would sustain the project, and the combined art organizations and artists would have adequate space to display their contributions.

The proposal centered on two projects, either to build on the property at 109th Street, as originally planned, or to enlarge the American Fine Arts Society building by purchasing the adjoining property. The latter was favored, but this involved obtaining the consent of the Architectural League and the Art Students League.

Howard Russell Butler had fathered the American Fine Arts Society, and it was through his vision and effort that the building was made possible. Without a dollar to start with, he raised $100,000, a sum which was matched by George Vanderbilt, and eventually a total fund of $400,000 was raised to cover the cost of the building. Thus the Society of American Artists, the Architectural League, and the Art Students League became the incorporated shareholders of the Society. After its merger with the Society of American Artists, the Academy had taken over the Society's stock and had purchased and received by gift further outstanding shares to increase its interest, so that each institution owned about one third

THE "WHITE ROOM" IN THE ACADEMY'S PRESENT HOME
AT 1083 FIFTH AVENUE

*The galleries were inaugurated in 1942 by a retrospective
exhibition entitled "Our Heritage," here illustrated.*

of the stock. Mr. Butler's plan was to buy the adjoining property to the west, with a fifty-foot front on West 57th Street, extending in the rear to a frontage of one hundred and ten feet on West 58th Street. This, combined with the American Fine Arts Building, would provide adequate wall space for the various art organizations exhibiting in the galleries.

A special meeting was called on December 21, 1925, to discuss the project, the representatives of the Academy being empowered to act if the plan was agreed to by the other two members of the American Fine Arts Society. Gifford Beal, speaking for the Art Students League, said that the school might be of advantage in permitting tax exemption, but the League itself might not benefit otherwise, and conceivably might have to bear greater responsibility, at the same time losing its identity. As it was understood that the Academy School would continue at West 109th Street, the question arose as to whether the additional building would be free of taxation. The Architectural League was thoroughly in favor of the project, Cass Gilbert suggesting that the title to the property be vested in the three joint owners. It was therefore voted that a committee be appointed to prepare and consider a plan for the purchase of the property, each society being represented by four members. An option to purchase was granted for thirty days.

Two meetings of the joint committee followed at which Mr. Butler proposed ten points for consideration and discussion. The Architectural League responded favorably. At the second meeting, the board of control of the Art Students League submitted a prepared statement which, after a formal preamble, asserted that

Said plan is not in the interest of the Art Students League and therefore finds itself unable to accept the same or to encourage the carrying out of such plan or any similar plan. The Board of Control of the Art Students League deems it proper to add that, having come to this decision, it will use all proper endeavor to prevent two-thirds of the outstanding stock of the American Fine Arts Society being voted in favor of any alienation of the property of the American Fine Arts Society, and failing in that endeavor, asks to have its stock appraised at its full market value and the amount thereof paid to the Art Students League. (Minutes)

Further conferences were held. The Academy and the Architectural League had no wish to alienate the Art Students League, and devised further plans for its protection. It was clear, however, that the Art

Students League was self-sufficient, having no need of expansion, whereas the Academy and other exhibiting societies needed more space and would profit by expansion. As the Art Students League was tax exempt, and as the new building, if erected, would probably have to be mortgaged, it was feared that the Art Students League, as an incorporated member of the American Fine Arts Society, would be subject to a greater burden. The board of control of the Art Students League, in accordance with its attorney, was therefore obdurate.

The option of purchase, having in the meantime expired, the property in question was withdrawn. Thus the final endeavor of the Academy to unite in a cooperative plan to further the interests of the art organizations of the city was frustrated, and the attainment of its goal still waited in the future.

At the annual meeting of Academicians in 1926, Edwin Blashfield made his final presidential address. In lamenting the loss of so many distinguished members during the year, including John Weir, Dwight Tryon, Paul Bartlett, Ben Foster, William H. Drake, Don Barber, and Joseph Pennell, he reminisced thoughtfully of earlier years. Speaking of the many members who had collaborated with *Harper's*, *Scribner's*, and the *Century*, he said

It was the heyday of American wood engraving when Cole and Wolf and others aroused lively encomiums in the press of London and Paris. In the elevators that took one upstairs, whether at Union Square or Franklin Square or at *Scribner's*, if you boarded them often enough, you were sure to meet Will Low, or Abbey or Reinhart of *Harper's*, Smith or Frank Millet, or Cox and Mowbray and, perhaps, George Inness with his big eyes and very long hair. And we think, too, of that sympathetic and most hospitable mansion on 17th Street where the Gilders, best of hosts, held open house, and Johnson and Brush were "de la maison" and Saint-Gaudens was almost sure to be present at the weekly receptions. Can't you, some of you, still hear the music of the Kneisel Quartette in his big studio, which was crowded on Sunday afternoons when it was too late to work, and his clay models were swaddled and wetted down for the night? Saint-Gaudens' studio was not far from the Greeley statue at 33rd Street but the Gilders were in East 17th Street, hard by the old Century, and to them came dramatic celebrities as well as artists, Americans from over-seas, Modjeska and Irving and Miss Terry and the Robertsons. . . . Those were great days which some of us remember, days spent in an old and different world that is passing—passing into our obituary list.

But, he concluded:

I cannot end upon a note of depression. We *are* in a changed world and *we* pass—but go into our schoolrooms upstairs and you will see on the walls more light and more color than ever before, and some drawings that it would be hard for any of us to emulate, and compositions showing thought and fancy and a perception of the requirements of decoration—Academicians die but the Academy lives and will live. (Minutes)

At the same meeting Cass Gilbert was elected president of the Academy. As one of the most distinguished of American architects, he brought added prestige to the Academy and with his executive ability was an able administrator of the council.

It is something of an experiment that an architect is elected President of the Academy. It is the first time in its history that this has been done, but it is not without precedent, for Sir Aston Webb, who retired recently from the Presidency of the Royal Academy in London, is an architect . . . so I feel that my election is more in recognition of architecture as a fine art than for any special qualifications I may be supposed to possess.

After long and faithful service, the veteran recording secretary, Douglas Volk, retired, and Hobart Nichols was elected to fill the vacancy. DeWitt Lockman, chairman of the school committee, read a long and illuminating report of the school's activities, stressing its need of further support. "With the school season of 1925–26 just ended, the National Academy of Design completed its one hundredth year as an educational institution, and worthily sustained its reputation as the leading art school in the City of New York. The registration during the centennial year was 574, and was, in fact, the largest registration in the history of the schools." Of this number 207 students were of American birth, 117 of Russian, and 58 of Italian; other nationalities were variously represented.

The report mentions the variety of nationalities represented in the schools. Interesting as this is, to my mind the far-reaching influence of the schools lies in the various classes of students reached, rather than in the nationalities represented. Many of our students who can hardly speak English, and would certainly not be encouraged in the paid schools, contribute designs which frequently receive prize awards. This, in itself, would be a sufficient justification, if any were needed, for the existence of the Schools. . . . And there is another thing to be said: I doubt if there is in the city an institution where the teachers give more time and attention to their students, and, incidentally, receive less remuneration for their service.

I have heard it suggested to let the Schools go. I have even heard the question: "Why keep up the Schools—they bring us in nothing?" Can you imagine the graduate of any university saying that of his Alma Mater? How many members of the Academy owe their training to these very Schools? . . . . The Schools are a part of the sacred trust bequeathed to us a century ago by the Founders of the Academy. It is our duty to see that this trust is properly discharged. . . . Successful schools now mean successful exhibitions in the near future. Unless the present generation of art students has the proper training, there will be no material worthy of exhibition in the building we plan to erect. (Minutes)

Although the number of students was almost too large to handle, and the chairman suggested a reduction in enrollment, nevertheless, in the next few years the number of students increased to over 600, with a long waiting list in addition.

Eugene Savage, having been commissioned by the Carnegie Foundation to make a survey of the art schools in the United States and Europe, presented a comprehensive report to the council of the Academy. The report suggested a regulated course of instruction, to cover a period of four to five years, with emphasis on composition and mural painting in its relation to architecture. It was thought that the curriculum followed in the Academy school covered the major conditions suggested, but that carrying out its further development would require improvements in accommodations and other necessary facilities.

With this in view, the president held conferences with Dr. Keppel of the Carnegie Corporation, and obtained a grant of $20,000. During the summer of 1929, renovations were completed, the alterations adding three classrooms and more suitable accommodations for the library. In recognition of these achievements, the Corporation continued the grant the following year, and for three years thereafter with reduced amounts. In addition to material improvements, the instruction in drawing and painting was supplemented by comprehensive lectures on the history of painting, architecture, ornament, stained glass, mosaic, fresco painting, and the graphic arts, as well as the required courses in perspective and anatomy. Special lectures were also given on technical methods and the chemistry of pigments. Karl Anderson, Sidney Dickinson, Leon Kroll, and Gifford Beal were added to the staff of instructors in drawing and painting. Arthur Covey conducted the class in mural painting and pictorial composition. The aim of the school was to offer a balanced system of art education, combining both practical study and theoretical knowledge. During these years, under the general direction of Robert Aitken, chairman of the school committee, and using the resources provided by the Carnegie Corporation, the Academy school attained its fullest development.

At the suggestion of Gari Melchers, chairman of the National Commission of Fine Arts, the Carnegie Corporation also made it possible to assemble all of the pictures purchased under the Henry W. Ranger Fund for exhibition at the National Gallery of Art in Washington. The exhibition was opened in December, 1929, and continued through January. "The assemblage in the National Gallery of representative examples of the works of American painters, and the period represented, will give to the Ranger Bequest great national importance. In the course of time, as the centuries pass, there will have been brought together an assemblage of art works such as no other agency or procedure can hope to surpass." (Minutes)

In a letter to the secretary, Charles Curran, President Gilbert expressed his desire to present a gold medal to be awarded by the Academy for distinguished service in the arts. "I believe that the Academy will uphold Academic standards and enlarge its influence for good, by recognizing the great and valuable services of patrons, as well as artists, in the development of the Fine Arts in this country and abroad. . . . The award of the medal should be made not only with great care but with appropriate ceremonies, so as to surround it with dignity and enhance the distinction of the award." (Minutes) With this in view, Elihu Root was chosen to be the first recipient of the award. On the occasion of its presentation in November, 1929, messages were read from President Hoover and Chief Justice Taft; the honored guests included Secretary of State Stimson, and Secretary of the Treasury Mellon. The medal was designed by Robert Aitken. The second award was made in 1932 during the Morse celebration at the Metropolitan Museum, a special reception being held in honor of the Academy. On the case of the medal was inscribed, "In Honor of Samuel Finley Breese Morse, the National Academy of Design presents this medal to his son, William Goodrich Morse."

In January, 1927, a special meeting of the exhibition committee, consisting of the council and the jury of selection, was called to discuss the project of inviting a group of the so-called younger artists to contribute to the 102d annual exhibition. The meeting took place at the residence of Cass Gilbert.

Recognizing the growing trend of the "modern" movement, many of the members felt that the jury of selection should be more liberal in its decisions and that the younger men should be more fully represented. After much discussion and divided opinion, a Committee of Solicitation was appointed with Gifford Beal as chairman. At a subsequent meeting a subcommittee composed of Louis Bouché, Richard Lahey, and Henry Schnakenberg was added. Mr. Beal reported that he was assured of approximately 75 works of the general character indicated. Edwin Blashfield spoke in favor of the idea, and Herbert Adams expressed the belief that, "it is possible to make this a very important thing for the Academy and for the country, but we can only do it in the most generous way possible." It was decided that the entire center gallery be given to the invited pictures.

Quite different from the work of the so-called radicals at the beginning of the century, less humanistic than the "Eight," the younger men, with a flair for color, reflected the growing influence of Cézanne and the vitalized expression of the French masters. Not altogether new or sensational, the exhibition nevertheless provided a favorable opportunity for the dissidents to display their talent. In retrospect, however, it is historically significant in the evolution of the Academy, inasmuch as many of those very exhibitors now look upon more recent innovations with conservative reserve. The artists represented who are now members of the Academy included: Guy Pene du Bois, Louis Bouché, Randall Davey, Charles Burchfield, Ernest Fiene, Reginald Marsh, Henry Mattson, Maurice Sterne, and Raphael Soyer.

Perhaps as a reaction from this generous gesture, the Academicians agreed to devote the autumn exhibition of 1929 to the works of members of the Academy exclusively. Special screens were installed in the Vanderbilt gallery to increase hanging space. As many of the Academicians had contributed only occasionally to the annual exhibitions, every effort was made to ensure the representation of the most distinguished members by important examples. Much favorable publicity was given to the exhibition—Cass Gilbert, Robert Aitken, Charles Dana Gibson, Hobart Nichols and others made radio addresses.

In an eloquent speech, Cass Gilbert alluded to the service of the artist during the war:

Do you remember when we went into the war, how the posters stirred the blood in your veins, and set your brain on fire with enthusiasm for the great cause? You enlisted, bought bonds, subscribed to the Red Cross and did all you could to help. The newspaper cartoons were more powerful than the editorials, and though the pen is said to be mightier than the sword, the pencil and the brush were mightier than either or both—for they *told* the story and millions answered their call . . . to be an artist in the true sense of the word is to live! (Minutes)

In 1929 Francis Jones, owing to ill health, retired as treasurer; he had served in that office for 22 years. His passing in 1932 was a sorrowful loss. "A man of rare personality and sane judgment, his counsel was sought by many institutions. He was for long a member of the board of directors of the Metropolitan Museum. He will be long remembered for his untiring and unselfish devotion to the interests of the Academy and other institutions of which he was a member." He was succeeded by Henry Prellwitz, with Frederick Ballard Williams as assistant treasurer.

At the annual meeting of 1933 Cass Gilbert made his valedictory address, declaring that his presidency of the Academy "had been his greatest honor and the experience had been one of great pleasure." In view of the serious financial conditions of the times, he advised against making plans for a new building until circumstances were more favorable. Alluding to several projects which had been under consideration during his administration, he called attention to the disastrous results which might have eventuated had they been carried out and faced with the Depression which followed. It was particularly unfortunate that this should have occurred during Gilbert's presidency, as his unquestioned ability and his many influential contacts would otherwise conceivably have resulted in the fulfillment of the plans.

Harry Watrous, who for so many years had served first as secretary and then as vice-president, succeeded Cass Gilbert, expressing the wish that he be honored by serving for one year. Robert Aitken was elected first vice-president, Hobart Nichols second vice-president, with Charles Chapman taking the latter's place as recording secretary. In this year the president's medal was awarded to Edwin Blashfield for distinguished service to the fine arts, and in 1938 Herbert Adams, past president of the Academy, was honored by the same distinction.

The heavy costs of the exhibitions and the school necessitated strict economy in administration. The autumn exhibition was discontinued. To permit a larger representation of the work of nonmembers, it was agreed that hereafter each exhibitor be limited to one example. In the annual exhibition of 1934, 1,873 pictures were submitted to the jury of selection, of which 337 were placed, 149 being exempt. In the graphic arts section, 1,422 examples were submitted, from which 177 were selected. The attendance had increased to over 24,000, no admission being charged. The sale of works declined. The enrollment in the school numbered over 600 students, its activities being furthered by a generous bequest of $30,000 from Albert Hallgarten.

At the annual meeting of 1934 Jonas Lie was elected president, Hobart Nichols, first vice-president; and Edward McCartan, second vice-president.

To promote the nomination of distinguished artists and to extend national representation in the Academy, one of the first endeavors of the new administration was the creation of a membership committee. This was composed of fifteen painters, five of whom were to serve for one year, five for two years, and five for three years. The committee was appointed by the president, with the approval of the council. The regular form of proposing a candidate for nomination was continued. It was also ordered that the jury of selection should be chosen by professional classification, the jury to be composed of nineteen painters, three sculptors, three architects, and three members of the graphic arts class. In judging the works presented, each class was to select only those works submitted in its own class, rather than, as heretofore, the jury acting as a whole. The exempt privilege was to be honored only in the class to which the member was elected. The latter part of the program proved highly satisfactory, but the membership committee caused much debate, as the candidates proposed by this committee were indicated on the ballot by a star, thus being given a preference over candidates proposed in the regular manner.

In the academy room of the Fine Arts Building a series of commemorative exhibitions was inaugurated, the works being chosen from examples in the permanent collection of the Academy. This was followed by several special exhibitions in the same gallery of works by contemporary members, the first exhibition being devoted to portraiture. The significance of the permanent collection was further emphasized by a request from the Museum of the City of New York that the Academy contribute 31 examples to an exhibition illustrative of the history of the city. An exhibition of the works by architects was included in the annual exhibition of 1935, with a view of making that class more active in the Academy.

During the administration of Jonas Lie, Edward Hendry was engaged as executive treasurer, working under the supervision of the treasurer and the finance committee. "In recognition of his invaluable work as accountant and financial advisor," a contract was signed to continue for ten years, thus relieving the treasurer of many burdensome details.

Although the enrollment of students at the school had somewhat declined, the standard of its activities was maintained by the school committee under the vigilant chairmanship of Edward McCartan. As the instructors were present only during criticisms twice each week, it was thought advisable to engage one instructor who would devote full time to the general supervision of the school and the conduct of the pupils. Charles Hinton, sculptor and mural painter, accepted this assignment, and remained in that capacity until the sale of the property ten years later. This proved a wise procedure, bringing to the school a continuity of administration, a faithful counselor, and a capable instructor. The enrollment during the decade of the 'thirties averaged about 400 students, the maximum being over 600, which resulted in overcrowding the classes.

The endeavor of President Jonas Lie was to extend the national representation in the membership of the Academy, and to further its usefulness in promoting American art. A firm believer in the fundamental purpose and significance of the Academy, he devoted his energy to stimulating the members by advocating national publicity. The agent in charge of the latter program received 4,185 items in reference to the Academy published in the press of 1936. To consolidate and inform the membership, the president sponsored the publication of a bulletin. "I believe that an institution such as ours should keep in sympathetic touch with its members, and with the public generally, and especially that part of the public which is interested in art. To promote this I established a bulletin, doing all the work myself, writing it, editing it, and making all the arrangements about it." Three issues were published but, owing to lack of funds, the venture was discontinued.

·XVI·

ART IN A WORLD AT WAR: THE NEW YORK WORLD'S FAIR · PRESIDENT
NICHOLS · THE ARCHER M. HUNTINGTON GIFT · THE MOVE TO FIFTH
AVENUE · A SECOND FIRE · SALE OF PROPERTY AT 109TH STREET ·
THE SECOND WORLD WAR · VICTORY SHIP SAMUEL F. B. MORSE · THE
ISIDOR FUND · THE ABBEY BEQUEST

WITH THE ADVENT of the New York World's Fair, to be held in the summer of 1939, extensive preparations were made by the council to celebrate
that occasion. In lieu of the annual exhibition, it was proposed to hold a
comprehensive exhibition of the combined work of the members of the
Academy during the summer period of the Fair. The plan required a
budget of $10,000, and special committees were appointed to raise funds.
The women's committee, with Mrs. Cass Gilbert as chairman, contributed $2,000. The exhibition was both retrospective and contemporary,
including works in painting, sculpture, architecture, and the graphic arts.
The historical section was of appropriate interest, illustrated by portraits
of the founders, past presidents, and various examples and documents
pertaining to the origin and growth of the Academy. The exhibition continued from May 8 to July 25, 1939. Being well represented by many of
the most prominent American artists of the nineteenth century, as well
as distinguished contemporaries, the display was an impressive one. But
as it was held in the summer season with the national focus upon the
World's Fair, the attendance was not as large as anticipated. However, it
formed a well conceived and justified contribution to the many art attrac-
tions presented by the various museums and galleries of the city during the
celebration of the Fair.

At the national exhibition of contemporary art held at the Fair, 25,000 paintings were submitted to the jury of selection; 65 examples by members of the Academy were presented, from which 40 were selected. In the autumn a special exhibition, exclusively by members of the Academy, was held in the art gallery on the Fair grounds under the auspices of the Public Works Administration.

Jonas Lie had been in ill health for some time. "During the last few years my entire time has been taken up with the work of the Academy and I have been able to do little or no work for myself." With the convening of the council in October, 1939, Mr. Lie felt it encumbent upon him to resign. His resignation was, therefore, accepted "on the grounds of ill health, with deepest appreciation of his unselfish and distinguished services to the National Academy and to American art, and with earnest solicitation for his speedy recovery."

As first vice-president, Hobart Nichols automatically became president to serve for the unexpired term of the retiring president. It was becoming apparent that the office of president was not only an honor but also a grave responsibility. Its duties occupied much of the time and consideration of one who, otherwise, would be engaged in professional activity. The material affairs and duties of the council consumed much of the time of administration. The exhibitions had once sustained the Academy; now their deficit, as well as the deficit of the school, proved an ever increasing burden. Theoretical plans in the interest of American art and artists were readily proposed, but the cost of carrying them out prohibited execution. Added to this, there was a continuous professional and public controversy arising from disparate views relative to modernistic aesthetics.

In this respect the endowed museums had a great advantage. Their exhibitions were continuous; the management and publicity could be carried out by a staff devoted solely to further their purpose; exhibitions could be arranged and presented without professional debate or the decision of juries of selection. The Academy could well carry out its program of the requirements of its schools and exhibitions within the premise of its artistic intention, but for artists engaged in professional creation, the material needs and functions of the Academy were a double and difficult burden.

Jonas Lie had exhausted his vitality in endeavoring to accomplish this double task, and the art world was greatly saddened by his untimely passing in the opening of the new year of 1940. "He was tireless in his devotion to any cause that he considered worthy, and he put tremendous energy into his office as the eighteenth President of the Academy. We who survive him shall profit by his example."

It was well for President Nichols to consider the desirability of continuing in office. He had served on its council for many years, and knew the trials and vicissitudes rather than its emoluments. Nevertheless, he worthily accepted the formal nomination and was unanimously elected president at the annual meeting of Academicians on April 24, 1940. At the same time Edward McCartan was elected first vice-president, and John Taylor Arms, second vice-president. Charles Curran continued as corresponding secretary.

Henry Prellwitz, treasurer of the Academy, died in March, 1940, having served in that office for twelve years, during the early part of which he had had little assistance. The esteem of his fellow administrators is expressed in the following words: "To fidelity to duty, unswerving devotion to the best interests and highest standards of the cause he served, a firmness in the conviction of right, but tempered with kindness, justice and respect for the feeling of others." He was succeeded by Frederick Ballard Williams, who had served with Mr. Prellwitz as assistant treasurer, Charles Keck being elected to the latter office.

In his first presidential address, in lamenting the loss of his predecessor, Mr. Nichols spoke with admiration of the accomplishment of Jonas Lie. "During the four years and six months of his administration, the Academy benefited by his dynamic and courageous leadership. At no time during its long history has there been such sharp division of opinion on the subject of art as there has been during the past decade. Mr. Lie insisted that the Academy should be liberal and absorb the best of the modern trends. To this end he worked diligently, with deep and sincere convictions." (Minutes)

The members were heartened by the president's announcement of the magnanimous gift by Archer M. Huntington of three adjoining properties, one of which was at 1083 Fifth Avenue. The adjoining property extended to the rear facing 89th Street. This gift had been formally approved at a special meeting of Academicians held on February 7. At the same time it was voted to sell the Academy property at West 109th Street, the negotiations relative to which were pending. It was proposed to remodel the buildings on Fifth Avenue to provide exhibition galleries and other proper facilities, with the ultimate thought of constructing a building for the school on the vacant lot.

The president also spoke of the successful conclusion of the 114th annual exhibition, which was formally opened by Mayor LaGuardia, with a spirited address broadcast on a national hook-up over station WOR. During the exhibition, the publicity committee, under the able direction of Robert Nisbet, arranged for several radio talks relative to the history of the Academy and its activities. The exhibition included 525 works in painting and sculpture, 194 of which were by members and 331 by nonmembers.

On May 27, 1940, the gift of Mr. Huntington was officially consummated, the donor having "further extended his generosity to the National Academy of Design by establishing a fund in perpetuity, two-fifths of the income of said fund to be placed to the credit of the National Academy of Design, thus enabling it to carry forward its project of utilizing the newly acquired property." In the following year Mr. Huntington was presented with the president's medal as a token of the deep appreciation not only of his gift to the Academy, but also in recognition of his great service to art in America. The presentation was made at an informal reception, as Mr. Huntington disliked ceremony and personal publicity.

The council was thus enabled to proceed with plans for remodeling the building, the design and execution of which was carried out by the distinguished architect, William A. Delano, during the summer and autumn of 1941.

Thus, nearly half a century after the demolition of its building on East 23d Street, the Academy was to be installed in its own home. It was therefore most appropriate that the inauguration of the galleries should be a tribute to its past members and the tradition of the Academy. Entitled "Our Heritage," the exhibition was formally opened by an imposing reception on January 8, 1942 and continued through February 7. Covering a period from the time of the first president, Samuel Morse, to the last deceased president, Jonas Lie, the "exhibition was acclaimed by the public and critics alike as an auspicious beginning of a new era for the Academy." Representing the professions included in the membership of the Academy, the display, selected mostly from examples in the permanent collection of the Academy and augmented by works loaned from other sources, was a virtual review of the important trends of American art during the long history of the Academy. In appreciation of the splendid accomplishment in the inauguration and administration of the new home of the Academy, the president was tendered a dinner given in his honor and was presented with a watch and chain as a token of esteem.

The significance and function of the new galleries was further augmented by the annual exhibitions of the American Water Color Society and the Society of American Etchers, later to be followed by those of the Audubon Artists, Allied Artists, and the National Association of Women Artists, the varied art organizations also occupying offices in the building. Thus the Academy had become a center, not only for its own activities, but also for the other art organizations governed by professional members, and had, in a limited way, carried out the plans of preceding administrations for a National Academy Association, the charter of which had not been renewed.

As the galleries of the American Fine Arts Society were no longer to be used by the Academy, and as the building had been heavily mortgaged, the council considered it advisable to liquidate its holding. The Art Students League had previously acquired the stock held by the Architectural League of New York and now entered into negotiations with the Academy to obtain sole control. The Academy owned 187 shares of stock, but its monetary value had so depreciated owing to the mortgage, that the council was glad to dispose of it for the sum of $5,000, thus being relieved of further responsibility and loss.

On March 27, 1941, a second fire started in the school building at 109th Street, destroying a third of the building. Fortunately, part of the art treasures had already been moved to the building on Fifth Avenue. The studios on the second floor were condemned for future use. As the property had been offered for sale, the estimated cost of reconstruction prohibited its consideration. But the council was reluctant to discontinue the school completely. Rooms were engaged for temporary quarters and Sidney Dickinson and Ivan Olinsky offered their services as instructors without remuneration. Later the required repairs were made to the lower floors of the school, permitting their use by a limited number of pupils. Karl Anderson and Jon Corbino joined the staff of instructors.

It was not until 1945 that negotiations for the sale of the 109th Street property were consummated and approved at a special meeting of Academicians on April 17 of that year. A contract was entered into with the trustees of the Women's Hospital, located on the adjoining property, whereby the Academy agreed to accept $25,000 on signing the contract and the balance of $200,000 on delivery of the deed on July 1, 1946. The transfer was not completed, however, until December 30, 1948, thus permitting the operation of the school until that time. During the war period the enrollment did not exceed 50 pupils, but before the termination of occupancy it had exceeded 100. The prizes were continued as well as the standard of achievement.

At the meeting of Academicians held December 22, 1941, Roy Brown offered a resolution, "That a section of painters in the Water Color class be included in the membership of the Academy." This was amended to the effect that the painters in water color be made a separate class, limited in number to 25 Academicians. As the resolution required an amendment to the constitution to make it operative, 27 members present signed a request that it be presented, after due notification, to a meeting of Academicians for ratification. A special meeting was accordingly held on January 28, 1942. The amendment was freely discussed, with differing opinions, and no decision reached. The question was ultimately decided at a meeting held on February 23, 1943, 41 Academicians being present. The amendment adopted was as follows: "The membership of the Academy shall consist of painters in oil, painters in water color, sculptors, architects and workers in the graphic arts, and shall be divided into three classes, viz. Academicians, Associates and Honorary Corresponding Members. The number of Academicians shall be limited to 225 and shall include not more than 125 painters in oil, 25 painters in watercolor, 50 sculptors, 25 architects and 25 workers in the graphic arts." The number of Associate Members continued to be unlimited.

Examples in water color had been included in the early exhibitions of the Academy, but after the formation of the American Water Color Society, work in that medium had been excluded from the Academy. Many of the painters worked in both water color and oil with eminent success. The revival and significance of water color in the second quarter of the present century made the exclusion of its practitioners seem unfavorable. Because of limited wall space, the water color section is, at present, represented only by the examples of members elected in that class.

With the entrance of the United States into the Second World War, the National Defense Artists' Committee was formed. The Academy received a citation from the Red Cross in acknowledgment of its efforts and contributions. Apart from the special interest in the demonstrations given in the galleries of the Academy, the current publicity called wide attention to the appeal. Katharine Cornell posed for Wheeler Williams, Cedric Hardwick for Jo Davidson. Charles Dana Gibson made drawings of Gertrude Lawrence and Katharine Cornell. Many of the members aided the government in official and civil capacities. In the armed forces the pictorial staff was represented by Captain Peter Hurd, Captain Ogden Pleissner, Captain Francis Bradford, Captain Floyd Gahman, Captain Samuel Chamberlain, and Captain Harry Camden. Commander Charles Bittinger was head of camouflage. Others who were in service included Commander William Platt, Lieutenant Colonel James Kellum Smith, Captain Sidney Waugh; Lieutenant Commander Lawrence Grant White; Lieutenant Commander Wheeler Williams. There were also many of the members on the assembly lines in war industry, or working in other helpful ways. Thirty-two students from the school were in the armed forces.

An event of unique significance to the Academy was the launching of the victory ship *Samuel F. B. Morse* at Baltimore on May 1, 1944. On that occasion a portrait of Morse by Alphaeus Cole was presented by the Academy and unveiled during the ceremony. This is the only ship of the navy in which a portrait of the man for whom the ship was named is displayed, special permission having been given by the Secretary of the Navy. The idea was promoted by Georg Lober, who represented the Academy at the launching. *Life* magazine publicized the event with a six-page illustrated story on the artist-inventor, much of the material for which was gathered from the archives of the Academy.

Thus it is demonstrated that the artists of our country have served not only in the cultural development of the arts, but in time of war their activity and inventions have been an important contribution to victory. The submarine, first demonstrated by Robert Fulton; the telegraph and other scientific marvels based upon the invention of Samuel Morse; the art of camouflage; and last but not least, pictorial publicity are among the many achievements arising from the peaceful arts in time of war.

In February, 1941, the sad news was received by the council of the passing of one of the most devoted and loved friends of the Academy,

Joseph Isidor. Mr. Isidor had been an annual donor to the library and was instrumental, under the recommendations of the library committee, of contributing many of its most treasured volumes. In his last will Mr. Isidor provided that upon the death of his wife, Rosa Kate Isidor, he desired that the Academy receive certain securities to be known as the "Joseph S. Isidor Fund," the income from such fund to be administered by the council, as it may seem fit, for the use of the academy school, $5,000 being set aside for the purchase of books for the library. "In the explanation of the foregoing provision, I wish to say that I have for many years derived great pleasure from my acquaintance with art and artists, and I desire that my name may be permanently associated with an effort to promote the interests and aid in the advancement of American art." (Minutes) Mrs. Isidor died on December 16, 1948. On March 9, 1950, the Treasurer received from the trustees of the estate $85,075.05 in securities having a book value of $61,776.55 and a cash principal of $23,298.50, with an accumulated income of $2,937.25.

The artists who had come into prominence in the early years of the century were now in advancing years, and many had joined their illustrious predecessors behind the veil of the departed. In November, 1942, the members received the sad notice of the passing of one of their most faithful and beloved members, Charles Courtney Curran. Mr. Curran had "served the Academy with honor as Corresponding Secretary for more than twenty years in which position, through his sterling character and unfailing courtesy, he endeared himself to the members of the Academy." He was succeeded by Georg Lober, who had served under Mr. Curran as assistant secretary, and who was thus enabled to carry on the continuity and the responsibilities of the office. At the annual meeting of 1942, J. Scott Williams was elected assistant corresponding secretary, and Raymond P. R. Neilson, recording secretary.

In the last will of Mary Gertrude Abbey, written in 1931, the council of the National Academy was appointed to perpetuate her desire in the administration of the conditions pertaining to a bequest in memory of her husband, Edwin Austin Abbey. The deed of trust created three funds known as the Abbey Mural Fund, the Abbey Scholarship Trust Fund, and the Abbey School Fund.

The original value of the Abbey Mural Fund, as stated in the deed of trust, amounted to approximately $300,000. However, after liquidating the securities for the purpose of distribution among the various beneficiaries, the Academy received a little in excess of $200,000 as the capital of the fund. It was the express desire of Mrs. Abbey that no part of principal should be used for any purpose other than to produce income and that the fund should not operate until after January 1, 1937. Upon receipt of the principal, the council of the Academy voted to allow the income to accumulate for a period of years, to increase the capital. Thus the first awards of the Mural Fund, under the provisions of the will, were not made until 1940.

Mural painting in America had had no tradition and little precedent before the advent of the Chicago World's Fair of 1893. It is true that the genius of John La Farge had revived ecclesiastical painting in works of imposing significance, but there had been little or no demand for the decoration of public buildings, and our painters were quite unpracticed in this art. The commission to decorate the interior of the Congressional Library at Washington offered the first liberal opportunity to create permanent works in mural painting, the example of which was followed in many state and municipal buildings. This was largely due to the revival of interest in architecture and to the helpful collaboration of architects. This had a particular relation to the significance of the Academy, as most of the artists engaged in both branches of the profession were sympathetically known to each other as fellow members.

The decorations of the Boston Public Library, executed by Puvis de Chavannes, John Singer Sargent, and Edwin Austin Abbey, created wide public attention as well as much interest and controversy in artistic circles. The commission given to Abbey furthered this branch of his art, and it may have been due to this development of mural painting in America that suggested the bequest of Mrs. Abbey.

The purpose of the bequest was three-fold: first, to found and maintain professorships and classes in decorative design and mural painting (the Edwin Austin Abbey Memorial Foundation for the Study of Mural Painting); second, to provide scholarships for advanced study in mural painting (the Incorporated Edwin Austin Abbey Memorial Scholarships for Mural Painting in the United States of America); and third, to make possible the awarding of commissions to distinguished artists to execute murals for buildings devoted to public service (the Edwin Austin Abbey Trust Fund for Mural Painting in the United States of America).

In regard to the commissions awarded under the Abbey Mural Fund, Mrs. Abbey expressed the wish that "only those artists who have proved themselves draughtsmen, designers and mural painters of a very high order shall be entrusted with said commissions." The award of commissions for mural decoration is made by the council of the Academy in accordance with the conditions of the trust. The first commission was given to Barry Faulkner, in 1940, to execute four murals on the walls of the Senate Chamber at Concord, New Hampshire, the work being completed in 1942. The second commission was awarded to Gifford Beal in 1943, to decorate the side wall of the School of Engineering at Princeton University, completed in 1945. The third and fourth commissions were awarded to Leon Kroll and Arthur Crisp in 1952. Mr. Kroll's decorations for the state capitol of Indiana were shown at the American Academy of Arts and Letters in January, 1953, before being installed at Indianapolis. Mr. Crisp's work is to decorate the state capitol at Columbus, Ohio.

In 1939, in accordance with the provisions of Mrs. Abbey's will pertaining to the Abbey Scholarship Trust Fund, the trustees of the fund, the National Academy of Design and Cornelius Smyth, formed and incorporated an association entitled the Incorporated Edwin Austin Abbey Memorial Scholarships for Mural Painting in the United States of America. The purpose of the corporation was to award, maintain, and manage the scholarships founded by Mrs. Mary Gertrude Abbey in memory of her husband, the late Edwin Austin Abbey. "To award scholarships to successful competitors for the purpose of enabling the holders to pursue their artistic studies and particularly the study of the art of mural painting in accordance with a course and under conditions from time to time prescribed by the corporation." The first meeting of the directors, held in 1939, called together Barry Faulkner, Arthur Covey, Harvey Wiley Corbett, Gifford Beal, and Leon Kroll. The first scholarship was awarded in 1941.

·XVII·

TOWARD OTHER TOMORROWS: THE EXHIBITION COMMITTEE · THE RE-
VISED MEMBERSHIP COMMITTEE · 125TH ANNIVERSARY · EXHIBI-
TION AND BANQUET IN HONOR OF SAMUEL F. B. MORSE · THE AMERICAN
HERITAGE · REVISIONS OF THE CONSTITUTION · THE SCHOOL MOVES
TO FIFTH AVENUE · THE "AVANT GARDE" · EVOLUTION OF THE ACAD-
EMY EXHIBITIONS

DURING THE ADMINISTRATION of Hobart Nichols two fundamental problems pertaining to the annual exhibitions and the method of nominating
and electing new members were given continuous considerations, both in
view of extending national representation in the Academy.

The first was implemented by establishing an exhibition committee to
be composed of the president, the first vice-president, the chairman of
the jury in each class to be represented in the exhibition, and one member,
either an Academician or an Associate, who is appointed by the president. The function of the committee is to prepare the annual schedule
of regular and special exhibitions, as well as to supervise the annual exhibitions of the Academy, and to solicit such works which, in its opinion,
would enhance the exhibition, the number of invited works being subject
to the approval of the council. Changes were also made in the jury of
selection, its membership being reduced to seven painters, three sculptors,
three water colorists, three architects, and three workers in the graphic
arts; each jury functions independently for its own class.

The problem of the membership committee and how it was to operate
proved more difficult to solve; its conferences covered a period of several
years and necessitated repeated amendments to the constitution. This

committee had originally been formed under the administration of Jonas Lie. As the committee was appointed by the president, it was considered to delegate too great authority in the selection of candidates for election. Consequently, the decision of the council, which authorized its enactment, was rescinded. John Taylor Arms, first vice-president of the Academy, reinaugurated this committee, with changes in the method of electing its members and the mode of its procedure. The purpose of Mr. Arms was to create a committee composed of members representing the several professions included in the membership of the Academy, whose sole function would be to propose artists of national distinction as Associate Members in their respective classes.

Under the previous constitution, any Academician or Associate could propose a candidate for Associate membership, provided his proposal was seconded and also sponsored by five additional members. Being thus nominated, the candidate was voted upon by all members present at the general meeting of Academicians and Associates. It could happen, therefore, that a candidate, being duly nominated and elected, might not receive the majority vote of his own professional class. To eliminate this possibility, the amendment proposed by Mr. Arms ruled that the candidate for nomination must be sponsored by the members of his own professional class, and that the proposal must receive the approval of the majority of the members of that class before the candidate would be eligible for election at the annual meeting held for that purpose. This mode of nomination and election was open to any member of the Academy but, as Mr. Arms contended, the candidates were apt to be limited to local artists, or personal friends of the proposers. The object of the membership committee was therefore to propose candidates nationally recognized in their respective professions, and in conference to deliberate upon their qualification. The committee was to be elected by the Academicians and to be so constituted that a certain proportion of new members would be elected each year, both in the Associate and in the Academician classifications.

The amendments to the constitution necessary for the enactment of this new method of nomination were duly ratified by the Academicians, and the first election under its ruling was highly approved. Thirty-eight candidates of eminence, in all classes, were elected at the general meeting of 1948. In the following year, however, many of the candidates proposed for nomination did not receive the approval of the majority of the members of their professional class, Raphael Soyer being the only candidate nominated and elected in the painter class. This necessitated a further amendment which provided that a candidate need receive the approval of the majority only of those voting, rather than that of the full membership of his professional class.

The final modification of Mr. Arms's original resolution did not take place until the succeeding administration. As now constituted, the membership committee is composed of 24 members—9 painters, 6 sculptors, 3 architects, 3 water colorists, and 3 from graphic arts. "The duties of the Membership Committee shall be to stimulate interest in and consideration of nationally recognized artists, and to suggest and propose such artists as candidates for nomination in their respective class." Each class meets separately and submits its report not later than twelve weeks before the general meeting. In addition to such proposals, any member may propose a candidate for nomination according to the previous provision, if the sponsors are of the same professional class as the candidate proposed. After all of the proposals have been received, the names of the candidates are mailed to the members of the class in which the candidate is proposed. "If a candidate receives the approval of a majority of those voting in his professional class, his name shall be submitted to all of the Academicians and Associates, to be voted upon at the General Meeting. Otherwise, his candidacy shall be considered as withdrawn." At the general meeting the affirmative votes of two thirds of the members voting constitutes election.

The nomination of candidates for Academicianship follows a similar method. Each Academician and Associate is privileged to propose the names of Associates in his own professional class, not to exceed the number of vacancies. Such proposals are mailed to each Academician of the class in which the candidate is proposed. "If a candidate receives the approval of a majority of the Academicians voting in the same professional class, his name shall be submitted to all of the Academicians. Otherwise, his candidacy shall be considered as withdrawn." The names of the approved candidates are then mailed to each Academician, with a record of the vote in each class. If, at the annual meeting of Academicians, the nominee shall receive a two-thirds affirmative vote, he is declared an Academician-elect. No Associate shall be a candidate for Academicianship at more than two successive annual meetings. Any member residing twenty-five miles or more from Columbus Circle is privileged to vote by mail. All voting is by secret ballot.

It is seen, therefore, that the candidate must have the approval of the members voting in his own professional class before being voted upon by the members of all classes. This preliminary screening has had a beneficial effect in electing artists of national reputation.

To inform the membership of the activities of the Academy and to solicit constructive suggestions, it was again proposed to publish a quarterly bulletin, to be edited by Eliot Clark. The first issue, published November, 1945, contained an illuminating commentary on the origin and significance of Academies by Albert Sterner.

It is a prevalent if erroneous idea that Academic training in the craft of the Fine Arts exerts a retarding influence on the creative faculties of the art student. This is a proverbial myth. Academies justly believe that no worth-while performance in any of the arts is possible without fundamental training, without knowledge, tested and traditionally handed on from craftsman to craftsman, as it was in the Mediaeval Guilds. What the eventual artist has to say, with this acquired technical knowledge, has nothing to do with an Academy or any other practical workshop. No Academy can or ever has destroyed or hindered the inevitable development of the rarely-born artist.

The bulletin noted that "by looking through the catalogs of this season's important exhibitions that a very large proportion of those represented are members of our 'non-progressive, moribund N. A. D.' Also many of the pictures were originally shown at the Academy Annuals."

In the second issue of the bulletin the editor contributed a "Retrospective Note of the National Academy Schools." The records of the school from the date of the fire in 1905 to 1946 showed a total enrollment of 17,690, the highest attendance in any one year (1927–28) being 687. Frederic Taubes was quoted in answers to "A Fair Question: Where do you stand with regard to Modern Art? To the right of the road, to the left, or in the middle?" He answered that "Good art does not walk on either side of the road, in fact, it doesn't walk at all—it soars. Good art is neither modern or old; what is modern today is de-modernized tomorrow, like ladies' hats. . . . There is just as much of the academic displayed in the exhibitions of the Museum of Modern Art as there is on the premises of the National Academy. There is as much of the academic among the abstractionists as there is among the haystack painters." Unhappily, after the first two issues, the bulletin was discontinued, owing to cost of publication and the burden of compilation.

At the annual meeting of 1946 President Hobart Nichols stated

Since reporting the state of the Academy at the last Annual Meeting, we have shared with our fellow Americans pride and relief on two great, historic days, VE Day and VJ Day, thus bringing to a close the most devastating war in the records of humanity. All normal activities were greatly affected, even in our country, which was spared the horror and destruction of combat on its soil. But fortunately, during these years of war, the Academy has carried on its activities with success and has added very considerably to its material wealth, through the generosity of Mr. Huntington and the wise investment of its funds. Never within my knowledge has the Academy been in such a secure position as it is at present. . . . Within the year we have negotiated for and finally purchased the adjoining property at No. 7 East 89th Street, and recently we have concluded the purchase of the adjoining property at 1082 Fifth Avenue.

Plans were considered for the erection of a school building on the lots facing 89th Street, but OPA regulations and shortage of materials prevented its operation.

The 121st annual exhibition was divided in two sections. The first was an open-jury show in which no work by members of the Academy was exempt, but which had a large number of invited works by nonmembers. Inaugurated as an experiment, this was met with the just complaint that nonmembers should be invited when that privilege was not extended to members. The second exhibition was composed of works by members only. A further innovation was the inauguration of the bi-annual exhibition of drawings under the chairmanship of John Taylor Arms. The exhibition received unusually favorable press comments. It was indeed a provocative and revealing testimony of the artists' formative creation, but after the second exhibition lack of public interest and the cost of presentation precluded its justifiable continuance.

In October, 1946, the Pepsi-Cola Company held its national exhibition in the galleries of the Academy. As there had been regional juries throughout the United States, the exhibition was thoroughly representative, while national publicity and promotion furthered a large attendance. Thus the new location of the galleries, with continuous exhibitions throughout the season, was becoming a familiar center of the art activities of the city. The Pepsi-Cola exhibition was continued the following year, but thereafter was discontinued. A feature of the annual exhibition of 1949 was the presentation of invited works by the candidates nominated for election. These were hung as a group, together with the work of members elected the previous year. The second half of the 123d annual exhibition was devoted to architectural drawings, water colors, and prints.

In reporting for the council at the annual meeting of 1948, President Nichols referred particularly to "the excellent work done by the Committee of Membership in this first year of its operation." Commending John Taylor Arms for his untiring effort in formulating this committee, Mr. Nichols asserted, "It is generally agreed that the Arms Amendment made it possible to elect the most distinguished group of new members that the Academy has considered in many years." At this same meeting Eliot Clark was elected corresponding secretary and Isabel Bishop, recording secretary; Dana Pond and Robert Brackman were elected members of the council.

At the annual meeting of 1949 Hobart Nichols retired from the presidency. In his valedictory address Mr. Nichols, after outlining the activities of the current year, concluded:

For the past full decade you have honored me with your confidence in the high office of President of the National Academy of Design, an office still considered by worthy people the greatest honor that an American artist can achieve. During this unusually long period of service, which I venture to hope, was not without success, I have had the unfailing support and encouragement of the membership-at-large, and particularly of a group of co-workers some of whose period of service equals my own. To all, I desire to register my sincere gratitude. But there is one member who has contributed more constructive ideas and given more lavishly of his valuable time than most of us. I refer to the retiring vice-president, John Taylor Arms. . . . The outstanding feature of my administration, indeed the chief pillar of its success, is of course, the great generosity and interest of Mr. Archer M. Huntington. He has enriched the Academy, actually and potentially, with gifts of real estate and money to more than a million dollars. He has done this unconditionally, which is characteristic of his generosity, and I feel that the Academy is obligated to use these funds and property with wisdom and prudence, and always for the permanent benefit of the Academy.

At the conclusion of the meeting a letter was read from the nominating committee, Ernest Roth, chairman: "The Nominating Committee, wishing to acknowledge Mr. Nichols's long and loyal services to the Academy and, realizing it has no power to take action, recommends that the Council, if possible, bestow on Mr. Nichols the title of President Emeritus." Mr. Georg Lober then presented this request to the assembled Academicians, which being duly seconded, was heartily and unanimously approved. In a brief word of appreciation of the honor conferred upon him, the retiring president said, in conclusion, that no words could express more simply his gratitude than "I thank you."

The president then announced that candidates nominated for office, council, and Academicianship were all elected: for president, DeWitt M. Lockman; first vice-president, Roy Brown; second vice-president, Ogden Pleissner; corresponding secretary, Eliot Clark; assistant corresponding secretary, Brenda Putnam; recording secretary, Salvatore Lascari; treasurer, Arthur Crisp; assistant treasurer, Charles Keck; members of council: Ralph Fabri and Ferdinand Warren to serve for three years; and Julius Delbos, to serve for one year. Thus the new president entered his office with but few members representing the previous administration.

Elected an Academician in 1921, DeWitt M. Lockman had previously served on the council and also as chairman of the school and library committees. He was thus thoroughly conversant with the functions of administration. His term of office coincided with the 125th Anniversary of the Academy, and as president he devoted his time and energy to the commemoration of that event.

Mr. Archer M. Huntington added to his magnanimous benefactions with a bequest of $200,000, the income from which was to be used in furthering public relations at the discretion of the president and the consent of the council. This happily provided funds to defray the cost of the celebration. The special tribute was in honor of the first president and founding father of the Academy, Samuel Finley Breese Morse. In cooperation with the Museum of Natural History, which placed at the disposal of the Academy one of its large halls, an exhibition was arranged of the works of Morse both as painter and scientist. The elaborate catalogue, in which all of the paintings exhibited were reproduced, was prefaced with a foreword by the president. The text told of the history of the Academy, of Morse the artist and Morse the scientist and was supplemented by contributions demonstrating the fundamental significance of his discovery in relation to the marvels that were to follow in radio, television, and the evolution of electronics. Seven thousand copies of the

catalogue were published and distributed to various institutions throughout the country.

It was indeed an impressive exhibition, demonstrating the fact that the
creative artist is a *seer*, envisioning the world of the unknown by means
of the known, the coordination of visual observation and intellectual
contemplation.

Preceding the exhibition in honor of its first president, a gala banquet
was given at the Waldorf-Astoria, attended by over 500 guests. A feature
of the occasion uniting past and present was a telegraphic message, sent in
cooperation with the government, whereby the words, "What hath God
wrought," were transmitted from the Smithsonian Institute at Washington and recorded by Morse's original instrument placed before the
speakers' dais. This was followed by a message of congratulation from the
Royal Academy in London delivered by the British representative,
Robert Wilberforce.

In sending his greetings and paying tribute to the Academy and its
founder as artist and inventor, President Truman, in his congratulations,
telegraphed in part: "On this memorable occasion, may I extend felicita-
tions to the National Academy of Design, founded by that illustrious and
versatile American, Samuel F. B. Morse, upon its long and splendid record
of achievement in the advancement of American art. The National Academy has been the inspiration and guiding force of art in America for a
century and a quarter."

Representatives of civic, educational, scientific, and art institutions
honored the speakers' table. It was most fitting that the chancellor of
New York University, Harry Woodburn Chase, should be present to
honor the man who, as artist and inventor, had been so closely associated
with that University; also present was Roland L. Redmond, president of
the Metropolitan Museum, with which institution the Academy has co-
operated from the first days of its organization. The venerable William
Adams Delano addressed the guests as president of the City Art Commission, and Walter P. Marshall as president of the Western Union Telegraph
Company. F. Trubee Davison, president of the American Museum of
Natural History, represented that vast field of learning and natural
science, in relation to which Charles Willson Peale, the renowned colonial painter, founded the first museum. It was a happy and memorable

occasion wherein art and science could join in proclaiming their mutual relation of enlightened vision and discerning understanding.

The celebration was concluded by an exhibition of the works of living members of the Academy, held in the galleries of the Academy in the autumn of that year.

Arthur Crisp succeeded Frederick Ballard Williams as treasurer of the Academy, his first endeavor being the reorganization of the administration of finance. The Fulton Trust Company of New York (now incorporated with the New York Trust Company), was appointed as custodian of all securities owned by the Academy and was to act in an advisory capacity with the treasurer and finance committee and, with their approval, to make all disbursements. The combined funds of the Academy had been placed in a general pool. As this included the restricted as well as the unrestricted resources of the Academy, the treasurer's next problem was to separate the two. This proved more complicated. The result, however, was clarifying to the extent that the council was informed precisely of its unrestricted funds and was thus, in consequence, enabled to regulate its expenditure in relation to its free income. A separate account is kept for each bequest. As the school, the exhibitions, and the maintenance of building operation and the staff combined to cause a heavy annual deficit, the perennial problem of the council has been to reduce expenses within the required program of its activities. Mr. Crisp has kept a vigilant eye on expenditures.

On the resignation of the recording secretary, Salvatore Lascari, Alphaeus Cole was appointed by the council to fill the vacancy, and was elected to that office at the annual meeting, to be followed on his retirement by Ralph Fabri.

At a special meeting of the council in March, 1950, Adolph Weinman, as chairman, presented the report of the nominating committee. "The Nominating Committee regrets that our President, who has worked so unceasingly for the Academy during the past year, has been ordered by his physician to abstain from any further responsibility or undue effort. Consequently he has asked the committee not to consider him as a candidate for renomination."

At the annual meeting of Academicians in May, 1950, Lawrence Grant White was elected president, with Sidney Waugh as first vice-president,

Walter Biggs and Gordon Grant being elected to the council. Mr. White, member of the firm of McKim, Mead and White, founded by his renowned father, Stanford White, is thus the second architect to preside over the Academy. Accustomed to administrative responsibility and active in the arts of design, Mr. White brings to the office sound and liberal judgment. The first duty of the new council was to incorporate the recent amendments to the constitution, to append the by-laws pertaining to meetings and committees, and to clarify other articles. This resulted in a revision of the constitution, under the chairmanship of the corresponding secretary, which on completion was ratified at a special meeting of Academicians March 14, 1951, to become effective April 25, 1951.

Under the new constitution an executive committee was added to the administration, composed of the president, the treasurer, and the corresponding secretary, the duty of which committee is to take action on such urgent matters that may arise in connection with administration, and to report such action to the council for ratification.

A new office was also added to the staff, Mr. Vernon C. Porter being engaged as director of the Academy. Mr. Porter had been previously director of the Riverside Museum and, more recently, assistant to the director of the Art Students League. His duty is to supervise the management and maintenance of the building, to have charge of the staff, to execute the instructions as ordered by the council, and, in addition, to direct the school under the supervision of the school committee. Having been trained in this double function, he is well able to direct his administration.

After the sale of the Academy property facing Cathedral Parkway, the school was temporarily discontinued until such time as new provision could be made. Plans have been designed for the erection of a building on the vacant lot adjoining the Academy on East 89th Street, but insufficient funds have delayed their execution. In the meantime, the large gallery B-1, with an entrance on East 89th Street, was altered, a new lighting system installed, and the basement provided with student lockers and other necessary requirements. Although it has deprived the Academy of one of its much needed exhibition rooms, it has provided an excellent studio for a limited number of students. Classes opened in October, 1950, with an enrollment of 131 students. Ogden Pleissner, Ivan Olinsky, and

Robert Philipp served as instructors in drawing and painting; Ralph Fabri, chairman of the school committee, served as instructor in the graphic arts and was replaced by Ernest Roth the following year. Mr. Pleissner retired after the first season, but served as chairman of the school committee, together with Robert Brackman and Henry Gasser. Louis Bouché was appointed to fill the vacancy, the class in etching being discontinued. Under the able direction of the instructors and the school committee, the classes have developed favorably, as indicated by the excellent work exhibited at the end of the school term. Plans are still under consideration for enlarging both the school and the galleries of the Academy.

As examples from the permanent collection of the Academy had not been publicly displayed since 1942 and, as the name "National Academy" was given in 1826, it was thought to be a propitious occasion to present a retrospective exhibition of American painting during the nineteenth century. Entitled "The American Tradition," the exhibition was held in the galleries of the Academy the first half of December, 1951. Representative of the national achievement in painting, it included the most honored names of the profession, and illustrated the great changes in style and technique during the first century of the Academy's heritage. Individual artists stand out prominently and the sequence of the American tradition is integrated in the influence of a particular period. Thus one could study, in the same gallery, the work of Sargent, Duveneck, Eakins, and Bellows; of Inness, Wyant, Homer, and Ryder; or, in the upper gallery, the naturalistic examples of Cole, Durand, Church, Kensett, Whittredge, and Cropsey. A unique contribution of the collection were the many examples of self-portraits, or of those by fellow members, of the artists represented. The greater number of the examples exhibited were selected from the permanent collection of the Academy but, where an artist was not properly represented in the Academy collection, his work was supplemented by important examples from various museums, art dealers, and private collections. The Academy is particularly indebted for the helpful assistance of the Metropolitan Museum.

The American Federation of Arts selected 28 examples from the exhibition for a rotary tour during 1952–53 and has recorded it as one of the most favored exhibitions of the season.

Through the interest and generosity of the Frick Art Reference Library, 750 photographs have been made of the paintings in the permanent collection prior to 1905. A duplicate set was presented to the Academy and is of great value for convenient reference.

In 1952 Charles Downing Lay was appointed archivist and Mary Bartlett Cowdrey of Smith College, assistant archivist. Miss Cowdrey is the author of the *National Academy of Design Exhibition Record, 1826–1860*, published by the New York–Historical Society in 1943. She has been authorized by the council to extend this work, compiled from the original exhibition catalogues, up until 1870, and it is hoped that it may be extended for every ten years thereafter. "Under the name of each exhibiting artist are grouped the titles of every work of art exhibited year by year, with the catalog numbers, the name of the owner in italics, or designation for sale, if the picture is so indicated in the original catalog. Whenever one work of art is associated with two artists' names, as collaborators or as artist and engraver, it is given under the name of each artist." Miss Cowdrey states in the introduction, "Students in the field of American art have been constantly turning to the Annual Exhibition catalogs of the National Academy of Design for specific information on the works of nineteenth century American artists. The demand on the material, increasing as it does year by year, made apparent the need for such a compilation of the early records as the present work. . . . Within the last few years many of the more important artists of the first half of the nineteenth century have been withdrawn from obscurity and honored by exhibitions, catalogs, check lists and monographs. To investigate thoroughly the work of any American artist after 1825, the research student must consult the National Academy records if for no other reason than to satisfy himself that the artist in question did not exhibit."

At the annual meeting of 1952 seven Associates were elected Academicians, of whom two were painters; sixteen Associates were elected, of whom three were painters. The council elected, as Honorary Corresponding Members, Sir Gerald Kelly, president of the Royal Academy of Arts; Sir Giles Gilbert Scott, president of the Royal Institute of British Architects, and Alfred Joseph Casson, president of the Royal Canadian Academy of Arts.

Eight Academicians passed away in the same year, and seven Associate members. As the Associate membership of the Academy is, by constitution, unlimited, it will be seen that although death deprives the Academy of its honored members, the renewal of life ever amplifies its membership and carries on the work of the departed in active memory of the enduring heritage of the founding fathers.

The period from 1925 to 1953 has been one of general world unrest— the revaluation of all values. Historically, it is marked by the Great Depression, the rise of totalitarian domination in Germany and Italy, the horrors of the Second World War, followed by the "cold war" of Communism against Freedom. The corresponding revolt in the arts is manifested by the disintegration of traditional continuity, the return to primitivism, and the analytical dissection of aesthetic values, the ultimate end of which is a complete divorce from all humanistic association. The revolt has many ramifications, all of which, in sincere effort, are an endeavor to seek new forms of vitalized expression. The movement is now a part of history. Whether it is a beginning or a dead end, future evolution can alone determine. The disintegration is, however, unparalleled in the history of art. At moments one witnesses the crosscurrents of time, as if in a dream the ancestors were in battle for survival.

Archaeology, research, and processes of reproduction have brought a visual nearness to the primordial imagery of man. This visual awareness has permeated modern imagery, but the significance of its original meaning and content is unrelated to the mind of modern man. Freudian psychoanalysis of dreams uncovered the nether world of the persistence of the subconscious and revealed the conflict between the intellect, the will, and the subliminal mind; of past and present; of time and eternity. The main currents of modernism are themselves in conflict: free emotional expressionism, conscious constructivism, and sublimated "pure art." All, however, are in conflict with optical and technical representation.

The revolution in art, called both "modern" and "international," began in Paris before the First World War and was closely related to sociological changes. The movement, in its inception, was a protest against the restrictions of the Salon and the closed jury system. An artist could be known only in exhibitions; if he was excluded, he was unknown. The program of personal publicity was initiated by Courbet, Whistler, Manet, and the Salon des Refusés. Collectively it was promoted by the inauguration of the Salon des Independents in 1884, and by the Salon d'Automne in 1905, in both of which any artist might exhibit on payment of a fee.

Pictorially it was a revolt against the tradition of the Renaissance and a return to the primitives.

Economically and politically, it was a contest between the "haves" and the "have nots." The socialists' plea for equality of opportunity and reward was equated with artistic equality and freedom of expression. Aesthetically it might be called the analytical era as opposed to the impressionistic era which had preceded it.

In France, the First World War held the movement in abeyance. The art schools were closed. Thereafter the progressive education of the student with its concomitant examinations and discipline was severed. Individual expression was stressed before the student was technically trained.

In America the so-called radicals of the 'eighties now became the deans of the Academy; to them "modern art" was anathema. But, as in France, the war brought a lull to the movement, and was followed by the trend of "regional art" and the national expansion of art consciousness.

After the Second World War, the modernist movement gained impetus. As in the 'seventies and 'eighties, students returning from abroad brought with them the new formulas. Art dealers promoted the "Ecole de Paris." Sales boomed in inflated figures. Regional art was forgotten; abstraction became the vogue. The French masters of the style were now of the older generation. Revolt could go no further. In America, the radicals of the first quarter of the century were in reaction. How is the new leaven to be formed and what direction is it to follow?

The modern movement may be timed in its evolution both geographically and anthropologically. Springing from Paris as a cosmopolitan art, it permeated the eastern states twenty-five years later as the *avant-garde*, and a decade later, like a tidal wave, reached the Pacific.

The "independents" in New York followed the pattern of Paris; while the Academy, like the Salon, followed "tradition." Likewise sociological changes and influences followed the revolution in Russia. Greenwich Village became the center of ferment. The art world seethed with contention. The post-impressionists were followed by the expressionists, the cubists, the abstractionists, and the purists. The art of representation was labeled "academic" or, more politely, "traditional." Art had been reduced to the level of promotion and publicity.

The Academy walls could not contain the vast annual production. The preference given to members, plus the jury system, precluded proper representation. As the Academy was unable to extend its galleries, it was natural that other organizations should be formed. This need was furthered by the Whitney Museum of American Art, followed by the Museum of Modern Art, devoted largely to foreign production. Selection, however, became more restricted, and the control passed from the artist to the professional director, both institutions being privately endowed to carry out the intended purpose.

The evolution of creative art cannot be stopped by lack of wall space, for quantity is not the equivalent of quality. The truly creative artist is as rare as the scientific seer. Whereas the geography of the earthly habitat has been explored and terra incognita is no more, the empyrean of the imagination remains ever undiscovered—the seeing eye guided by inner illumination, the reflection of the infinite visualized in the finite, the seer and the source united.

Although the Academy is now past its 125th anniversary, the unknown artist is still discovered on its walls. The artists on the jury of selection have still a keen eye in anticipation of a new find, and the unknown of today becomes the known of tomorrow.

This is as it should be. Evolution does not follow a straight line. Action and reaction are resolved in synthesis. In the continuity of time the end is also the beginning. Evolution follows a slow underlying rhythm; like the sea, the tempest disturbs its surface. The eye records the image as the ear records the sound, but both have meaning only in the reflection of the mind.

With the ever changing trends of fashion, the Academy in its long history has undergone periodical criticism. The word itself, in Greece once held in reverence, has become a misnomer; but its proper meaning should revive its significance as the education of the artist and the cultivation of the individual.

During this crisis, the Academy has continued a natural evolution. Without a predetermined aesthetic policy, which was not inherent in its purpose, this has been inevitable. As an organization, the newly elected Associate members, reflecting their generation, have equal power relative to the selection and display of exhibitions, while the Academicians represent the continuity of an earlier genesis. It is apparent, however, that the aesthetic criterion cannot be determined by age, or timeliness equated with time. The long history of the Academy exhibitions illustrates this evolution. There is, in consequence, no sporadic break. This has engendered a stabilizing condition in a time of revolution and a fortification for the many who carry on the tradition.

The initial intention and purpose of the Academy is as vital today as it was at the time of its inception: the dual purpose of the training of the artist, and the presentation of his work. But education can impart only the tools of knowledge and the science of the craft. It remains for the artist to express himself.

APPENDIX

FOUNDERS

FIRST FIFTEEN

Thomas S. Cummings
M. I. Danforth
William Dunlap
Asher B. Durand
John Frazee
Charles C. Ingham
Henry Inman

G. Marsiglia
Peter Maverick
S. F. B. Morse
Edward C. Potter
Hugh Reinagle
Ithiel Town
W. G. Wall

Charles C. Wright

SECOND FIFTEEN

Frederick S. Agate
Alexander Anderson
Thomas Cole
James Coyle
John Evers
William Jewett
William Main

John Paradise
J. Parisen
Rembrandt Peale
Nathaniel Rogers
Martin E. Thompson
John Vanderlyn
Samuel L. Waldo

D. W. Wilson

PRESIDENTS

Samuel F. B. Morse, 1826–1845
Asher B. Durand, 1845–1861
Samuel F. B. Morse, 1861–1862
Daniel Huntington, 1862–1870
Henry P. Gray, 1870–1871
William Page, 1871–1873
J. Q. A. Ward, 1873–1874
Worthington Whittredge, 1874–1877
Daniel Huntington, 1877–1891
Thomas W. Wood, 1891–1899

Frederick Dielman, 1899–1909
John W. Alexander, 1909–1915
J. Alden Weir, 1915–1917
Herbert Adams, 1917–1920
Edwin H. Blashfield, 1920–1926
Cass Gilbert, 1926–1933
Harry W. Watrous, 1933–1934
Jonas Lie, 1934–1939
Hobart Nichols, 1939–1949
DeWitt M. Lockman, 1949–1950

Lawrence Grant White, 1950–

MEMBERS

Abbey, Edwin Austin,* 1852–1911. Painter, A.N.A. 1901, N.A. 1902
Adams, Herbert,* 1858–1945. Sculptor, A.N.A. 1898, N.A. 1899
Adams, Joseph Alexander, 1803–1880. Graphic Artist, A.N.A. 1833
Adams, Kenneth Miller, 1897–. Painter, A.N.A. 1938
Adams, Wayman, 1883–. Painter, A.N.A. 1921, N.A. 1926
Adams, William Apthorp, 1797–1881. Artist, H.M. (a) 1841
Agate, Alfred T., 1818–1846. Painter, A.N.A. 1832, H.M. (p) 1840
Agate, Frederick Style, 1803–1844. Painter, Founder, N.A. 1826

Aitken, Robert Ingersoll, 1878–1949. Sculptor, A.N.A. 1909, N.A. 1914
Albee, Grace, 1890–. Graphic Artist, A.N.A. 1941, N.A. 1946
Albee, Percy F., 1883–. Painter, A.N.A. 1943
Albert, Ernest, 1857–1946. Painter, A.N.A. 1922
Albright, Ivan LeLorraine, 1897–. Painter, A.N.A. 1942, N.A. 1950
Albright, Malvin (Zsissly), 1897–. Painter, A.N.A. 1948, N.A. 1952
Aldrich, Chester Holmes, 1871–1940. Architect, A.N.A. 1928, N.A. 1939
Aldrich, William Truman, 1880–. Architect, A.N.A. 1939, N.A. 1944
Alexander, Francis, 1800–1881. Painter, H.M. (p) 1839
Alexander, John White,* 1856–1915. Painter, A.N.A. 1901, N.A. 1902
Allan, John, 1777–1863. Antiquarian, H.M. (a) 1843
Allen, Charles Curtis, 1886–1950. Painter, A.N.A. 1933, N.A. 1945
Allen, Junius, 1898–. Painter, A.N.A. 1934, N.A. 1941
Allen, Theodore, 1800–1850. Patron, H.M. (a) 1837
Allen, Thomas,* 1849–1924. Painter, A.N.A. 1884
Allston, Washington, 1779–1843. Painter, H.M. (p) 1827
Amateis, Edmond Romulus, 1897–. Sculptor, A.N.A. 1936, N.A. 1942
Ames, Joseph, 1816–1872. Painter, A.N.A. 1869, N.A. 1870
Anderson, Alexander, 1775–1870. Engraver, Founder, N.A. (Elect) 1826, H.M.
    (p) 1843
Anderson, Karl, 1874–. Painter, A.N.A. 1913, N.A. 1923
Angel, John, 1881–. Sculptor, A.N.A. 1944, N.A. 1948
Anshutz, Thomas Pollock, 1851–1912. Painter, A.N.A. 1910
Arms, John Taylor, 1887–1953. Graphic Artist, A.N.A. 1930, N.A. 1933
Armstrong, David Maitland,* 1836–1918. Architect, A.N.A. 1906
Asplund, Tore, 1903–. Aquarellist, A.N.A. 1949, N.A. 1951
Atterbury, Grosvenor, 1869–. Architect, A.N.A. 1918, N.A. 1940
Audubon, John James, 1785–1851. Painter, H.M. (p) 1833
Audubon, John Woodhouse, 1812–1862. Painter, A.N.A. 1840, H.M. (p) 1843,
    A.N.A. 1847
Audubon, Victor Gifford, 1809–1860. Painter, A.N.A. 1840–1844, A.N.A. 1845,
    N.A. 1846
Auerbach-Levy, William, 1889–. Painter, A.N.A. 1926
Augur, Hezekiah, 1791–1858. Sculptor, ARTIST 1827, H.M. (p) 1828
Ayres, Louis, 1874–1947. Architect, A.N.A. 1935, N.A. 1936

Bacher, Otto Henry,* 1856–1909. Graphic Artist, A.N.A. 1906
Bacon, Henry, 1866–1924. Architect, A.N.A. 1913, N.A. 1917
Bacon, Peggy (Brook), 1895–. Graphic Artist, A.N.A. 1947
Baer, William Jacob, 1860–1941. Painter, A.N.A. 1913
Baker, George Augustus, Jr., 1821–1880. Painter, A.N.A. 1843–1845, 1846, N.A.
    1851
Ball, Hugh Swinton, ?–1838. Sculptor, H.M. (a) 1837
Ballin, Hugo,* 1879–. Painter, A.N.A. 1906, A.N.A. 1912(?), N.A. 1940
Barber, Donn, 1871–1925. Architect, A.N.A. 1923
Barnard, George Grey, 1863–1938. Sculptor, A.N.A. (Elect) 1902
Barry, Charles A., 1830–1892. Artist, A.N.A. (Elect) 1860

Barse, George Randolph, Jr.,* 1861–1938. Painter, A.N.A. 1898, N.A. 1900
Bartlett, Paul Wayland,* 1865–1925. Sculptor, A.N.A. (Elect) 1902, A.N.A. 1916, N.A. 1917
Bartolini, Lorenzo, 1777–1850. Sculptor, H.M. (p) 1833
Bates, Earl Kenneth, 1895–. Painter, A.N.A. 1942
Baum, Walter Emerson, 1884–. Painter, A.N.A. 1945
Baumgartner, Warren W., 1894–. Aquarellist, A.N.A. 1945, N.A. 1950
Beach, Chester, 1881–. Sculptor, A.N.A. 1908, N.A. 1924
Beal, Gifford R., 1879–. Painter, A.N.A. 1908, N.A. 1914
Beal, Reynolds, 1867–1951. Painter, A.N.A. 1909
Beard, James Henry, 1814–1893. Painter, H.M. (p) 1847, N.A. 1872
Beard, William Holbrook, 1825–1900. Painter, A.N.A. 1861, N.A. 1862
Beaux, Cecilia,* 1855–1942. Painter, A.N.A. 1894, N.A. 1902
Beckwith, James Carroll,* 1852–1917. Painter, A.N.A. 1886, N.A. 1894
Belcher, Hilda, 1881–. Painter, A.N.A. 1926, N.A. 1932
Bell, Edward August,* 1862–1953. Painter, A.N.A. 1901
Bellows, Albert Fitch, 1829–1883. Painter, A.N.A. 1859, N.A. 1861
Bellows, George Wesley, 1882–1925. Painter, A.N.A. 1909, N.A. 1913
Bellows, Rev. Henry Whitney, 1814–1882. Clergyman, H.M. (a) 1849
Belluschi, Pietro, 1899–. Architect, A.N.A. 1953
Bennett, William James, 1787–1844. Painter, A.N.A. 1827, N.A. 1828
Benson, Eugene, 1839–1908. Painter, A.N.A. 1863–1888
Benson, Frank Weston,* 1862–1951. Painter, A.N.A. 1897, N.A. 1905
Benvenuti, Pietro Aretino, 1769–1844. Painter, H.M. (p) 1829
Berman, Eugene, 1899–. Painter, A.N.A. 1950
Berneker, Louis Frederick, 1875–1937. Painter, A.N.A. 1931
Berninghaus, Oscar Edward, 1874–1952. Painter, A.N.A. 1926
Besnard, Paul Albert, 1849–1934. Painter, H.C.M. France 1932
Betts, Louis, 1873–. Painter, A.N.A. 1912, N.A. 1915
Bicknell, Frank Alfred, 1866–1943. Painter, A.N.A. 1913
Bierstadt, Albert, 1830–1902. Painter, H.M. (p) 1858, N.A. 1860
Biggs, Walter, 1886–. Aquarellist, A.N.A. 1944, N.A. 1947
Birch, Thomas, 1779–1851. Painter, H.M. (p) 1833
Birney, William Verplanck, 1858–1909. Painter, A.N.A. 1900
Bishop, Isabel (Wolff), 1902–. Painter, A.N.A. 1940, N.A. 1941
Bitter, Karl Theodore Francis,* 1867–1915. Sculptor, A.N.A. 1902, N.A. 1903
Bittinger, Charles, 1879–. Painter, A.N.A. 1912, N.A. 1937
Blake, Theodore Evernghim, 1869–1949. Architect, A.N.A. 1948
Blakelock, Ralph Albert, 1847–1919. Painter, A.N.A. 1913, N.A. 1916
Blashfield, Edwin Howland,* 1848–1936. Painter, A.N.A. 1882, N.A. 1888
Blauvelt, Charles F., 1824–1900. Painter, A.N.A. 1856, N.A. 1859
Blomfield, Sir Reginald, 1856–1942. Architect, H.C.M. England 1933
Blondell, Jacob De, 1817–1877. Painter, A.N.A. 1854
Blum, Robert Frederick,* 1857–1903. Painter, A.N.A. 1888, N.A. 1893
Blume, Peter, 1906–. Painter, A.N.A. (Elect) 1948
Blumenschein, Ernest Leonard, 1874–. Painter, A.N.A. 1910, N.A. 1927
Blumenschein, Mary Shepard Greene, 1869–. Painter, A.N.A. 1913

Bogaerts, Felix (Guillaume Marie), 1805–1851. Author, Professor of History, H.M. (a) 1846
Bogardus, Margaret, 1804–1878. Painter, A.N.A. 1842–1844, A.N.A. 1845
Bogert, George Hirst,* 1864–1944. Painter, A.N.A. 1899
Boggs, William Brenton, 1809–1875. Painter, A.N.A. (Elect) 1841
Bogle, James, 1817–1873. Painter, A.N.A. 1849, N.A. 1861
Bohm, Max, 1868–1923. Painter, A.N.A. 1917, N.A. 1920
Bohrod, Aaron, 1907–. Painter, A.N.A. 1951, N.A. (Elect) 1953
Bolton, William Jay, 1816–1884. Painter, A.N.A. 1843–1844, A.N.A. 1845
Bonfield, George R., 1802–1898. Painter, H.M. (p) 1845
Bonnat, Leon Joseph Florentin, 1833–1922. Painter, H.C.M. France 1917
Borg, Carl Oscar, 1879–1947. Painter, A.N.A. 1938
Borglum, Solon Hannibal, 1868–1922. Sculptor, A.N.A. 1911
Borie, Adolphe, 1877–1934. Painter, A.N.A. 1917, N.A. 1934
Boring, William Alciphron, 1859–1937. Architect, A.N.A. 1913
Bosa, Louis, 1905–. Painter, A.N.A. 1952
Bosley, Frederick Andrew, 1881–1942. Painter, A.N.A. 1931
Boston, Joseph H.,* 1860–. Painter, A.N.A. 1901
Bosworth, William Welles, 1869–. Architect, A.N.A. 1918, N.A. 1928
Botts, Hugh, 1903–. Graphic Artist, A.N.A. 1942
Bouché, Louis, 1896–. Painter, A.N.A. 1948, N.A. 1950
Boughton, George Henry, 1833–1905. Painter, H.M. (p) 1858, N.A. 1871
Boutelle, De Witt Clinton, 1820–1884. Painter, A.N.A. 1850–1851, A.N.A. 1852
Bower, Alexander, 1875–1952. Painter, A.N.A. 1931, N.A. 1950
Bowers, Edward, ?–? Painter, A.N.A. (Elect) 1861
Boyd, Fiske, 1895–. Graphic Artist, A.N.A. 1948
Boyle, Ferdinand Thomas Lee, 1820–1906. Painter, A.N.A. 1849–1888
Boyle, John J., 1852–1917. Sculptor, A.N.A. 1910
Brackman, Robert, 1896–. Painter, A.N.A. 1932, N.A. 1940
Bradford, Francis Scott, 1898–. Painter, A.N.A. 1932
Bradford, William, 1827?–1892. Painter, A.N.A. 1874
Brandegee, Robert Bolling,* 1848–1922. Painter, A.N.A. 1907
Brandt, Carl Ludwig, 1831–1905. Painter, A.N.A. 1862, N.A. 1872
Bransgrove, Stephen, 1900–. Painter, A.N.A. 1933–1934
Breckenridge, Hugh Henry, 1870–1937. Painter, A.N.A. 1913
Bredin, Rae Sloan, 1881–1933. Painter, A.N.A. 1921
Brent, Henry Johnson, 1811–1880. Painter, H.M. (a) 1849, H.M. (p) 1851
Brevoort, James Renwick, 1832–1918. Painter, A.N.A. 1861, N.A. 1863
Bricher, Alfred Thompson, 1839–1908. Painter, A.N.A. 1879
Bridges, Fidelia, 1834–1923. Painter, A.N.A. 1873
Bridgman, Frederic Arthur,* 1847–1928. Painter, A.N.A. 1874, N.A. 1881
Brinckerhoff, Arthur Freeman, 1880–. Architect, A.N.A. 1948
Brinley, Daniel Putnam, 1879–. Painter, A.N.A. 1930
Bristol, John Bunyan, 1826–1909. Painter, A.N.A. 1859, N.A. 1875
Brockhurst, Gerald Leslie, 1890–. Painter, A.N.A. (Elect) 1951
Brook, Alexander, 1898–. Painter, A.N.A. 1948, N.A. 1951
Bros, Robert, 1902–. Sculptor, A.N.A. 1950

Brown, Archibald Manning, 1881–. Architect, A.N.A. 1942, N.A. (Elect) 1953
Brown, Arthur, Jr., 1874–. Architect, A.N.A. 1943, N.A. (Elect) 1953
Brown, Glenn, 1854–1932. Architect, A.N.A. 1927
Brown, Henry Kirke, 1814–1886. Sculptor, A.N.A. 1847, N.A. 1851
Brown, John Appleton,* 1844–1902. Painter, A.N.A. 1896
Brown, John George, 1831–1913. Painter, A.N.A. 1861, N.A. 1863
Brown, Roy Henry, 1879–. Painter, A.N.A. 1921, N.A. 1926
Browne, Belmore, 1880–. Painter, A.N.A. 1928
Browne, Charles Francis, 1859–1920. Painter, A.N.A. 1913
Browne, George Elmer, 1871–1946. Painter, A.N.A. 1919, N.A. 1928
Browne, Syd, 1907–. Aquarellist, A.N.A. 1951
Bruce, Edward, 1879–1943. Painter, A.N.A. 1935
Bruen, George W., 1795–1849. Patron, H.M. (a) 1841
Bruestle, George Matthew, 1871–1939. Painter, A.N.A. 1927
Brunner, Arnold W., 1857–1925. Architect, A.N.A. 1910, N.A. 1916
Brush, George de Forest,* 1855–1941. Painter, A.N.A. 1888, N.A. (Elect) 1901,
    1906, N.A. 1908
Brussel-Smith, Bernard, 1914–. Graphic Artist, A.N.A. (Elect) 1952
Bryant, Henry, 1812–1881. Painter, A.N.A. 1837
Bryant, William Cullen, 1794–1878. Poet, H.M. (a) 1833
Buehr, Karl Albert, 1866–1952. Painter, A.N.A. 1922
Bulfinch, Charles, 1763–1844. Architect, H.M. (p) 1827
Buller, Cecil, ?–. Graphic Artist, A.N.A. 1949
Bunce, William Gedney,* 1840–1916. Painter, A.N.A. 1902, N.A. 1907
Bunner, Andrew Fisher, 1841–1897. Painter, A.N.A. 1880
Burchfield, Charles Ephraim, 1893–. Aquarellist, A.N.A. (Elect) 1944, A.N.A.
    1952
Burroughs, Bryson,* 1869–1934. Painter, A.N.A. 1904, N.A. 1930
Burroughs, Edith Woodman, 1871–1916. Sculptor, A.N.A. (Elect) 1913
Butler, Charles, 1870–1953. Architect, A.N.A. 1953
Butler, George Bernard,* 1838–1907. Painter, A.N.A. 1871, N.A. 1873
Butler, Howard Russell,* 1856–1934. Painter, A.N.A. 1897, N.A. 1900

Cafferty, James H., 1819–1869. Painter, A.N.A. 1849, N.A. 1853
Calder, Alexander Stirling,* 1870–1945. Sculptor, A.N.A. 1906, N.A. 1913
Calverley, Charles, 1833–1914. Sculptor, A.N.A. 1871, N.A. 1874
Camden, Harry Poole, 1900–1943. Sculptor, A.N.A. (Elect) 1942
Camuccini, Vincenzo, 1773–1844. Painter, H.M. (p) 1829
Canina, Cav. Luigi, 1795–1856. Architect, H.M. (p) 1843
Carey, Edward L., 1805–1845. Patron, H.M. (a) 1842
Carlsen, Dines, 1901–. Painter, A.N.A. 1922, N.A. 1941
Carlsen, Emil,* 1853–1932. Painter, A.N.A. 1904, N.A. 1906
Carlson, John Fabian, 1875–1945. Painter, A.N.A. 1911, N.A. 1925
Carpenter, Francis Bicknell, 1830–1900. Painter, A.N.A. 1852
Carrère, John Merven, 1858–1911. Architect, A.N.A. 1908, N.A. 1910
Carrigan, William L., 1868–1939. Painter, A.N.A. 1936
Carroll, John, 1892–. Painter, A.N.A. 1948, N.A. 1950

Carroll, Nicholas, ?–1855. Patron, H.M. (a) 1839
Carter, Clarence Holbrook, 1904–. Aquarellist, A.N.A. 1949
Caser, Ettore, 1880–1944. Painter, A.N.A. 1931
Casilear, John William, 1811–1893. Painter, A.N.A. 1833, N.A. 1851
Cassatt, Mary, 1855–1926. Painter, A.N.A. (Elect) 1909
Casson, Alfred Joseph, 1898–. Painter, H.C.M. Canada 1952
Castellon, Federico, 1914–. Graphic Artist, A.N.A. 1947
Catherwood, Frederick, ?–1854. Architect, H.M. (p) 1837
Catlin, George, 1796–1872. Painter, N.A. 1826–1828
Cecere, Gaetano, 1894–. Sculptor, A.N.A. 1935, N.A. 1938
Chamberlain, Samuel, 1895–. Graphic Artist, A.N.A. 1939, N.A. 1945
Champney, James Wells, 1843–1903. Painter, A.N.A. 1882
Chapin, Cornelia Van Auken, 1895–. Sculptor, A.N.A. 1940, N.A. 1945
Chapin, Rev. Edwin Hubbell, 1814–1880. Clergyman, H.M. (a) 1854
Chapin, Francis, 1899–. Painter, A.N.A. 1951, N.A. (Elect) 1953
Chapman, Carlton Theodore,* 1860–1925. Painter, A.N.A. 1900, N.A. 1914
Chapman, Charles Shepard, 1879–. Painter, A.N.A. 1919, N.A. 1926
Chapman, John Gadsby, 1808–1889. Painter, H.M. (p) 1832, N.A. 1836
Chase, Adelaide Cole,* 1868–1944. Painter, A.N.A. 1906
Chase, Harry, 1853–1889. Painter, A.N.A. 1883
Chase, William Merritt,* 1849–1916. Painter, A.N.A. 1888, N.A. 1890
Cheffetz, Asa, 1896–. Graphic Artist, A.N.A. 1938, N.A. 1944
Cheney, John, 1801–1885. Engraver, H.M. (p) 1833
Cheney, Seth Wells, 1810–1856. Graphic Artist, A.N.A. 1848
Choate, Nathaniel, 1899–. Sculptor, A.N.A. 1940
Church, Frederic Edwin, 1826–1900. Painter, A.N.A. 1848, N.A. 1849
Church, Frederick Stuart,* 1842–1924. Painter, A.N.A. 1883, N.A. 1885
Ciampaglia, Carlo, 1891–. Painter, A.N.A. 1936
Cicognara, Count Leopold, 1767–1834. Author, H.M. (a) 1833
Clark, Eliot Candee, 1883–. Painter, A.N.A. 1917, N.A. 1944
Clark, Walter,* 1848–1917. Painter, A.N.A. 1898, N.A. 1909
Clarke, Gilmore David, 1892–. Architect, A.N.A. 1944, N.A. 1946
Clarke, Thomas Shields, 1860–1920. Sculptor, A.N.A. 1902
Clarkson, Ralph, 1861–1942. Painter, A.N.A. 1910
Clinedinst, Benjamin West,* 1859–1931. Painter, A.N.A. 1894, N.A. 1898
Clonney, James Goodwyn, 1812–1867. Painter, A.N.A. 1834
Clover, Lewis P., Jr., 1819–1896. Painter, A.N.A. 1840
Coffin, William Anderson,* 1855–1925. Painter, A.N.A. 1898, N.A. 1912
Cogdell, John Stephano 1778–1847. Lawyer, ARTIST 1827, H.M. (a) 1828
Cohen, Lewis, 1857–1915. Painter, A.N.A. 1911
Cohen, Mendes Isaac, 1796–1879. Financier, H.M. (a) 1832
Coit, Daniel Wadsworth, 1787–1876. Patron, H.M. (a) 1832
Colden, David Cadwallader, 1797–1850. Patron, H.M. (a) 1839
Cole, Alphaeus Philemon, 1876–. Painter, A.N.A. 1930, N.A. 1941
Cole, Thomas, 1801–1848. Painter, Founder, N.A. 1826
Cole, Timothy, 1852–1931. Graphic Artist, A.N.A. 1906, N.A. 1908

Coleman, Charles Caryl, 1840–1928. Painter, A.N.A. 1865
Collens, Charles, 1873–. Architect, A.N.A. 1953
Collins, Alfred Quinton,* 1855–1903. Painter, A.N.A. (Elect) 1900
Colman, Samuel,* 1832–1920. Painter, A.N.A. 1854, N.A. 1862
Colyer, Vincent, 1825–1888. Painter, A.N.A. 1849–1850, 1851
Coman, Charlotte Buell, 1834–1924. Painter, A.N.A. 1910
Connaway, Jay Hall, 1893–. Painter, A.N.A. 1933, N.A. 1943
Cook, Howard Norton, 1901–. Graphic Artist, A.N.A. 1948, N.A. 1949
Cook, Walter, 1846–1916. Architect, A.N.A. 1906, N.A. 1912
Cooke, Edward William, 1811–1880. Painter, H.M. (p) 1858
Cooke, George, 1793–1848. Painter, A.N.A. 1833–c.1838
Cooper, Colin Campbell, 1856–1937. Painter, A.N.A. 1908, N.A. 1912
Cooper, James Fenimore, 1789–1851. Writer, H.M. (a) 1831
Cooper, Mario Ruben, 1905–. Aquarellist, A.N.A. 1950, N.A. 1952
Corbett, Harvey Wiley, 1873–. Architect, A.N.A. 1926, N.A. 1930
Corbino, Jon, 1905–. Painter, A.N.A. 1938, N.A. 1940
Cornelius, Peter Joseph Von, 1783–1867. Illustrator, H.M. (p) 1845
Cornoyer, Paul, 1864–1923. Painter, A.N.A. 1909
Cornwell, Dean, 1892–. Painter, A.N.A. 1934, N.A. 1940
Corr, Erin, 1803–1862. Engraver, H.M. (p) 1833
Costigan, John Edward, 1888–. Painter, A.N.A. 1924, N.A. 1928
Cotton, William Henry, 1880–. Painter, A.N.A. 1916
Couse, Eanger Irving, 1866–1936. Painter, A.N.A. 1902, N.A. 1911
Covey, Arthur Sinclair, 1877–. Painter, A.N.A. 1929, N.A. 1934
Cox, Allyn, 1896–. Painter, A.N.A. 1940
Cox, Kenyon,* 1856–1919. Painter, A.N.A. 1900, N.A. 1903
Cox, Louise Howland King,* 1865–1945. Painter, A.N.A. 1902
Coyle, James, 1798–1828. Painter, Founder, N.A. 1826
Cozzens, Abraham (Abram) M., 1811–1868. Patron, H.M. (a) 1843
Craig, Thomas Bigelow, 1849–1924. Painter, A.N.A. 1897
Cram, Ralph Adams, 1863–1942. Architect, A.N.A. (Elect) 1914, A.N.A. 1938
Cranch, Christopher Pearce, 1813–1892. Painter, A.N.A. 1850, N.A. 1864
Cranch, John, 1807–1891. Painter, A.N.A. 1853
Crane, Bruce,* 1857–1937. Painter, A.N.A. 1897, N.A. 1901
Crawford, Thomas G., 1813–1857. Sculptor, H.M. (p) 1838
Cresson, Margaret French, 1889–. Sculptor, A.N.A. 1942
Cret, Paul Philippe, 1876–1945. Architect, A.N.A. 1935, N.A. 1938
Crisp, Arthur, 1881–. Painter, A.N.A. 1920, N.A. 1937
Cropsey, Jasper Francis, 1823–1900. Painter, A.N.A. 1844, N.A. 1851
Cross, John Walter, 1878–1951. Architect, A.N.A. 1942
Crowninshield, Frederic, 1845–1918. Painter, A.N.A. 1905
Csoka, Stephen, 1897–. Graphic Artist, A.N.A. 1945, N.A. 1948
Cumming, William, 1769–1852. Painter, H.M. (p) 1827
Cummings, Henry Richards, ?–?, H.M. (a) 1862
Cummings, Thomas Agustus, 1825–1859. Painter, A.N.A. 1852
Cummings, Thomas Seir, 1804–1894. Painter, Founder, N.A. 1826

Curran, Charles Courtney,* 1861–1942. Painter, A.N.A. 1888, N.A. 1904
Curry, John Steuart, 1897–1946. Painter, A.N.A. 1937, N.A. 1943
Cushing, Howard Gardiner,* 1869–1916. Painter, A.N.A. 1906

Dabo, Leon, 1868–. Painter, A.N.A. 1934, N.A. 1944
Daguerre, Louis Jacques Mande, 1789–1851. Painter, H.M. (p) 1839
Daingerfield, Elliott,* 1859–1932. Painter, A.N.A. 1902, N.A. 1906
Dallas, Jacob A., 1825–1857. Graphic Artist, A.N.A. 1854
Dallin, Cyrus Edwin, 1861–1944. Sculptor, A.N.A. 1912, N.A. 1930
Dalton, Peter, 1894–. Sculptor, A.N.A. 1943, N.A. 1952
Dana, Richard Henry, 1787–1879. Writer, H.M. (a) 1849
Dana, William Parsons Winchester, 1833–1927. Painter, A.N.A. 1862, N.A. 1863
Danforth, Moseley Isaac, 1800–1862. Graphic Artist, Founder N.A. 1826, H.M. (p) 1827
Daniel, Lewis C., 1901–1952. Graphic Artist, A.N.A. 1948
Darley, Felix Octavius Carr, 1822–1888. Graphic Artist, H.M. (p) 1851, N.A. 1852
Dassel, Hermine (nee Borchard), ?–1857. Painter, H.M. (p) 1850
Davey, Randall, 1887–. Painter, A.N.A. 1937, N.A. 1938
Davidson, George, 1889–. Painter, A.N.A. 1936
Davidson, Jo, 1883–1952. Sculptor, A.N.A. 1944
Davis, Alexander Jackson, 1803–1892. Architect, ARTIST, 1827 A.N.A. 1828–c.1838
Davis, Charles Harold,* 1856–1933. Painter, A.N.A. 1901, N.A. 1906
Davis, Gladys Rockmore, 1901–. Painter, A.N.A. 1940, N.A. 1943
Davis, Isaac P., 1771–1855. Antiquarian, H.M. (a) 1845
Day, Frank Miles, 1861–1918. Architect, A.N.A. 1910
Day, James Francis,* 1863–1942. Painter, A.N.A. 1906
Dearth, Henry Golden,* 1863–1918. Painter. A.N.A. 1902, N.A. 1906
Deas, Charles, 1818–1867. Painter, A.N.A. 1839
DeCamp, Joseph Rodefer, 1858–1923. Painter, A.N.A. (Elect) 1902
de Coux, Janet, 1904–. Sculptor, A.N.A. 1940
de Creeft, Jose, 1884–. Sculptor, A.N.A. (Elect) 1948
de Forest, Lockwood, 1850–1932. Painter, A.N.A. 1891, N.A. 1898
de Francisci, Anthony, 1887–. Sculptor, A.N.A. 1934, N.A. 1937
de Haas, Mauritz Frederick Hendrick, 1832–1895. Painter, A.N.A. 1862, N.A. 1867
DeHaven, B. Franklin, 1856–1934. Painter, A.N.A. 1902, N.A. 1920
Dehn, Adolph, 1895–. Graphic Artist, A.N.A. (Elect) 1942
Deines, Ernest Hubert, 1894–. Graphic Artist, A.N.A. 1943
De Kay, James Ellsworth, M.D., 1792–1851. Naturalist, H.M. (a) 1830
De Keyser, Nicaise, 1813–1887. Painter, H.M. (p) 1846
de Kuyper, Jean Baptiste, ?–? Sculptor, H.M. (p) 1846
Delano, William Adams, 1874–. Architect, A.N.A. 1934, N.A. 1937
Delaroche, Paul Hippolyte, 1797–1856. Painter, H.M. (p) 1845
Delbos, Julius, 1879–. Aquarellist, A.N.A. 1945, N.A. 1948
De Luce, Percival, 1847–1914. Painter, A.N.A. 1897

DeLue, Donald, 1900–. Sculptor, A.N.A. 1940, N.A. 1943
De Maine, Harry, 1880–1952. Aquarellist, A.N.A. 1951
de Marco, Jean, 1898–. Sculptor, A.N.A. 1952
De Martini, Joseph, 1896–. Painter, A.N.A. 1950, N.A. (Elect) 1953
Demetrios, George, 1896–. Sculptor, A.N.A. 1949
DeRose, Anthony Lewis, 1803–1836. Painter, A.N.A. 1829, N.A. 1833
Derrick, William Rowell, 1857–1941. Painter, A.N.A. 1922
Derujinsky, Gleb, 1888–. Sculptor, A.N.A. 1933, N.A. 1953
Dessar, Louis Paul,* 1867–1952. Painter, A.N.A. 1899, N.A. 1906
Dessoulavy, Thomas, ?–? Painter, H.M. (p) 1833
Detwiller, Frederick Knecht, 1882–1953. Painter, A.N.A. 1939
De Veaux, James, 1812–1844. Painter, H.M. (p) 1844
Dewey, Charles Melville,* 1849–1937. Painter, A.N.A. 1903, N.A. 1907
Dewey, Rev. Orville, 1794–1882. Clergyman, H.M. (a) 1840
Dewing, Thomas Wilmer,* 1851–1938. Painter, A.N.A. 1887, N.A. 1888
Dickinson, Edwin, 1891–. Painter, A.N.A. 1948, N.A. 1950
Dickinson, Sidney Edward, 1890–. Painter, A.N.A. 1921, N.A. 1927
Dielman, Frederick,* 1847–1935. Painter, A.N.A. 1881, N.A. 1883
Dike, Philip Latimer, 1906–. Aquarellist, A.N.A. 1950, N.A. 1953
Dix, Charles Temple, 1838–1873. Painter, A.N.A. (Elect) 1861
Dix, John Adams, 1798–1879. Statesman, H.M. (a) 1836
Dixon, Thomas, 1792–1862. Patron, H.M. (a) 1827
Dodd, Lamar, 1909–. Painter, A.N.A. 1952
Dodge, John Wood, 1807–1893. Painter, A.N.A. 1832
Dolph, John Henry,* 1835–1903. Painter, A.N.A. 1877, N.A. 1898
Dorn, J. (Joseph?), 1759–1841. Painter, H.M. (p) 1829
Dougherty, Paul,* 1877–1947. Painter, A.N.A. 1906, N.A. 1907
Doughty, Thomas, 1793–1856. Painter, H.M. (p) 1827
Downing, Andrew Jackson, 1815–1852. Horticulturist, H.M. (a) 1845
Drake, William Henry, 1856–1926. Painter, A.N.A. 1902
Duble, Lu, 1896–. Sculptor, A.N.A. 1942
duBois, Guy Pene, 1884–. Painter, A.N.A. 1937, N.A. 1940
Dubois, Mary Ann Delafield, 1813–1888. Sculptor, A.N.A. (Elect) 1842
Dufner, Edward, 1872–. Painter, A.N.A. 1910, N.A. 1929
Duggan, Peter Paul, c.1810–1861. Painter, A.N.A. 1849, N.A. 1851
Du Mond, Frank Vincent,* 1865–1951. Painter, A.N.A. 1900 N.A. 1906
Dunlap, William, 1766–1839. Painter, Founder, N.A. 1826
Dunn, Harvey, 1884–1952. Painter, A.N.A. 1935, N.A. 1945
Dunsmore, John Ward, 1856–1945. Painter, A.N.A. 1925
Durand, Asher Brown, 1796–1886. Painter, Founder, N.A. 1826
Durand, John, 1822–1908. Writer, H.M. (a) 1854
Duveneck, Frank,* 1848–1919. Painter. A.N.A. 1905, N.A. 1906

Eakins, Thomas,* 1844–1916. Painter, A.N.A. 1902, N.A. 1902
Eames, John Heagan, 1900–. Graphic Artist, A.N.A. (Elect) 1953
Earle, Lawrence Carmichael, 1845–1921. Painter, A.N.A. 1897
Eastlake, Sir Charles Lock, 1793–1865. Painter, H.M. (p) 1845

Eastman, Seth, 1808–1875. Illustrator, H.M. (a) 1838

Eaton, Charles Harry, 1850–1901. Painter, A.N.A. 1893

Eaton, Charles Warren, 1857–1937. Painter, A.N.A. 1901–1910

Eaton, Joseph Oriel, 1829–1875. Painter, A.N.A. 1866

Eberle, Abastenia St. Leger, 1878–1942. Sculptor, A.N.A. 1920

Eby, Kerr, 1889–1946. Graphic Artist, A.N.A. 1930, N.A. 1934

Edmonds, Francis William, 1806–1863. Painter, A.N.A. 1829–1830(?)–, A.N.A. 1837, N.A. 1840

Edwards, Charles, 1797–1868. Lawyer, H.M. (a) 1833

Edwards, George Wharton, 1864–1950. Painter, A.N.A. 1930, N.A. 1945

Eggers, Otto R., 1882–. Architect, A.N.A. 1948, N.A. 1951

Ehninger, John Whetton, 1827–1889. Painter, A.N.A. (Elect) 1854, A.N.A. 1858, N.A. 1860

Eichenberg, Fritz, 1901–. Graphic Artist, A.N.A. 1947, N.A. 1949

Ellerhusen, Ulric Henry, 1879–. Sculptor, A.N.A. 1932, N.A. 1934

Ellett, Thomas Harlan, 1880–1951. Architect, A.N.A. 1942, N.A. 1945

Elliott, Charles Loring, 1812–1868. Painter, A.N.A. 1845, N.A. 1846

Emerson, William, 1801–1868. Lawyer and Lecturer, H.M. (a) 1833

Emmet, Lydia Field, 1866–1952. Painter, A.N.A. 1909, N.A. 1912

Engelmann, Godefroy, 1814–1897. Lithographer, H.M. (p) 1848

Etnier, Stephen, 1903–. Painter, A.N.A. 1950, N.A. 1953

Evans, Rudulph, 1878–. Sculptor, A.N.A. 1918, N.A. 1929

Evers, John, 1797–1884. Painter, Founder, N.A. 1826

Eyre, Wilson, Jr., 1858–? Architect, A.N.A. 1910–1914

Fabri, Ralph, 1894–. Graphic Artist, A.N.A. 1944, N.A. 1946

Falconer, John M., 1820–1903. Painter, H.M. (a) 1851

Fanshaw, Samuel Raymond, 1814–1888. Painter, A.N.A. 1841

Farndon, Walter, 1876–. Painter, A.N.A. 1928, N.A. 1937

Farnsworth, Jerry, 1895–. Painter, A.N.A. 1933, N.A. 1935

Faulkner, Barry, 1881–. Painter, A.N.A. 1926, N.A. 1931

Faxon, William Bailey,* 1849–1941. Painter, A.N.A. 1906

Ferguson, Duncan, ?–? Painter, A.N.A. 1832–c.1837

Ferguson, Henry A., 1842–1911. Painter, A.N.A. 1884

Fields, Mitchell, 1901–. Sculptor, A.N.A. 1945

Fiene, Ernest, 1894–. Painter, A.N.A. 1948, N.A. 1952

Fink, Frederick, 1817–1849. Painter, H.M. (p) 1839

Fisher, Alanson, 1807–1884. Painter, A.N.A. 1842–1844, A.N.A. 1845

Fisher, Alvan, 1792–1863. Painter, H.M. (p) 1827

Fisher, Anna S., ?–1942. Painter, A.N.A. 1920, N.A. 1932

Fisher, John Thomas, 1806–1860. Patron, H.M. (a) 1847

Fiske, Gertrude, 1879–. Painter, A.N.A. 1922, N.A. 1930

Fitch, John Lee, 1836–1895. Painter, A.N.A. 1870

Fjelde, Paul, 1892–. Sculptor, A.N.A. 1949

Flagg, Charles Noel, 1848–1916. Painter, A.N.A. 1909

Flagg, George Whiting, 1816–1897. Painter, H.M. (a) 1842, H.M. (p) 1844, N.A. 1851

Flagg, Jared Bradley, 1820–1899. Painter, H.M. (p) 1847, N.A. 1849
Flagg, Montague,* 1842–1915. Painter, A.N.A. 1906, N.A. 1910
Flameng, François, 1856–1923. Painter, H.C.M., France, 1919
Flanagan, John, 1865–1952. Sculptor, A.N.A. 1911, N.A. 1928
Folinsbee, John Fulton, 1892–. Painter, A.N.A. 1919, N.A. 1928
Folo, Giovanni (Johannes), 1764–1836. Engraver, H.M. (p) 1836
Foote, Will Howe, 1874–. Painter, A.N.A. 1910
Foster, Ben,* 1852–1926. Painter, A.N.A. 1901, N.A. 1904
Foster, Will (William Frederick), 1882–1953. Painter, A.N.A. 1929
Fowler, Frank,* 1852–1910, Painter, A.N.A. 1892, N.A. 1900
Franzen, August,* 1863–1938. Painter, A.N.A. 1906, N.A. 1920
Fraser, Charles, 1782–1860. Painter, H.M. (p) 1830
Fraser, James Earle, 1876–1953. Sculptor, A.N.A. 1912, N.A. 1917
Fraser, Laura Gardin, 1889–. Sculptor, A.N.A. 1924, N.A. 1931
Frazee, John, 1790–1852. Sculptor, Founder, N.A. 1826, A.N.A. 1836, H.M. (p) 1840
Frazier, Kenneth,* 1867–1949. Painter, A.N.A. 1906
Fredericks, Alfred, ?–1907? Painter, A.N.A. 1863–1888
Freedlander, Joseph Henry, 1870–1943. Architect, A.N.A. 1913, N.A. 1932
Freeman, James Edward, 1808–1884. Painter, A.N.A. 1831, N.A. 1833
Freer, Frederick Warren,* 1849–1908. Painter, A.N.A. 1887
French, Daniel Chester,* 1850–1931. Sculptor, A.N.A. 1900, N.A. 1901
French, Frank, 1850–1933. Painter, A.N.A. 1922
Friedlander, Leo, 1890–. Sculptor, A.N.A. 1936, N.A. 1949
Frieseke, Frederick Carl, 1874–1939. Painter, A.N.A. 1912, N.A. 1914
Frishmuth, Harriet W., 1880–. Sculptor, A.N.A. 1925, N.A. 1929
Fromkes, Maurice, 1872–1931. Painter, A.N.A. 1927
Frothingham, James, 1786–1864. Painter, A.N.A. 1828, N.A. 1831
Frothingham, Sarah C., 1821–1861. Painter, A.N.A. 1840–1844, A.N.A. 1845
Fry, Sherry Edmundson, 1879–. Sculptor, A.N.A. 1914, N.A. 1930
Fuller, Dudley B., 1800–1868. Merchant, H.M. (a) 1841
Fuller, George,* 1822–1884. Painter, A.N.A. 1853
Fuller, Henry Brown,* 1867–1934. Painter, A.N.A. 1906
Fuller, Lucia Fairchild,* 1870–1924. Painter, A.N.A. 1906
Fulton, Julia (Blight), 1810–1848. Painter, ARTIST 1827, A.N.A. 1828–C.1832
Furness, William Henry, Jr., 1827–1867. Painter, H.M. (p) 1862

Gaertner, Carl Frederick, 1898–1952. Painter, A.N.A. 1952
Gahman, Floyd, 1894–. Painter, A.N.A. 1943
Gannam, John, 1905–. Aquarellist, A.N.A. 1950
Garber, Daniel, 1880–. Painter, A.N.A. 1910, N.A. 1913
Garfield, Abram, 1872–. Architect, A.N.A. 1949
Gasser, Henry, 1909–. Aquarellist, A.N.A. 1948, N.A. 1950
Gaugengigl, Ignaz Marcel,* 1855–1932. Painter, A.N.A. 1906
Gaul, William Gilbert,* 1855–1919. Painter, A.N.A. 1879, N.A. 1882
Gauley, Robert David, 1875–1943. Painter, A.N.A. 1908
Gay, Edward, 1838–1928. Painter, A.N.A. 1869, N.A. 1907

Gay, Henry B., 1821?–1862. Painter, H.M. (a) 1853
Gay, Walter, 1856–1937. Painter, A.N.A. (Elect) 1904–1906
Gehron, William, 1887–. Architect, A.N.A. (Elect) 1953
Geiffert, Alfred, Jr., 1890–. Architect, A.N.A. 1951
Genth, Lillian Mathilde, 1876–1953. Painter, A.N.A. 1908
Geyer, Harold Carl, 1905–. Graphic Artist, A.N.A. 1950
Gibbes, Robert Wilson, M.D., 1809–1866. Scientist, H.M. (a) 1849
Gibson, Charles Dana, 1867–1944. Graphic Artist, A.N.A. 1918, N.A. 1932
Gibson, (John ?), 1790–1866. Sculptor, H.M. (p) 1833
Gifford, Robert Swain,* 1840–1905. Painter, A.N.A. 1867, N.A. 1878
Gifford, Sanford Robinson, 1823–1880. Painter, A.N.A. 1850, N.A. 1854
Gignoux, Regis François, 1816–1882. Painter, A.N.A. 1843, N.A. 1851
Gilbert, Arthur Hill, 1894–. Painter, A.N.A. 1930
Gilbert, Cass, 1859–1934. Architect, A.N.A. 1906, N.A. 1908
Gilbert, Cass, Jr., 1894–. Architect, A.N.A. 1932
Gilbert, Grove Sheldon, 1805–1885. Painter, H.M. (p) 1848
Giles, Howard Everett, 1876–. Painter, A.N.A. 1918, N.A. 1929
Gilmor, Robert, 1774–1848. Merchant, H.M. (a) 1833
Gimber, Stephen Henry, 1810–1862. Engraver, A.N.A. 1830–c.1833
Girard, Alexis François, 1789–1870. Engraver, H.M. (p) 1848
Girometti, Pietro, 1812–1859. Sculptor, H.M. (p) 1833
Githens, Alfred Morton, 1876–. Architect, A.N.A. 1948
Glackens, William J.,* 1870–1938. Painter, A.N.A. 1906, N.A. 1933
Glass, James W., Jr., 1825–1857. Painter, H.M. (p) 1847
Goetz, ———, ?–? H.M. 1833
Gonzalez, Xavier, 1899–. Painter, A.N.A. (Elect) 1953
Goodhue, Bertram Grosvenor, 1869–1924. Architect, A.N.A. 1917, N.A. 1923
Gore, John Christopher, ?–? Painter, H.M. (p) 1833
Gorsline, Douglas Warner, 1913–. Painter, A.N.A. 1943, N.A. 1947
Gourlie, John Hamilton, ?–1891. Painter, H.M. (a) 1853
Gracie, William, 1788–1842. Merchant, H.M. (a) 1827
Grafly, Charles Allan,* 1862–1929. Sculptor, A.N.A. 1902, N.A. 1905
Grain, Frederick, ?–c.1879. Painter, A.N.A. 1836
Gramatky, Hardie, 1907–. Aquarellist, A.N.A. 1948, N.A. 1950
Grant, Gordon Hope, 1875–. Graphic Artist, A.N.A. 1942, N.A. 1947
Granville-Smith, Walter, 1870–1938. Painter, A.N.A. 1908, N.A. 1915
Graves, Abbott Fuller, 1859–1936. Painter, A.N.A. 1926
Gray, Henry Peters, 1819–1877. Painter, A.N.A. 1841, N.A. 1842
Gray, Mary, 1891–. Painter, A.N.A. 1929
Greacen, Edmund William, 1876–1949. Painter, A.N.A. 1920, N.A. 1935
Greacen, Nan (Faure), 1908–. Painter, A.N.A. 1940
Greatorex, Eliza, 1820–1897. Graphic Artist, A.N.A. 1869–1888
Green, Frank Russell, 1856–1940. Painter, A.N.A. 1897
Greene, Edward D. E., 1823–1879. Painter, A.N.A. 1853, N.A. 1858
Greenleaf, James Leal, 1857–1933. Architect, A.N.A. 1924
Greenough, Horatio, 1805–1852. Sculptor, H.M. (p) 1828

Gregory, John, 1879–. Sculptor, A.N.A. 1927, N.A. 1934
Grier, Sir Edmund Wyly, 1862–. Painter, H.C.M., Canada, 1937
Griffin, Walter, 1861–1935. Painter, A.N.A. 1912, N.A. 1922
Grimes, Frances, 1869–. Sculptor, A.N.A. 1931, N.A. 1945
Griswold, Casimir Clayton, 1834–1918. Painter, A.N.A. 1866, N.A. 1867
Groll, Albert Lorey, 1866–1952. Painter, A.N.A. 1906, N.A. 1910
Grosz, George, 1893–. Painter, A.N.A. (Elect) 1950
Grover, Oliver Dennett, 1861–1927. Painter, A.N.A. 1913
Gruppe, Karl Heinrich, 1893–. Sculptor, A.N.A. 1939, N.A. 1950
Guerin, Jules, 1866–1946. Painter, A.N.A. 1916, N.A. 1931
Gugler, Eric, 1889–. Architect, A.N.A. 1942, N.A. 1946
Guy, Seymour Joseph, 1824–1910. Painter, A.N.A. 1862, N.A. 1865

Hackley, Rev. Charles William, 1809–1861. Clergyman, H.M. (a) 1844
Haggin, Ben Ali, 1882–1951. Painter, A.N.A. 1912
Hale, Lilian Wescott, 1881–. Painter, A.N.A. 1927, N.A. 1931
Hale, Philip Leslie, 1865–1931. Painter, A.N.A. 1917
Hall, Anne, 1792–1863. Painter, ARTIST 1827, A.N.A. 1828, N.A. 1833
Hall, Basil, 1788–1844. Author, H.M. (a) 1828
Hall, Charles Henry, 1781–1852. Patron, H.M. (a) 1831
Hall, Frederick Garrison, 1878–1946. Painter, A.N.A. 1938
Hall, George Henry, 1825–1913. Painter, A.N.A. 1853–1855, 1863, N.A. 1868
Halleck, Fitz-Greene, 1790–1867. Poet, H.M. (a) 1841
Hamersley, Dr. Andrew, ?–1862. Physician, H.M. (a) 1839
Hamilton, Hamilton, 1847–1928. Painter, A.N.A. 1886, N.A. 1889
Hamilton, William R., ?–? Painter, A.N.A. 1833
Hancock, Walker, 1901–. Sculptor, A.N.A. 1936, N.A. 1939
Hansen, Armin Carl, 1886–. Painter, A.N.A. 1926, N.A. 1948
Hardenbergh, Henry J., 1847–1918. Architect, A.N.A. 1910
Hardin, Adlai Stevenson, 1901–. Sculptor, A.N.A. 1951
Harding, Chester, 1792–1866. Painter, H.M. (p) 1828
Harding, George, 1882–. Painter, A.N.A. 1940, N.A. 1945
Harkness, Albert, 1886–. Architect, A.N.A. 1951
Harmon, Arthur Loomis, 1878–. Architect, A.N.A. 1935, N.A. 1944
Harper, William St. John, 1851–1910. Painter, A.N.A. 1892
Harris, Joseph T., ?–? Painter, A.N.A. 1839
Harrison, Alexander,* 1853–1930. Painter, A.N.A. 1898, N.A. 1901
Harrison, Lowell Birge,* 1854–1929. Painter, A.N.A. 1902, N.A. 1910
Harrison, Wallace Kirkman, 1895–. Architect, A.N.A. 1938, N.A. 1948
Hart, James McDougal, 1828–1901. Painter, A.N.A. 1858, N.A. 1859
Hart, William, 1823–1894. Painter, A.N.A. 1854, N.A. 1858
Hartley, Jonathan Scott,* 1845–1912. Sculptor, A.N.A. 1879, N.A. 1891
Harvey, George, 1799–1878. Painter, A.N.A. 1828
Haseltine, Herbert, 1877–. Sculptor, A.N.A. 1940, N.A. 1946
Haseltine, William Stanley, 1835–1900. Painter, A.N.A. 1860, N.A. 1861
Hassam, Childe,* 1859–1935. Painter, A.N.A. 1902, N.A. 1906

Hastings, Thomas, 1860–1929. Architect, A.N.A. 1906, N.A. 1909
Hatch, George Whitefield, 1805–1867. Engraver, ARTIST 1827, A.N.A. 1828–c.1844
Havens, James Dexter, 1900–. Graphic Artist, A.N.A. 1951
Haviland, John, 1792–1852. Architect, H.M. (p) 1827
Hawthorne, Charles Webster, 1872–1930. Painter, A.N.A. 1908, N.A. 1911
Hays, William Jacob, Jr., 1872–1934. Painter, A.N.A. 1909
Hays, William Jacob, Sr., 1830–1875. Painter, A.N.A. 1852–1860
Healy, George Peter Alexander, 1813–1894. Painter, H.M. (p) 1843
Heintzelman, Arthur William, 1891–. Graphic Artist, A.N.A. 1933, N.A. 1937
Heitland, Wilmot Emerton, 1893–. Aquarellist, A.N.A. 1949, N.A. 1951
Helck, Clarence Peter, 1893–. Aquarellist, A.N.A. 1945, N.A. 1950
Heller, Helen West, ?–. Graphic Artist, A.N.A. 1948
Hennessy, William John, 1839–1917. Painter, A.N.A. 1861, N.A. 1863
Henri, Robert,* 1865–1929. Painter, A.N.A. 1905, N.A. 1906
Henry, Edward Lamson, 1841–1919. Painter, A.N.A. 1867, N.A. 1869
Hepburn, Andrew Hopewell, 1880–. Architect, A.N.A. 1948
Hering, Henry, 1874–1949. Sculptor, A.N.A. 1928, N.A. 1937
Herter, Albert,* 1871–1950. Painter, A.N.A. 1902, N.A. 1943
Hewitt, Edward Shepard, 1877–. Architect, A.N.A. 1942, N.A. 1948
Hewlett, James Monroe, 1868–1941. Architect, A.N.A. 1929, N.A. 1931
Hibbard, Aldro Thompson, 1886–. Painter, A.N.A. 1923 N.A. 1933
Hicks, Thomas, 1823–1890. Painter, A.N.A. 1841, N.A. 1851
Higgins, Eugene, 1874–. Painter, A.N.A. 1921, N.A. 1928
Higgins, William Victor, 1884–1949. Painter, A.N.A. 1921, N.A. 1935
Hildebrandt, Howard Logan, 1872–. Painter, A.N.A. 1921, N.A. 1932
Hill, John Henry, 1839–? Engraver, A.N.A. (Elect) 1858
Hill, John William, 1812–1879. Painter, A.N.A. 1833
Hills, Laura Coombs,* 1859–1952. Painter, A.N.A. 1906
Hinton, Charles Louis, 1869–1950. Sculptor, A.N.A. 1916, N.A. 1941
Hirons, Frederic Charles, 1882–1942. Architect, A.N.A. 1932
Hitchcock, George, 1850–1913. Painter, A.N.A. 1909
Hoeber, Arthur, 1854–1915. Painter, A.N.A. 1909
Hoffman, Harry Leslie, 1874–. Painter, A.N.A. 1930
Hoffman, Malvina, 1887–. Sculptor, A.N.A. 1925, N.A. 1931
Holabird, John Augur, 1886–1945. Architect, A.N.A. 1937, N.A. 1944
Homer, Winslow, 1836–1910. Painter, A.N.A. 1864, N.A. 1865
Hone, Philip, 1781–1851. Merchant, H.M. (a) 1827
Hope, James, 1818–1892. Painter, A.N.A. 1871
Hopkins, James R., 1877–. Painter, A.N.A. 1921
Hopkinson, Charles Sydney,* 1869–. Painter, A.N.A. 1927, N.A. 1929
Hoppin, Thomas Frederick, 1816–1873. Artist, H.M. (p) 1844
Hord, Donal, 1902–. Sculptor, A.N.A. 1943, N.A. 1951
Hosack, Dr. David, 1769–1835. Scientist, H.M. (a) 1827
Hotchkiss, T. H., ?–1869. Painter, A.N.A. (Elect) 1859
Hovenden, Thomas,* 1840–1895. Painter, A.N.A. 1881, N.A. 1882
Howard, Cecil De Blaquiere, 1888–. Sculptor, A.N.A. 1944, N.A. 1948

Howard, John Galen, 1864–1931. Architect, A.N.A. 1910
Howe, George, 1886–. Architect, A.N.A. 1951
Howe, William Henry,* 1844–1929. Painter, A.N.A. 1894, N.A. 1897
Howells, John Mead, 1868–. Architect, A.N.A. 1944
Howland, Alfred Cornelius, 1838–1909. Painter, A.N.A. 1873, N.A. 1882
Hows, John Augustus, 1832–1874. Painter, A.N.A. 1862
Hoyle, Raphael, 1804–1836. Painter, A.N.A. 1829, N.A. 1831
Hoyt, Burnham, 1887–. Architect, A.N.A. (Elect) 1953
Hubbard, Richard William, 1816–1888. Painter, A.N.A. 1851, N.A. 1858
Hubbell, Henry Salem,* 1870–1949. Painter, A.N.A. 1906
Hudson, Eric, 1868–1932. Painter, A.N.A. 1926
Hughes, Robert Ball, 1806–1868. Sculptor, H.M. (p) 1830
Humphreys, William, 1794–1865. Engraver, H.M. (p) 1833
Hunt, William Morris, 1824–1879. Painter, A.N.A. (Elect) 1871
Hunter, Rev. John, D.D., ?–1862. Painter, H.M. (a) 1848
Huntington, Anna Vaughn Hyatt, 1876–. Sculptor, A.N.A. 1916, N.A. 1922
Huntington, Daniel, 1816–1906. Painter, A.N.A. 1839, N.A. 1840
Huntley, Victoria Hutson, 1900–. Graphic Artist, A.N.A. 1942
Hurd, Peter, 1904–. Painter, A.N.A. 1941, N.A. 1942
Hurley, Edward Timothy, 1869–1950. Graphic Artist, A.N.A. 1948
Hutchins, Robert S., 1907–. Architect, A.N.A. 1949
Hutchison, Frederick William, 1875?–1953. Painter, A.N.A. 1922, N.A. 1935
Hyde, William Henry,* 1858–1943. Painter, A.N.A. 1900

Ingham, Charles Cromwell, 1796–1863. Painter, Founder, N.A. 1826
Inman, Henry, 1801–1846. Painter, Founder, N.A. 1826
Inman, John, 1805–1850. Author, H.M. (a) 1828
Inman, John O'Brien, 1828–1896. Painter, A.N.A. 1865
Inness, George,* 1825–1894. Painter, A.N.A. 1853, N.A. 1868
Inness, George, Jr.,* 1854–1926. Painter, A.N.A. 1893, N.A. 1899
Inslee, William, ?–? Painter, ARTIST 1827, A.N.A. 1828–c.1837
Ipsen, Ernest Ludwig, 1869–1951. Painter, A.N.A. 1913, N.A. 1924
Irvine, Wilson Henry, 1869–1936. Painter, A.N.A. 1926
Irving, John Beaufain, 1826–1877. Painter, A.N.A. 1869, N.A. 1872
Irving, Washington, 1783–1859. Writer, H.M. (a) 1841
Irwin, Benoni, 1840–1896. Painter, A.N.A. 1889
Isham, Samuel,* 1855–1914. Painter, A.N.A. 1900, N.A. 1906

Jackson, Frederic Ellis, 1879–1950. Architect, A.N.A. 1947
James, Henry, 1811–1882. Author, H.M. (a) 1854
Jazet, Jean Pierre Marie, 1788–1871. Engraver, H.M. (p) 1848
Jelinek, Hans, 1910–. Graphic Artist, A.N.A. 1952
Jennewein, Carl Paul, 1890–. Sculptor, A.N.A. 1929, N.A. 1933
Jewett, William, 1795–1874. Painter, Founder, N.A. (Elect) 1826, A.N.A. 1847
Jewett, William Smith, 1812–1873. Painter, A.N.A. 1845
Jocelyn, Nathaniel, 1796–1881. Painter, ARTIST 1827, H.M. (p) 1828, N.A. 1846
Johansen, John Christen, 1876–. Painter, A.N.A. 1911, N.A. 1915

Johnson, David, 1827–1908. Painter, A.N.A. 1859, N.A. 1861
Johnson, Eastman,* 1824–1906. Painter, A.N.A. 1859, N.A. 1860
Johnson, Frank Tenney, 1874–1939. Painter, A.N.A. 1929, N.A. 1937
Johnston, Francis, 1761–1829. Architect, H.M. (p) 1827
Jones, Alfred, 1819–1900. Graphic Artist, A.N.A. 1844, N.A. 1851
Jones, Francis Coates,* 1857–1932. Painter, A.N.A. 1885, N.A. 1894
Jones, Hugh Bolton,* 1848–1927. Painter, A.N.A. 1881, N.A. 1883
Jones, Thomas D., 1808–1881. Sculptor, A.N.A. 1853
Jones, Thomas Hudson, 1892–. Sculptor, A.N.A. 1932
Jongers, Alphonse,* 1872–1945. Painter, A.N.A. 1906
Josset, Raoul, 1900–. Sculptor, A.N.A. (Elect) 1953
Judson, Sylvia Shaw, 1897–. Sculptor, A.N.A. 1948

Kalish, Max, 1891–1945. Sculptor, A.N.A. 1933
Kappes, Alfred,* 1850–1894. Painter, A.N.A. 1887, N.A. (Elect) 1894
Kautzky, Theodore, 1896–1953. Aquarellist, A.N.A. 1947, N.A. 1950
Kayn, Hilde B., 1906–1950. Painter, A.N.A. 1943
Kebbon, Eric, 1890–. Architect, A.N.A. 1952
Keck, Charles, 1875–1951. Sculptor, A.N.A. 1921, N.A. 1928
Keith, Dora Wheeler,* 1857–1940. Painter, A.N.A. 1906
Keller, Henry George, 1870–1949. Painter, A.N.A. 1939
Kellogg, Miner Kilbourne, 1814–1889. Painter, H.M. (p) 1851
Kelly, Sir Gerald, 1879–. Painter, H.C.M. England 1950
Kemble, Gouverneur, 1786–1875. Patron, H.M. (a) 1854
Kemble, William, ?–1881. Merchant, H.M. (a) 1854
Kendall, William Mitchell, 1856–1941. Architect, A.N.A. 1930, N.A. 1935
Kendall, William Sergeant,* 1869–1938. Painter, A.N.A. 1901, N.A. 1905
Kensett, John Frederick, 1818–1872. Painter, A.N.A. 1848, N.A. 1849
Kent, Norman, 1903–. Graphic Artist, A.N.A. 1945, N.A. 1949
Kent, Rockwell, 1882–. Graphic Artist, A.N.A. 1948
Kerckhove, Joseph Romain Louis, Vicomte de, 1789–? Physician, H.M. (a) 1846
Keyes, Bernard M., 1898–. Painter, A.N.A. 1938
Keyes, Bessie Potter Vonnoh,* 1872–. Sculptor, A.N.A. 1906, N.A. 1921
Kilham, Walter Harrington, Jr., 1904–. Architect, A.N.A. 1949
Kimball, Richard Arthur, 1899–. Architect, A.N.A. (Elect) 1953
King, Charles Bird, 1785–1862. Painter, H.M. (p) 1827
King, Frederic Rhinelander, 1887–. Architect, A.N.A. 1951
King, Paul, 1867–1947. Painter, A.N.A. 1918, N.A. 1933
Kingman, Dong, 1911–. Aquarellist, A.N.A. 1948, N.A. 1951
Kinney, Troy, 1871–1938. Graphic Artist, A.N.A. 1933
Kirk, Frank C., 1889–. Painter, A.N.A. 1944
Kiselewski, Joseph, 1901–. Sculptor, A.N.A. 1936, N.A. 1944
Klauder, Charles Zeller, 1872–1938. Architect, A.N.A. 1938
Kline, William Fair, 1870–1931. Painter, A.N.A. 1901
Kloss, Gene, 1903–. Graphic Artist, A.N.A. 1950

Koch, John, 1909–. Painter, A.N.A. 1953
Kohn, Robert David, 1870–1953. Architect, A.N.A. 1953
Konti, Isidore, 1862–1938. Sculptor, A.N.A. 1906, N.A. 1909
Korbel, Mario Joseph, 1882–. Sculptor, A.N.A. 1937, N.A. 1944
Kosa, Emil J., Jr., 1903–. Aquarellist, A.N.A. 1948, N.A. 1951
Kost, Frederick Weller,* 1861–1923. Painter, A.N.A. 1900, N.A. 1906
Kreis, Henry, 1899–. Sculptor, A.N.A. 1948, N.A. 1951
Kroll, Leon, 1884–. Painter, A.N.A. 1920, N.A. 1927
Kronberg, Louis, 1872–. Painter, A.N.A. 1935, N.A. 1943
Kuntze, Edward J., 1826–1870. Sculptor, A.N.A. 1869
Kupferman, Lawrence Edward, 1909–. Graphic Artist, A.N.A. 1943
Kuyper, Jean Baptiste de, 1807–1852. Sculptor, H.M. (p) 1846
Kyle, Joseph, 1815–1863. Painter, A.N.A. 1849

La Beaume, Louis, 1873–. Architect, A.N.A. 1944, N.A. 1949
Laborde, Leon Emmanuel Simon Joseph, Comte de, 1807–1869. Art Writer,
    H.M. (a) 1848
Lacombe, Theodore, ?–? Journalist, H.M. (a) 1851
Laessle, Albert, 1877–. Sculptor, A.N.A. 1927, N.A. 1932
La Farge, Christopher Grant, 1862–1938. Architect, A.N.A. 1910
La Farge, John,* 1835–1910. Painter, A.N.A. 1863, N.A. 1869
Laloux, Victor, 1850–1937. Architect, H.C.M. France, 1932
Lamb, William F., 1883–1952. Architect, A.N.A. 1942, N.A. 1950
Lambdin, George Cochran, 1830–1896. Painter, H.M. (p) 1862, N.A. 1868
Lambdin, James Reid, 1807–1889. Painter, H.M. (p) 1839
Landacre, Paul, 1893–. Graphic Artist, A.N.A. 1939, N.A. 1946
Landeck, Armin, 1905–. Graphic Artist, A.N.A. 1937, N.A. 1942
Lang, Louis, 1814–1893. Painter, A.N.A. 1850, N.A. 1852
Lankes, Julius J., 1884–. Graphic Artist, A.N.A. 1941
Lanman, Charles, 1819–1895. Painter, A.N.A. 1842
Lantz, Michael, 1908–. Sculptor, A.N.A. 1951
Lascari, Hilda Kristina, 1885–1937. Sculptor, A.N.A. 1935
Lascari, Salvatore, 1884–. Painter, A.N.A. 1934, N.A. 1945
Lathrop, Dorothy Pulis, 1891–. Graphic Artist, A.N.A. 1949
Lathrop, Francis,* 1849–1909. Painter, A.N.A. 1906
Lathrop, Gertrude Katherine, 1896–. Sculptor, A.N.A. 1932, N.A. 1940
Lathrop, William Langson, 1859–1938. Painter, A.N.A. 1902, N.A. 1907
Latilla, Eugene, ?–1861. Architect, H.M. (p) 1846
Laufman, Sidney, 1891–. Painter, A.N.A. 1939, N.A. 1945
Launitz, Robert Eberhardt, 1806–1870. Sculptor, A.N.A. 1832, N.A. 1833
Lawrence, Sir Thomas, R.A., 1769–1830. Painter, H.M. (p) 1827
Lawrie, Alexander, 1828–1917. Painter, A.N.A. 1868–1874, 1876–1882
Lawrie, Lee, 1877–. Sculptor, A.N.A. 1927, N.A. 1932
Lawson, Ernest, 1873–1939. Painter, A.N.A. 1908, N.A. 1917
Lay, Charles Downing, 1877–. Architect, A.N.A. 1945, N.A. 1948
Lay, Oliver Ingraham, 1845–1890. Painter, A.N.A. 1876

Lazarus, Jacob Hart, 1822–1891. Painter, A.N.A. 1849

Leake, Gerald, 1885–. Painter, A.N.A. 1937

Le Clear, Thomas, 1818–1882. Painter, A.N.A. 1861, N.A. 1863

Lee, Arthur, 1881–. Sculptor, A.N.A. (Elect) 1929

Lee, George Washington, 1803–1842. Patron, H.M. (a) 1832

Le Grice, Count Hawks, ?–? Foreign Correspondent, H.M. (a) 1832

Leigh, William Robinson, 1866–. Painter, A.N.A. 1953

Leighton, Clare Veronica Hope, 1901–. Graphic Artist, A.N.A. 1945, N.A. 1949

Leith-Ross, Harry, 1886–. Painter, A.N.A. 1928, N.A. 1936

Le Mercier, Rose Joseph, 1803–1887. Lithographer, H.M. (p) 1848

Lentelli, Leo, 1879–. Sculptor, A.N.A. 1928, N.A. 1943

Leslie, Charles Robert, 1794–1859. Painter, H.M. (p) 1827

Leupp, Charles M., 1808–1859. Patron, H.M. (a) 1843

Leutze, Emanuel, 1816–1868. Painter, H.M. (p) 1843, N.A. 1860–1868

Lever, Richard Hayley, 1876–. Painter, A.N.A. 1925, N.A. 1933

Lewis, Arthur Allen, 1873–. Graphic Artist, A.N.A. 1929, N.A. 1935

Lie, Jonas, 1880–1940. Painter, A.N.A. 1912, N.A. 1925

Limbach, Russell T., 1904–. Graphic Artist, A.N.A. 1952

Lindeberg, Harry Thomas, 1880–. Architect, A.N.A. 1942, N.A. 1949

Linton, William James, 1812–1897. Graphic Artist, A.N.A. 1870, N.A. 1882

Lipparini, Ludovico, 1800–1856. Painter, H.M. (p) 1833

Lippincott, William Henry, 1849–1920. Painter, A.N.A. 1885, N.A. 1897

Litchfield, Electus Darwin, 1872–1952. Architect, A.N.A. 1951

Livingston, Montgomery, 1816–1855. Painter, A.N.A. 1842, H.M. (p) 1847

Llewellyn, Sir William, 1863–1941. Painter, H.C.M. England 1932

Lober, Georg John, 1892–. Sculptor, A.N.A. 1932, N.A. 1935

Locke, Charles Wheeler, 1899–. Painter, A.N.A. 1945, N.A. 1951

Lockman, De Witt McClellan, 1870–. Painter, A.N.A. 1917, N.A. 1921

Lockwood, Robert Wilton,* 1862–1914. Painter, A.N.A. 1902, N.A. 1912

Loeb, Louis,* 1866–1909. Painter, A.N.A. 1901, N.A. 1906

Loggie, Helen A., ?–. Graphic Artist, A.N.A. 1949

Long, Robert Carey, 1819?–1849. Architect, H.M. (p) 1849

Longacre, James Barton, 1794–1869. Engraver, ARTIST 1827

Longman, Evelyn Beatrice (Batchelder), 1874–. Sculptor, A.N.A. 1909, N.A. 1919

Loomis, Chester,* 1852–1924. Painter, A.N.A. 1906

Loop, Henry Augustus, 1831–1895. Painter, A.N.A. 1859, N.A. 1861

Loop, Jeanette Shepherd Harrison, 1840–1909. Painter, A.N.A. 1873

Lopez, Charles Albert,* 1869–1906. Sculptor, A.N.A. 1906

Lovet-Lorski, Boris, 1894–. Sculptor, A.N.A. 1945

Low, Mary Fairchild,* 1858–1946. Painter, A.N.A. 1906

Low, Will Hicok,* 1853–1932. Painter, A.N.A. 1888, N.A. 1890

Lucas, Albert Pike, 1862–1945. Painter, A.N.A. 1921, N.A. 1927

Lucioni, Luigi, 1900–. Painter, A.N.A. 1937, N.A. 1941

Lukeman, Henry Augustus, 1871–1935. Sculptor, A.N.A. 1909

Lupton, Frances Platt Townsend (Lancaster), ?–? Painter and Sculptor, ARTIST
    1827, A.N.A. 1828–1832

Lyman, Joseph, 1843–1913. Painter, A.N.A. 1886

MacCameron, Robert Lee, 1866–1912. Painter, A.N.A. 1910

MacEwen, Walter, 1860–1943. Painter, A.N.A. 1903–1920

Mack, Warren Bryan, 1896–1952. Graphic Artist, A.N.A. 1944

MacLane, Jean (Johansen), 1879–. Painter, A.N.A. 1912, N.A. 1926

MacLaughlin, Donald Shaw, 1876–1938. Graphic Artist, A.N.A. 1935, N.A. (Elect) 1938

MacLeary, Bonnie, 1892–. Sculptor, A.N.A. 1930

MacMonnies, Frederick William,* 1865–1937. Sculptor, A.N.A. 1901, N.A. 1906

MacNeil, Hermon Atkins,* 1866–1947. Sculptor, A.N.A. 1905, N.A. 1906

MacRae, Emma Fordyce (Swift), 1887–. Painter, A.N.A. 1930, N.A. 1951

Maginnis, Charles Donagh, 1867–. Architect, A.N.A. 1941, N.A. 1942

Magonigle, Harold Van Buren, 1867–1935. Architect, A.N.A. 1924

Magrath, William, 1838–1918. Painter, A.N.A. 1873, N.A. 1876

Main, William, 1796–1876. Graphic Artist, Founder, N.A. 1826, A.N.A. 1836–1838

Manship, Paul Howard, 1885–. Sculptor, A.N.A. 1914, N.A. 1916

Mapes, James Jay, 1806–1866. Painter, H.M. (a) 1833

Marchant, Edward Dalton, 1806–1887. Painter, A.N.A. 1833

Marin, John, 1875–1953. Aquarellist, A.N.A. (Elect) 1944–1946

Mark, Louis, 1788?–? Statesman, H.M. (a) 1829

Marsh, Fred Dana,* 1872–. Painter, A.N.A. 1906

Marsh, Reginald, 1898–. Painter, A.N.A. 1937, N.A. 1943

Marsiglia, Gerlando, 1792–1850. Painter, Founder, N.A. 1826

Martin, Homer Dodge,* 1836–1897. Painter, A.N.A. 1867, N.A. 1874

Martino, Antonio Pietro, 1902–. Painter, A.N.A. 1938, N.A. 1942

Martino, Giovanni, 1908–. Painter, A.N.A. 1943, N.A. 1944

Martiny, Philip,* 1858–1927. Sculptor, A.N.A. 1902

Mason, Abraham John, 1794–c.1884. Engraver, A.N.A. 1830

Mason, Rev. Cyrus, 1799–1865. Clergyman, H.M. (a) 1842

Mason, Maud Mary, 1867–. Painter, A.N.A. 1934

Mason, Roy Martell, 1886–. Painter, A.N.A. 1930, N.A. 1940

Mastro-Valerio, Alessandro, 1887–1953. Graphic Artist, A.N.A. 1951

Matteson, Tompkins Harrison, 1813–1884. Painter, A.N.A. 1847

Mattson, Henry Elis, 1887–. Painter, A.N.A. 1948, N.A. 1951

Maverick, Emily, 1803–1850. Engraver, ARTIST 1827, A.N.A. 1828–1830

Maverick, Maria, 1805–1832. Engraver, ARTIST 1827, A.N.A. 1828–1830

Maverick, Peter, 1780–1831. Graphic Artist, Founder, N.A. 1826

May, Edward Harrison, 1824–1887. Painter, A.N.A. 1849, N.A. (Elect) 1876

Mayer, Constant, 1832–1911. Painter, A.N.A. 1866

Maynard, George Willoughby,* 1843–1923. Painter, A.N.A. 1881, N.A. 1885

Mayr, Christian, 1805?–1850. Painter, A.N.A. 1836, N.A. 1849

McCartan, Edward, 1879–1947. Sculptor, A.N.A. 1922, N.A. 1925

McCord, George Herbert, 1848–1909. Painter, A.N.A. 1880

McCormick, Howard, 1875–1943. Graphic Artist, A.N.A. 1928

McCoy, John W., II, 1910–. Aquarellist, A.N.A. 1945, N.A. 1950

McEntee, Jervis, 1828–1891. Painter, A.N.A. 1860, N.A. 1861

McFee, Henry Lee, 1886–1953. Painter, A.N.A. 1948, N.A. 1950

McIlhenney, Charles Morgan, 1858–1904. Painter, A.N.A. 1892
McKim, Charles Follen, 1847–1909. Architect, A.N.A. 1905, N.A. 1907
Mead, William Rutherford, 1846–1928. Architect, A.N.A. 1908, N.A. 1910
Meakin, Lewis Henry, 1850–1917. Painter, A.N.A. 1913
Mechau, Frank, 1904–1946. Painter, A.N.A. 1937
Meeks, Everett Victor, 1879–. Architect, A.N.A. 1937, N.A. 1949
Meem, John Gaw, 1894–. Architect, A.N.A. 1942
Megarey, John, 1818–1845. Painter, A.N.A. (Elect) 1844
Meiere, Hildreth, ?–. Painter, A.N.A. 1942
Meissner, Leo John, 1895–. Graphic Artist, A.N.A. 1945
Melchers, Gari,* 1860–1932. Painter, A.N.A. 1904, N.A. 1906
Mellon, Eleanor M., 1894–. Sculptor, A.N.A. 1938, N.A. 1950
Mengs, Raphael, ?–? Painter, H.M. (p) 1829
Menihan, John C., 1908–. Graphic Artist, A.N.A. 1948
Mestrovic, Ivan, 1883–. Sculptor, A.N.A. (Elect) 1948
Metcalf, Eliab, 1785–1834. Painter, H.M. (p) 1829
Meyer, Herbert, 1882–. Painter, A.N.A. 1939, N.A. 1942
Meyerowitz, William, 1893–. Painter, A.N.A. 1943
Mielatz, Charles Frederick William, 1864–1919. Graphic Artist, A.N.A. 1906
Mignot, Louis Remy, 1831–1870. Painter, A.N.A. 1858, N.A. 1859
Miller, Barse, 1904–. Aquarellist, A.N.A. 1944, N.A. 1947
Miller, Charles Henry,* 1842–1922. Painter, A.N.A. 1873, N.A. 1875
Miller, George, ?–? Painter, A.N.A. 1833–c.1838
Miller, Kenneth Hayes, 1876–1952. Painter, A.N.A. 1942, N.A. 1944
Miller, Richard Emil, 1875–1943. Painter, A.N.A. 1913, N.A. 1915
Milles, Carl, 1875–. Sculptor, A.N.A. 1948, N.A. (Elect) 1953
Millet, Clarence, 1897–. Painter, A.N.A. 1943
Millet, Francis Davis,* 1846–1912. Painter, A.N.A. 1881, N.A. 1885
Minor, Robert Crannell,* 1840–1904. Painter, A.N.A. 1888, N.A. 1897
Mixter, Felicie Waldo Howell, 1897–. Painter, A.N.A. 1922, N.A. 1945
Moeller, Louis Henry Charles, 1855–1930. Painter, A.N.A. 1884, N.A. 1895
Moffett, Ross E., 1888–. Painter, A.N.A. 1937, N.A. 1942
Mooney, Edward Ludlow, 1813–1887. Painter, A.N.A. 1839, N.A. 1840
Moore, Charles Herbert, 1840–1930. Painter, A.N.A. (Elect) 1861
Moore, E. Bruce, 1905–. Sculptor, A.N.A. 1937, N.A. 1942
Mora, Francis Luis,* 1874–1940. Painter, A.N.A. 1904, N.A. 1906
Moran, Edward, 1829–1901. Painter, A.N.A. (Elect) 1872–1873, A.N.A. 1874
Moran, Thomas,* 1837–1926. Painter, A.N.A. 1881, N.A. 1884
Morgan, Wallace, 1873–1948. Graphic Artist, A.N.A. 1945, N.A. 1947
Morgan, William, 1826–1900. Painter, A.N.A. 1862
Morghen, Raphael, 1758–1833. Engraver, H.M. (p) 1830
Morris, Benjamin Wistar, 1870–1944. Architect, A.N.A. 1927, N.A. 1941
Morrison, Hector, 1814–1877. H.M. (a) 1842
Morse, Samuel Finley Breese, 1791–1872. Painter, Founder, N.A. 1826
Morton, Dr. Alexander Hamilton, 1804–1895. Surgeon, H.M. (a) 1833
Morton, Henry Jackson, 1807–1890. Painter, A.N.A. 1828–1884
Morton, Jacob, 1761–1836. Soldier, H.M. (a) 1827

Morton, John Ludlow, 1792–1871. Painter, ARTIST 1826, A.N.A. 1828, N.A. 1831
Moschcowitz, Paul,* 1876–1942. Painter, A.N.A. 1906
Mosler, Henry, 1841–1920. Painter, A.N.A. 1895–1906
Mount, Henry Smith, 1802–1841. Painter, ARTIST 1827, A.N.A. 1828
Mount, Shepard Alonzo, 1804–1868. Painter, A.N.A. 1833, N.A. 1842
Mount, William Sidney, 1807–1868. Painter, A.N.A. 1831, N.A. 1832
Mowbray, Harry Siddons,* 1858–1928. Painter, A.N.A. 1888, N.A. 1891
Mueller, Hans Alexander, 1888–. Graphic Artist, A.N.A. 1948
Mulhaupt, Frederick John, 1871–1938. Painter, A.N.A. 1926
Murphy, Alice Harold, 1896–. Graphic Artist, A.N.A. 1949
Murphy, Frederick Vernon, 1879–. Architect, A.N.A. 1951
Murphy, Hermann Dudley, 1867–1945. Painter, A.N.A. 1930, N.A. 1934
Murphy, John Francis,* 1853–1921. Painter, A.N.A. 1885, N.A. 1887
Murray, John R., 1775–1851. Merchant, H.M. (a) 1839
Myers, Jerome, 1867–1940. Painter, A.N.A. 1920, N.A. 1929

Nason, Thomas Willoughby, 1889–. Graphic Artist, A.N.A. 1936, N.A. 1940
Neagle, John, 1796–1865. Painter, ARTIST 1827, H.M. (p) 1828
Neal, David Dolhoff, 1838–1915. Painter, A.N.A. (Elect) 1871
Nebel, Berthold, 1889–. Sculptor, A.N.A. 1932, N.A. 1946
Nehlig, Victor, 1830–1909. Painter, A.N.A. 1863, N.A. 1870
Neilson, Dr. John, Jr., 1799–1851. Physician, H.M. (a) 1833
Neilson, Raymond Perry Rodgers, 1881–. Painter, A.N.A. 1925, N.A. 1938
Nelson, Edward D., ?–1871. Painter, H.M. (a) 1854
Nelson, George Laurence, 1887–. Painter, A.N.A. 1929, N.A. 1942
Nettleton, Walter,* 1861–1936. Painter, A.N.A. 1905
Newcombe, George W., 1799–1845. Painter, A.N.A. 1832
Newell, George Glenn, 1870–1947. Painter, A.N.A. 1918, N.A. 1937
Newman, Allen George, 1875–1940. Sculptor, A.N.A. 1926
Newton, Gilbert Stuart, 1794–1835. Painter, H.M. (p) 1827
Nichols, Edward W., 1820–1871. Painter, A.N.A. (Elect) 1858, A.N.A. 1861
Nichols, Henry Hobart, 1869–. Painter, A.N.A. 1912, N.A. 1920
Nichols, Spencer Baird, 1875–1950. Painter, A.N.A. 1922, N.A. 1933
Nickerson, Jennie Ruth (Greacen, Jr.), 1905–. Sculptor, A.N.A. 1945
Nicoll, James Craig, 1847–1918. Painter, A.N.A. 1880, N.A. 1885
Niehaus, Charles Henry, 1855–1935. Sculptor, A.N.A. 1902, N.A. 1906
Niemeyer, John Henry,* 1839–1932. Painter, A.N.A. 1906
Nims, Jeremiah, 1814–1841. Painter, A.N.A. 1841
Nisbet, Robert Hogg, 1879–. Painter, A.N.A. 1920, N.A. 1928
Noble, John, 1874–1934. Painter, A.N.A. 1924, N.A. 1927
Noble, John Alexander Harrison, 1913–. Graphic Artist, A.N.A. 1951
Noble, Thomas Satterwhite, 1835–1907. Painter, A.N.A. 1867–1884

Oakley, George, 1793–1869. Painter, ARTIST 1827, A.N.A. 1828
Oakley, Violet, 1874–. Painter, A.N.A. 1918, N.A. 1929
Oberhardt, William, 1882–. Graphic Artist, A.N.A. 1945
Oberteuffer, George, 1878–1940. Painter, A.N.A. 1937, N.A. 1938

Ochtman, Dorothy, 1892–. Painter, A.N.A. 1929
Ochtman, Leonard,* 1854–1934. Painter, A.N.A. 1898, N.A. 1904
O'Connor, Andrew, Jr., 1874–1941. Sculptor, A.N.A. 1919–1929
O'Connor, Robert Barnard, 1895–. Architect, A.N.A. (Elect) 1953
Oddie, Walter Mason, 1805–1865. Painter, A.N.A. 1833
O'Donovan, William Rudolf,* 1844–1920. Sculptor, A.N.A. 1878
Oertel, Rev. Johannes Adam Simon, 1823–1909. Engraver, A.N.A. 1856–1884
Ogilvie, Clinton, 1838–1900. Painter, A.N.A. 1864
O'Hara, Eliot, 1890–. Aquarellist, A.N.A. 1944, N.A. 1948
Olinsky, Ivan Gregorewitch, 1878–. Painter, A.N.A. 1914, N.A. 1919
Olinsky, Tosca, 1909–. Painter, A.N.A. 1945
Olmsted, Frederick Law, 1870–. Architect, A.N.A. 1914, N.A. 1929
Olsen, Herbert Vincent, 1905–. Aquarellist, A.N.A. 1951
Orr, Douglas William, 1892–. Architect, A.N.A. 1948
Osgood, Samuel Stillman, 1808–1885. Painter, A.N.A. 1842–1844, 1845–1860
O'Toole, Cathal Brendan, 1904–. Painter, A.N.A. 1939, N.A. 1944

Paddock, Willard Dryden, 1873–. Sculptor, A.N.A. 1922
Page, Marie Danforth, 1869–1940. Painter, A.N.A. 1927
Page, William, 1811–1885. Painter, A.N.A. 1831, N.A. 1836
Palmer, Erastus Dow, 1817–1904. Sculptor, H.M. (p) 1849
Palmer, Walter Launt,* 1854–1932. Painter, A.N.A. 1887, N.A. 1897
Panton, Henry, 1816?–1879. Painter, H.M. (a) 1853
Paradise, John, 1783–1833. Painter, Founder, N.A. 1826
Paradise, John Wesley, 1809–1862. Graphic Artist, A.N.A. 1833
Paradise, Phil, 1905–. Aquarellist, A.N.A. (Elect) 1953
Parisen, J., ?–? Painter, Founder, N.A. 1826, ARTIST 1827–1828
Parker, Charles, ?–? H.M. (a) 1846
Parker, John Adams, Jr., 1829–1900. Painter, A.N.A. 1868–1888
Parker, Lawton S., 1868–. Painter, A.N.A. 1916
Parrish, Maxfield,* 1870–. Painter, A.N.A. 1905, N.A. 1906
Parshall, De Witt, 1864–. Painter, A.N.A. 1910, N.A. 1917
Parshall, Douglas, 1899–. Painter, A.N.A. 1927
Parsons, Charles, 1821–1910. Painter, A.N.A. 1862
Parton, Arthur, 1842–1914. Painter, A.N.A. 1871, N.A. 1884
Parton, Henry Woodbridge, 1858–1933. Painter, A.N.A. 1921, N.A. 1929
Partridge, Roi, 1888–. Graphic Artist, A.N.A. 1940, N.A. 1949
Patania, Chev. Joseph, ?–? Painter, H.M. (a) 1841
Paxton, William McGregor, 1869–1941. Painter, A.N.A. 1917, N.A. 1928
Peabody, Robert Swain, 1845–1917. Architect, A.N.A. 1910
Peale, Rembrandt, 1778–1860. Painter, Founder, N.A. 1826, H.M. (p) 1827
Peale, Rosalba, 1799–1874. Painter, ARTIST 1827, H.M. (p) 1828
Pearce, Charles Sprague,* 1851–1914. Painter, A.N.A. 1906
Pearson, Joseph Thurman, Jr., 1876–1951. Painter, A.N.A. 1913, N.A. 1919
Peele, John Thomas, 1822–1897. Painter, A.N.A. 1846–1888
Peixotto, Ernest Clifford, 1869–1940. Painter, A.N.A. 1909
Pellew, John C., 1903–. Aquarellist, A.N.A. 1951, N.A. 1952

Pennell, Joseph, 1860–1926. Graphic Artist, A.N.A. 1907, N.A. 1909
Perit, Peletiah, 1785–1864. Patron, H.M. (a) 1843
Perkins, Thomas Handasyde, 1764–1854. Patron, H.M. (a) 1828
Perrine, Van Dearing, 1869–. Painter, A.N.A. 1923, N.A. 1931
Perry, Enoch Wood, 1831–1915. Painter, A.N.A. 1868, N.A. 1869
Perry, William Graves, 1883–. Architect, A.N.A. 1942
Petersen, Martin, 1870–. Graphic Artist, A.N.A. 1943
Pettrick, Ferdinand Friedrich August, 1798–1872. Sculptor, H.M. (p) 1837
Philip, Frederick William, 1814–1841. Painter, A.N.A. 1833
Philipp, Robert, 1895–. Painter, A.N.A. 1935, N.A. 1945
Piccirilli, Attilio, 1866–1945. Sculptor, A.N.A. 1909, N.A. 1935
Piccirilli, Furio, 1870–1949. Sculptor, A.N.A. 1918, N.A. 1936
Picknell, William Lamb,* 1853–1897. Painter, A.N.A. 1891
Pike, John, 1911–. Aquarellist, A.N.A. 1944, N.A. 1948
Pilot, Robert W., 1898–. Painter, H.C.M. Canada 1952
Pittman, Hobson, 1900–. Painter, A.N.A. 1950, N.A. (Elect) 1953
Pitz, Henry Clarence, 1895–. Aquarellist, A.N.A. 1951
Platt, Charles Adams,* 1861–1933. Architect, A.N.A. 1897, N.A. 1911
Platt, Eleanor, 1910–. Sculptor, A.N.A. (Elect) 1948
Platt, William, 1897–. Architect, A.N.A. 1942, N.A. 1948
Pleissner, Ogden M., 1905–. Painter, A.N.A. 1938, N.A. 1940
Polasek, Albin, 1879–. Sculptor, A.N.A. 1926, N.A. 1933
Pollia, Joseph P., 1893–. Sculptor, A.N.A. (Elect) 1953
Pond, Dana, 1881–. Painter, A.N.A. 1943, N.A. 1945
Poole, Abram, 1883–. Painter, A.N.A. 1933, N.A. 1938
Poor, Henry Varnum, 1888–. Painter, A.N.A. (Elect) 1948
Poore, Henry Rankin, 1859–1940. Painter, A.N.A. 1888
Pope, John, 1821–1881. Painter, A.N.A. 1858
Pope, John Russell, 1874–1937. Architect, A.N.A. 1919, N.A. 1924
Porter, Benjamin Curtis,* 1845–1908. Painter, A.N.A. 1878, N.A. 1880
Post, George Browne, 1837–1913. Architect, A.N.A. 1906, N.A. 1908
Post, William Merritt, 1856–1935. Painter, A.N.A. 1910
Potter, Edward C., 1800–1826. Painter, Founder, N.A. 1826
Potter, Edward Clark,* 1857–1923. Sculptor, A.N.A. 1905, N.A. 1906
Potthast, Edward Henry,* 1857–1927. Painter, A.N.A. 1899, N.A. 1906
Potts, Rev. George, D.D., 1802–1864. Clergyman, H.M. (a) 1841
Powell, Arthur James Emery, 1864–. Painter, A.N.A. 1921, N.A. 1937
Powell, William Henry, 1823–1879. Painter, A.N.A. 1840–1844, A.N.A. (Elect)
    1846–1847, A.N.A. 1854
Powers, Hiram, 1805–1873. Sculptor, H.M. (p) 1837
Poynter, Sir Edward John, 1836–1919. Painter, H.C.M. England 1917
Pratt, Bela Lyon, 1867–1917. Sculptor, A.N.A. 1910
Pratt, Robert M., 1811–1880. Painter, A.N.A. 1849, N.A. 1851
Prellwitz, Edith Mitchill,* 1865–1944. Painter, A.N.A. 1906
Prellwitz, Henry,* 1865–1940. Painter, A.N.A. 1906, N.A. 1912
Prendergast, Charles E., 1869–1948. Painter, A.N.A. 1939
Preston, William Campbell, 1794–1860. Lawyer, H.M. (a) 1846

Proctor, Alexander Phimister,* 1862–1950. Sculptor, A.N.A. 1901, N.A. 1904
Prud'homme, John Francis Eugene, 1800–1892. Graphic Artist, A.N.A. 1837, N.A. 1846
Pushman, Hovsep T., 1877–. Painter, A.N.A. (Elect) 1934–1936
Putnam, Brenda, 1890–. Sculptor, A.N.A. 1934, N.A. 1936
Pyle, Howard, 1853–1911. Painter, A.N.A. 1905, N.A. 1907

Quartley, Arthur,* 1839–1886. Painter, A.N.A. 1879, N.A. 1886
Quinn, Edmond Thomas, 1868–1929. Sculptor, A.N.A. 1920

Rand, Ellen Emmet, 1876–1941. Painter, A.N.A. 1926, N.A. (Elect) 1934
Rand, J., ?–? Painter, A.N.A. 1833–1838
Ranger, Henry Ward, 1858–1916. Painter, A.N.A. 1901, N.A. 1906
Ranney, William Tylee, 1813–1857. Painter, A.N.A. 1850
Recchia, Richard Henry, 1885–. Sculptor, A.N.A. 1941, N.A. 1944
Redfield, Edward Willis,* 1869–. Painter, A.N.A. 1904, N.A. 1906
Reed, Doel, 1894–. Graphic Artist, A.N.A. 1942, N.A. 1952
Reed, Luman, 1787–1836. Patron, H.M. (a) 1834
Rehn, Frank Knox Morton,* 1848–1914. Painter, A.N.A. 1899, N.A. 1908
Reid, Robert,* 1862–1929. Painter, A.N.A. 1902, N.A. 1906
Reinagle, Hugh, 1790–1834. Painter, Founder, N.A. 1826
Reinhart, Benjamin Franklin, 1829–1885. Painter, A.N.A. 1871
Reinhart, Charles Stanley,* 1844–1896. Painter, A.N.A. 1891
Remington, Frederic, 1861–1909. Painter, A.N.A. 1891
Renier, Joseph Emile, 1887–. Sculptor, A.N.A. 1937
Renwick, James, 1790–1863. Physicist, H.M. (a) 1841
Retszch, Friedrich August Moritz, 1779–1857. Illustrator, H.M. (p) 1836
Reynard, Grant Tyson, 1887–. Graphic Artist, A.N.A. 1940
Ricci, Jerri, 1916–. Aquarellist, A.N.A. 1951
Ricci, Ulysses Anthony, 1888–. Sculptor, A.N.A. 1942
Rice, William Morton Jackson,* 1854–1922. Painter, A.N.A. 1900
Richards, Thomas Addison, 1820–1900. Painter, A.N.A. 1848, N.A. 1851
Richards, William Trost, 1833–1905. Painter, H.M. (p) 1862, N.A. 1871
Richardson, Andrew, 1799–1876. Painter, A.N.A. 1832, N.A. 1833
Riggs, Robert, 1896–. Graphic Artist, A.N.A. 1939, N.A. 1946
Ritchie, Alexander Hay, 1822–1895. Painter, A.N.A. 1863, N.A. 1871
Ritman, Louis, 1889–. Painter, A.N.A. 1943, N.A. 1950
Ritschel, William, 1864–1949. Painter, A.N.A. 1910, N.A. 1914
Rittenberg, Henry R., 1879–. Painter, A.N.A. 1920, N.A. 1927
Robb, James, 1814–1881. Banker, H.M. (a) 1847
Robbins, Horace Wolcott, 1842–1904. Painter, A.N.A. 1864, N.A. 1878
Roberts, Priscilla, 1916–. Painter, A.N.A. (Elect) 1951
Robinson, William S., 1861–1945. Painter, A.N.A. 1901, N.A. 1911
Rogers, John, 1829–1904. Sculptor, A.N.A. 1862, N.A. 1863
Rogers, Nathaniel, 1788–1844. Painter, Founder, N.A. 1826, A.N.A. 1836
Roll, Alfred Philippe, 1847–1919. Painter, H.C.M. France 1919
Rolshoven, Julius, 1858–1930. Painter, A.N.A. 1926

Romanelli, Romano, 1882–. Sculptor, H.C.M. Italy 1933
Rondel, Frederick, 1826–1892. Painter, A.N.A. 1861
Rook, Edward Francis, 1870–. Painter, A.N.A. 1908, N.A. 1924
Root, John Wellborn, 1887–. Architect, A.N.A. 1951
Rosen, Charles, 1878–1950. Painter, A.N.A. 1912, N.A. 1917
Rosenberg, Louis Conrad, 1890–. Graphic Artist, A.N.A. 1932, N.A. 1936
Rossiter, Thomas Pritchard, 1818–1871. Painter, A.N.A. 1840, N.A. 1849
Roth, Ernest David, 1879–. Painter, A.N.A. 1920, N.A. 1928
Roth, Frederick George Richard,* 1872–1944. Sculptor, A.N.A. 1906, N.A. 1906
Rothermel, Peter Frederick, 1817–1895. Painter, H.M. (p) 1847
Rouland, Orlando, 1871–1945. Painter, A.N.A. 1936
Rowse, Samuel Worcester, 1822–1901. Crayon Artist, H.M. (p) 1858
Rox, Henry, 1899–. Sculptor, A.N.A. 1952
Rudy, Charles, 1904–. Sculptor, A.N.A. 1952
Ruggles, Edward, 1814–1867. Physician, H.M. (a) 1851
Rungius, Carl Clemens Moritz, 1869–. Painter, A.N.A. 1913, N.A. 1920
Ruzicka, Rudolph, 1883–. Graphic Artist, A.N.A. (Elect) 1941
Ryder, Albert Pinkham,* 1847–1917. Painter, A.N.A. 1902, N.A. 1906
Ryder, Chauncey Foster, 1868–1949. Painter, A.N.A. 1913, N.A. 1920
Ryder, Platt Powell, 1821–1896. Painter, A.N.A. 1868
Ryerson, Margery Austen, 1886–. Painter, A.N.A. 1944
Ryland, Robert Knight, 1873–1951. Painter, A.N.A. 1940

Saarinen, Eero, 1910–. Architect, A.N.A. (Elect) 1952
Saarinen, Eliel, 1873–1950. Architect, A.N.A. 1940, N.A. 1946
Saint-Gaudens, Augustus,* 1848–1907. Sculptor, A.N.A. 1888, N.A. 1889
Saintin, Jules Emile, 1829–1894. Painter, A.N.A. (Elect) 1858–1860, A.N.A. 1861
Salvatore, Victor D., 1885–. Sculptor, A.N.A. 1947
Sample, Paul Starrett, 1896–. Painter, A.N.A. 1937, N.A. 1941
Samstag, Gordon, 1906–. Painter, A.N.A. 1939
Sanford, Marion, 1904–. Sculptor, A.N.A. 1944
Sargent, Henry, 1770–1845. Painter, H.M. (p) 1840
Sargent, John Singer,* 1856–1925. Painter, A.N.A. 1891, N.A. 1897
Sartain, William,* 1843–1924. Painter, A.N.A. 1880
Satterlee, Walter, 1844–1908. Painter, A.N.A. 1879
Savage, Eugene Francis, 1883–. Painter, A.N.A. 1924, N.A. 1926
Sawyer, Helen (Farnsworth), 1900–. Painter, A.N.A. 1938, N.A. 1950
Schinkel, Karl Friedrich, 1781–1841. Architect, H.M. (p) 1834
Schlaikjer, Jes Wilhelm, 1897–. Painter, A.N.A. 1932, N.A. 1948
Schlegel, Fredolin, ?–? Painter, A.N.A. 1856–1879
Schmitz, Carl Ludwig, 1900–. Sculptor, A.N.A. 1948
Schoff, Stephen Alonzo, 1818–1904. Engraver, A.N.A. 1844–1884
Schofield, Walter Elmer,* 1867–1944. Painter, A.N.A. 1902, N.A. 1907
Schoolcraft, John Lawrence, c.1804–1860. Patron, H.M. (a) 1845
Schreyvogel, Charles, 1861–1912. Painter, A.N.A. 1901
Schultheiss, Carl Max, 1885–. Graphic Artist, A.N.A. 1944, N.A. 1946
Schwarz, Frank Henry, 1894–1951. Painter, A.N.A. 1934

Schweitzer, Gertrude, 1911–. Aquarellist, A.N.A. 1945, N.A. 1951
Scott, Sir Giles Gilbert, 1880–. Architect, H.C.M. England 1950
Scott, Julian, 1846–1901. Painter, A.N.A. 1870
Scudder, Janet, 1873–1940. Sculptor, A.N.A. 1920
Sedgwick, Theodore, 1811–1859. Lawyer, H.M. (a) 1841
Sellstedt, Lars Gustaf, 1819–1911. Painter, A.N.A. 1871, N.A. 1874
Selous, Henry Courtney, 1803–1890. Illustrator, H.M. (p) 1839
Sepeshy, Zoltan Leslie, 1898–. Painter, A.N.A. 1947, N.A. 1948
Serpell, Susan Watkins, 1875–1913. Painter, A.N.A. 1912
Severn, Joseph, 1793–1879. Painter, H.M. (p) 1833
Sewell, Lydia Amanda Brewster, 1859–1926. Painter, A.N.A. 1903
Sewell, Robert Van Vorst, 1860–1924. Painter, A.N.A. 1901
Seyffert, Leopold Gould, 1887–. Painter, A.N.A. 1916, N.A. 1925
Seymour, Daniel, 1809–1850. Patron, H.M. (a) 1847
Shannon, Sir James Jebusa, 1862–1923. Painter, A.N.A. (Elect) 1908
Shattuck, Aaron Draper, 1832–1928. Painter, A.N.A. 1858, N.A. 1861
Shaw, Joshua, 1776–1860. Painter, H.M. (p) 1828
Sheets, Millard Owen, 1907–. Aquarellist, A.N.A. 1944, N.A. 1947
Shegogue, James Hamilton, 1806–1872. Painter, A.N.A. 1841, N.A. 1843
Shepley, Henry Richardson, 1887–. Architect, A.N.A. 1939, N.A. 1943
Sherwood, Rosina Emmet,* 1854–1948. Painter, A.N.A. 1906
Shinn, Everett, 1876–1953. Painter, A.N.A. 1935, N.A. 1943
Shirlaw, Walter,* 1838–1909. Painter, A.N.A. (Elect) 1878–1879, A.N.A. 1887, N.A. 1888
Shrady, Henry Merwin, 1871–1922. Sculptor, A.N.A. 1909
Shumway, Henry Colton, 1807–1884. Painter, A.N.A. 1831, N.A. 1832
Shurtleff, Roswell Morse, 1838–1915. Painter, A.N.A. 1880, N.A. 1890
Simmons, Edward Emerson, 1852–1931. Painter, A.N.A. (Elect) 1901
Singer, William Henry, Jr., 1868–1943. Painter, A.N.A. 1916, N.A. 1931
Sluyter, James Schureman, 1822–1864. Lawyer, H.M. (a) 1858
Smedley, William Thomas,* 1858–1920. Painter, A.N.A. 1897, N.A. 1905
Smillie, George Henry, 1840–1921. Painter, A.N.A. 1864, N.A. 1882
Smillie, James, 1807–1885. Graphic Artist, A.N.A. 1832, N.A. 1851
Smillie, James David, 1833–1909. Painter, A.N.A. 1865, N.A. 1876
Smith, Allen, Jr., 1810–1890. Painter, A.N.A. 1833–1883
Smith, Howard Everett, 1885–. Painter, A.N.A. 1921
Smith, James Kellum, 1893–. Architect, A.N.A. 1942, N.A. 1944
Smith, Thomas Lochlan, 1835–1884. Painter, A.N.A. 1869
Smith, William Arthur, 1918–. Aquarellist, A.N.A. 1949, N.A. 1952
Snell, Henry Bayley,* 1858–1943. Painter, A.N.A. 1902, N.A. 1906
Snowden, George Holburn, 1902–. Sculptor, A.N.A. 1937, N.A. 1941
Sonntag, William Louis, 1822–1900. Painter, A.N.A. 1860, N.A. 1861
Soyer, Raphael, 1899–. Painter, A.N.A. 1949, N.A. 1951
Spear, Arthur Prince, 1879–. Painter, A.N.A. 1920
Speicher, Eugene Edward, 1883–. Painter, A.N.A. 1912, N.A. 1925
Speight, Francis, 1896–. Painter, A.N.A. 1937, N.A. 1940

Spencer, Frederick R., 1806–1875. Painter, A.N.A. 1837, N.A. 1846
Spencer, Lillie Martin, 1811–1902. Painter, H.M. (p) 1850
Spencer, Robert, 1879–1931. Painter, A.N.A. 1914, N.A. 1920
Spicer-Simson, Theodore, 1871–. Sculptor, A.N.A. 1951
Springweiler, Erwin Frederick, 1896–. Sculptor, A.N.A. 1947
Spruance, Benton Murdoch, 1904–. Graphic Artist, A.N.A. 1948
Staigg, Richard Morrell, 1817–1881. Painter, A.N.A. 1856, N.A. 1861
Stanton, Daniel, ?–? Painter, H.M. (a) 1843
Stearns, Junius Brutus, 1810–1885. Painter, A.N.A. 1848, N.A. 1849
Stebbins, Emma, 1815–1882. Sculptor, A.N.A. (Elect) 1842
Steele, Theodore Clement, 1847–1926. Painter, A.N.A. 1913
Sterne, Maurice, 1878–. Painter, A.N.A. 1935, N.A. 1944
Sterner, Albert, 1863–1946. Painter, A.N.A. 1910, N.A. 1934
Stevens, William Lester, 1888–. Painter, A.N.A. 1935, N.A. 1943
Stewart, Albert T., 1900–. Sculptor, A.N.A. 1937, N.A. 1945
Stillman, William James, 1828–1901. Painter, A.N.A. 1854–1887
Stoddard, Alice Kent (Pearson, Jr.), 1883–. Painter, A.N.A. 1938
Stone, Edward Durell, 1902–. Architect, A.N.A. (Elect) 1953
Stone, William Oliver, 1830–1875. Painter, A.N.A. 1856, N.A. 1859
Story, George Henry, 1835–1922. Painter, A.N.A. 1875
Story, Julian Russell,* 1857–1919. Painter, A.N.A. 1906
Strang, Samuel Augustus, 1823–1894. H.M. (a) 1854
Strickland, William, c.1787–1854. Architect, H.M. (p) 1827
Stuart, Gilbert, 1755–1828. Painter, H.M. (p) 1827
Stuempfig, Walter, Jr., 1914–. Painter, A.N.A. 1951, N.A. (Elect) 1953
Sturges, Jonathan, 1802–1874. Patron, H.M. (a) 1837
Sully, Jane Cooper (Darley), 1807–1877. Painter, H.M. (p) 1830
Sully, Thomas, 1783–1872. Painter, H.M. (p) 1827
Suydam, James Augustus, 1817–1865. Painter, H.M. (p) 1858, N.A. 1861
Swain, William, 1803–1847. Painter, A.N.A. 1836
Swartwout, Egerton, 1870–1943. Architect, A.N.A. 1927, N.A. 1934
Symons, George Gardner, 1861–1930. Painter, A.N.A. 1910, N.A. 1911

Taft, Lorado, 1860–1936. Sculptor, A.N.A. 1909, N.A. 1911
Tait, Arthur Fitz-William, 1819–1905. Painter, A.N.A. 1855, N.A. 1858
Talbot, Jesse, 1806–1879. Painter, A.N.A. 1842–1844
Tanner, Henry Ossawa, 1859–1937. Painter, A.N.A. 1909, N.A. 1927
Tarbell, Edmund Charles,* 1862–1938. Painter, A.N.A. (Elect) 1894–1896,
     A.N.A. 1904, N.A. 1906
Taylor, John Williams, 1897–. Painter, A.N.A. (Elect) 1953
Taylor, Prentiss, 1907–. Graphic Artist, A.N.A. 1948
Teague, Donald, 1897–. Aquarellist, A.N.A. 1945, N.A. 1948
Tenerani, Pietro, 1798–1869. Sculptor, H.M. (p) 1847
Terry, Luther, 1813–1869. Painter, H.M. (p) 1846
Thayer, Abbott Handerson,* 1849–1921. Painter, A.N.A. 1898, N.A. 1901
Theed, William, Jr., 1804–1891. Sculptor, H.M. (p) 1836

Thompson, Alfred Wordsworth,* 1840–1896. Painter, A.N.A. 1873, N.A. 1875
Thompson, Cephas Giovanni, 1809–1888. Painter, A.N.A. (Elect) 1846–1848, A.N.A. 1861
Thompson, Jerome, 1814–1886. Painter, A.N.A. 1851
Thompson, Launt, 1833–1894. Sculptor, A.N.A. 1859, N.A. 1862
Thompson, Leslie Prince, 1880–. Painter, A.N.A. 1922, N.A. 1937
Thompson, Martin E., 1786–1877. Architect, Founder, N.A. 1826, A.N.A. 1836
Thompson, Thomas, 1775–1852. Painter, A.N.A. 1834
Thon, William, 1906–. Aquarellist, A.N.A. 1949
Thorndike, George Quincy, 1825–1886. Painter, A.N.A. 1861
Thorne, William,* 1863–. Painter, A.N.A. 1902, N.A. 1913
Thorwaldsen, Albert Bertel, 1770–1844. Sculptor, H.M. (p) 1829
Tiffany, Louis Comfort,* 1848–1933. Painter, A.N.A. 1871, N.A. 1880
Toombs, Henry Johnston, 1896–. Architect, A.N.A. 1951
Torrey, Manasseh Cutler, 1807–1837. Painter, A.N.A. 1833
Town, Ithiel, 1784–1844. Architect, Founder, N.A. 1826, A.N.A. 1836, H.M. (p) 1839
Towne, John, 1787–1851. Patron, H.M. (a) 1846
Townsend, Ernest Nathaniel, 1893–1945. Painter, A.N.A. 1941
Trebilcock, Paul, 1902–. Painter, A.N.A. 1932
Trench, Joseph, ?–? Architect, H.M. (p) 1850
Trentenova, Raymond, 1792–1832. Sculptor, H.M. (p) 1829–1830, 1832
Trowbridge, Samuel Breck Parkman, 1862–1925. Architect, A.N.A. 1913
Tryon, Dwight William,* 1849–1925. Painter, A.N.A. 1890, N.A. 1891
Turner, Charles Yardley,* 1850–1918. Painter, A.N.A. 1883, N.A. 1886
Turner, Helen Maria, 1858–. Painter, A.N.A. 1913, N.A. 1921
Turner, Janet Elizabeth, 1914–. Graphic Artist, A.N.A. 1952
Twibill, George W., 1806?–1836. Painter, A.N.A. 1832, N.A. 1833
Twitchell, Asa Weston, 1820–1904. Painter, H.M. (p) 1854
Tylee, Daniel, 1782–1852. ARTIST 1827, H.M. (a) 1828
Tyler, George Washington, 1805–1833. Painter, A.N.A. 1832
Tyson, Carroll Sargent, 1877–. Painter, A.N.A. 1941, N.A. 1944

Ufer, Walter, 1876–1936. Painter, A.N.A. 1920, N.A. 1926
Ulrich, Charles Frederick,* 1858–1908. Painter, A.N.A. 1883
Unwin, Nora Spicer, 1907–. Graphic Artist, A.N.A. (Elect) 1953

Van Alen, William, 1882–. Architect, A.N.A. 1943
Van Boskerck, Robert Ward,* 1855–1932. Painter, A.N.A. 1897, N.A. 1907
Vanderlyn, John, 1775–1852. Painter, Founder, N.A. (Elect) 1826
Van Elten, Hendrik Dirk Kruseman, 1829–1904. Painter, A.N.A. 1871, N.A. 1883
Van Laer, Alexander Theobald, 1857–1920. Painter, A.N.A. 1901, N.A. 1909
Van Soelen, Theodore, 1890–. Painter, A.N.A. 1933, N.A. 1940
Vedder, Elihu,* 1836–1923. Painter, A.N.A. 1863, N.A. 1865
Ver Bryck, Cornelius, 1813–1844. Painter, A.N.A. 1836, N.A. 1841
Vernet, Emile Jean Horace, 1789–1863. Painter, H.M. (p) 1845

Verplanck, Gulian Crommelin, 1786–1870. Author, H.M. (a) 1830
Vincent, Harry Aiken, 1864–1931. Painter, A.N.A. 1920
Vinton, Frederic Porter,* 1846–1911. Painter, A.N.A. 1882, N.A. 1891
Vogel von Vogelstein, Baron Karl Christian, 1788–1868. Painter, H.M. (p) 1833
Volk, Douglas,* 1856–1935. Painter, A.N.A. 1898, N.A. 1899
Volkert, Edward Charles, 1871–1935. Painter, A.N.A. 1921
Vollmering, Joseph, 1810–1887. Painter, A.N.A. 1853
Vonnoh, Robert William,* 1858–1933. Painter, A.N.A. 1899, N.A. 1906

Walcott, Harry Mills,* 1870–1944. Painter, A.N.A. 1903
Waldo, Samuel Lovett, 1783–1861. Painter, Founder, N.A. (Elect) 1826, A.N.A. 1847
Walker, Charles Howard, 1857–1936. Architect, A.N.A. 1911
Walker, Charles Wellington, 1889–. Architect, A.N.A. 1952
Walker, Henry Oliver,* 1843–1929. Painter, A.N.A. 1894, N.A. 1902
Walker, Horatio,* 1858–1938. Painter, A.N.A. 1890, N.A. 1891
Walker, Ralph Thomas, 1889–. Architect, A.N.A. 1948, N.A. 1949
Walker, Thomas Read, 1806–1880. Lawyer, H.M. (a) 1842
Wall, William Guy, 1792–1864. Painter, Founder, N.A. 1826, H.M. (p) 1831
Waltman, Harry Franklin, 1871–1951. Painter, A.N.A. 1917
Wappers, Baron Gustave Egide Charles, 1803–1874. Painter, H.M. (p) 1833
Ward, Aaron, 1790–1867. General, Lawyer, H.M. (a) 1834
Ward, Edgar Melville, 1839–1915. Painter, A.N.A. 1875, N.A. 1883
Ward, John Quincy Adams, 1830–1910. Sculptor, A.N.A. 1862, N.A. 1863
Ward, Lynd Kendall, 1905–. Graphic Artist, A.N.A. 1945
Warneke, Heinz, 1895–. Sculptor, A.N.A. 1939
Warner, Everett Longley, 1877–. Painter, A.N.A. 1913, N.A. 1937
Warner, Olin Levi,* 1844–1896. Sculptor, A.N.A. 1888, N.A. 1889
Warren, Andrew W., ?–1873. Painter, A.N.A. 1863
Warren, Ferdinand E., 1899–. Painter, A.N.A. 1940, N.A. 1948
Washburn, Cadwallader, 1866–. Graphic Artist, A.N.A. 1940
Waterman, Marcus, 1834–1914. Painter, A.N.A. 1861–1884
Watkins, Franklin Chenault, 1894–. Painter, A.N.A. (Elect) 1951
Watrous, Harry Willson,* 1857–1940. Painter, A.N.A. 1894, N.A. 1895
Watson, Stuart (Stewart), ?–? Painter, A.N.A. 1836, H.M. (p) 1858
Watt, William G., 1867–1924. Graphic Artist, A.N.A. 1922
Watts, Robert, M.D., 1812–1867. Professor of Anatomy, H.M. (a) 1845
Waugh, Frederick Judd, 1861–1940. Painter, A.N.A. 1909, N.A. 1911
Waugh, Samuel Bell, 1814–1885. Painter, A.N.A. 1845, H.M. (p) 1847
Waugh, Sidney Biehler, 1904–. Sculptor, A.N.A. 1936, N.A. 1938
Webb, Jacob Louis,* 1856–1928. Painter, A.N.A. 1906
Webb, Sir T. Aston, 1849–1930. Architect, H.C.M. England 1919
Weems, Katharine Ward Lane, 1899–. Sculptor, A.N.A. 1934, N.A. 1939
Weidenaar, Reynold Henry, 1915–. Graphic Artist, A.N.A. 1949
Weinedel, Carl, 1795–1845. Painter, A.N.A. 1839–1845
Weinman, Adolph Alexander,* 1870–1952. Sculptor, A.N.A. 1906, N.A. 1911

Weir, John Ferguson, 1841–1926. Painter, A.N.A. 1864, N.A. 1866
Weir, Julian Alden,* 1852–1919. Painter, A.N.A. 1885, N.A. 1886
Weir, Robert Walter, 1803–1889. Painter, A.N.A. 1828, N.A. 1829
Weldon, Charles Dater, 1844–1935. Painter, A.N.A. 1889, N.A. 1897
Wendt, William, 1865–1946. Painter, A.N.A. 1912
Wengenroth, Stow, 1906–. Graphic Artist, A.N.A. 1938, N.A. 1941
Wenzler, Henry Antonio (Anthon[y] Henry), ?–1871. Painter, A.N.A. (Elect)
    1848–1849, A.N.A. 1850, N.A. 1860
West, William Edward, 1788–1857. Painter, H.M. (p) 1832
Wetherill, Elisha Kent Kane, 1874–1929. Painter, A.N.A. 1927
Wheelwright, Edmund March, 1854–1912. Architect, A.N.A. (Elect) 1910
Wheelwright, Robert, 1884–. Architect, A.N.A. 1952
Whitaker, Frederic, 1891–. Aquarellist, A.N.A. 1945, N.A. 1951
White, Edwin D., 1817–1877. Painter, A.N.A. 1848, N.A. 1849
White, John Blake, 1781–1859. Lawyer, H.M. (a) 1837
White, Lawrence Grant, 1887–. Architect, A.N.A. 1943, N.A. 1948
Whitehorne, James, 1803–1888. Painter, A.N.A. 1829, N.A. 1833
Whitney, Gertrude Vanderbilt, 1876–1942. Sculptor, A.N.A. 1940
Whittemore, William John, 1860–. Painter, A.N.A. 1897
Whittredge, Thomas Worthington, 1820–1910. Painter, A.N.A. 1860, N.A. 1861
Whorf, John, 1903–. Aquarellist, A.N.A. 1944, N.A. 1947
Wickey, Harry Herman, 1892–. Graphic Artist, A.N.A. 1939, N.A. 1946
Wickwire, Jere Raymond, 1883–. Painter, A.N.A. 1936
Wiggins, Guy, 1883–. Painter, A.N.A. 1916, N.A. 1935
Wiggins, John Carleton,* 1848–1932. Painter, A.N.A. 1890, N.A. 1906
Wightman, Thomas, 1811–1888. Painter, A.N.A. 1849
Wiles, Gladys, ?–. Painter, A.N.A. 1934
Wiles, Irving Ramsay,* 1861–1948. Painter, A.N.A. 1889, N.A. 1897
Wilgus, William John, 1819–1853. Painter, H.M. (p) 1839
Williams, Edgar Irving, 1884–. Architect, A.N.A. (Elect) 1953
Williams, Frederick Ballard, 1871–. Painter, A.N.A. 1907, N.A. 1909
Williams, John Alonzo, 1863–1951. Aquarellist, A.N.A. 1945, N.A. 1947
Williams, John Scott, 1877–. Painter, A.N.A. 1935, N.A. 1938
Williams, Keith Shaw, 1905–1951. Painter, A.N.A. 1939, N.A. 1942
Williams, Penry, 1798–1885. Painter, H.M. (p) 1833
Williams, Wheeler, 1897–. Sculptor, A.N.A. 1938, N.A. 1940
Williams, William George, 1801–1846. Soldier, H.M. (a) 1832
Williamson, John, 1826–1885. Painter, A.N.A. 1861
Wilmarth, Lemuel Everett, 1835–1918. Painter, A.N.A. 1871, N.A. 1873
Wilson, D. W., ?–1827. Painter, Founder, N.A. 1826, ARTIST 1827
Wilson, Edward Arthur, 1886–. Graphic Artist, A.N.A. 1949
Wilson, Matthew, 1814–1892. Painter, A.N.A. 1843–1888
Winkler, John W., 1890–. Graphic Artist, A.N.A. 1936, N.A. 1943
Winner, William E., ?–1883. Painter, H.M. (p) 1850
Winter, Andrew, 1892–. Painter, A.N.A. 1931, N.A. 1938
Winter, Ezra Augustus, 1886–1949. Painter, A.N.A. 1924, N.A. 1928
Witt, John Harrison, 1840–1901. Painter, A.N.A. 1885

Woelfle, Arthur William, 1873–1936. Painter, A.N.A. 1929
Wolf, Henry, 1852–1916. Graphic Artist, A.N.A. 1905, N.A. 1908
Wood, Grant, 1892–1942. Painter, A.N.A. (Elect) 1937–1938
Wood, Thomas Waterman, 1823–1903. Painter, A.N.A. 1868, N.A. 1871
Woodbridge, Frederick James, 1900–. Architect, A.N.A. 1953
Woodbury, Charles Herbert,* 1864–1940. Painter, A.N.A. 1906, N.A. 1907
Wortman, Denys, 1887–. Graphic Artist, A.N.A. 1945, N.A. 1947
Wotherspoon, William Wallace, 1821–1888. Painter, A.N.A. 1848
Wright, Catharine Morris, 1899–. Painter, A.N.A. 1933
Wright, Charles Cushing, 1796–1854. Graphic Artist, Founder, N.A. 1826, A.N.A. 1836
Wright, Frank Lloyd, 1869–. Architect, A.N.A. (Elect) 1952
Wright, George Hand, 1872–1951. Graphic Artist, A.N.A. 1935, N.A. 1939
Wust, Alexander, 1837–1876. Painter, A.N.A. 1861
Wyant, Alexander Helwig,* 1836–1892. Painter, A.N.A. 1868, N.A. 1869
Wyatt, Richard James, 1795–1850. Sculptor, H.M. (p) 1832
Wyeth, Andrew Newell, 1917–. Aquarellist, A.N.A. 1944, N.A. 1945
Wyeth, Newell Convers, 1882–1945. Painter, A.N.A. 1940, N.A. 1941

Yates, Cullen, 1866–1945. Painter, A.N.A. 1908, N.A. 1919
Yewell, George Henry, 1830–1923. Painter, A.N.A. 1862, N.A. 1880
Young, Charles Morris, 1869–. Painter, A.N.A. 1913
Young, Mahonri MacKintosh, 1877–. Sculptor, A.N.A. 1912, N.A. 1923

Zantzinger, Clarence Clark, 1872–. Architect, A.N.A. 1942, N.A. 1945
Zuloaga y Zanora, Ignacio, 1870–1945. Painter, H.C.M. Spain 1933

FELLOWS IN PERPETUITY

NAMES PRECEDED BY ASTERISK INDICATE ACTIVE MEMBERS

Adams, Edward D.
Adams, Kempton
Agar, John G.
Aiken, Charles Wilson
Aiken, Jonas B.
Allen, William M.
Andrews, Blandina B.
Andrews, Loring
Andrews, William Loring
Appleton, Thomas G.
Arnold, Aaron
Arnold, B. G.
Arnold, Richard
* Arthur, Mrs. George D.
Aspinwall, William H.
Bacon, Francis McN.
* Bacon, Francis McN., Jr.
Barbey, Mrs. Mary L.
Battell, Joseph
Belden, Mrs. Charles D.
Blodgett, William T.
Bradford, Alexander W.
* Braman, Helen S.
Bristed, Charles A.
Brown, James
Brown, James, Jr.
* Brown, John Crosby
Brown, Mrs. Thomas McKlee
* Burr, Mrs. Charles P.
Burr, Henry A.

* Buttolph, Mrs. Edna Gibson
Caldwell, Mrs. Rossie A.
Caldwell, Samuel B.
Caldwell, Susan B.
Caldwell, Wilhelmina
Camp, Hugh N.
Casilear, John W.
Casilear, John W., Jr.
Caswell, John
Cenci, Beatrice Fiorenzo
Cenci, Mme. Eleanor
Chaplin, Trescott Fox
Chittenden, S. B.
Clark, David Crawford
Clark, George Crawford
Clark, L. C.
Clark, Louis C.
Coleman, William T.
Constable, James M.
Cornell, Birdsall
* Countryman, Mrs. M. Alden
Coxe, Rev. Dr. A. Cleveland
Coxe, Reginald Cleveland
Crane, Mrs. Dr.
Denny, John T.
Denny, Col. and Mrs. Thomas
Dodge, Mrs. Melissa P.
Dodge, William E.
Dodge, William E., Jr.
Dows, David

* Dows, David, Jr.
Dows, Margaret E.
* Dudley, Miss Fannie G.
* Dudley, Miss Laura Fellows
Ely, David J.
Faile, Thomas H.
Fellows, Mrs. Laura A.
Field, Benjamin H.
Fogg, William H.
Foote, Julia Jerome
Ford, Henry William
Ford, Howard
Friedsam, Col. Michael
Fry, John Heming
Gandy, Miss Katherine
Gandy, Sheppard
Gelston, Margaret L.
Gelston, Mary J.
Gerry, Louisa M.
* Gerry, Mr. and Mrs. Robert L.
Gibert, Fred E.
Gibson, Charles Dana Townsend
Gibson, Mrs. E. F. H.
Grafton, J.
Gray, Horace
Gray, Samuel S.
Green, Andrew H.
Grinnell, Moses H.
Griswold, George
Guion, W. H.
Hallet, Samuel
Hatch, George W.
Hatch, Warner D.
Haughwaut, E. V.
Havemeyer, William F.
Hicks, Benjamin D.
Higgins, Abion W.
Hitchcock, Miss S. M.
Hitchcock, Thomas
Hoag, D. T.
Hoe, Laura
Hoe, Robert
Hoe, Robert, Jr.
* Hoe, Robert, 4th
Hoe, Thyrza
Howland, Meredith
Hoyt, Edwin

* Huntington, Archer M.
Hurlbut, Henry A.
Hurlburt, Mr. and Mrs. William H.
Iselin, Adrian
Jerome, Addison G.
Jerome, Leonard W.
Jesup, Maria V. A.
Jesup, Morris K.
* Johnson, Mrs. Dorothy Aiken
Johnston, J. Boorman
Johnston, John T.
Jones, Constance Andrew
Jones, David
Jones, John Divine
* Jones, Mrs. Loring P.
Jones, Walter R.
Kemble, Gouverneur
Kennedy, Robert Lenox
Kensett, Thomas
Kernochan, Mrs. Catherine L.
Lane, Fred A.
Lane, Josiah
Lang, Florence Osgood Rand
Laurence, Alice Jerome
Learned, Edward
Learned, Edward Kernochan
Learned, Edward McA.
Lenox, Henrietta A.
Lenox, James
Livingston, Robert J.
Lockwood, Legrand
Lorillard, Peter
* Lovett, Mrs. Adele Brown
Low, A. A.
* Low, A. Augustus
* Lowther, Mrs. Millie Rader
Ludington, C. H.
Ludlum, Nicholas
Lummis, Charles A.
Lummis, William
Maitland, Robert Lenox
Marquand, Henry G.
Mason, Sidney
McKaye, James
McKie, Thomas
Miller, George N.
Miller, Dr. George Norton

Minturn, Robert B.
Morgan, Alexander C.
* Morgan, Mrs. Alexander C.
Morgan, Elisha E.
Morgan, Henry T.
Morgan, J. Pierpont
Morris, Harrison S.
* Morris, Mrs. Harrison S.
Morse, Charles Walker
Morse, Samuel F. B.
Morton, Levi P.
Munson, Henry A.
Munson, Walstein E.
Niblo, William
O'Brien, John
O'Brien, Robert
O'Brien, William
Ogden, William B.
Olyphant, Robert M.
Olyphant, Capt. Robert M.
Paine, John
Parish, Daniel
* Parish, Edward Codman
Parish, Henry
Pell, Alfred
* Pell, Claiborne
* Pell, Herbert C., Jr.
Phelps, Royal
Phoenix, Mrs. M. W.
Pierrepont, Henry E.
Rader, Max
Rainsford, George L.
Randolph, Franklin Fitz
Randolph, Hector Craig Fitz
* Reese, Mrs. S. M. Page
Reese, William A.
Remsen, Robert George
Remsen, William
Rhinelander, William C.
Robbins, George A.
Roberts, Caroline D.
Roberts, Marshall O.
Sandford, James T.
Sandford, Josephine L.
Scott, William
Sheldon, Edwin Bernon
Sheldon, Edwin H.
Shepard, Elliott F.

Skiddy, Francis
Spencer, Lorillard
Spencer, Lorillard, Jr.
Speyer, James
Stephenson, George S.
Steward, D. Jackson
Stewart, A. T.
Stillman, C. C.
Stokes, James
Stuart, Alexander
Stuart, Robert L.
Stuyvesant, Rutherford
Suydam, Mrs. Ferdinand
Suydam, James A.
Swan, Benjamin L., Jr.
Swan, Benjamin L., Sr.
Taber, Henry M.
Thorne, Edwin
Thorne, Jonathan
* Thorne, Oakleigh
* Thorne, Samuel
Thorne, Thomas P.
Tilden, William
Travers, Maria Louisa
Travers, William R.
Vanderbilt, Cornelius
Vanderbilt, Mrs. Cornelius
Von Hesse, Mrs. Emily
Warburg, Felix M.
Ward, Ann Maria
Ward, Augustus H.
* Watson, Thomas J.
Webb, Mrs. Henrietta A.
Webb, William H.
Wetmore, Samuel
Wetmore, Sarah Taylor
Wetmore, Maj. and Mrs. William B.
Wiggins, Carleton
* Wiggins, Guy Carleton
* Williams, Blair S.
Williams, John S.
* Williams, John S. 2nd
Williams, Perry P.
Winthrop, Henry
Wolfe, Catherine Lorillard
Wolfe, John
Wolfe, John David
Young, Edmond M.

FELLOWS FOR LIFE

Benedict, James
Benson, Bernhard
Bull, Ernest M.
Case, Mrs. George B.
Coolidge, Mrs. Calvin
Davies, J. Clarence
Deitsch, Samuel L.
de Laittre, Mrs. Karl
Egan, Mrs. Eloise
Ely, Miss Fanny Griswold
Ettl, Alexander J.
Frick, Miss Helen Clay
Harrison, Richard C.
Jones, Mrs. A. S. H.
Maitland, Robert L.

McClellan, Gen. George B.
Moore, Joseph T.
Mott, Hopper Lenox
Parkin, William
Philipp, Mrs. J. Peterson
Pratt, Mrs. Ruth Baker
Rhoades, Miss C. Harsen
Roosevelt, Mrs. Franklin D.
Salzbrenner, Albert
Timme, Dr. Walter
Train, Mrs. Helen Coster
Vassar, George, Jr.
Weber, Mrs. Sybilla
White, Henry C.
Zabriskie, George A.

ANNUAL SUBSCRIBERS (1953)

Birch, Stephen, Jr.
Blake, Edwin M.
Bliss, Hon. Robert Woods
Brennan, Mary M. (Mrs. M. F.)
Brown, Mrs. Stephen H.
Chabot, Anna Clemens
Chadbourne, Mrs. Thomas L.
Colgate, Henry A.
Colgate, Mr. and Mrs. Russell
Crary, C. J.
Cuff, Frank B.
Darlington, Mrs. Herbert S.
Dawes, Dexter B.
Day, Elizabeth N.
Desmond, Mrs. Thomas C.
Egan, Mrs. Eloise
Emmons, Mrs. Arthur B.
Engel, Michael M.
Erickson, Mrs. A. W.
Fazzano, Joseph R.
Ferris, Miss Eleanor
Fischer, Albert L.
Frederick, Mrs. Leopold
Gaisman, Henry J.
Garvan, Mrs. Francis P.
Havemeyer, Horace
Herman, Mrs. Helen S.
Howell, Alfred C.

Jones, Mrs. R. V.
Karasick, Mr. and Mrs. Samuel
Ketcham, Miss F. H.
Key, Mrs. Edmund, Jr.
Kress, Samuel H.
Levi, Mr. and Mrs. Julian C.
Mather, Frank J., Jr.
Meyer, Frederick W.
Moore, Mr. E. A.
Morris, John B., Jr.
Obst, Hans A.
Paddock, Josephine
Philipp, Mrs. Jane Peterson
Quantrell, Ernest E.
Reichert, Louis
Rosenthal, William
Rutherford, Mrs. T. B.
Scoville, Grace
Sedgwick, Mr. and Mrs. F. M.
Smillie, Ralph
Sparrow, Mrs. Edward W.
Trees, Clyde C.
Walker, Charles Wellington
Walker, Ralph
Watrous, Col. and Mrs. L.
Weintraub, Mrs. S.
Wensley, Mr. and Mrs. R. L.
Young, Howard

Zabriskie, George A.

PRIZES, SCHOLARSHIPS, DONATIONS

THE INCORPORATED EDWIN AUSTIN ABBEY MEMORIAL SCHOLARSHIPS FOR MURAL PAINTING IN THE U.S.A. Bequest of Mary Gertrude Abbey as a memorial to her husband. Provides scholarships for study of mural painting.

THE EDWIN AUSTIN ABBEY MEMORIAL TRUST FUND FOR MURAL PAINTING IN THE U.S.A. Bequest of Mary Gertrude Abbey as a memorial to her husband. Provides for mural embellishment of public buildings.

THE EDWIN AUSTIN ABBEY MEMORIAL FOUNDATION FOR THE STUDY OF MURAL PAINTING. Bequest of Mary Gertrude Abbey as a memorial to her husband. Provides for professorships and classes in mural painting.

THE BENJAMIN ALTMAN FUND. Income used as prizes for figure and landscape paintings in annual exhibition.

THE ALBERT H. BALDWIN FUND. Bequest of Emily H. Barhydt in memory of her brother. Income used for prizes in graphic arts or water-color painting in Academy classes.

THE HELEN FOSTER BARNETT FUND. Income used for a prize in sculpture by an artist under 35 years of age in annual exhibition.

THE EDWIN HOWLAND BLASHFIELD FUND. Income devoted to general uses and purposes of the Academy.

THE ARNOLD W. BRUNNER FUND. Bequest of Emma Beatrice Brunner in memory of her husband. Income devoted to general uses and purposes of the Academy.

THE HOWARD RUSSELL BUTLER FUND. Income devoted to paying attendance fees to members of the council.

THE INA THERESA CAMPBELL FUND. Income devoted to general uses and purposes of the Academy.

THE HENRY LEGRAND CANNON FUND. Income used for an unrestricted prize.

THE MARY HINMAN CARTER MEMORIAL PRIZE. Bequest of Mrs. Russell S. Carter in memory of her daughter. Income used for an Academy school prize.

THE ANDREW CARNEGIE FUND. Income used for a prize in oil painting in annual exhibition. Fund transferred from Society of American Artists to the Academy when merged in 1906.

THE THOMAS B. CLARKE FUND. Income used for a prize in figure composition in annual exhibition.

THE NORMAN W. DODGE PRIZE. For a painting by a woman artist in the annual exhibition. Discontinued.

THE FREDERIC F. DURAND FUND. Income devoted to general uses and purposes of the Academy.

THE BENJAMIN DUVEEN FUND. Income devoted to general uses and purposes of the Academy.

THE CHARLES LORING ELLIOTT MEDAL FUND. Bequest of Mrs. Charles Loring Elliott in memory of her husband. Medal used in the Academy school for excellence in drawing.

THE HARRIOT ERVING FUND. Income devoted to general uses and purposes of the Academy.

THE WILLIAM H. FOGG MEMORIAL FUND. Bequest of Mrs. Elizabeth H. Fogg. Income used for scholarships in the Academy school.

THE SAMUEL GOULDING FUND. Income devoted to the perpetual care and preservation of the Goulding portraits in permanent collection of the Academy.

THE DESSIE GREER FUND. Income used for an unrestricted prize in annual exhibition.

THE JULIUS HALLGARTEN PRIZE FUNDS. The income provides (1) for 3 prizes in annual exhibition to artists under 35 and (2) for scholarships in the Academy school.

THE JULIUS HALLGARTEN MEMORIAL FUND. Bequest of Albert N. Hallgarten in memory of his father. Income used for a traveling scholarship for a student in the Academy school.

THE HARPER BROTHERS FUND. Income devoted to general uses and purposes of the Academy.

THE ARCHER M. HUNTINGTON FUND. Income devoted to general uses and purposes of the Academy.

THE ARCHER M. HUNTINGTON PUBLICITY FUND. Income devoted to special activities of the Academy at the discretion of the President.

THE HUNTINGTON FUND (Helen G. Granville Barker). Income devoted to the general uses and purposes of the Academy.

THE GEORGE INNESS GOLD MEDAL. Donor, George Inness, Jr., N.A., in memory of his father. Awarded at the annual exhibition. Discontinued.

THE JOSEPH S. ISIDOR SUSTAINING FUND. Income devoted to (1) general uses and purposes of the Academy school and (2) additions to the library of the Academy.

THE JOSEPH S. ISIDOR MEMORIAL MEDAL. Income used for a medal awarded to a figure composition in annual exhibition.

THE JOHN STEWART KENNEDY FUND. Income devoted to general uses and purposes of the Academy.

THE RICHARD LAWRENCE MAKIN FUND. Income used for sustaining the exhibition program or for general uses and purposes of the Academy.

THE ISAAC N. MAYNARD PRIZE FUND. Income used for a prize for a portrait in oil or in sculpture in annual exhibition.

THE HELEN K. MC CARTHY MEMORIAL PRIZE. For a landscape painting by a woman artist in the annual exhibition. Discontinued.

THE EDWARD MOONEY MEMORIAL FUND. Bequest of Ella Mooney. Income used for a traveling scholarship for a student in the Academy school.

THE EDWARD C. MOORE, JR. FUND. Income devoted to the general uses and purposes of the Academy.

THE SAMUEL FINLEY BREESE MORSE GOLD MEDAL FUND. Income used for a gold medal award at the annual exhibition.

THE J. FRANCIS MURPHY MEMORIAL PRIZE. Awarded to a landscape in oil in annual exhibition. Discontinued.

THE ADOLPH AND CLARA OBRIG PRIZE FUND. Income used for prizes in oil and water-color paintings in annual exhibitions.

THE EDWIN PALMER MEMORIAL PRIZE FUND. Bequest of Eleanor P. Palmer in memory of her husband. Income used for a prize for a marine painting in annual exhibition.

THE WALTER L. PALMER MEMORIAL FUND. Income devoted to sustaining the exhibition program.

PRESIDENT'S MEDAL. Donor, Cass Gilbert, N.A. Awarded for distinguished services in the Fine Arts. Discontinued.

THE THOMAS R. PROCTOR PRIZE FUND. Income used for a prize in portraiture in oil painting or in sculpture in annual exhibition.

THE HENRY WARD RANGER FUND. Income used for the purchase of paintings by American artists for temporary distribution to museums, etc., subject to recall and review by the National Gallery of Art for their permanent collection, ten years after the death of the artist.

THE J. SANFORD SALTUS GOLD MEDAL FUND. Income used for a gold medal awarded a painting or sculpture in annual exhibition.

THE JULIA A. SHAW MEMORIAL PRIZE. Donor, Samuel T. Shaw, in memory of his mother. Prize to a woman artist in annual exhibition. This prize was awarded prior to 1907 by the Society of American Artists. Discontinued.

SAMUEL T. SHAW, PATRON. Activity devoted to purchase of oil paintings from the annual exhibitions. Discontinued.

THE ELLIN P. SPEYER PRIZE FUND. Donor, James Speyer, in memory of his wife. Income used for a prize in annual exhibition for painting or sculpture of animals, or work illustrating kindliness to same.

THE S. J. WALLACE TRUMAN PRIZE. Bequest of Ella W. Everett. Income used for a prize in landscape painting in annual exhibition.

THE ELIZABETH N. WATROUS GOLD MEDAL FUND. Income used for a gold medal award in sculpture in annual exhibition.

THE HARRY W. WATROUS PRIZE FUND. Income used for an additional cash prize to winner of Elizabeth N. Watrous medal.

THE DR. SEWARD WEBB PRIZE. Award to an artist in annual exhibition by the Society of American Artists. Discontinued.

THE NORA D. WOODMAN FUND. Bequest given as a memorial to her grandfather, Asher B. Durand, N.A. Devoted to general uses and purposes of the Academy.

SOURCES

National Academy of Design, Minutes, 1826–1952
——Constitutions
——Catalogues, 1826–1952
——Exhibition Record, 1826–1860, The New-York Historical Society
Society of American Artists, Catalogues
——Constitutions

Cowdrey, Bartlett. American Academy of Fine Arts and American Art-Union, Volume I: Introduction, 1816–1852. With a History of the American Academy by Theodore Sizer, a History of the American Art-Union by Charles E. Baker, and a foreword by James Thomas Flexner.
——American Academy of Fine Arts and American Art-Union, Volume II: Exhibition Record, 1816–1852. New York, 1953. The New-York Historical Society.
Cummings, Thomas S., N.A. Historic Annals of the National Academy of Design (1825–1863). Philadelphia, 1865.
Dunlap, William, N.A. History of the Rise and Progress of the Arts of Design in the United States. New York, 1834.
Isham, Samuel, N.A. The History of American Painting. New York, 1936.
Noble, Louis L. The Course of Empire, Voyage of Life, and other pictures of Thomas Cole, N.A. His letters and miscellaneous writings. New York, 1853.
Tuckerman, Henry T. Book of the Artists—American Artist Life. New York, 1867.

ACKNOWLEDGEMENTS

MY THANKS and appreciation are due to Lawrence Grant White, President of the National Academy, for his encouragement and painstaking reading of the manuscript; to the editorial judgment and helpful suggestions of Dr. William Bridgwater and Miss Joan McQuary, and to Miss Eugenia Porter for the production and design of the book; to Miss Matilda Berg for compiling the comprehensive index; to Vernon C. Porter, Director of the Academy, and Miss Alice Melrose for compiling the appendix and the verification of names and dates; above all to Archer M. Huntington for his generosity in making possible the publication of the History, sponsored by the National Academy of Design.

E. C.

INDEX